A Dynamic Systems Approach to
Development of Cognition and Action

MIT Press/Bradford Books Series in Cognitive Psychology
Stephen E. Palmer, editor

A Dynamic Systems Approach to Development: Applications, edited by Linda B. Smith and Esther Thelen, 1993

A Dynamic Systems Approach to the Development of Cognition and Action, Esther Thelen and Linda B. Smith, 1994

A Dynamic Systems Approach to the Development of Cognition and Action

Esther Thelen and Linda B. Smith

A Bradford Book
The MIT Press
Cambridge, Massachusetts
London, England

Second printing, 1995

This book was set in Palatino by DEKR Corporation and was printed and bound in the United States of America.

Library of Congress Cataloging-in-Publication Data

Thelen, Esther.
 A Dynamic systems approach to the development of cognition and
action / Esther Thelen and Linda B. Smith.
   p.   cm.—(MIT Press/Bradford book series in cognitive psychology)
 "A Bradford book."
 Includes bibliographical references and index.
 ISBN 0-262-20095-3
 1. Cognition in infants. 2. Perceptual-motor processes. 3. Motor
ability in infants. 4. Developmental psychobiology. I. Smith,
Linda B. II. Title. III. Series.
 BF720.C63T48   1994
 155.42'2235—dc20   93-6037
                                                              CIP

For David and Maurice

Contents

Series Foreword

The series on Cognitive Psychology presents a collection of definitive books on cognition viewed from a psychological perspective. It includes undergraduate and graduate textbooks, major reference works, and research monographs on the cutting edge of psychological knowledge, and on occasion, as the situation warrants, a few edited volumes. Books in the series concern a wide variety of topics in cognition, including perception, attention, imagery, memory, learning, categorization, language, problem solving, thinking, and cognitive development. Although the primary emphasis is on presenting psychological theories and findings, most volumes in the series have an interdisciplinary flavor, attempting to develop important connections between cognitive psychology and the related fields of anthropology, computer science, education, linguistics, neuroscience, and philosophy.

Stephen E. Palmer

Acknowledgments

The intellectual climate at Indiana University provides both the energy and challenge for new ideas. The Dynamics Group of the IU Cognitive Science Program set the zeitgeist. We began meeting in 1987 with Bob Port, John Merrill, Janet Metcalfe, Helga Winold, and Jung Suh, and we continue our study and discussion with Tim van Gelder, Geoff Bingham, Bev Ulrich, Jim Townsend, Dave Jones, and Jonni Kanerva. This group has been financially supported by the Indiana University Dean of Faculties Multidisciplinary Ventures Fund. We also thank Rich Shiffrin, Director of the Cognitive Science Program, for his support, leadership, and openness, and our colleagues in Cognitive Science, especially Michael Gasser, for their continual thoughtful criticisms.

Our fellow developmentalists at Indiana have helped us think about developmental process and provided unparalleled collegiality. We thank Jeff Alberts, Susan Jones, Meredith West, Sheila Walker, Steve Barlow, Bev Ulrich, and Alexandra Quittner. The students and postdoctoral associates in our seminars and laboratories worked hard to keep us honest. We especially thank Karen Adolph, Deborah Davis, Daniela Corbetta, Lisa Gershkoff-Stowe, Steve Goldinger, Diana Heise, Jodi Jensen, Kathi Kamm, Don Katz, Jürgen Konczak, Teresa Mitchell, Mike Muchisky, Laura Namy, Brigette Oliver, Michael Schoeny, Maria Sera, Gregory Smith, John Spencer, and Beatrix Vereijken. We are also grateful to Peggy Intons-Peterson, Chair of the Department of Psychology, for maintaining so well the intellectual and collegial life that is Indiana's hallmark.

Since 1987, our understanding of development and dynamic systems have grown through interchanges with our colleagues and friends throughout the world who have also been attempting to understand development and cognition as a complex dynamic system. We thank all the participants in the 1989 workshop who so heartily dared to consider something new: Dick Aslin, Bennett Bertenthal, George Butterworth, Carol Eckerman, Gene Goldfield, Alan Fogel, Scott Kelso, Darren Newtson, and Peter Wolff. Conversations over the years with Scott Kelso, Gregor Schöner, Alan Fogel, Susan Oyama, Patrick Bateson, Karl Newell, Jane Clark, Carolyn Heriza, Michael Turvey, Peter Kugler, Blandine Bril, Claes von Hofsten, Judy DeLoache, and Dedre Gentner have been a continuing source of inspiration. Kathryn Hirsch-Pasek, Alan Fogel, and Michael Tucker provided tough yet sympathetic readings of the manuscript, the very best kind of help. We offer also our special thanks to Clark Presson not only for his insightful comments on the manuscript, but also for his persistent interest in this project, his always wise questions about development, and for his friendship. Karen Adolph and Peter Schiller kindly allowed us to use their unpublished work.

We owe a special debt of gratitude to two distinguished scholars of development, Eleanor J. Gibson and Gerald M. Edelman. Their influence on this book is everywhere. Jackie Gibson spent a month at Indiana University as a member of the IU Advanced Study Institute. She continually challenged and inspired. Gerry Edelman, whose brilliant and provocative talk at IU generated days of e-mail debate, is rare among brain scientists in taking human development seriously. We hope we have done his theory justice here.

Part of the fun of Indiana is our supportive and able staff. Amber Cox creatively and ably made many of the graphics. Karen Jukes typed and assembled the manuscript with patience and good humor. Finally, Mary Buuck and Dexter Gormley helped in so many ways—graphics, finding references, taking photos, fixing leaking roofs—that we truly could not have finished this book without them. Don Katz, John Spencer, and Teresa Treat took time from graduate studies to help with the index.

The taxpayers of the United States and the state of Indiana have supported our research for many years through grants from the National Institutes of Health, the National Institute of Mental Health, and Indiana University, and we thank them.

Finally, our families are our joy, our energy, and our serenity. We are most thankful to David, Jennifer, and Jeremy Thelen and Maurice, Gordon, and Evann Smith for giving us both comfort and space to grow.

Introduction

People lead lives of both thought and action. One of the enduring puzzles of human existence is how we acquire physical and mental activities of such great complexity from our simple origins as a single cell. How do we come to understand the world so we can act within it? How do we construct a social and physical reality? Where do our rich mental lives of metaphor, fantasy, and invention come from? At the same time, what enables our brains to control our limbs and body segments to perform intricate and skilled actions? For thousands of years, philosophers and other scholars of the mind have recognized that clues to these profound questions may be found in the developing child.

Like so many before us—Baldwin, Darwin, Gesell, Piaget, Werner—we approach the mystery of human development with the conviction that the acquisition of mental life is continuous with all biological growth of form and function. Because humans can perform so many special activities, it is easy to think of our ontogeny as special. What we argue in this book is that while the endpoints of human development are complex and unique, the processes by which we reach those endpoints are the same as those that govern development in even simple organisms, and to some degree, even in complex, nonliving systems.

Thus, in our approach to fundamental questions of mental life, we invoke principles of great generality. These are principles of nonlinear dynamic systems, and they concern problems of emergent order and complexity: how structure and patterns arise from the cooperation of many individual parts. Nonlinear systems principles originated in physics, chemistry, and mathematics. Although a few visionary biologists have recognized the relevance of nonlinear dynamics to the study of biological systems (e.g., von Bertalanffy, 1968; Waddington, 1977), only within the last few years have these principles been rigorously and formally applied (e.g., Glass and Mackey, 1988; Kelso, Mandell, and Shlesinger, 1988). Such principles describe systems of diverse material substrates that live in many different time scales. We believe these principles are especially powerful in integrating organic ontogeny at every level from morphology to behavior. We devote the first section of the book to describing principles of dynamic systems and to reinterpreting behavioral and developmental data in dynamic terms.

But even the most potent general principles are insufficient; developmentalists also need to understand process and mechanism at the level of the phenomena of real life. What are the organic and environmental factors that engender change? How can we begin to untangle the complex web of causality when real infants live and develop in a world filled with people, things, and events in continuous interaction? A major task of this book, therefore, is to instantiate dynamic principles into the realm of process and mechanism. We seek to demonstrate that these general principles *do* capture both the essence of ontogeny and its local details and variations, and indeed can offer new and powerful explanations of experimental data from infants and children.

We are especially dedicated to showing that behavior and development are dynamic at many levels of explanation, in particular, that phenomena described at the level of behavior are congruent with what is known about the brain and how it works. We are not seeking reductionist explanations, but harmonious ones. Neuroanatomy and physiology support all behavior, although, as we argue later, they are not logically causal. Thus, we will ground our thinking about process and mechanism in a developmental theory of the brain.

What Development Looks Like: The View from Above

What does it mean to say that an organism "develops"? We seek here to find commonalities across all development, from the first cleavage of the fertilized egg, through the earliest somatic and morphological differentiation, the complex processes of neurogenesis and emerging physiological competences, and their ultimate expression in behavior throughout the life span. What unites these diverse processes that occur over time? We look at ontogeny first with our lowest level of magnification.

Over the broad sweep of time, the most global quality of developing organisms is that they go from being small and simple to being bigger and more complex. By complexity, we mean simply an increase in the number of different parts and activities, and the relations among them. Development is linear and quantitative, as growth is always incremental. At the same time, development is also nonlinear and qualitative, since complexity invokes new forms and abilities.

There is a remarkable *orderliness* to this process. Within any species, development normally proceeds with inexorable regularity and even inevitability. We can describe quite precisely the behavioral and physiological repertoire of the human newborn and predict with great certainty that all intact humans will walk, speak the language of their culture, form social relationships, reach reproductive maturity, and engage in certain mental operations. We can circumscribe the ages and sequences of these events, and many others, with significant reliability. Our everyday language reflects this orderliness when we speak of "stages of child (or adult) development," "developmental milestones or timetables," and even the "ticking of the biological clock."

The sweep of development is more than just orderly, it is *progressive* or directional. The changes, both qualitative and quantitative, are not reversible. Once a new structure emerges, or a growth level is attained, or a behavior performed, the organism does not revert back to earlier forms. Certain functions may decline in old age or with disease, but the developmental process does not become undone; the organism does not look like an immature form. Although certain behaviors may appear childlike, age or brain damage does not create an immature organism.

Across all species, the direction of development leads toward increasing nutritional independence from the parent animal and the attainment of reproductive maturity. Seeking food and mates requires an accurate match between those properties in the environment necessary for the realization of those goals and the perceptual and motor apparatus of the animal. Development progresses toward such an adaptive match.

The orderly, progressive, incremental, and directional qualities of development in the broadest sweep give rise to the impression of a *teleological* process, one guided by design. How can organisms move so surely toward the goal of adaptive, adult functioning in so determined a fashion without a plan? Where is the guidebook for this inevitable change from simple to more complex? It seems like this destiny must be written, somewhere, somehow, as instructions to be read as ontogeny proceeds.

Developmentalists have devoted considerable effort to uncovering the grand ontogenetic plan. The classic "nature-nuture" controversy, a standard in every textbook, is a reflection of the quest for understanding where development *comes from*. At one extreme, the developmental ground plan is seen as residing entirely within the organism, as a set of genetic blueprints, which contains all the information needed for the final adult form and which needs only to be "read" sequentially over time. At the other extreme, the organism is viewed as containing none of the information for its final destiny, but as absorbing structure and complexity from the order in the environment through experience with the environment.

Surprisingly, several current approaches to development continue to side with either a version of genetic determinism or bald environmentalism. However, most developmentalists at least pay lip service to the view that development is a function of the *interaction* between genetically determined processes and input from the environment. Interactionism and transactionalism are everyone's comfortable buzzwords, and the proffered "solution" to the nature-nurture dichotomy.

There are several reasons why the commonly accepted interactionist position is inadequate to explain the grand sweep of developmental progress. First and foremost is the serious logical impasse created by seeking the developmental plan in *any* preexisting agency, a point most recently made by Oyama (1985) in compelling detail. Remember that the premier developmental question is how organic form is created—the emergence of *novelty and complexity* in structure and function. Invoking any prior plan *within* the organism leads to infinite regress. For example, we ask where does the structure of the mind come from? If it comes from the structure of the central nervous system (CNS), where is that encoded? If the structure of the nervous system is entirely encoded in the genes, how does a sequential one-dimensional chemical code lead to an elaborated, three-dimensional and functionally specific structure? Where are the *rules* that govern this transition from code to organism? Thus, we have to postulate yet *another* set of instructions, and so on. In essence, genetic determinism just sidesteps the question of origins and dumps the problem onto the laps of the evolutionists, who must account for behavioral novelty. If we propose, in contrast, that the structure of the mind comes from information or knowledge from the world, how is that information evaluated? By what criteria does the organism know what is "good"? What is to be paid attention to and be assimilated into the mental repertoire? Again, this requires another level of representations of the final developmental product.

The dilemma of where the information for the adult resides does not disappear with interactionism. Interactionist positions, as presently formulated, only combine *two* logically untenable views, without any notion of how their combination resolves the fundamental regressive nature of both of them. Information is *both* within the organism *and* "out there" and combines in some unspecified way. The genes alone cannot specify the end-state of the developmental process, as they play out in a continuous, and essential, supporting matrix of the cell, tissue, organism, and environment. Extragenetic factors are themselves also insufficient specifiers of the egg-into-adult transformation. Interactionist positions do not make it clear how combining two imperfect codes creates the complete blueprint. If genes and environment "combine," we must specify how their interactions over time create new forms and new behaviors.

Maturationism, environmentalism, and interactionism are imperfect developmental theories because they essentially *prescribe* the adult form before it develops. These views take no account of *process*, of how new form and function are realized over time. Development is not the specification of the outcome—the product—but is the route by which the organism moves from an earlier state to a more mature state. By assuming prescription or teleology, we simply finesse process since the outcome is encapsulated in the plan.

The view from above, therefore, lends itself to explanations that provide a source of order and information for ontogenetic innovations. But conventional theories are logically unsatisfactory, as they provide no principled account of what moves the system forward. Conventional approaches are also deficient because they also fail to account for developmental processes at a closer level of observation.

What Development Looks Like: The View from Below

The grand sweep of development seems neatly rule-driven. In detail, however, development is messy. As we turn up the magnification of our microscope, we see that our visions of linearity, uniformity, inevitable sequencing, and even irreversibility break down. What looks like a cohesive, orchestrated process from afar takes on the flavor of a more exploratory, opportunistic, syncretic, and function-driven process in its instantiation. In succeeding chapters, we provide many concrete examples of the messy, fluid, context-sensitive nature of behavioral development.

First, development appears to be modular and heterochronic. That is, not all of the structures and functions of the animal develop apace or as a unified whole. We observe enormous species differences in the relative maturity of component structures and functions at birth, presumably in response to selective pressures. Although many species are born altricial or precocial in both sensory and motor capabilities (horses vs. rats), the newborns of other species are a mixed bag. Humans, for example, have precocial sensory functions, but altricial motor abilities at birth. Anokhin (1964) pointed out that the developmental process can be remarkably responsive to ecological demands on the young; even single neural tracts can be selectively accelerated to provide necessary function. There are equally striking disparities in the relative rates of growth and change of perceptual, motor, cognitive, and social elements within the species. That is, each component may have its own characteristic developmental trajectory, exhibiting times of accelerated change, times of slow, linear increment, and times of quiescence. The paradox is that the organism moves along as an adapted, integrated whole as the component structures and processes change in fits and starts.

Most remarkably, when we experimentally dissect an ontogenetic phenomenon, we often discover that elements of a seemingly integrated behavioral performance can be detected long in advance of the fully functional behavior. That is, under special conditions, the organism may demonstrate *precocial* abilities in one domain. Other elements appear to mature more slowly and can never be isolated from mature performance. One striking example of precocial abilities from the animal literature is weaning in rat pups. Rat pups do not normally eat and drink independently for about 3 weeks after birth. However, Hall and Bryan (1980) demonstrated that even newborn rat pups will ingest liquid or semisolid food from the floor of a test chamber when the temperature of the chamber is sufficiently warm. Why should such components be available but "waiting in the wings"? What, then, drives the organism to new levels of performance? How do these cryptic precursors become manifest?

The boundaries of progressive stages are equally blurred by seeming regressions in performance and losses of previously well-established behaviors. Some of these losses appear species-wide, as in the universal decline of suckling behaviors in mammals, and may be adaptive solutions to ontogenetic changes in life demands. Other losses are more immediately context-bound and short-term, especially when new abilities are first emerging.

Thus, although orderly and switch-like from afar, developmental change is more tentative and fluid from close up. In immature animals, performance seems to be variable and easily disrupted. When we observe behavioral development under stable and uniform conditions, it looks itself stable and uniform. If we only ask one set of questions, we elicit a restricted set of answers. Only when we introduce instabilities, novelty, and variability into the context do we elicit and test the range of response capabilities of the animal. Under challenges of variability, we often discover a flexibility of solutions not apparent under more restricted conditions.

At the close-up range, therefore, the rules seem not to hold. What determines the behavioral performance seems less like the grand plan or timetable than the immediacy of the situation or the task at hand. Our efforts to organize developmental phenomena into lawful relations appear stymied by the phenomena themselves.

Goals for a Developmental Theory

What, then, do we require of a developmental theory that spans levels, domains, and species? In table I.1, we list six goals we believe are essential, and we elaborate them further below. The primary thrust of development is the generation of novel structure and behavior. A developmental explanation must do better than assuming it was all there to begin with. So the first need is for a principled understanding of where novelty comes from. This explanation must encompass two, seemingly paradoxical, levels. At low magnification, events seem planful. Development proceeds with clocklike qualities, measuring off events in time with

Table I.1
Goals for a Developmental Theory

---

1. To understand the origins of novelty.
2. To reconcile global regularities with local variability, complexity, and context-specificity.
3. To integrate developmental data at many levels of explanation.
4. To provide a biologically plausible yet nonreductionist account of the development of behavior.
5. To understand how local processes lead to global outcomes.
6. To establish a theoretical basis for generating and interpreting empirical research.

---

global precision and regularity. Likewise, the process seems to have global teleology; it is goal-directed and common to all intact individuals. At closer range, however, we must explain diversity, flexibility, and asynchrony: how to account for the mobility of behavior units and the ability of even young organisms to reorganize their behavior around context and task.

It is our basic assumption that the end-state of the organism is not instantiated at the beginning of the journey toward maturity. Thus, our principles must explain how global developmental trajectories can arise from diverse, heterogeneous, mobile, and dynamic local effects. We will argue that these variable, fluid, task-sensitive local effects are not just noise in a grand developmental plan, but are *the processes that engender developmental change*. Indeed, it is the very nature of such local complexity to produce behavior with global simplicity. We have as a recurring theme, therefore, the necessity for compatibility among time scales. As developing organisms perceive and act in daily life, there must be continuity between these activities and changes over a long time scale.

At the same time, we seek a biologically valid, but nonreductionist, account of the development of behavior. At first glance, this may seem a contradiction in terms. When developmental psychologists invoke the "biological bases" of behavior, they usually mean the neurophysiological, hormonal, or genetic aspects of human functioning: behavior is assumed to be "based" on these more fundamental processes. No one would question that the nervous system, the hormonal system, and the genes are essential contributors to human behavior. It is, however, a serious error to partition the contributors to development into those that somehow reside within the organism as biological, genetic, innate, and therefore primary, and those outside the organism, which may include the everyday features of the physical and social environment, as only supportive and nonbiological.

We hope to show at many levels that no one element alone has causal primacy or forms the basis for behavior. The ontogenetic niche, as West and King (1987) have named the normal and expected environment, determines developmental outcome as surely as the "wetware" within the bounds of the organism itself. A language environment for a developing human is as biological as a left hemisphere. The boundaries between what is "innate" and what is "acquired" become so blurred as to be, at the very least, uninteresting, compared to the powerful questions of developmental process.

Thus, here we turn the reductionist-dichotomous paradigm on its head to ask how behavior arises from a multitude of underlying contributing elements. It is not so much how the whole can be understood as a function of the pieces, but how the pieces can come together to produce the whole. At the same time that we reject a simple reductionist view of organic development, we also believe strongly, like others before us, that cognitive growth is an extension of adaptive ontogeny in general. This means that while cognition may not be understood solely in terms of neural structures, accounts of cognitive change must be entirely harmonious with what is known about the structure and function of the nervous system and its development.

Our commitment to a biologically consistent theory means that we categorically reject machine analogies of cognition and development. For several decades, the preeminent metaphor for understanding human cognition has been the digital computer. The brain may well share certain operations with a digital computer, but it is different from a machine on the most fundamental thermodynamic level, as we detail in succeeding chapters. A developmental theory must be appropriate to the organism it serves; thus, we deliberately eschew the machine vocabulary of processing devices, programs, storage units, schemata, modules, or wiring diagrams. We substitute, instead, a vocabulary suited to a fluid, organic system, with certain thermodynamic properties.

We propose here a radical departure from current cognitive theory. Although behavior and development appear structured, there are no structures. Although behavior and development appear rule-driven, there are no rules. There is complexity. There is a multiple, parallel, and continuously dynamic interplay of perception and action, and a system that, by its thermodynamic nature, seeks certain stable solutions. These solutions emerge from relations, not from design. When the elements of such complex systems cooperate, they give rise to behavior with a unitary character, and thus to the illusion of structure. But the order is always executory, rather than rule-driven, allowing for the enormous sensitivity and flexibility of behavior to organize and regroup around task and context.

By this view, cognition—mental life—and action—the life of the limbs—are like the emergent structure of other natural phenomena. For example, in certain meteorological contexts, clouds form into thunderheads that have a particular shape, internal complexity, and behavior. There is a clear order and directionality to the way thunderheads emerge over time. Likewise, in the establishment of ecological communities in the colonization of an island or in the growth of a secondary forest, the types and abundance of various plants and animals follow a well-defined sequence leading to the climax ecosystem. Again, there is order, direction, and structure just as there is in development. But there is no design written anywhere in a cloud or a program in the genes of any particular species that determines the final community structure. There is no set of instructions that causes a cloud or a group of plants and animals to change form in a particular way. There are only a number of complex physical and biological systems interacting over time, such that the precise nature of their interactions leads inevitably to a thunderhead or to a forest. We suggest that action and cognition are also emergent and not designed.

Our dynamic approach shares many similarities with the "general systems" principles of von Bertalanffy (1968), Laszlo (1972), and others, and the organismic view of development associated with the eminent biologists Waddington (1966, 1977) and Weiss (1969). Systems and organismic accounts have long been a powerful "root metaphor" in developmental psychology (Reese and Overton,

1970; see, e.g., Brent, 1978, 1984; Bronfenbrenner, 1979; Fogel, 1993; Gesell, 1946; Gottlieb, 1991a,b; Horowitz, 1987; Kitchener, 1982; Lerner, 1978; Overton, 1975; Piaget, 1971; Sameroff, 1983; Werner, 1957; Wolff, 1987). Systems notions appear and reappear in developmental accounts because they provide a logically compelling formulation for the complexities of developmental change. Developmental data from many content domains are interpretable only with systems principles which stress wholeness, self-organization, nonlinearity, developmental buffering or equifinality, and hierarchical levels of organization.

Unfortunately, there is a major gap between the post hoc invocation of systems principles and their translation into *empirical studies of developmental process* (Thelen, 1989). This is especially true in accounts of cognitive development. Piaget, for example, offers *equilibration* as the fundamental process of acquiring new structures (Chapman, 1988). Piaget adapted his formulations of equilibration deliberately from the embryologist Waddington (Haroutunian, 1983), and the root metaphor is both organic and systemic. Nonetheless, in the enormous corpus of research and theory inspired by Piaget, there is little discussion or investigation of the process itself. Instead, focus has been on the nature of the structural outcome. Left unanswered by researchers are questions such as: What is equilibration? Why and how does the organism seek a stable relationship with its environment? What moves the organism to seek new levels of problem solving?

In our dynamic account, we embrace systems principles and the organic metaphor. But we strive to expand these ideas into more detailed and useful models of major developmental phenomena. To do this, we follow current trends in biology. In the recent past, the biological study of the whole organism has been overshadowed by the remarkable and compelling advances made by reductionist paradigms in genetics and molecular biology. The tide is turning now with the emerging study of complex systems rooted in powerful mathematical and physical principles. Such principles have allowed the synthetic behavior of biological systems at more macro levels to be modeled in an elegant and formal manner (see, e.g., Baltes, 1987; Fogel, 1993; Gleick, 1987; Haken, 1977; Kelso, Mandell, and Shlesinger, 1988). We, in turn, base our model of developmental change on a semiformal adaptation of the dynamic principles which are proving so insightful for understanding the behavior of systems at many levels of organization. We hope, in this way, to give substance and generality to ideas which have been historically attractive to developmentalists.

We hope to give substance to theorizing about systems in development by outlining and demonstrating concrete and realizable empirical instantiations of these principles. We attempt to translate systems principles into programs of research. Developmentalists may believe in nonlinearity, emergent properties, and multiple causality, but many conventional experimental methods and analyses are ill-suited to detect such phenomena. We believe that commitment to holistic thinking will require adopting some new and unconventional empirical strategies, as well as using and interpreting our conventional strategies in new ways.

The second way we go beyond description and structural constructs is to suggest a *neurologically plausible* mechanism of the ontogeny of cognition and action that is entirely harmonious with general dynamic principles. To do this we invoke the selectionist theory of Gerald M. Edelman (1987, 1988, 1992), an inclusive and elegant account that encompasses embryology, neuroembryology, and behavior. Edelman's *theory of neuronal group selection* fits our basic requirement for a plausible account of ontogeny: that there be no homunculus in the brain or in the genes directing the process. We must emphasize here, as we do later in the book, that this is not a reductionist retreat. Rather, we believe it adds to the power of a dynamic explanation to demonstrate dynamic principles at work at several levels of analysis. That is, events at the behavioral level are mirrored and supported by neural and morphological dynamics. And equally important, we believe, Edelman's account provides remarkable, enduring insight into our concern for time scales, or how local processes build into the global outcome.

Readers will also recognize that our developmental account is both inspired by and consistent with tenets of ecological psychology, especially the work of Eleanor J. Gibson (1969, 1988). In particular, we invoke Gibson's beliefs that the world contains information and that the goal of development is to discover relevant information in order to make a functional match between what the environment affords and what the actor can and wants to do. We share her beliefs in the primacy of perception and action as the basis for cognition, and in the fundamental role of exploration. We will show how experiments conducted from a Gibsonian perspective are congruent with, and amplify, dynamic principles. Finally, we recognize that our developmental account is also compatible with the school of developmental theorists who trace their heritage to Vygotsky (e.g., Cole, 1985; Luria, 1976; Rogoff, 1982; Vygotksy, 1978, 1986; Wertsch, 1985) and who emphasize the contextual, historical, and cultural origins of human thought. Indeed, as we suggest in the final chapter, a dynamic account provides a biological rationale for contextualism and offers a potential reconciliation and integration of processes at both macro- and microlevels of analysis.

The heart of our enterprise, therefore, is to demonstrate that these principles *explain developmental data* in ways that are both logically satisfying and useful, and plausible at many levels of analysis. We emphasize from the start that our search for more powerful explanatory principles for development has been primarily data-driven. Both of us faced a decade's research that we could not interpret using available models. The data were intriguing and perplexing, but we clearly needed new ways to make sense of them. We each soon realized that the puzzles in our own data sets were not unique, but mirrored the larger issues for developmental study as a whole.

Unquestionably, the largest corpus of theory-driven developmental data lies in the domain of cognition. Literally thousands of papers have been published on the milestone events of early mental life, such as the acquisition of symbolic reasoning and language. Because cognitive processes are both extraordinarily complex and usually opaque—i.e., only by indirect means can they be measured—they present the greatest theoretical challenge. Action theory, the concerns of perception and movement, proceeds with more observables and is more directly amenable to dynamic analysis. Thus, we begin with the development of locomotion. Locomotor development illustrates both the nature of the theoretical challenge and the application of the principles to a developmental problem that is more transparent and more accessible. Understand that we do not wish, by this organization, to characterize action as "mere" motor development or to assign primacy to either movement or cognition. Indeed, we will spend considerable effort building an argument for the inextricable causal web of perception, action, and cognition.

Plan of the book

With these overall goals in mind, we now summarize the organizational thread of the book, which is divided into three main sections. In the first section, we address developmental processes in the most general terms. All developing organisms, including the thinking and acting human, share a common set of characteristics and raise a common set of fundamental logical and philosophical questions. Dynamic systems principles, in turn, offer a broad, theoretically cogent approach to these problems. In the first chapter, we raise these questions using a well-studied example in human motor development: the ontogeny of erect locomotion. We also show that similar issues pervade the study of behavioral development in other vertebrate species. We then see, in chapter 2, how the current crisis in cognitive development mirrors these very same issues. We conclude here that current developmental theories of cognition and action are insufficient to explain these universal puzzles of development. In chapter 3, we introduce the concepts of nonlinear dynamic systems in general terms. We return to the example of learning to walk in chapter 4 to elaborate a dynamic approach to development. In this chapter we introduce, within the context of research and data on infant locomotion, the developmental meaning of attractors, phase shifts, time scales, dynamic stability, and variability. We illustrate the application of dynamic principles to empirical work.

The second major section of the book, chapters 5, 6, and 7, brings dynamic principles into issues of process and mechanism. Here we address the relation between multiple levels—morphology, neural processes, and behavior—and multiple time scales—real time, developmental time—in engendering developmental change. In chapter 5, therefore, we begin with a discussion of the dynamic nature of the brain. We follow with an extended explication of Edelman's theory of neuronal group selection. This entails a diversion into neural embryology to establish the anatomical basis of diversity, the key to selectionist theory. The chapter concludes with illustrations of dynamic processes in neural development.

In chapters 6 and 7, we build support for a selectionist theory. Chapter 6 commences with a discussion of the philosophical nature of categories. The ability to form perceptual categories is the foundation of human cognition and action. The point of this chapter is to show the fundamental dynamic properties of categories of thought and action and their development. We illustrate these dynamics through a computer simulation and by offering a new interpretation of how infants learn the properties of objects. Chapter 7 reviews further evidence from human infant studies for the process of development as dynamic selection. Here we build support for the unity of perception and action in category formation. First, we show that the primitive state is one of intermodal and cross-modal integration. Next, we argue for the critical role of movement in the formation of dynamic representations. And third, we show how this perception-action unity is revealed in both real and developmental time in studies of infant learning and memory.

We use the final section of the book, chapters 8, 9, 10, and 11, to show how dynamic principles and their process instantiations address the enduring puzzles of development we identified in the first section. Chapter 8 addresses the question of context specificity—the messy local variability contained within the global order. Using examples from infants learning about slopes, and knowing what is possible and impossible about the behavior of objects, we show how the local details—the variability and sensitivity of everyday behavior—are part and parcel of the developmental pathway. The chapter concludes with a discussion of the development of novel word interpretations. A theme repeated in this chapter is continuity of time scales.

Chapter 9 is about variability and selection. Here we discuss a study of learning to reach, a foundational skill. The point of this chapter is to show the real process of individual exploration of the natural variability of a system and how adaptive patterns of action are selected dynamically from this variability. This work addresses also the origins of new forms.

Likewise, chapter 10 is about emergence of novelty, and specifically, the phase shift in the so-called A-not-B error of late infancy. This has been a well-studied but poorly understood phenomenon. We analyze the multiple levels of causality and recast an explanation in dynamic terms. Here again, we echo the themes of context specificity, stability, and change, and the evolving dynamic landscape.

In chapter 11, our final chapter, we take a stab at what we have called the "hard problems." We begin with the issue of motivation: What starts the processing going? We suggest that motivation is a constant and distributed property of the developmental process landscape, a property that imparts meaning and value to the individual's actions within that landscape. We then go on to address the critical question of whether a dynamic account of early cognition and action can be extended to so-called higher cognitive processes. Can we extend a non-symbolic, nonrepresentational cognition beyond the sensorimotor period to account for higher-order reasoning, language, logic, and metacognition—"thinking about thinking"? We conclude here that as all mental activity is emergent, situated, historical, and embodied, there is in principle no difference between the processes engendering walking, reaching, and looking for hidden objects and those resulting in mathematics and poetry. Our developmental theorizing leads us to a view of cognition as seamless and dynamic.

A Dynamic Systems Approach to the Development of Cognition and Action

PART I

The Nature of Development: A Dynamic Approach

Chapter 1

Lessons from Learning to Walk

In the Introduction, we claimed that developing organisms shared a number of very general, and sometimes paradoxical, characteristics that posed a challenge to developmental theory. In this chapter, we substantiate our claims by exploring in detail a relatively well-studied ontogenetic phenomenon outside the cognitive sphere—the development of locomotion. We show how the systematic dissection of locomotor development raised fundamental issues about the nature of development which were inadequately addressed by prevailing theory. While the bulk of this chapter is concerned with human locomotion, we demonstrate that locomotor development in other vertebrate species—cat, chick, and frog—illustrates identical problems of ontogenetic process. Then, in chapter 2, we build a parallel story for emerging human cognition.

Learning to Walk: The Views from Above

There is a long and venerable tradition in developmental psychology of studies of learning to walk. Some of the most methodologically elegant and theoretically generative early work in the scientific study of human development came from the motor domain (e.g., Gesell, 1939; McGraw, 1932, 1940, 1945; Shirley, 1931). These early investigators had varied motives for studying motor processes: to establish developmental norms, to resolve the nature-nurture controversy, and to understand the developmental process and its underlying neurological basis. They began, as in any scientific endeavor, by describing the phenomenon, in this case, the progression of behavioral forms leading to clear developmental milestones.

Their efforts led to exquisite catalogs of motor types, with Gesell, for example, describing 23 stages and 28 substages of prone behavior (Gesell and Ames, 1940). These workers produced similar catalogs for nearly all motor behaviors, including prone progression, sitting, standing, swimming, and stair climbing, and Gesell later extended the stage concept to a host of mental and social activities. As an illustration, McGraw's sketch of the "seven phases of erect locomotion" (1945) is reproduced in figure 1.1. She proposed that infants progressed sequentially through these identifiable stages of reflex stepping, static phase, transition phase, deliberate stepping, independent stepping, and heel-toe progression to finally achieve the last phase, integrated walking.

What, then, moves the organism through these sequential stages? Both McGraw and Gesell invoked maturational processes as the primary driver of developmental change. For example, McGraw believed that her locomotor phases

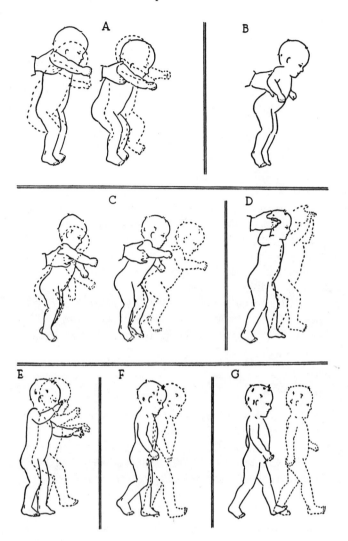

Figure 1.1
The seven stages of erect locomotion. (Reprinted with permission from McGraw, 1945.)

(and other motor changes) were driven primarily by changes in the motor cortex and its inhibitory influence on lower brain centers. "Certain qualities of movements signify grossly the level of neural maturation," McGraw claimed (1946, p. 359).

The story is a believable one. The first assumption in this neural-maturational approach is that the cerebral cortex is the agent of diverse, plastic, and purposeful behavior. Newborns, in contrast, are dominated by "primitive subcortical nuclei" (McGraw, 1945, p. 10). Their behavior is largely reflexive, and they exhibit phylogenetically old patterns, such as residual swimming movements and the Moro reflex. We also know that the cortex is unmyelinated and histologically immature at birth and that cortical areas become more highly differentiated and more complex during the first year. Thus, as the cortex matures, it progressively inhibits the limited and stereotyped subcortical output and increasingly takes over the control of the neuromuscular system.

This fits neatly onto McGraw's picture of the progression toward independent walking. According to McGraw (1945), the stepping movements seen in the first month or two of life are "controlled at a nuclear level" (p. 76) and are likely remnants of primitive functioning. The increase in such stepping seen between birth and 1 month is due to "advances in the subcortical centers" (p. 78). The subsequent decline of stepping movements within the next months is due to "cortical inhibitory processes," (p. 79) which are rapidly maturing at the same time postural mechanisms are advancing. In the next, or transition, stage, leg movements are variable, and it is difficult to tell whether they are reflexive or deliberate. Posture continues to improve. The "onset of cortical participation" can definitely be detected in phase D (see figure 1.1), when the child performs deliberate steps, although it is not complete. Postural and forward propulsion mechanisms become integrated in the phase of independent stepping, although the movement is not refined or integrated. When coordination improves, infants initiate stance with a definite heel-strike to toe-off progression. The final stage sees locomotion as smooth and automatic.

It must be noted here that McGraw's causal simplicity does not do justice to her descriptive and theoretical richness. She consistently described a multidetermined, gradual process, yet she felt it necessary to instantiate the driving force in structure, in this case, tissues in the brain. Indeed, both McGraw and Gesell in their later writings acknowledged the complexities of the processes they described. McGraw reminds readers that, "as yet no architectural features in the nervous system have been ascertained which clearly demarcate 'maturation' and 'learning' as two distinct features of growth" (1945, p. 121). Yet, she believes that "the qualities of learning appear concurrently with the beginning of cortical participation in each function" (1945, p. 122). In the preface to the 1962 edition of her 1945 book, *The Neuromuscular Maturation of the Human Infant*, McGraw looked back at her efforts to relate behavioral development to "maturation of the neural tissues, particularly those of the brain" (p. xi) as largely unsuccessful. This was in part because of methodological limitations, but more fundamentally a result of the unwarranted belief that complex functioning could be understood by histological changes in the brain or by assuming simple localization of function. Gesell (1945), too, evolved a sophisticated theory that acknowledged both the dynamic and nonlinear nature of developmental processes.

Despite the later reservations of these pioneers, however, the message from the volumes of developmental norms of the 1930s and 1940s and of illustrations such as figure 1.1 fell on many accepting ears. Development was a linear, stagelike progression through a sequence of increasingly more functional behaviors, driven toward adult forms by a grand plan (and scheduled by a grand timekeeper). This is what ontogeny looked like when the magnification was low, when the details from the individual subjects were averaged, and a series of more-or-less finely sculpted categories were imposed upon them.

Several more contemporary accounts of infant locomotion have echoed this tradition of unitary causality. Forssberg (1985), for example, speculated that newborn stepping was the ontogenetic manifestation of a phylogenetically old spinal pattern generator that only gradually comes under higher-level control. He focused especially on the observation that both newborns and new walkers strike the ground with their flat foot or toe rather than with the heel, as is characteristic of more mature human walkers. Most nonhuman animals also have the digitigrade (toe-first) gait. Infants retain the ancestral pattern throughout infancy and even for several months after they acquire independent locomotion. Only when the old pattern generator is replaced by a specifically human pattern generator do infants use the typical heel-strike.

In a recent paper, Konner stated baldly that locomotor development was a "paradigmatic case" (1991, p. 199) of neural growth directing behavioral change. "Motor development sequences are largely genetically programmed," he wrote (1991, p. 199). His evidence for this was the same as McGraw's: that the corticospinal tracts controlling the lower limbs become myelinated late in the first year, the same time as walking develops. "Thus, the development of improved function in this tract as a result of myelination is a likely candidate for a neural basis of the maturation of walking" (p. 201) as well as for the waning of the infantile reflexes. The basis for a phylogenetic origin of motor sequences, Konner claimed, is their universal limited range of timing of onset: all humans learn to walk the same way.

In a more cognitivist spirit, Zelazo (1984) proposed that "higher order influences" were the prime movers of the developmental progression leading to independent walking. The first function of these cognitive processes was to convert the reflexive repertoire of the young infant into instrumental actions. In a now classic paper, Zelazo, Zelazo, and Kolb (1972) showed that when newborn stepping was deliberately practiced, it did not disappear, but indeed increased in frequency. The authors interpreted this retention as the capture of the primitive pattern by higher influences in the form of instrumental learning. Thus, the stepping patterns of the newborn disappeared, not because of inhibition by the cortex, but through "disuse." Practice enhanced the precocious conversion of newborn stepping into an intentional act.

Secondly, according to Zelazo (1984), higher influences organized the onset of independent walking by providing the processing speed necessary to associate events rapidly and thus allow infants to integrate their movements with their intended goals. He proposed that a global cognitive change in such processing capabilities underlies a number of qualitative changes at about 1 year, including the onsets of functional play, first words, and bipedal locomotion. Whatever the postural and biomechanical requirements, infants would not walk until their representational abilities were sufficient to direct their movements toward intentional actions (Zelazo, 1984).

Deficiencies of Single-Cause Explanations

We believe that both the traditional maturationist and the more contemporary neurophysiological and cognitivist explanations for the development of walking are seriously deficient on both logical and empirical grounds. These appear to be pitfalls of developmental theory in general, and we will later express the same reservations about current formulations of cognitive change.

From the low-magnification view, the stages and phases of Gesell and McGraw capture a grand sweep of development in summary form. Such behavioral catalogs are not only an entirely reasonable and appropriate way to approach development, they may indeed be essential. What happened in the case of motor development (and arguably, in cognitive studies in the wake of Piaget) was that the catalog became reified as the process. That is, what started out as descriptive ended up as explanatory. (This critique has been leveled at stage theory in general, e.g., by Brainerd, 1978). It has been accepted dogma in many developmental textbooks that the stagelike progression of motor development, leading to a species-typical outcome (all human infants sit, walk, and climb), is evidence for "maturation," or a "biological" process uncontaminated by "experience." Here was a subtle shift from description to causality. *The equality of the outcome became the singularity of the process.* The very act of describing and classifying a continuous stream of changes into universal types made it easy to invoke a universal classifier, an agent (the brain) who knows the stagelike outcomes ahead of time and guides the organism to those outcomes.

This invocation of a single neurological or mentalistic causality for ontogenetic change has a number of critical consequences. First, the assumption of prior causality effectively stops other efforts to understand process. With all the cards in the hands of "biology," there is little else for the behavioral scientist to do, a conclusion that no doubt led to the nearly universal disinterest in motor development studies for nearly 40 years. For example, by every measure, children's mental operations become faster and more complex with age and their brains become bigger and more functionally differentiated. In one sense, a bigger brain and more processing capacity underlie all developmental change—motor, perceptual, cognitive, affective, social. If this were a sufficient explanatory principle, no further work would be necessary, but it clearly is not. Invoking a "switch" to a new pattern generator is equally post hoc and without process.

In addition, this development-by-design argument leads to a logical impasse (Oyama, 1985). Ultimately, invoking mental growth as an explanatory primitive leads to genetic nativism: it was all there to begin with, encoded in the genes, and only needs to be read from the genetic code into the neural structures with the passage of time. The interesting questions are thus finessed. Why do infants walk when they do? By what developmental pathways is this outcome assured? What are the necessary and sufficient conditions for the appearance of new forms?

Both the maturationist and cognitivist views of locomotor development assign a causal primacy to the mental structures that provide *intentionality* to the act of walking. That is, the shift from reflexive or more primitive movement to adaptive action is at the level of conscious control of the leg movements. Here we challenge the implicit assumption of such single cause models that a behavior such as walking "resides" in any single instantiation in the central nervous system (CNS) as either a neural or cognitive code. This assumption, that any behavior can be reduced to an *essential* that is represented in a privileged form within the organism, is widespread and seductive, but ultimately illusory. To illustrate this point, we make a brief digression to consider recent work on the neurophysiology of locomotion in nonhuman animals. We choose this example, first because it will later become relevant when we examine human locomotion in more detail, but also because neurophysiologists have tended to assign essence to lower rather than higher functions in the CNS. The fallacy of single causation is similar, however.

Central Pattern Generators and Locomotion

The question asked by motor neurophysiologists is: How is locomotion controlled by the CNS? One striking observation from a number of vertebrate species was that the pattern of locomotor movements appeared to be generated from the spinal cord. In the cat, for example, investigators surgically severed the brain from the spinal cord and cut the roots to the spinal cord carrying sensory information from the limbs, effectively isolating the spinal cord from both higher brain and peripheral influences. When the spinal cord was appropriately stimulated and the cat given postural support, it would indeed walk on a treadmill with coordination patterns within the joints of one limb and between the four limbs that were very similar to locomotion in the intact cat. Researchers could even paralyze the cat's muscles and detect patterns of neural firing *in the spinal cord* that corresponded to the alternating flexions and extensions of the muscles in normal locomotion. In other words, the spinal cord was sending the locomotor messages even in the absence of functioning recipients (see reviews by Grillner, 1975, 1981, 1985).

Such discoveries led neurophysiologists to hypothesize a *central pattern generator* (CPG), or a network of neurons in the spinal cord that could autonomously generate the muscle-specific neural activations of natural locomotion in the absence of sensory input (see Delcomyn, 1980; Grillner, 1975, 1981; for reviews). A unit of the CPG was envisioned to control the pattern of coordination in each limb, and these units, were, in turn, coupled to one another to activate the separate limbs in the precise sequencing needed for gait.[1] Control was essentially hierarchical, with the brain turning on the CPG and the CPG directing the muscles. The role of sensory input was to modulate this chain of command. (Please note that there is no neurophysiological evidence for a CPG in humans, although the concept is repeatedly invoked; e.g., see Forssberg, 1985.)

The CPG seems like an attractive concept because it captures the *essence* of quadruped locomotion: a fundamental neural structure that encodes the pattern of movement. We ask, however, whether an essence of locomotion, or of any behavior, exists in a privileged form within the organism. What can spinal cats really do? Without higher brain centers, cats cannot maintain any postural control of the hindlimbs and the muscle tone necessary to support the weight alone is lacking. Cats cannot initiate or guide their movements, nor can they anticipate obstacles and correct their steps. In short, such cats cannot walk. Real-life cat behavior poses difficult conceptual problems for the CPG. How does the pattern generator handle walking backward or walking over highly variable terrain? Cats can still walk, for example, when a limb joint is immobilized by a cast. This requires reorganization of the muscle firing patterns. How does the CPG do this? Do CPGs exist for other limb behaviors such as scratching or shaking off a foreign substance? If so, how does the cat switch between them? Do cats have CPGs in anticipation of novel movements for situations not previously encountered?

At best, the CPG is a highly impoverished essence of locomotion. The cat may be generating patterns of movement but it is not walking. It is only walking when it shows independent, functionally appropriate behavior. So even if the CPG existed, it is not doing the interesting work. At worst, the concept is vacuous because every real-life action requires that the CPG be plastic, responsive, and adaptive to changes both within the cat and in the cat's world. Where, then, does walking reside?

While the isolated cat spinal cord can produce patterned neural impulses under special experimental conditions, the CPG is a neural abstraction. Walking in intact animals is not controlled by an abstraction, but in a continual dialogue with the periphery, and this system is much more complicated. What look like immutable and essential characteristics of the CPG when cats are studied in special circumstances are, under closer scrutiny, labile and plastic (Pearson, 1987; Smith, 1986). The nervous system must be this way because the output devices (limbs and body segments) demand it. Real-life cats (and other terrestrial vertebrates) have to support bodies on their limbs and maintain an erect posture against gravity. The moving limbs themselves have mass, and muscles have elastic and viscous qualities. Muscle functions are highly complex, with some muscles activating more than one joint. When the animal moves, all of these peripheral structures and forces are continuously changing. These complexities cannot be handled by a simplified code isolated from the output (Smith and Zernicke, 1987). Rather, muscle activation patterns reflect and respond to the dynamic needs of the animal and its moving limbs. What sculpts movement patterns are these peripheral demands, not cartoons of the movement that exist beforehand (Hasan and Stuart, 1988). Cats and humans do not walk in abstractions. They walk in a gravity-dominated, variable, and changing world for different functional purposes.

Indeed, whenever function is considered, neuroscientists find that sensory information is dominant (Patla, 1991). For example, even spinal cats will speed up their steps when the treadmill belt is faster. Proprioception is critical to the timing of the steps in response to the treadmill, and indeed it has now been conclusively shown that the initiation of a swing is triggered by receptors signifying muscle stretch. As the body moves forward on the standing leg, the calf muscles are stretched, but they are unloaded as the leg is fully stretched. This unloading, not an autonomous signal, maintains the stance in the opposite leg and triggers the muscles initiating swing (Pearson, Ramirez, and Jiang, 1992).

Even in simpler animals, the hierarchical model of brain to spinal cord to muscles appears to be wrong. In her recent review of the CPG concept in cockroaches, eels, and cats, Cohen argues for heterarchical rather than hierarchical control; connections between the elements—spinal cord, brain, sensory input, muscles, and limbs—are dense and multiply interconnected. Locomotor patterns are as much controlled by mechanical considerations at the periphery as controlling them, for instance. She writes:

> It is not possible to speak of the command neurons driving the CPG since they are both driving each other. It is not possible to regard the sensory input as regulating or entraining the CPG, because the CPG is filtering the input. Each level of the system contributes to the output, and each level helps to shape the final output of the system, and each is shaped in turn by the others. As a consequence of the mutual interactions within the system, each portion of the system contributes its own peculiar properties and constraints to the final output. (Cohen, 1992, p. 117)

Where then, does locomotion reside?

The notion of the CPG as the essence of locomotion does not fit the data. It is precisely a similar confrontation with the data that raises our third and most serious objection to single-cause models in development. *They simply do not account for what we really observe in developing organisms.* Our theories must account for what we find when we look beyond categories and stages and when we turn up the microscope. In the remainder of this chapter, we document how a closer look at learning to walk demands new formulations.

Learning to Walk: A Confrontation with More Data

Whatever descriptive categories we accept for the development of human upright locomotion, we can detect several rather dramatic transitions. The first is the intriguing "disappearance" at about 2 months of age of the coordinated, steplike movements performed by newborns when they are held erect. The second is the reappearance of stepping movements while infants bear their weight on their feet during the second half of the year. Finally, the first independent steps at about 1 year stand as a third milestone event. We have rejected "brain matura-tion" as an explanatory principle for these changes on several logical grounds. Now we see that this single cause also lacks empirical substance. What do these transitions look like under more careful scrutiny? What happens when we turn up the power of our microscope?

The first transition is especially puzzling. Newborn infants are motorically immature, so it is surprising to see them precociously lift and lower their legs in alternating and steplike fashion. It further defies our notions of progressive development to observe the normal *loss* of a well-articulated movement, as infants steadfastly refuse to step after a month or two.

Many scholars have used newborn stepping as an example of so-called re-gressive or U-shaped development (Bower, 1976; Strauss, 1982; Oppenheim, 1981), as this phenomenon raises questions about continuity and the nature of ontogenetic precursors, as well as about the functions of behaviors that disappear. What seems clear is that stepping in the newborn period is involuntary. (Many have used the term *reflexive,* but stepping, for a number of reasons, is not a reflex in the accepted sense; see Thelen and Fisher, 1982.) It is also obvious that stepping movements toward the end of the first year have a more intentional character.

Both the McGraw and the Zelazo accounts focused on the dimension of intentionality as the key element in transforming newborn steps to later steps, but they hypothesized different routes to voluntary behavior. McGraw suggested that the involuntary patterns must be suppressed for volition to emerge; Zelazo spoke of these patterns as captured by higher centers and converted to voluntary acts through association processes. Loss of the movement pattern occurred by inhibition in the former and by disuse in the latter.

It is easy to move from the descriptive statement that changes in intentionality *accompany* the loss and recovery of stepping, to making intentionality the *agent* of those changes. If we forget about any single causation and look at the behavior itself and the contexts in which it is performed, a different picture emerges.

Stepping movements in the newborn period are not random thrashings of the legs, but organized movements with a recognizable structure in time and space. Specifically, infants lift their legs by flexing and extending their hips, knees, and ankles nearly simultaneously, often alternating movements between the two legs. The timing of the flexion phase is remarkably consistent, usually around 0.3 second, with the extension considerably more variable. A distinctive pattern of muscle activations underlying these movements can be detected by electromyography (EMG) (Thelen and Fisher, 1983).

What is developmentally important is that while these kinematic and EMG patterns are characteristic of newborn stepping movements, they are not unique to them. Thelen and Fisher (1983) found that newborn stepping was nearly identical in kinematic details (the coordination of the joints and the timing of the phases of cyclic flexions and extensions of the legs) and in underlying muscle activation patterns with another common newborn movement, kicking in the supine position. Both kicking and stepping increased as infants became more behaviorally aroused, and these rate adjustments occurred in similar phases of the movement cycle in both actions. Infants who were lifted from supine when kicking looked liked infants who were stepping when upright. The evidence suggested that what had previously been considered as distinct and separate behaviors were manifestations of the same motor output performed in two different postures.

Most significant was that while infants clearly stopped stepping when they were about 2 months old, *they continued to kick* throughout the first year when they were supine, prone, or sitting. It seemed unlikely that either cortical inhibition or disuse would selectively act on upright leg cycles and not on supine leg cycles. Since only postural set distinguished a continuous from a discontinuous developmental course, the disappearance of the movement pattern seemed hardly inevitable.

Indeed, on closer look, the transition from stepping to no-stepping was much more labile than previously imagined. Remember that Zelazo et al. (1972) reported a practice effect: infants given daily exercise in spontaneous stepping retained the movement pattern throughout the first year. But stepping was also a function of rather nonspecific states of the infant. At all ages, step (and kick) rate and strength were directly correlated with general level of arousal. Infants who were stepping little when alert and happy began stepping movements when fussy. The decline in step rate between 2 and 6 weeks was most rapid in infants who had the highest rate of weight gain (Thelen, Fisher, Ridley-Johnson, and

Griffin, 1982). Step rate was also affected by simple environmental manipulations. When infants were held upright in torso-deep warm water, stepping movements increased in both number and vigor. Three-month-old infants who did not normally step performed frequent steps when their legs were submerged (figure 1.2). Conversely, the addition of small weights to the legs of stepping infants suppressed the movements (Thelen, Fisher, and Ridley-Johnson, 1984).

Very simple changes in the infants or their environmental contexts shifted the developmental path of a transition believed to be the inevitable consequence of brain maturation. Does stepping really "disappear"? What is the nature of a structural mechanism that is affected by posture or by adding weights to the leg?

The picture becomes even more complex when we look at the second transition, the "reappearance" of stepping movements when infants are supporting their weight on their feet. Normally, this transition is late in the first year, at 8 to 10 months. Again, however, a mechanical manipulation revealed a different developmental course. Thelen (1986) discovered that 7-month-old infants, who normally did not step, performed highly coordinated, alternating steps when they were supported with their feet on the slowly moving belts of a small, motorized treadmill. Stepping began immediately when the treadmill was turned on, and like adults, infants adjusted their step rate to the speed of the treadmill. As the

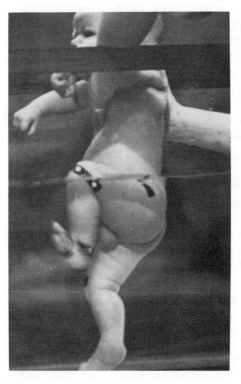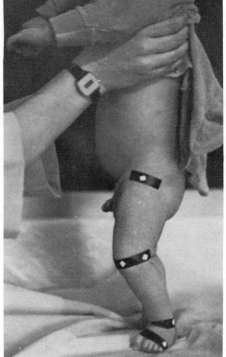

Figure 1.2
Upright stepping restored when leg mass is reduced by submersion. This 3-month-old infant was tested with feet on the table and submerged in warm water, as described in Thelen et al., 1984.

treadmill speed was increased, infants increased their step rate by decreasing the stance or support phase of the step, a phase-dependent correction typical of adult locomotion in many species, including humans. Even more remarkable were infants' abilities to make functionally appropriate corrections to the bilateral coordination of their treadmill stepping. Thelen, Ulrich, and Niles (1987) tested another group of 7-month-old infants on a treadmill constructed with two parallel belts whose speed could be independently adjusted so that each leg could be driven at a different speed. Under this unusual challenge, infants maintained perfectly alternating steps (figure 1.3). This required asymmetrical adjustments: precisely slowing down the stance phase on the faster leg and speeding up the stance phase on the slower leg to maintain a step rate intermediate between the fast and the slow belts.

The discovery of treadmill stepping in 7-month-old infants raised the question of the ontogenetic origins of this behavior. In a longitudinal study of nine infants tested monthly on the treadmill, Thelen and Ulrich (1991) found one infant stepping well *at 1 month* of age, several stepping at 2 to 3 months, and the remainder performing well-coordinated steps by 4 months. Coordination and adjustment to speed changes continued to improve, and then leveled off at about 6 months.

There are a number of characteristics of treadmill stepping that add to this developmental puzzle. First, treadmill stepping appeared to be a completely involuntary action. Until about 8 or 9 months infants paid little attention to their moving legs and seemed neither distressed nor surprised at their activity. Their movements seemed "captured" by the treadmill. Later in the first year, infants did seem to notice the treadmill, but this attention *inhibited* rather than facilitated the response. In fact, older infants who were standing and stepping on their own frequently refused the treadmill.

While involuntary, however, treadmill stepping was not reflexive, in the sense that a reflex is a stereotyped response to phasic stimuli, and where the magnitude of the response is independent of the strength of the stimuli. Rather, treadmill stepping was flexible and adaptive in a functionally specific way. That is, infants maintained an alternating gait pattern when faced with speed changes and even when their legs were moving at different speeds (see figure 1.3). Clearly, something about the mechanical stretching of the legs backward by the treadmill belt organized the two legs into a functional synergy, that is, a cooperative unit responsive to its own behavior and to perturbations from external sources.

The implications of this phenomenon are profound: mechanisms are in place early in development that detect the movement of the legs as they are pulled back, and translate these perceptions into a highly structured movement that is responsive to the dynamic context of the legs. It is important to note here that treadmill stepping is *at every age* kinematically more mature-looking than steps performed without the treadmill (if any steps are indeed taken). That is, treadmill steps are more consistently alternating, and the pattern of excursions of the joints looks more like mature locomotion than the pattern in newborn stepping, or for that matter, deliberate steps taken alone several months before walking (Thelen and Cooke, 1987). Indeed, some infants even show a proportion of treadmill steps with a distinct heel-strike (Thelen, Bril, and Breniere, 1992). Heel-strike was previously considered a defining character of mature locomotion (Forssberg,

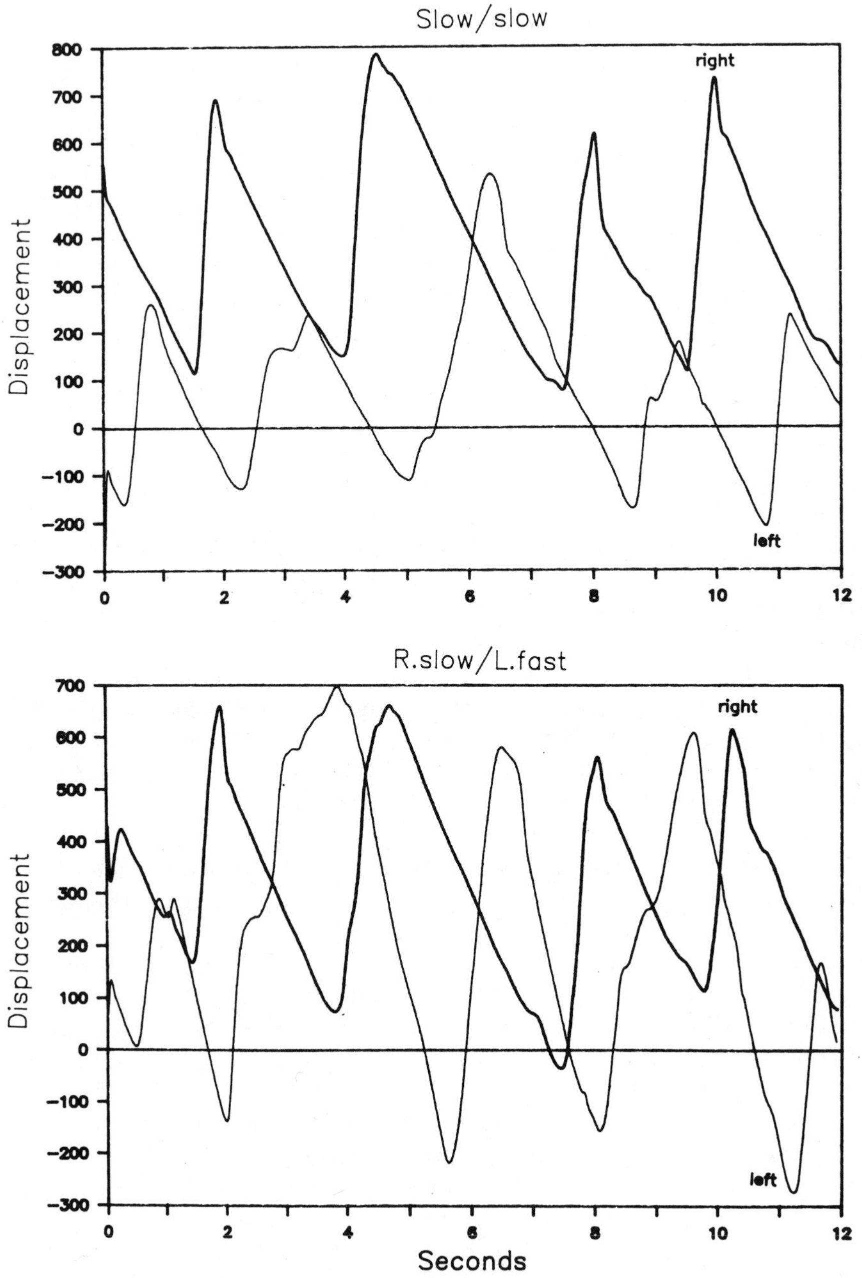

Figure 1.3
Displacements of the right (R) and left (L) feet forward and backward of a single infant on a split-belt treadmill, with the belt speeds adjusted to be both slow, both fast, or one slow and one fast. Movement in the positive direction is the stance phase. The figure illustrates the influence of the belt speed on step rate (infants take fewer steps on the slow treadmill) and the maintenance of regularly alternating steps in both the tied- and split-belt conditions. (From Thelen, Ulrich, and Niles, 1987.)

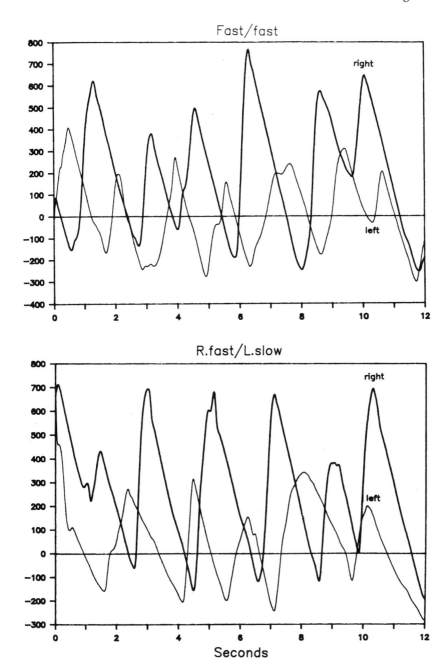

Figure 1.3 (continued)

1985; Sutherland, Olshen, Cooper, and Woo, 1980). Patterns of equivalent maturity are never seen without the treadmill, and indeed not until infants are walking well with support, that is, making real forward progression. In short, the treadmill acted to reveal a developmental progression believed to be organically determined.

Deconstructing Developmental Stages

What do the data from newborn and treadmill stepping mean, then, for the linear progress of McGraw's seven phases toward upright locomotion? First, these data suggest that a seemingly unitary behavior is composed of many subcomponents. Behavior on the treadmill exposes a component of locomotion—the responsive patterning of the legs—entirely divorced from both intentionality to move and the ability to support the weight on the feet. Behavior on the treadmill is also separate from autonomous stepping, as performance on the treadmill is improving dramatically *at the same time* that stepping alone is decreasing.

Second, not only are these components distinct but they develop at dramatically different rates. The neuromuscular mechanism for treadmill stepping is available very early in the first year; the ability to stand upright emerges many months later. Although independent walking requires the ability both to support the weight on the legs and to move the legs in an alternating pattern of swing and stance, these are highly decomposable properties with entirely different developmental paths. When infants were supported by others and the dynamic movement of the legs was simulated by the treadmill, the stepping configuration emerged reliably by 3 or 4 months. On the other hand, 9- or 10-month-old infants who can stand quite well by themselves cannot step.

A similar heterochrony is evident in the intentional aspect of leg motor control. Treadmill stepping is likely involuntary through 7 months, but infants can use their legs for other voluntary activities such as activating an interesting mobile as early as 2½ to 3 months of age (e.g., Rovee and Rovee, 1969). Intentionality on treadmills is not conjoint with intentionality when kicking a mobile. Voluntary use of the legs is not a unitary ability developing in a linear or incremental fashion throughout the first year, but is tied to the context.

Third, these studies show that walking development is sensitive to organic and environmental events to a degree not previously suspected. Whatever the course of brain development, *behavioral expression* is entirely context-dependent. By testing infants in the upright posture, one may conclude that stepping movements disappear. In the supine position, leg movements not only persisted during the first year but showed an elaborated developmental course, which included increasing individuation of the joints and changing patterns of interlimb coordination (Thelen, 1984). On the treadmill, leg movements also persisted, but with an entirely different ontogenetic profile, that of gradual improvement in alternate interlimb phasing and decreasing variability in all aspects of the movement (Thelen and Ulrich, 1991).

The point here is that without a context, *there is no essence* of leg movements during the first year. Leg coordination patterns are entirely situation-dependent—whether the infant be calm or excited; upright, supine, or prone; deliberately using the legs for exploration or locomotion; on a treadmill; submerged in water; or standing alone. There is, likewise, *no essence* of locomotion either in the motor cortex or in the spinal cord. Indeed, it would be equally credible to assign the essence of walking to the treadmill than to a neural structure, because it is the action of the treadmill that elicits the most locomotor-like behavior.

As we document further in chapter 4, locomotor development can only be understood by recognizing the *multidimensional* nature of this behavior, a multi-dimensionality in which the organic components and the context are equally causal and privileged. That is, while neural and anatomical structures are nec-essary for the expression of the behavior, the sufficiency of a behavioral outcome is only completed with the task and context. The very same muscles, joints, and nervous system that produce stepping when the treadmill is turned on produce feet-stuck-to-the-ground behavior when the motor is off, or foot-in-the-mouth behavior when the baby is lying down. At the same time, there are a variety of ways to step on the treadmill—with legs rotated outward or inward, landing on the toes or flat foot, and so on.

The concept of a grand developmental plan incorporating a species-typical endpoint does not explain the fluid nature of leg movement coordination in the first year. In the next chapter, we argue that cognitive development is equally modular, heterochronic, context-dependent, and multidimensional. But to in-crease the generality of our points here, we look briefly at locomotor development in three other vertebrate species. Human bipedal locomotion is without question the most biomechanically demanding, and that human infants take longer to learn to walk alone than other species is no surprise. The processes, however, are characteristics of behavioral development in general. Locomotion in three nonhuman vertebrates—frog, chick, and cat—have the same qualities of apparent homogeneity of process from afar, but modularity, heterochrony, context depen-dency, and multidimensionality when viewed from close up.

Locomotor Development in the Bullfrog

Like other amphibians, the bullfrog (*Rana catesbeiana*) lives two dramatically different lives. As a tadpole for nearly 2 years, it is aquatic, herbivorous, and actively seeks food and avoids prey. As a frog, it is terrestrial, air-breathing, and carnivorous, but quite inactive, as it sits and waits for prey to happen by. The bullfrog's locomotion during these two life stages is also behaviorally and ana-tomically distinct. Tadpoles swim by means of tail oscillations, which are con-trolled by spinal motoneurons which innervate the axial muscles of the body and tail. In contrast, frogs step, hop, or swim using their hindlimbs, while the forelimbs are used for support. The motoneurons that innervate the hindlimbs to produce alternate or synchronous locomotor movements are completely dif-ferent from those used for tail oscillations (Stehouwer and Farel, 1983).

Metamorphosis, a period of profound, but rapid physiological and morpho-logical change, separates these two life stages. During the 2 weeks of metamorphosis,

> The bullfrog becomes semiterrestrial, the eyes migrate dorsomedially, the forelimbs erupt, the tail degenerates, larval mouthparts degenerate and the

adult jaw structure is attained, the long coiled intestine of the primarily herbivorous tadpole is replaced by the stout intestine befitting the carnivorous frog, and the gills are replaced by the skin and lungs as primary organs of respiration. (Stehouwer, 1988, p. 384)

Although frogs do not use the hindlimbs alone for locomotion until the end of the metamorphic period, anatomical changes long predate this period. Stehouwer and Farel (1983) detected the underlying neural activity for hindlimb stepping and kicking in the isolated spinal cord during early and intermediate tadpole stages, even before the morphological differentiation of the hindlimbs. Hindlimbs themselves erupt later in the larval period, but are nonfunctional. Thus, both the neurological substrate for locomotion and the limbs themselves are precociously accelerated in relation to their behavioral expression.

The behavioral expression of locomotion, however, appears to be, at least in part, environmentally mediated. Stehouwer and Farel (1984) tested metamorphic bullfrogs in three substrate conditions: (1) deep water, (2) a slippery, wet surface (presumably a transition surface), and (3) a dry, rough surface simulating dry land. Both hard surfaces elicited significantly accelerated locomotor patterns in the use of hindlimb stepping and the cessation of tail beating. That is, the tactile or proprioceptive stimuli, or both, from the surface were sufficient to elicit behavioral patterns not normally seen until later stages in development.

Terrestrial locomotion in the frog requires more than hindlimb movements. In addition to the physiological adaptations to life on land, the frog must develop forelimb postural support and new patterns of eye movements. These changes accompany the bullfrog's *preference* for dry land at the end of the metamorphic period, and its locomotor adaptation to it (Stehouwer, 1988). As in human infants, functional locomotion arises as a confluence of organismic and environmental factors. Although elements of the behavior may be precociously elicited, these are not privileged components; contact with a surface is as necessary as the underlying neural substrate.

Locomotor Development in the Chick

In the frog, neural patterns appropriate for hindlimb locomotion were detected in the spinal cord, but the behavior was expressed only in context. Limb movement patterns in the developing chick are similarly organized.

Like human infants, embryonic and newly hatched chicks perform a variety of patterned leg movements. In the egg, chicks spontaneously move their legs in jerky, seemingly random actions interspersed with periods of coordinated flexions and extensions (Watson and Bekoff, 1990). At the time of hatching, however, a distinctive synchronous thrusting movement of both legs appears, which assists the chick in escaping from the shell. After hatching, these movements are not seen again. Instead, chicks can step with alternate legs, hop by using both legs together, and even swim when placed in water.

Although patterned neural activity can be detected in the isolated chick embryo spinal cord (Bekoff, 1976), these developmental transitions and regressions result not from basic remodeling of a CPG, but from ontogenetically appropriate contextual changes. For example, the initiation of hatching movements appear to be posture-dependent. Hatching movements can be elicited in post-hatching chicks by enclosing them in glass eggs or otherwise restraining them. Bekoff and Kauer (1984) found that such a manipulation "restored" the precise leg motor output patterns normally seen only during normal hatching. The trigger appeared to be the bending of the neck into the typical embryonic position, a posture that would normally occur as the embryo grew larger in the shell (Bekoff and Kauer, 1982). Hatching movements do not "disappear" from the repertoire, but the context for their elicitation normally does.

Likewise, Bekoff (1985) produced distinctive patterns of muscle activations in chicks by other contextual manipulations. Flexor and extensor burst character-istics depended on whether the chick bore weight on the limbs. The muscle patterns of swimming chicks were more like those seen in spontaneous embry-onic motility, conditions where the legs are not loaded, than those seen in chicks walking down a runway. In addition, surgically disrupting the sensory input from the legs in chicks immediately after hatching restored a more hatching-like rather than locomotor-like pattern of coordination.

In chicks, as in frogs and humans, a dialogue with the periphery is an essential motor-driving developmental change. One must question both the usefulness, and indeed the reality, of any privileged code such as a CPG when behavioral output is never isolated from a behavioral situation. Examples of "pure" motor output, typically thought of as the embryonic condition or when the animal is tested on a treadmill, are no more than specific contexts. Locomotor development in the cat provides a final example.

Locomotor Development in the Cat

Similar themes of heterochrony and context specificity recur in the development of locomotion in the cat. Although it was widely believed that kittens do not support their weight and step until the end of their second week after birth, Bradley and Smith (1988a,b) detected stepping by day 3 in all the kittens they tested. The key to this precocial ability was strictly in the testing context. Newborn kittens who are removed from their mothers become highly aroused and will typically drag their bellies forward by moving their forelimbs. However, when Bradley and Smith placed the kittens only a short distance from the mothers, the kittens supported their weight and stepped with both fore- and hindlimbs to return to their mothers. The authors concluded that this situation, which both minimized stress and optimized motivation to move overground, was "the only reliable condition for inducing weight-supported hindlimb stepping" (1988, p. 48).

Newborn kittens also stepped on the treadmill when their trunk was well supported, but these steps were difficult to elicit because the kittens became highly upset and locked their limbs in either tight flexion or extension. Indeed, Bradley and Smith (1988) report that while the kittens normally dragged their hindlimbs on the treadmill, they would perform weight-supported steps when they attempted to push off the belt and climb onto the examiner's hand!

These earliest stepping attempts had muscle activation patterns that shared many characteristics with treadmill and overground locomotion in adult cats. There were a number of context-sensitive alterations in the adultlike patterns, however. Normal alternation of flexor and extensor activity was disrupted in stressful situations. When very young kittens were bearing their weight, they "stiffened" their limbs by contracting both flexor and extensor muscles simultaneously. This co-contraction, usually believed to be a more "primitive" pattern than alternating flexors and extensors, is very often seen in human infants as well during weightbearing. However, this limb stiffening, rather than a mark of neural immaturity, may be an ad hoc strategy for stabilizing the joints before more adultlike postural control has developed.

The demonstration that newborn kittens can be coaxed to perform locomotor actions several weeks before they commonly walk by themselves indicates that locomotor development in cats, as well as in frogs, chicks, and humans, is modular and context-sensitive. Cats can generate patterned limb activity very early in life, but *walking alone* requires more—postural stability, strong muscles and bones, motivation to move forward, a facilitative state of arousal, and an appropriate substrate. Only when these components act together does the cat truly walk.

In each of these cases, it is tempting to assign the "essence" of locomotion to CPGs that appear to encode some abstraction of locomotion. Neural structures can produce highly structured firing patterns even when they are severed from their normal input and output connections. This autonomous activity alone is not natural behavior, although it may be a component of it. Most important, isolated neural structures at whatever level have no mechanisms for generating new forms other than their intrinsic processes, vaguely named maturation. With further investigation, we have seen, however, that there is no essence; there is only performance within a specifying context. We believe that this is the fundamental insight that will allow us to build a useful developmental model. In the next chapter, we pursue the same line of reasoning in the cognitive domain.

Note

1. The question of whether a dedicated neural structure provides the essential characteristics of vertebrate locomotion can be asked separately from the important evidence that many neural structures, including those in vertebrate spinal cord, produce autonomous oscillations, with complex coupling, frequency, and phase relations. That these oscillations are possibly essential in producing coordinated behavior is discussed in chapter 6. Here we argue against the notion that the neural network contains some privileged icon of the behavior, abstracted from the complex motivational and environmental contexts in which it is performed.

Chapter 2

The Crisis in Cognitive Development

In this chapter, we offer an overview of current theorizing about cognitive development. Our question is, What theoretical tools are currently available for understanding the development of mind and are these tools sufficient to the task? We find explanations in cognitive development wanting in the same ways that single causes, maturation, and central pattern generators (CPGs) are found wanting as explanations of walking. We begin with a brief history of the fall of Piaget's logicomathematical theory of cognitive development.

Piaget: The View from Above

Piaget (e.g., 1951, 1954, 1970) emphasized the grand sweep of development. In Piaget's view, the child's mental life marches forward in one direction toward greater logical heights. The march is composed of qualitatively distinct and invariantly ordered stages. In infancy, children are sensorimotor organisms; their mental life is what is perceived and acted on. In the preschool years, children represent their world in symbols, but these symbols are still perceptual, rigid, and cannot be mentally manipulated. In the school years, children reason logically, mentally manipulating ideas, but these ideas are concrete, not abstract. Finally, in adolescence, the full power of the mind is realized in abstract logical thought.

Viewed from afar, cognitive development fits Piaget's description. If one looks at children of different ages and their approach to a variety of tasks, ignoring all the details and subtleties of performance, what does one see? One sees children who at different ages interact with their world in qualitatively different ways. We may not know how to theoretically describe the differences, but the behavior of a 1-year-old is not at all like that of a 3-year-old who does not behave as he or she will at age 8 or 18 years. Moreover, when we present children with the same tasks that Piaget did, we get the same results. The infant seamlessly shifts attention when an object goes out of view. The 3-year-old, however, systematically searches for missing objects. The 8-year-old can make inferences about space from memory, and the 18-year-old can reason about abstract entities and space devoid of contextual support. At a global level, the intellectual differences between children of different ages are very much as Piaget described them.

Nonetheless, the scientific consensus is that the part of Piaget's theory that posited monolithic changes in the logicomathematical structures that underlie cognition is wrong. Piaget's cognitive theory fit the orderliness of development on the large scale, but it dramatically failed to capture the complexity and messiness of cognitive development in detail. Piaget's theory failed when developmentalists turned up the microscope. When researchers such as Rochel Gelman (1972) and Margaret Donaldson (1978) tinkered with some Piagetian tasks—when they reduced the memory, altered the language, took children's hands out from under their fannies so they could count—they found fragile and shifting competences. When we reify Piagetian tasks and observe cognition under stable and uniform conditions, we find stable stages of cognition. But if we vary the tasks and nudge and push at the child's mind, we see instabilities, context dependencies, and fluidity in cognition.

Turning up the microscope resulted in serious challenges to three central claims of Piagetian theory, claims of (1) an impoverished beginning state, (2) global discontinuities in cognition across stages, and (3) monolithic cognitive growth. According to Piaget, infants start their cognitive construction of the world with nothing more than reflexive responses to external stimuli. But the data show this not to be so. The beginning state is not impoverished; the human infant is highly "competent" and possesses highly structured perceptual and conceptual skills (e.g., Cohen and Salapatek, 1975). According to Piaget, advances in children's representations are discontinuous across stages. However, there is evidence that precursors to mature thought can be detected early in life. For example, infants show elements of abstract numerical thought (e.g., Wynn, 1992), a complex naive physics (Spelke, 1990), and "theories" of causality (Bullock, Gelman, and Baillargeron, 1982). There is a common core, a continuity, in the thinking of babies and adults. According to Piaget, the developmental revolutions in cognitive structure control and pervade all of cognition. Yet we see wide discrepancies in individual competencies across domains: the 2-year-old who uses symbols in play (Bates, 1979) cannot use a scale replica as a symbol (DeLoache, 1987); the preschooler who is fluent in the powerful operations of language cannot make logical inferences (Inhelder and Piaget, 1964). All of cognition does not move forward in lockstep. Cognitive development does not look like a marching band; it looks more like a teeming mob. Piaget's theory fails to fit the view from below.

The View from Below: Transitive Inference Making

The complexity of cognitive development is clarified by considering facts about cognitive development in one domain—transitive inference making. This task domain is not special; it serves as just one of many possible data sets suggesting the fluid, context-dependent character of developing cognition (see Smith, Sera, and Gattusso, 1988).

A transitive inference task is one in which we infer a third relation from two others. For example, we might infer "the blue rod is longer than the yellow rod" from "the blue rod is longer than the green rod" and "the green rod is longer than the yellow rod." According to Piaget, preschool children cannot make transitive inferences because they do not possess the mental operations to do so. Inhelder and Piaget (1964) empirically supported this claim with repeated demonstrations of preschool children failing to make transitive inferences. Piaget also pointed to other difficulties that the young child has with quantitative dimensions, for example, difficulties in seriating objects (e.g., from tallest to shortest).

In 1971, Bryant and Trabasso showed that preschool children can make transitive inferences. They suggested the child's problem was remembering the premises. Thus in the example of colored rods, if children forget or confuse what color is longer than what other color, they cannot successfully make a transitive inference. Accordingly, Bryant and Trabasso drilled preschool children until they perfectly remembered the premise information. The stimulus series, premises, and questions are given in figure 2.1. In this task (as in Piaget's task), children never actually see the objects, they only hear and learn verbal descriptions.

Bryant and Trabasso's results were clear. When preschool children perfectly learn the premise information, preschool children make transitive inferences. Subsequent research (Trabasso and Riley, 1975) further demonstrated that preschool children make inferences in the same way adults do. Both children and adults show a "distance effect"; they take more time to judge which of two items is longer if the items are close (e.g., green and red in figure 2.1) than if they are

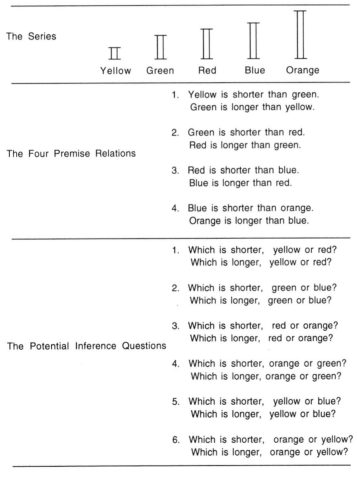

The Series

Yellow   Green   Red   Blue   Orange

The Four Premise Relations

1. Yellow is shorter than green.
   Green is longer than yellow.

2. Green is shorter than red.
   Red is longer than green.

3. Red is shorter than blue.
   Blue is longer than red.

4. Blue is shorter than orange.
   Orange is longer than blue.

The Potential Inference Questions

1. Which is shorter, yellow or red?
   Which is longer, yellow or red?

2. Which is shorter, green or blue?
   Which is longer, green or blue?

3. Which is shorter, red or orange?
   Which is longer, red or orange?

4. Which is shorter, orange or green?
   Which is longer, orange or green?

5. Which is shorter, yellow or blue?
   Which is longer, yellow or blue?

6. Which is shorter, orange or yellow?
   Which is longer, orange or yellow?

Figure 2.1
Stimuli, premises, and inference questions of the sort used by Bryant and Trabasso.

far (e.g., green and orange) in the series. This distance effect makes sense if one is answering the inference question from a perceived series. But in Bryant and Trabasso's experiments, children did not actually *see* the objects all lined up in a row. Instead, they must have imagined the series from the verbal descriptions between pairs of objects. This is a remarkable achievement. Preschool children cannot successfully seriate real objects, but they apparently can mentally seriate imagined objects. Moreover, both children and adults seem to be making inferences in much the same way. Children's thinking is continuous with adults' thinking.

What are we to make of these results? Is children's thinking just like adults? It is not that simple. In order to show that children can make transitive inferences, the children must be drilled on the premises for many trials and they must learn the premises in both directions. One cannot simply teach the child that "red is longer than green." One must teach the child that "red is longer than green" *and* "green is shorter than red." Without explicit and extensive training of the premises phrased in both directions, the preschool child encodes and remembers only categorical information—"red is long"—and not the critical comparative information. This fact is important. It is not that young children have difficulty remembering, as we might have difficulty remembering a list of facts. Rather, young children *systematically misremember* the information.

Moreover, the way young children misremember—interpreting "red is longer than green" as "red is long"—seems, as Piaget pointed out, just like their failures in seriation tasks. According to Piaget, seriation is like transitive inference making because both require the recognition that an individual object can be at the same time more than some objects and less than others. In one seriation task, Piaget asked children to insert objects in an already completed series. What young children do is insert the object so that it is longer than both adjacent items (figure 2.2A) or so that it is smaller than both adjacent items (figure 2.2B). The traditional Piagetian interpretation is that the child can think of the inserted object in only one way at a time—as short or as long.

This same difficulty is seen when children are shown seriated sticks and asked to draw them (Sinclair de Zwart, 1969). When drawing a series, preschool children draw "short ones and long ones" (figure 2.2C) or "short-long-short-long . . ." (figure 2.2D). The difficulty here is not memory; the series stays in view while the child draws. The same categorical treatment of dimensions is seen in how children talk about series. Children describe seriated objects as "the little ones and the big ones" (Ehri, 1976; Sera and Smith, 1987; Smith, Rattermann, and Sera, 1988). Children's misremembering of premises in a transitive inference task, their failures in seriating objects, how they talk about quantitative dimensions—all seem to fit together just as Piaget said they did.

What is the nature of the developmental process that it looks like this? Preschool children can make transitive inferences and apparently by the same mechanism as do adults, but they cannot remember comparative sentences. Preschool children can seriate in their minds but not in reality. Preschool children can make transitive inferences but need very special task support to do so. In their daily lives, preschool children rarely make transitive inferences. In daily life, the premises are not drilled or stated in both directions. Instead, in their daily interaction with the world, preschool children operate much as Piaget described

A   B

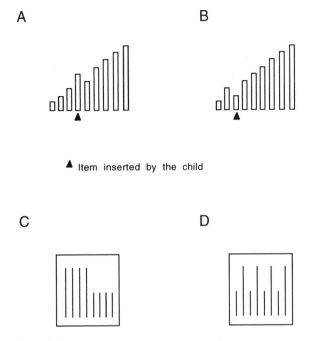

▲ Item inserted by the child

C   D

Figure 2.2
Illustrations of preschool children's responses to seriation tasks: (*A and B*) inserting an item in a series; (*C and D*) copying a series.

them. These data about transitive inference making in preschool children pose the same problem for developmental theory as do the data about walking in infancy. On the treadmill, infants display remarkable competence in stepping. In their daily life, they look like McGraw described them. They don't walk.

How can we explain both the continuities and discontinuities in development, the asynchronies and similarities in children's performances in related tasks, the mix of competence and incompetence? Our goal in this book is to provide a framework for explaining, in detail, data such as these. We believe that the explanation depends on the reconciliation of the global directionality of development with its complex, heterochronic underpinnings. Piaget in his early writings (1952) and some later ones (1976, 1985, 1987) expressed a similar view. Next in our brief overview, we ask how contemporary theorizing deals with the data.

Competence versus Performance

The mix of competence and incompetence that characterizes the young child led some developmentalists to make a distinction between competence and performance (Gelman, 1972; Donaldson, 1978). The well-taken point is that performance is not a perfect window on underlying cognition. For example, as adults, we automatically make transitive inferences if given the premises. Yet few of us would readily make transitive inferences if the premises were in pig Latin. The idea is that the young child might often be trying to reason in pig Latin; the young child might possess considerable cognitive competence but because of immature memory, attention, and language skills, that competence might rarely be fully realized in performance.

The distinction between competence and performance has been a major methodological force for the past 20 years, since Gelman's classic paper on number (Gelman, 1969) The modus operandi of this approach is clear: Define the *essence* of some knowledge structure, do a thorough task analysis, strip away the supporting process and performance variables that could limit successful use of the essential knowledge structure, and see if children possess the "essential" knowledge. Researchers have followed this strategy in cognitive domain after cognitive domain and unmasked cognitive competencies well beyond what scholars thought possible in the 1960s. This approach has led to a mountain of good data. It has not led to good theory.

The theoretical problem with the competence-performance distinction is the same one we encountered with the proposal of a CPG as "the essence" of walking. It is the fallacy of single causation. What is competence if it is so severely limited? What is performance if it is not intimately related to competence? The CPG is at best an impoverished competence because the meat in the story of walking is how a CPG is labile and plastic and accommodates to the continually changing demands of real terrain. The transitive inference making skills of preschoolers also seems barely a shadow of the inferences that adults routinely make in everyday conversation. And the "performance" limitations in preschoolers' inferences—understanding comparative terms and conceptualizing dimensions as continual—seems central, not peripheral, to the "competence." The problem with the competence-performance distinction is that no one competence alone is ever enough in any domain. This is why there is no agreed upon set of competencies. The developmentalist who studies language cites performance limitations in concepts (e.g., Clark, 1972; Hood and Bloom, 1979). The developmentalist who studies concepts cites performance limitations in language (Donaldson, 1978). One investigator's competence is another's performance limitation. There is no way out of this quandary because real on-line cognition about the real world requires it all—concepts and language and memory and attention and more.

The competence-performance distinction as used by developmentalists derives from Chomsky's (1965, 1986) notion of a competence model. However, the theoretical assumptions of such a distinction have not been well articulated by developmentalists and may be unknown to many. Chomsky seeks a theory of human linguistic competence. Such a theory would be a theory of language universals; it would explicitly characterize the formal properties that define the range of possible human languages. Such a theory would directly predict the range of grammars of human language that actually occur. Linguistic competence theories are strictly formal accounts of linguistic structure, excluding meaning and saying *nothing* about the relationship between speakers and their worlds.

This distinction between competence and what is involved in *any* use of that competence is illustrated in figure 2.3. Linguistic competence, the language universals, is an abstract knowledge set. This knowledge or competence sits atop two other levels, as shown in figure 2.3: the general purpose (cognitive) system

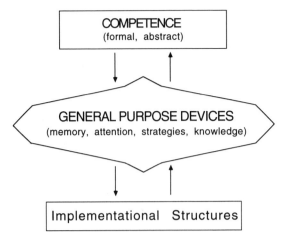

Figure 2.3
Illustration of the competence-performance distinction.

and the implementational level that actually deals with energy and the physical world. In this system, competence is the abstract-symbolic knowledge. According to Chomsky (1965, 1968) its structure is independently determined by distinct biological constraints on human language; its structure is not determined by the vagaries of real-time language use, memory, attention, or other "performance" factors. However, real language use and language acquisition always depend on all three levels.

If one accepts this description of linguistic competence and language use, it becomes obvious how one can theoretically ask about competence vs. performance in development. Is the child's language a reflection of linguistic competence—knowledge of abstract syntactic rules? Or is it a reflection of general processing limits? It also becomes clear that although one can ask the question, one cannot empirically answer it. There is no direct window on competence. Real language use and real language acquisition always involve more than competence. The lack of empirical constraints on competence models has led to some strange conclusions. Developmental psychologists who have accepted the idea of competence as distinct from performance have concluded as much as virtually full-blown grammars from one- and two-word utterances (Bloom, 1973; see also Gleitman and Wanner, 1982).

The distinction between competence and performance does not make sense if cognition is determined by highly interactive systems always in contact with each other and the external world, always and simultaneously influencing each other. The distinction between competence and performance also does not make easy *biological* sense. Where could competence—the formal properties of grammar—reside? If competence is "genetic" as Chomsky suggests, how is it specified in the brain? Abstract formal constraints are fine for disembodied logical systems. But people are biological entities; they are embodied, living process. If competence in the Chomskyean sense is part of our biology, then it must also be embodied in living real-time process.

Nativism

Some developmentalists have focused on the directional qualities of development and the many demonstrations of early competence and have concluded that there is an innate design. This rationalist-nativist view was well articulated by Keil (1981). He argued for strong innate constraints that are highly restrictive and that uniquely and specifically determine what is known. Under these assumptions, the empirical and theoretical job for developmentalists is to specify the innate designs. Keil argued for the theoretical specification of constraints in the Chomskyean (1965) sense—as formal restrictions that limit the class of logically possible knowledge structures in the domain.

This search for innate constraints on human cognition emphasizes what is constant across development—what does not change. The search for innate constraints has led to a number of very specific proposals. For example, from their extensive studies of the development of counting, Gelman and Gallistel (1978) proposed universal principles that constrain all human counting systems. These postulated universal principles are: (1) one-to-one counting—in counting, each object is assigned only one number; (2) stable ordering—there is an invariant sequence of number names; (3) the cardinal principle—the last ordinal number counted equals the numerosity of the set; (4) the "doesn't matter" principle—the assignment of number names to particular objects, though fixed for the duration of a count, is arbitrary. Gelman and Gallistel presented evidence that as soon as children can be tested, they present evidence for each of these principles—at least in some simplified context. The conclusion is innate principles for counting.

Gelman and Gallistel's principles emphasized the continuity between the beginning mind and the mature mind. Knowledge, or at least the core of it, is *static,* unchanging. This view of development fits the earliest developmental theories (see Ausabel, 1957); the child is a miniature adult. Keil (1981; see also Fodor, 1983) argued that such constancy in the form of highly specific innate blueprints is a *logical necessity.* If cognitive development proceeds primarily through the process of hypothesis testing and induction, then the hypotheses and inductive devices must be constrained in the input they take and the structure of their output.

The logical argument is built on Quine's (1960) riddle concerning the indeterminacy of translation. Imagine that you are in a new land with a foreign language. In this land, you pick up words and phrases and ultimately achieve some fluency. But you would be unable to achieve even the most limited fluency—a word or two—if you did not construe the world in the same way as the natives. When a rabbit hops by and the native says "rabbit," is he saying "hopping," "white," "furry," "long ears," "rabbit," "rabbit parts," all of these, or some of these? In fact, people do not have the problems in learning a language that Quine pointed to—neither adults in a foreign land nor the young child learning his first language. People tend to understand one another, to parse the world in a similar way for the purpose of talking about it. This understandability between humans points to commonalities across humans. Theorists such as Keil infer hard-wired blueprints from these commonalities. Innate constraints—blueprints for thought—limit the kinds of hypotheses that can be formed and the data relevant to hypothesis testing. The nativists then offer the *logical* argument that there is nothing truly new in development.

Quine's riddle concerning the indeterminacy of translation and the nativist arguments that follow from it presume that *cognitive* learning proceeds by a process of induction, that is, by the generation of hypotheses and their confirmation by empirical experience. Thus, according to Osherson, Stob, and Weinstein (1986), the learning of representations and beliefs consists of:

1. a learner,
2. a thing to be learned,
3. an environment in which the thing to be learned is exhibited to the learner,
4. the hypotheses that occur to the learner about the thing to be learned on the basis of the environment.

Learning is said to be successful in a given environment if the learner's hypothesis about the thing to be learned eventually becomes stable and accurate. (Osherson, Stob, and Weinstein, 1986, p. 7)

There is much about learning construed in this way that we find problematic—that there is a "thing" to be learned, that successful learning means an internally represented belief (a hypothesis) that is accurate and stable. But most important for understanding the pull of nativism on cognitive theorists is the fact that learning construed in this way is well understood to be nearly impossible. Without limits on the kinds of hypotheses formed, no single induction will be uniquely determined by the empirical data (see Goodman, 1955). For example, the continued experience of hearing rabbits called *rabbit* is consistent with the induction that *rabbit* means rabbit, with the induction that *rabbit* means rabbit parts, and with the induction that *rabbit* means rabbit up until February 2020. Here lies the argument for innate ideas: If cognitive learning consists *only* of inductions, and if a single set of empirical data (the experiences of an individual) support multiple inductions, some accurate and some not, then the only possibility is that knowledge is innate.

An example of this kind of reasoning can be seen in the bold nativist proposals of Spelke, Breinlinger, Macomber, and Jacobson (1992). In an elegant series of habituation studies, they asked what 3- and 4-month-old infants know about falling objects. In brief, they found that infants looked more at (found more surprising) perceptual events that violated reasonable expectations about what falling objects do. Spelke et al. used these results to argue for three strong proposals about the origins of knowledge: (1) infants possess an innate set of core beliefs, (2) these beliefs are strictly conceptual (based on representations) and do not depend on perception and action, and (3) these beliefs do not change with development.

How does evidence from a *perceptual* task and 3- and 4-month-olds (who have been viewing the world since birth) compel such strong nativist-rationalist conclusions? Spelke et al. assume that infants' looking behavior is controlled by conceptual *representations* (beliefs about falling objects) and not perceptual *processes*; they do so because infants show organized patterns of looking at events involving *novel* objects and motions. By the "logic" outlined above, it then follows that there can be only two possible origins for these beliefs: inductions from experience or innate specifications. Spelke et al. find induction wanting and thus conclude that the beliefs are innate:

> Consider an infant who must predict the resting positions of falling objects. Three of the many possible inductions consistent with the behavior of a falling object, and stated in terms of the relation of the object to surrounding surfaces, are these:
>
> 1. A falling object will land on some surface.
> 2. A falling object will land on the first surface in its path.
> 3. A falling object will land in a place it can reach by moving continuously such that no part of it passes through any surface in its path.
>
> Informally, the simplest of these inductions appears to be Induction 1. The findings . . . suggest that young infants do *not* make this induction: Four-month-old infants do not appear to infer that a falling object will land on a surface rather than in midair. . . . Why do infants respond to the regularity captured by Induction 3 rather than captured by Induction 1? (Spelke et al., 1992, p. 627)

Spelke et al. offer the answer that the generalization of induction 3 must be innately known. It is the failure of induction, not direct evidence from infants, that compels nativism.

In our view, the nativists make two errors, one an error of reasoning, the other an error of fact. Cognitivists assume that cognition consists of represented beliefs and that these can only be innate or induced from experience. When they cannot find inductive learning procedures that will work to explain performance, they reason that there is no development. The error in reasoning is that the nativists forget that their initial premises may be wrong: Development may be something other than induction; cognition may be something other than represented hypotheses and beliefs.

The nativists' second error is the denial of the empirical fact of development. Despite the seemingly hidden competencies revealed in special tasks and amid the continuities across development, children do develop; babies and adults are not the same. The fact of development is not explained by a list of innate ideas. Just as the assumption of a built-in CPG does not explain the development of walking, the assumption of built-in representations about moving objects does not explain the changes in infants' and children's thinking. When we attend to the fact of development, theoretical constructs such as "continuity" and "innate" lose their power.

What Is Continuity?
What does it mean for cognition to be "continuous" across development? How much and in what way must the end-state be contained in the organism from the beginning for development to be "continuous"?

In his argument for the continuity of human cognition, Keil (1981) contrasts discontinuous cognitive development with two forms of continuous development. These views are illustrated schematically in figure 2.4. Sequence (*A*) is

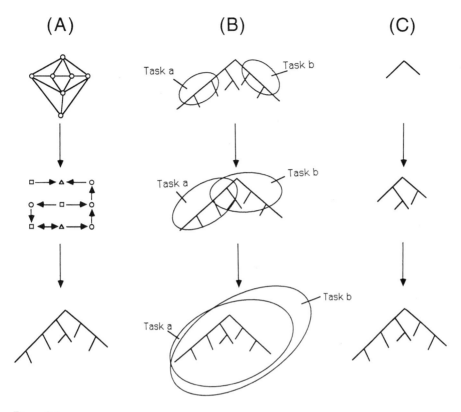

Figure 2.4
Illustrations of three kinds of developmental sequences: (A) qualitative change; (B) accessible; (C) constrained development. (Redrawn from Keil, 1981.)

Piaget's view, the stage-theoretic description of cognitive development as qualitative reorganizations. Keil rejects this description on two grounds: (1) empirical evidence—he cites the demonstrations of precocial competence and continuity that have dominated the cognitive development literature for the last 20 years, and (2) theoretical parsimony—he argues that continuous change is easier to explain than qualitative reorganizations.

We do not think sequence (A) can be so easily dismissed. Development at the macrolevel—under low magnification—looks like sequence (A). Infants do not walk, then they do. Children do not make transitive inferences, and then they do. Using high magnification, we see tiny streams of continuity. These streams are important, but they are only one part of the developmental story. The evidence suggests both continuities and discontinuities, and we must explain them both. Sequence (A) cannot be rejected on grounds of theoretical parsimony either—at least not from the nativist view. It is not at all clear that writing an end-state knowledge structure into the genome is any simpler—for more continuous forms of development—than writing a sequence of qualitative unfoldings into the genes. Both seem implausible.

Sequence (B) illustrates one way in which the end-state might be there from the very beginning. In this view, cognitive development is seen as increasing access to constant knowledge structures. The idea is that certain knowledge structures are in place early in development, but are *welded* to specific functional tasks (see Rozin, 1976; Pylyshyn, 1978). For example, infants may possess considerable knowledge about the sound structure of speech and use that knowledge in acquiring and using spoken language—the functional task this knowledge most directly serves. But with development, knowledge about the sound structure of language becomes accessible to other cognitive tasks and is used to serve other functions—learning to read, poetry, theories of language (e.g., see Walley, 1993). Considerable evidence about cognitive development fits this idea of initial inaccessible knowledge structures that are tightly tied to a single functional task but that become accessible and general with development. Nativists like data fitting this description. The structure is all there; it just has to become accessible and general. But how does it become accessible? These data and the accessibility story point to the discontinuity of cognitive development as well as its continuity. Accessibility to seemingly constant underlying cognitive structures is itself a discontinuity in need of explanation.

Further, early welded knowledge and increased accessibility to that knowledge are no more likely a marker of "innate ideas" than of acquired ones. The motor sequence in tying shoelaces is a tight encapsulated knowledge structure and we have little access to its internal structure. It is not innate knowledge. *Early* welded knowledge is no sure sign of innate knowledge either. Both ducklings and human infants *learn* about their mothers' voices before they are born (Gottlieb, 1991c; DeCasper and Fifer, 1980).

Sequence (C) illustrates the view of cognitive development that Keil favors and that underlies the Chomskyean endeavor. The beginning state is continuous with the end-state because the beginning state contains constraints that allow development to go forward only in certain ways. In this view, then, there is structural change, but it is highly constrained. The knowledge structures at all ages, while different, share important formal properties. There is little direct evidence for or against this view of cognitive development. The questions to be answered are: What are the constraints like? How are they "built in"? How do they operate?

We wonder if *each* of the questions were answered whether the innate constraints would look at all like blueprints for a final structure. The development of walking, for example, is highly constrained by the biomechanics of legs and muscles. These constraints are not a prescription for a final product. The development and shape of thunderheads on a hot summer day is highly constrained by the interactions of a number of complex physical systems. Yet there is no set of formal rules in clouds *directing* their growth into thunderheads. Constraints need not be by blueprint or design.

What does it mean, then, to say that development is continuous or discontinuous? Development is always continuous in time; there is a line in time with no gaps that takes each individual from infancy to adulthood. Change somehow happens in real time, second to second, minute to minute. There are also discontinuities. Infants are not miniature adults. Any theory of development, including those outlined in figure 2.4, must, in order to be a complete theory of development, explain both the continuities and discontinuities. It makes *no* sense to ask if development is one or the other.

What Does Innate Mean?

Do the continuities in development reflect an "innate" core? If so, what does it mean to say that some knowledge is innate? Nativist-rationalists typically envision abstract blueprints or sketches of knowledge that are icons of the end-states they constrain. Thus, the innate constraint on number knowledge is number knowledge; the innate constraint on grammar is an internal grammar; the innate constraint on knowledge about falling objects is knowledge about falling objects. These are clearly vacuous proposals.

In their discussion of the origins of knowledge about falling objects, Spelke et al. concede us this point. They write about nativism:

> It rejects several classes of explanations for the foundations of cognition, but it offers no explanation in their place. The apparent emptiness and arbitrariness of nativist proposals in psychology are characteristic, and they lead characteristically to discontent. If cognition is built on other psychological processes such as perceiving and acting, then the task of explaining the origins of thought falls naturally to the psychologist, among other scientists. If cognition is part of humans' psychological beginnings, however, psychologists cannot contribute to the explanation of its origins. That explanatory task falls entirely to other disciplines. (Spelke et al., 1992, p. 629)

Spelke et al. accept this consequence of their strong nativist proposals and in doing so make transparent the dualism behind their theorizing: Mind is distinct from body. We reject the idea that the "origins of knowledge" is a scientific question outside the scope of psychology. Indeed, we believe that developmental psychology is in grave danger if it gives itself the right to say "innate" whenever there is (as yet) no developmental theory and then frees itself from saying what "innate" means by saying that solving that problem is someone else's job. Whose job could it be? Certainly not biology; "innate ideas" is not a biologically plausible construct.

A more biologically plausible version is one in which the initial structure of the organism, the activities that structure engenders, and the typical environment in which they occur conjoin to direct development along a typical course. And in the cases in which these developmental processes are beginning to be understood, the "constraints" on development do not look like innate ideas and miniature versions of the end-state. Thus, pecking in newly hatched chicks develops from the passive bending of the neck as the heartbeat causes the head to rise and fall in the egg and not from an innate icon of pecking (Kuo, 1967), and in these same chicks the recognition of mealworms develops from the experience of seeing their own feet after hatching, not from an innate description of mealworms (Wallman, 1979).

Newport (Johnson and Newport, 1989; Newport, 1990) offers a profound example closer to home—from human language learning. In her study of American Sign Language as a first language and English as a second language, she has found consistent differences between people who learned the language very early in life and those who learned it later. The persons Newport studied were all at the time of the study adults, all had used American Sign Language or English as their principal language for at least 20 years, and all were "fluent."

Nonetheless, those who had learned the language early in life, in the preschool years, showed a greater sensitivity and knowledge of deep syntactic regularities in the language than those who learned the language later. Why should this be so? Why should young children who are, if anything, cognitively deficient, learn deeper and more abstract regularities than older persons? By innate design?

Newport speculates that young children learn deep syntactic properties more readily than adults precisely because young children are cognitively "deficient." Newport suggests that when mature persons with all their cognitive resources try to learn a language, they attend to and remember all that they hear and the full range of meanings in the context. Very young children are, however, cognitively deficient. They cannot hear, or remember, or think about it all. They can only pick up bits and pieces of language. Newport's idea is that the deep properties of language structure are more transparent in relations between bits and pieces than in the intact whole. Perhaps language evolved to make use of cognitive immaturity rather than the cognitively immature being prescient to the deep structural properties of language. Language acquisition may be "constrained," but not by an abstract blueprint for language. As Lehrman pointed out in 1970, the idea of innate blueprints may be seductive but meaningless. At best the claim for an "innate blueprint" is shorthand for an unexplained developmental process.

Nativists argue for the *logical* necessity of innate ideas. They ask how the finely honed components of a mature mind could come about without the outcome being specified in detail in the organism at the start. An answer is suggested by Robert Cairns's (1988) analogy between evolution and development: evolution is to biology what development is to psychology—the process behind the structure. In this book, we propose a developmental process that is like evolutionary process. Evolutionary process is mindless and opportunistic. There is no design, no blueprints, no "pregiven" specifications for the species that can emerge. There is no end-state—only context-specific adaptations. Yet from the opportunistic and context-specific, we get marvelous species of many kinds, each reflecting its unique evolutionary history and each finely honed to its place in the whole. Might not the developmental process over developmental time work like this? Might not the origins of knowledge in an individual emerge in opportunistic and context-specific psychological processes that reflect the unique developmental history of the individual and that fit together to make a living and thinking whole?

Modularity

The rationalist-nativist approach emphasizes continuity in domain-specific knowledge across development, and *dis*continuity in cognitive structures across different domains. Fodor (1972) has been particularly critical of the Piagetian view of cognitive structures as all-encompassing:

> Classical developmental psychology invites us to think of the child as a realization of an algebra which can be applied, relatively indifferently, to a wide variety of types of cognitive integrations, but which differs in essential respects from the mathematics underlying adult mentation. The alternative

is that the child is a bundle of special purpose computational systems which are formally analogous to those that are involved in adult cognition. . . . Cognitive development on this view, is the maturation of the processes such systems subserve. (Fodor, 1972, p. 93)

Fodor (1983) developed the idea of special-purpose computational systems into the modularity hypothesis. The modularity hypothesis is a claim about the architecture of cognition. Most discussions of this hypothesis in the literature focus on the structure of the end-state. Do we have a highly interactive cognitive system in which different sources of knowledge communicate freely in a seamless whole? Or are we comprised of highly autonomous modular systems in which subsystems are blind to one another's internal states and communicate only at input and output?

The idea of autonomous systems composed of encapsulated subsystems is the core of the modularity hypothesis. According to Fodor, a modular cognitive faculty means "one that has access, in the course of its computations, to *less than all* of the information at the disposal of the organism whose cognitive faculty it is" (Fodor, 1987, p. 25). Because of this informational encapsulation, modular faculties are not intelligent in the general problem-solving sense and are "unlabile" and fixed, but fast in real time. Fodor (1987) points to the Müller-Lyer illusion and its persistence in spite of knowledge as an instance of informational encapsulation. Fodor concludes that the cognitive mechanisms that mediate visual size perception must be informationally encapsulated. Importantly, according to the modularity hypothesis, not everything is modular—just some knowledge domains. Marked context effects are the hallmark of seamless, general-purpose, cognitive mechanisms—everything affects everything else. Intransigent process in the face of changing information is the signal of modular faculties. Most empirical work has been directed to the modularity of subsystems in mature language and mature vision (see Garfield, 1987).

The modularity hypothesis is consistent with the developmental evidence—to a degree. Cognitive development does not march forward across all domains in synchrony. There are heterogeneous systems. But we do not endorse the modularity hypothesis. We have three questions that are not well answered by modularity theory.

First, what are the boundaries for an autonomous module? Fodor's idea is that autonomous modular faculties such as language are composed of informationally encapsulated subsystems, whereas general problem solving is not. But language understanding in its *entirety*—that is, including the meaning of what is uttered—is by Fodor's own view a mix of both encapsulated subsystems and broadly interactive ones. The proposed separate modules of language appear to strongly interact with one another in real-time language use (see Kelly, 1992; Pinker, 1987, 1989; Tucker and Hirsh-Pasek, 1993). Analogously, the *immediate* visual experience of objects involves general knowledge (Rock, 1973) and some informationally encapsulated devices (see Stillings, 1987). If real language understanding and real visual experience are a mix of informationally encapsulated devices and general purpose mechanisms, we must do more than draw sharp lines between components. We must explain how they mix together to make a whole.

Second, where do modules and informationally encapsulated subsystems come from? As Karmiloff-Smith (1992) argued, the architecture of the adult need not be isomorphic to the architecture of the child; but rather may be a product of development. "Informationally encapsulated" units do develop; the Müller-Lyer illusion does (see Pick and Pick, 1970). Moreover, the driving force behind developmental change in informationally encapsulated models need not be maturation, as Fodor suggests; rather, "informationally encapsulated" units may emerge with learning. The Stroop effect in adults is informationally encapsulated, rather like the Müller-Lyer illusion that Fodor cites as evidence of vision's modularity. When asked to name the color of the ink, we cannot stop ourselves from reading the word spelled out by the ink. Our knowledge of the trick, our best efforts, are to little avail. But the informationally encapsulated (automatic by Shiffrin and Schneider, 1977) mechanisms in reading are a product of development (cf. Greenfield, 1991; Tucker and Hirsh-Pasek, 1993). Evidence from the development of language itself strongly suggests this possibility: syntax appears to depend on (or be bootstrapped out of) semantics (Pinker, 1987, 1989; Tucker and Hirsh-Pasek, 1993). However, virtually all of the empirical research and theoretical work on the question of cognition is composed of modular systems and involves the study of *adult* vision and *adult* language. This work is irrelevant to our questions about development. All the facts possible about the architecture of the end-state won't tell you how it got there. Anatomical forays into the fully mature are not embryology.

Third, how are the heterogeneous modules related to each other, and when do these relations emerge? There *must* be deep correspondences between the heterogeneous systems that make up mind. Even if cognitive modules are separate "organs" of mind, they still have to fit together to form a functional whole. For example, the long necks of giraffes, which are adapted for eating, require special cardiovascular support. It is not enough that each piece does its job well; the pieces must fit together. Because of this fitting together, the nature of one piece constrains the nature of others. Because of this fitting together, there *will* be *developmental* interactions between heterogeneous systems. And, there *must* be real-time interactions if cognition and behavior in the moment is to be coherent and adaptive.

Again, an analogy to evolution is helpful. The analogy is between the evolution of species and the development of heterogeneous subsystems. At a given point in evolutionary time, the morphology of a species is stable, but that stability is a local phenomenon. There is change over evolutionary time. Similarly, at a given point in developmental time, we may see stable and seemingly "encapsulated" modules. But over the lifespan of the individual, over developmental time, the internal structure of modules, indeed their existence, may change as a product of the interactions in the whole. Across evolutionary time, change in one species' behavior has effects on other species. Across developmental time, change in one mental module will necessitate change in others. There can be no complete encapsulation in a dynamic system.

We also reject Fodor's program of research for studying modular systems. According to Fodor, the modular systems are studiable because they are highly constrained. The "general cognitive processes" by which various modules interact and communicate are not studiable by Fodor's claim because they are unconstrained—anything can influence anything else. The central tenet of dynamic systems is that order, discontinuities, and new forms emerge precisely from the complex interactions of many heterogeneous forces. By our view, the power source of human cognitive development is not in the separate modules but in their mutual interactions.

Human Information Processing

A human information processing approach to cognitive development attributes developmental change to the development of general purpose mechanisms, knowledge acquisition, and their interaction. In contrast to modularity theories, the emphasis is on general-purpose cognition—the general problem-solving part of mind. The general mechanisms posited derive from adult cognitive theories and the overriding metaphor is mind as machine. The studied processes consist of encoding, retrieval, interference, attention, feature integration, strategies, and rules. These components have been derived from a chronometric approach to mind and are components of a description of the temporal steps from input to output (e.g., Posner, 1980). The research strategy in both the adult literature and developmental literature is to isolate components responsible for a particular performance pattern. In developmental research, the principal research question is which component is responsible for the better performance of older than younger children in some task.

With the advance of research and data in this framework, the approach itself has come to an impasse. Consistent with Fodor's description of general-purpose cognition, the results suggest almost seamless interactions of knowledge sources. In brief, everything matters and everything develops. For example, infants' success in the A-not-B search task diagnostic of stage 4 in Piaget's theory of sensory-motor development depends on encoding, memory retrieval, attention, spatial strategies, task-specific knowledge, and more (see Wellman, Cross, and Bartsch, 1986). The greater success of older children than younger children in transitive inference making (Smith, Sera, and Gattusso, 1988a,b), reasoning about pendulums (Siegler, 1978), class inclusion reasoning (Trabasso, 1977), and a variety of other well-researched tasks involves a complex of cognitive mechanisms. The evidence clearly shows that everything does get better with development; every step in the modal model of mind becomes more efficient. The question, What develops?, when phrased as encoding vs. retrieval or attention vs. knowledge, has thus become inappropriate. What develops cannot be framed in terms of either-or. Everything develops. And performance in any one task involves real-time contributions from many mechanisms and processes.

Further, the precise mix of mechanisms and processes appears intimately linked to the specific task at hand and the individual's expertise in that task. What is known and how that knowledge is organized and interconnected determines how it is encoded, retrieved, attended to, and strategically used. Thus, a 10-year-old chess expert will appear "more mature" at various stages of information processing when in a chess task than will a novice adult in the same task or the same child in an unfamiliar task (see Chi, 1978; Chi and Koeske, 1983). Performance in any one task is multiply determined and the determinants seem task-specific. As a result of these facts, information processing models in the cognitive development literature often involve many processes and mechanisms and proposals about developmental change. The processes and mechanisms postulated in models are closely linked to the experimental paradigm they seek to explain. The literature is thus replete with seemingly unrelated models; models of analogy (Gentner, 1989) contain no overlapping mechanisms with models of naive physics (Siegler, 1978), which in turn contain no overlapping mechanisms with models of perceptual classification (e.g., Smith, 1989).

The task domains that are separately studied and modeled in the information processing approach are not the (somewhat) principled modules (e.g., syntax) of the nativist-rationalist approach. The task domains are merely experimental paradigms. We are not arguing that such task-specific models are inherently or even empirically wrong. We believe them to be, in the very detail of their task analyses, useful grist for the theoretical mill. But such task-specific models are by themselves as theoretically inadequate as a list of empirical facts. The larger truths about development and cognition that extend across tasks must be abstracted and interconnected.

Cognitive development can be conceptualized as having two principal questions: (1) What develops? and (2) How does it develop? The information processing approach has concentrated on what develops. We find its answers rich in detail but lacking in illumination of the bigger picture. More problematic is the information processing approach's total disregard for the mechanisms of development (see Siegler, 1989, for discussions of this failing). How do we get from the immature flow chart to the mature one? What propels development forward? There is no cognitive theorist in the brain to draw a new box or write a new rule.

Connectionism

Both the nativist-rationalist approach and the human information processing approach view cognition as the manipulation of structured symbolic representations. In these approaches, the cognitive world is divisible into two parts: first, the enduring structures, and second, the processes on those structures. Cognitive structures are symbols and their connections; they are representations, rules, and concepts—the substance of cognition. Processes are such mechanisms as memory, attention, spreading activation, and, depending on the kind of theory, also combination and analysis mechanisms that operate on structures. In many ways, the stalled progress of theory in cognitive development is the direct consequence of this structure-process distinction (see Smith and Thelen, 1993). This structure-process distinction promotes the Balkanization of developmental phenomena into domain-specific competencies and modules, the denial of development by rationalist-nativists, and task-specific models of information processing. This crisis in theory derives from the attempt to retain the idea that constant knowledge structures direct cognition in the face of data showing both continuity and discontinuity, both global structure and local variability.

Recently, a new approach, connectionist modeling, has emerged in which the distinctions between structure and process are blurred. Connectionist modeling is sometimes characterized as "brain-style" or "neural" network modeling (Rumelhart, 1989) because, like the brain, the connectionist network is made up of many, many units. These units, like neurons, only fire or not fire, and like neurons, individual units in a connectionist network have no intrinsic meaning; they do not represent or "stand for" anything. Rather, knowledge and meaning are distributed across units—in patterns of activation. Connectionist models are also like the brain in that they are plastic; connectionist models *modify themselves* by changing the strengths of connections between units in response to their interaction with the environment. This kind of theorizing is sufficiently new that its full potential as models of development has not been fully explored. They have just begun to be seriously applied to real developmental phenomena (Gasser and Smith, 1991; Plunkett and Marchman, 1989; Rumelhart and McClelland, 1986; L. B. Smith, 1993b). Connectionist models are of considerable interest to us because they share our key assumption that there is *only process*.

Connectionism is like the dynamic systems theory we propose in three ways. First, it offers an explanation of the structure of behavior without putting an icon of the structure in the head; it promises rule-like behavior without rules, global order without design. In both connectionist models and our dynamic systems theory of cognition, knowledge is not enduring rules or conceptual structures. Instead, knowledge is assembled in real time, in context from units that do not in and of themselves look like or contain the resultant knowledge.

Second, connectionism and our dynamic systems theory both view knowledge as a pattern of activity in time as opposed to a structure, an object-like entity. This is a developmentally powerful idea. If we think of knowledge as an entity, then the only way we can get change in knowledge is by adding, subtracting, combining, and taking apart entities. In such an ontology there is no such thing as truly new knowledge. However, if we think of knowledge not as entity but as process, change is less problematic. Processes may *sometimes* be in stable equilibrium and *appear* entity-like. But processes are dynamic; they are inherently temporal and thus changeable.

Third, by viewing mental life as only process, connectionism and our dynamic systems theory offer a potential resolution of the problem of the simultaneous global order of behavior and its local continuities and discontinuities. The resolution is reminiscent of that between classical physics and quantum theory (Smolensky, 1986). Quantum mechanics is the microlevel from which the kinds that populate the macrolevel of classical physics emerge. It is *not* that classical physics is *reduced* to quantum mechanics. Quantum mechanics does not *explain* the action of objects as objects at the macrolevel. But quantum mechanics does explain transitions and changes in the objects. The interactions, the *dynamics* of quanta, explain how the objects of the macrolevel *change*. Objects are no less real because they consist of processes between particles. But the power of explanation is in the dynamics of the processes, in the view from below examined from above. The explanatory power is in the *joint* consideration of the micro- and macrolevels.

This is not traditional reductionism. In 1975, in *The Language of Thought*, Fodor argued against trying to explain one level of phenomena by looking to the next lower level, because there were unlikely to be "nice" reductions. Rather, Fodor argued that reductions between levels, between, for example, cognition and biology, are likely to be nonsensical. The nonsense derives from the (likely) unsystematic relation between the concepts of mind and the concepts of brain. Again, we see the dualist underpinnings of contemporary theorizing.

Fodor (1975) argued that the situation might look like that in figure 2.5. $P_1x \rightarrow P_2y$ is a law at the macrolevel, the level of behavior we seek to explain. For example, P_1 might be an intent to drink coffee from a cup on the desk. P_2y might be the act of bringing the coffee cup to the lips. So the "law" $P_1x \rightarrow P_2y$ reads "intent to drink coffee $\rightarrow$ grasping cup and bringing to mouth." The relevant entities, or kinds, for the macrolevel are P states—intentions and actions. Below P states, however, are N (neuroscience) states. N states make up the microstructure. The N states that coincide with P_1 might be thirst, caffeine withdrawal, stress, habit. The N states that correspond to grasping the cup will be a variety of highly distinct movements depending on where the cup is relative to the hand, etc. Fodor's point is that the N states are unlikely to hang together in coherent sets that are alike in any way. Thus, P_1x is a syncretic disjunctive set of N states. P_2x is a syncretic disjunctive set of N states. Although we can write one law on the P level (e.g., psychology), a diverse set of functions take the N states that coincide with P_1 to the N states that coincide with P_2. Indeed, there may even be exceptions. Stress, even when writing, does not always lead to coffee. Since this is so, Fodor concludes, "reductionism loses its ontological bite, since we can no longer say that every event which consists of satisfaction of a P-predicate consists of the satisfaction of an N-predicate" (p. 22). Fodor argues that there is nothing to gain by reducing P's to N's. The states that matter for laws about behavior are intentions and actions, not conglomerates of unrelated stresses and thirsts and addictions and muscle movements.

Fodor is right. We have nothing to gain from traditional reductionism. The state of affairs illustrated in figure 2.5 is probably correct. But the proper theoretical response to the truth of figure 2.5 is not the narrowing of focus to only one level. If we want to explain the dynamics of cognitive structures—how they emerge and change and break apart—we cannot write theories at only the macrostructural level. Nor will we succeed only by looking at the microlevel. If the picture is figure 2.5 is correct about the relation between higher and lower levels

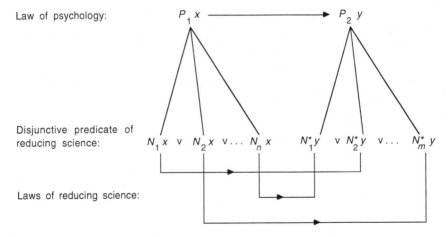

Figure 2.5
Illustration of Fodor's (1975) argument about the futility of reductionism.

of analyses (e.g., between intents and muscle movements, between symbols and subsymbols, cognition and sensation, psychology and neuroscience), then we will only be able to understand how a law such as $P_1x \to P_2y$ emerges in development, dissolves with trauma, and functions in context when we understand the interaction and dynamics of P states and N states as a system. Explanation requires that we keep both the view from above *and* the view from below. Connectionism is promising, because like dynamic systems, it is attempting to do just that.

Connectionism *is* promising, and it is a formal approach that is intimately related to dynamic systems theory. And there are a number of interesting connectionist models that instantiate dynamic systems (though not developmental dynamics), e.g., Jordan (1990), Hanson (1990), Mjolsness, Sharp, and Reinitz (1990). Connectionist models may be thought of as one formalism through which dynamic systems theories may be realized. But all connectionist models to date fail as theories of development. They fail because they fail to take the structure of the brain and biological process seriously, because they fail to take the complexity of the developmental task seriously, and because they fail to take developmental data seriously. These may not be failures in principle. But we believe there is a failure of spirit—a shrinking away from the most radical implications of the idea of connectionism itself. We consider these failures in turn.

The first failure is a failure to acknowledge and make use of the heterogeneous structures of the brain. Although connectionism is neutral on nature-nurture issues (Rumelhart and McClelland, 1986; Smolensky, 1986), little serious attention has been paid in this literature to developmentally or neurally reasonable assumptions about starting structures. Instead, connectionist modelers pride themselves on building cognitions by connecting homogeneous nodes. Connectionism is *patently* not "brain-style" modeling in the sense of modeling of the diverse, complex, and heterogeneous structures of the brain. In contrast to connectionism, we seek a biologically based theory of development and take seriously what is known about brain structure and plasticity.

The second failure probably derives from the first. Networks of nodes yield only *toy* systems capable of solving single problems (e.g., recognizing the past tense, or lifting a block). But individual children simultaneously solve many problems and perform many different tasks. These different tasks seem to make use of subsets of the same components. We use our mouths for smiling, talking, and sucking. We look at a single object and sometimes name it, sometimes name a property, sometimes count it, sometimes pick it up, sometimes throw it. We do not want to explain how one little task *might be* accomplished. We want to explain how children do all the tasks they do. Where do both the global order of development across, and the messy variability between, tasks come from? We want to explain a larger problem than most connectionists; we want to explain the developmental trend in its full complexity in intact whole systems. Moreover, we believe that the *causal forces* behind development—the forces that drive change—lie in the solving of diverse tasks and in the interaction of *heterogeneous* systems.

The third failure is one that abounds in psychology (see Smith and Sera, 1992). It is a failure to take the question of development and the data about development as fundamental to explanation. Thus, our goals differ from the specific goals of most connectionist theories. The goal of (much) connectionist modeling is a mathematical analysis of the theoretical space. On what set of initial assumptions and with what theoretical tools can one get the end-state? The goal with differing initial assumptions and theoretical tools is the same for formal theorists of the Chomskyean approach. Our goal is different. Our eyes are not on the end-state but on development itself. Our goal is not to explore theoretical possibilities, but the data at hand. We are driven by the data of developmental change itself. Why does development look the way it does? Why does it dip and dive and rise as it does? We seek an account of development, not an account of the end-state.

The fourth failure is a failure of insight. Much connectionist theory strives to answer old questions in new ways, without realizing that the questions themselves are the wrong ones. Traditional cognitive psychology seeks to understand what is stable and constant—for example, how different individuals in different contexts can mean the same thing by the word *cat*. Traditional theory explains the stability of cognition in terms of representations. Thus, the reason we all have the same understanding of the word *cat* is because we all possess a representation of what it means to be a cat. Cognition in the traditional view consists of accessing and mentally manipulating such representations.

For connectionists, knowledge consists of the correspondence between an emergent global state of a network and properties of the world. Thus we have knowledge of the meaning of *cat* when a stable pattern of network activity emerges in the context of *cat*. In this way, connectionism shows how ephemeral constructs such as representations might emerge from real processes. Given this formulation of the problem, it is enticing to equate the emergent global states with representations (see, for example, Clark and Karmiloff-Smith, 1993). However, unlike symbolic representations, global patterns of network activity are continuous, not discrete, and are not decomposable into elements that in their configuration represent the structure of reality. Table 2.1, adapted from Varela, Thompson, and Rosch (1991), summarizes (in its first two columns) the differences between traditional theory and connectionism.

All in all, we find connectionism too much like traditional cognitive theory in that it is trying to solve the same theoretical problem. Connectionism is still trying to explain the stability of cognition, and it measures its success by the very yardsticks of traditional theory: Can it get symbol-like behavior without symbols? Rule-like behavior without rules? Can it get patterns of network activity to *act like representations*? To our mind, connectionism has not come far enough.

The central theoretical problem is not stability but change. How do minds change? Where does new knowledge, new understanding, new behavior come from? How does the organism continually adapt and create new solutions to new problems? The answer we present in this book makes no use of representations or representation-like processes. The yardstick by which we measure our theory is thus not rule-like nor symbol-like behavior (though we specifically consider a dynamic systems account of symbolic reasoning in chapter 11). The third column of table 2.1 contrasts a dynamic systems theory of cognition with traditional theory and connectionism.

Table 2.1
Three kinds of theories about cognition (adapted from Varela, Thompson, and Rosch, 1991)

	Traditional Theory	Connectionism	Dynamic Systems
What is cognition?	Symbolic computation—rule-based manipulation of symbols	The emergence of global states in a network of simple components	A history of activity that brings forth change and activity
How does it work?	Through any device that can manipulate symbols	Through local rules and changes in the connectivity of elements	Through the self-organizing processes of interconnected sensorimotor subnetworks
What does a good cognitive system do?	Represent the stable truths of the real world	Develop emergent properties that yield stable solutions to tasks	Become an active and adaptive part of an ongoing and continually changing world

Teleology: Beyond the End-state in Developmental Theory

The focus on stability is a focus on the end-state. Thus, traditional cognitive theory is fixed on ultimate accurate representations of reality and connectionism is fixed on asymptotic activity. This end-state focus has captured just about all developmental theorizing as well. Theorists as diverse as Darwin, Baldwin, Piaget, and Werner all viewed development as a process of "getting better"—as a generative force for the improvement of mankind. Development is a movement more or less steadily toward a goal. Degree of development is measured by distance from a goal. Sometimes the goal is the end-state, the adult standard (e.g., language), and sometimes the goal is functional and adaptive value. Either way, we as developmental theorists seem in our theories to know where development is inevitably going or ought to be going.

The danger of teleology in developmental theory is that it finds its way into the mechanisms of development. The end-state is the mechanism in nativist-rationalist approaches. The end-state (in more or less complete form) is written into the organism and propels it to where it must go. The end-state is implicitly in specific teaching mechanisms such as the one used by Rumelhart and Mc-Clelland (1986) in their connectionist model of the acquisition of the past tense. The end-state, what the *correct* answer is, does all the work. Similarly, the end-state is intimately involved in most information processing theories or hypothesis-testing accounts. Developmental transitions and changes come about when the strategies and rules a child possesses *do not work*. In these accounts, the mechanism of development *is* the evaluation of how well development is doing. The child somehow knows that he does not know enough and so develops some more. By putting the end-state in the mechanism, we presuppose what it is we are trying to explain.

Conclusion

We believe that we can get beyond teleology by studying the processes of development. In this book, we present a theory of change that rejects many of the usual ideas about cognitive development: in our view, development does not "know" where it is going from the start. There are no constraints on development that act like levies on a flooding river, keeping it from going where it ought not to go. There is no set end-state other than the end of life itself. We propose instead that development is the outcome of the self-organizing processes of continually active *living* systems.

The dynamic systems theory that we present here is related to several classic ideas about development (see particularly Piaget, 1952; Waddington, 1977; Werner, 1957). It is also related to new and exciting ideas among our contemporaries; we are not alone in recognizing that the current crisis in cognitive development lies in the emphasis on constancy and the consequent failure to study processes of change (see particularly Bates, 1979; Bates and Elman, 1993; Fischer and Bidell, 1991; Fogel, 1993; Siegler, 1989, 1991). We turn now to an introduction to dynamic systems theory.

Chapter 3

Dynamic Systems: Exploring Paradigms for Change

If the future is already in some way contained in the present, which also contains the past, what is the meaning of an arrow of time? The arrow of time is a manifestation of the fact that the future is not given, that, as the French poet Paul Valery emphasized, "time is construction."
—Prigogine and Stengers (1984, p. 16)

Development of the nervous system, from fertilized egg to mature brain, is not a programmatic but a historical phenomenon under which one thing simply leads to another.
—Stent (1984, p. 156)

Adaptive behavior is an emergent property which spontaneously arises through the interaction of simple components. Whether these components are neurons, amino acids, ants, or bit strings, adaptation can only occur if the collective behavior of the whole is qualitatively different from that of the sum of the individual parts. This is precisely the definition of nonlinear.
—Farmer and Packard (as quoted in Gleick, 1987, p. 339)

A chemist adds a few simple chemicals—bromate ions in a highly acidic medium—in a shallow glass dish, and watches a remarkable series of events (figure 3.1):

> A dish, thinly spread with a lightly colored liquid sits quietly for a moment after its preparation. The liquid is then suddenly swept by a spontaneous burst of colored centers of chemical activity. Each newly formed region creates expanding patterns of concentric, circular rings. These collide with neighboring waves but never penetrate. In some rare cases, rotating one-, two-, or three-armed spirals may emerge. Each pattern grows, impinging on its neighboring patterns, winning on some fronts and losing on others, organizing the entire surface into a unique pattern. Finally, the patterns decay and the system dies, as secondary reactions drain the flow of the primary reaction. (Madore and Freedman, 1987, p. 253)

Some years later, another group of chemists study the same chemical reaction—the so-called Belousov-Zhabotinskii reaction—but instead of just mixing the

Figure 3.1
The Belousov-Zhabotinskii reaction. Chemicals in a flat dish produce concentric circles and spiral waves. These complex forms can be modeled by a simple simulation (right panels). (From Madore and Freedman, 1987. Reprinted by permission.)

chemicals in the dish, they have discovered a way of feeding the chemicals into the reaction chamber in a precisely controlled flow (figure 3.2). As the reaction oscillates, they measure, over time, the concentration of one of the ions produced. These ions also oscillate with a fixed period. As the chemists increase the flow of the reactants in a smooth and continuous manner, they find remarkable and curious results. Although they increase the reactants gradually, the oscillation periods increase by *precise doublings* of the original period. Then, at a critical flow rate, the reaction seems to go wild; the ions fluctuate erratically and seemingly randomly. Nonetheless, by the simple procedure of plotting the concentrations of ions in this erratic time series—a value at one time vs. the value after a time delay—a wonderful and complex pattern is revealed (figure 3.3). The changes look random, but are not; the ions fluctuated in a complex but deterministic manner known mathematically as *chaos*. And to add to the puzzle, even small amounts of impurities in the chemicals disrupted this sequence of doubling

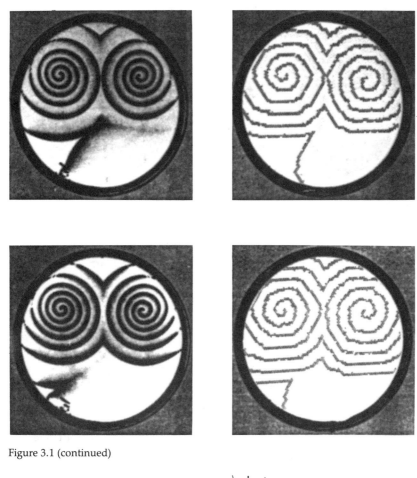

Figure 3.1 (continued)

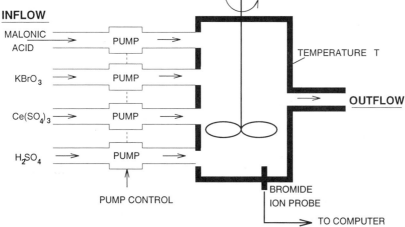

Figure 3.2
Schematic representation of the chemical reactor used to study the oscillations in the Belousov-Zhabotinskii reaction. The different reaction paths depend on the inputs controlled by the pump. (From Prigogine and Stengers, 1984. Reprinted by permission.)

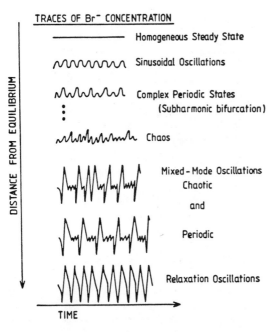

Figure 3.3
Temporal oscillations of the concentration of the bromine ion in the Belousov-Zhabotinskii reaction. Although the concentration of the reactants is increased gradually, the products of the reaction appear in qualitatively distinct time-based patterns. (From Prigogine and Stengers, 1984. Reprinted by permission.)

periods to chaos to another ordering of discrete states (Swinney, Horsthemke, McCormick, Noszticzins, and Tam, 1988).

Now, remember Chemistry 1, especially the seemingly endless exercises spent "balancing" equations. So many moles of substance A mixed up with so many moles of substance B yielded so many moles of substance C plus so many moles of substance D. In these simple chemical reactions, everything in the right-hand side of the equation was accounted for by the terms on the left-hand side. Matter and energy were conserved. The reactions had a beginning state and an end-state, but no history. What were important were the reactants and the products of the chemical reaction; time was not a measured dimension, and the process by which the substances reacted was not considered. The reactants reached an equilibrium state and stayed there. The reaction was entirely linear. Ions of sodium and chloride combined to produce NaCl, no matter if there were just a few ions or countless billions. In many cases, it did not matter if your test tube was not completely rinsed out, as the reaction proceeded to completion even with some impurities in the solution. Although some chemical reactions do not proceed along these simple lines, those chosen by teachers and textbook authors model a class of deterministic, linear physical systems whose properties could be completely described and understood at the level of the instruction.

Imagine now how our views of the physical world might have been changed if, on the first day of Chemistry 1, the instructor had demonstrated the Belousov-Zhabotinskii reaction. We would see the seemingly spontaneous generation of elaborate patterns in space and in time from mixing some simple, inert chemicals. We would wonder how these chemicals *knew* to produce circular and spiral patterns and oscillations of such precise and fixed nature as though driven by a set clock. We would be puzzled by how the equations would not "balance" as the oscillations of the ion concentrations did not match the input. We could ask how a tiny impurity or small changes in the concentration of the chemical appeared to reset the clock and change the nature of the patterns.

In short, the Belousov-Zhabontinskii reaction would disturb our conventional ideas of how the world worked. These inert molecules *cooperated* with one another to produce complexity from the most simple of precursors, to generate patterns without a designer, and to set time ticking off without a watchmaker. What seemed to be random was not. Something happened to the simple laws of cause and effect. Nothing about the nature of bromide ions and the acid medium could have predicted this outcome, an outcome so remarkable that Prigogine and Stengers (1984) claim that if this reaction and others like it had not been observed, no one would have believed them possible.

The task of this chapter is to outline a science of change. In the first two chapters we argued that current theorizing in action and cognition lacked a principled basis for understanding developmental process. Many of the major theoretical systems, maturationist, neurological, rationalist-nativist, and information processing, have a teleological core. This core presumes an end-state before the developmental process begins and thus, in the words of Prigogine and Stengers (1984), negates the "arrow of time" (p. 16). At best, these approaches freeze development as a series of stagelike end-states, which do indeed capture the broad sweep of ontogeny. At worst, they are tautological and often vacuous: organisms develop because everything is getting better. Reductionist approaches describe the messy details, but leave the details without coherence. The questions of what develops and how it develops are unanswered.

For our approach to development, we use the science of the Belousov-Zhabotinskii chemical reaction rather than the science of our beginning chemistry class. This is a relatively new science that discards simple cause-and-effect models, linearity, determinism, and reductionist analysis. Instead, it is a science for systems with a history, systems that change over time, where novelty can be created, where the end-state is not coded anywhere, and where behavior at the macrolevel can, in principle, be reconciled with behavior at the microlevel.

What we invoke here are principles for the *global properties of complex systems*, i.e., principles that apply not only to bromide ions in acid media but to the myriad time and space patterns that arise from this combination. It seems increasingly evident that such principles may apply to complex systems *irrespective of their material substrates*. This means that systems of different levels of diversity and complexity, and whose constituent elements are completely dissimilar, may share general modes of behavior. Reductionist approaches, in contrast, seek the essence of a system in a unique and privileged component of that system.

The new science that can extract common principles in the behavior of chemical reactions, clouds, forests, and embryos is variously called the study of *dynamic, synergetic, dissipative, nonlinear, self-organizing,* or *chaotic* systems. (We adopt here *dynamic systems* as the descriptor to emphasize that these are systems that change continuously over time.) The roots of the study of complex systems are in physics and mathematics and are highly abstract. Two highly readable, nonmathematical treatments which capture the paradigm-breaking nature of dynamic systems are Prigogine and Stengers' (1984) *Order Out of Chaos: Man's New Dialogue with Nature* and Gleick's (1987) *Chaos: Making a New Science.*[1]

There has been an explosion of interest in dynamic systems over the last decade, and especially in the last 5 years. Although not long ago terms like *fractals, chaos, strange attractors,* and *Mandelbrot sets* were the domains of a few visionary (and believed to be quite eccentric!) mathematicians, they have now become the buzzwords of popular science and Sunday supplements. It is no wonder that these ideas have captured the public imagination. These mathematicians have opened our eyes to the remarkable geometric complexity and even eerie beauty that can be generated by seemingly simple equations. They have described how events over time can look random but be highly deterministic. They have emphasized the role of scale changes and abrupt phase shifts and bifurcations—the essential nonlinearity of many everyday phenomena. And equally important, mathematicians have provided the tools to capture complex phenomena in formal and elegant terms.

The power and generality of dynamic approaches are best reflected, however, in their wide application to the real world. The list is long and diverse: weather, laser beams, chemical reactions, galaxy formations, liquid flow patterns, the formation of snowflakes, leaf patterns, slime molds, biological rhythms, lung tissue morphology, morphogenesis, nerve impulse patterns, neural network behavior, heart rhythms, motor coordination, perceptual systems, economic patterns, and so on. Although the science is yet in its infancy, the list grows every day. With each year, there are an increasing number of conferences, papers, and volumes, and a growing excitement and fascination with a hitherto unknown way of looking at the world.

Under what imaginable principles can these diverse phenomena possibly be subsumed? What is common among systems so very different in spatial and temporal scale and whose elements range from simple collections of molecules, to complex cells and tissue components, to the most macroscopic events of human behavior? How, in turn, can these principles help us to understand how humans learn to move and think?

Our aim here is to distil the conceptual essence of dynamic systems and to show how these general principles provide a theoretically satisfying and *useful* way of looking at early human development. Although the elegance of dynamic studies has been in their mathematical formalisms, this is a strictly nonmathematical approach. A number of biological systems have been formally modeled, but their behavior is considerably simpler than that of developing humans (see, e.g., Schöner and Kelso, 1988; West and Goldberger, 1987; Cohen, Holmes, and Rand, 1982). Developmental data that are sufficiently fine-grained, non-noisy, and stationary to be amenable to appropriate mathematical analysis do not yet exist. Although it is not yet clear that developmental systems can easily be modeled using available nonlinear techniques, generating such data is certainly a high-priority goal. Even in the absence of the elegant mapping of data to theory that characterizes much other work in dynamic systems, the concepts remain powerful organizers of existing data and a fruitful source of new questions.

The Behavior of Dynamic Systems: An Overview

The central question is how complex systems, including developing humans, produce *patterns that evolve in time*. Recall the Belousov-Zhabotinskii reaction. Certain features of that reaction apply to dynamic systems in general. The chemists began with a mix of chemicals, a system with very many individual ions of several types. The behavior of the individual ions cannot be described nor can their possible numbers of combinations be enumerated. The degrees of freedom are very, very large.

When the reaction begins, however, the patterns show a spatial and temporal order that *can* be described because their dimensions are far fewer than those of the participating elements. In fact, the spatial patterns in the Belousov-Zhabotinskii reaction were simulated by a computer program that sets up very simple initial conditions (see Madore and Freedman, 1987). When the program runs, the sequence of patterns emerges. Likewise, the oscillations of the bromide ions can be described as rather simple mathematical functions. Their behavior is captured by *low-dimensional dynamics.*

At the same time that the initial degrees of freedom are compressed to produce more patterned behavior, the resulting patterns themselves are not simple, but undergo elaborate changes in space and time, including multiple stable patterns, discontinuities, resilience to perturbations, and shifts into deterministic chaos.

This sequence of *complexity to simplicity to complexity* captures the essence of dynamic systems whatever the material substance of the elements: simple molecules, photons, biological molecules, cells, tissues, organs, neurons, networks of neurons, organisms, or social systems. These characteristics are summarized in figure 3.4. In the remainder of this chapter, we describe in more detail the general principles of pattern formation in dynamic systems. Following this more general treatment, we characterize developing organisms in a dynamic framework. We conclude with a discussion of early embryogenesis, the sine qua non of the emergence of form.

Principles of Dynamic Systems

Complexity and Systems Far from Thermal Equilibrium

Developing humans, and all biological systems, belong to a class of systems that are both *complex* and that exist *far from thermal equilibrium*. We have already spoken of the complexity as consisting of very many individual elements, and in the case of biological systems, of enormous heterogeneity. This heterogeneity is manifest at all levels of organization, from the molecular components of the cells, to the diversity of tissue types and organ systems, to the functionally defined subsystems in physiology and behavior such as those used in respiration, digestion, reproduction, movement, perception, cognition, affect, and so forth. Any be-

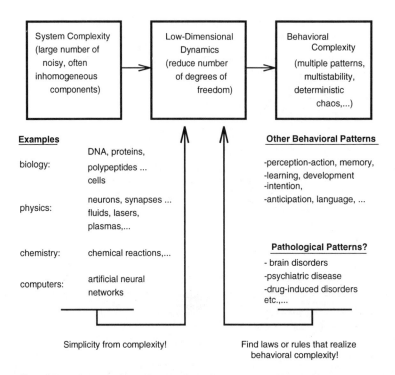

| System Complexity (large number of noisy, often inhomogeneous components) | → | Low-Dimensional Dynamics (reduce number of degrees of freedom) | → | Behavioral Complexity (multiple patterns, multistability, deterministic chaos,...) |

Examples

biology: DNA, proteins, polypeptides ... cells

physics: neurons, synapses ... fluids, lasers, plasmas,...

chemistry: chemical reactions,...

computers: artificial neural networks

Simplicity from complexity!

Other Behavioral Patterns

-perception-action, memory,
-learning, development
-intention,
-anticipation, language, ...

Pathological Patterns?

- brain disorders
-psychiatric disease
-drug-induced disorders
etc.,...

Find laws or rules that realize behavioral complexity!

Figure 3.4
Features of complex systems and strategies for understanding them. (From Kelso, Mandell, and Shlesinger, 1988. Reprinted by permission.)

havioral act, the reach for the cup of coffee sitting beside the word processor, for example, clearly involves an interwoven hierarchy of enormous complexity, ranging from the physiological and neurological pathways of thirst (or caffeine dependency), which in turn involve cellular processes of electrolyte or neurotransmitter balance, or both, and which trigger visual and motor networks to search and reach for the cup, again relying on processes like chemical changes in the retina and in muscle cells and membrane changes in tens of thousands of motoneurons. These activities, in turn, are supported by anatomical structures and vegetative physiological processes operating on many levels and time scales. For even the most simple functional actions, we can hardly imagine the enormous dimensionality of the participating elements and processes and their potential interactions. In order for biological systems to survive, all the components must be *coordinated* to an exquisite degree, and it is the nature of this coordination that concerns us. The molecules in the Belousov-Zhabotinskii reaction were also highly coordinated, and it is no coincidence, perhaps, that the reaction patterns also had a strong biological flavor. The key condition for biological coordination—and for the coordination of the Belousov-Zhabotinskii reaction—is the way energy flows through these systems.

We are more or less bored by the conventional chemistry class exercises because the latter operate in an energy domain we have come to expect for chemical reactions, that of *equilibrium* or *near-equilibrium thermodynamics*. A system is at thermodynamic equilibrium when the energy and momentum of the system are uniformly distributed and there is no flow from one region to another. When we add alcohol to water or dissolve salt in water, the molecules or ions mix or react completely. Unless we add more energy or matter, the system is stable; nothing new can emerge. We have created a *closed* system, which has run down to a state of *entropic equilibrium*. This is an example, of course, of the second law of thermodynamics: systems in nature tend to a state of thermal symmetry where the disorder is maximum (maximum entropy), and there is zero information and loss of the ability do to work. For systems near thermodynamic equilibrium, equilibrium can be thought of as an "attractor" state, a stable place where the system settles, whatever its initial conditions and whatever path the system takes to reach equilibrium. Salt in water will reach thermodynamic equilibrium regardless of whether we added a few molecules of NaCl to the water or several spoonfuls, or whether the water was initially hot or cool (Kugler and Turvey, 1987; Prigogine and Stengers, 1984; Yates, 1987).

The Belousov-Zhabotinskii reaction is surprising because it violates our expectations of how inert chemicals are supposed to act; its order increases, not decreases. It behaves like an *open system*, that is, one that is stable yet *far from thermodynamic equilibrium*. Far-from-equilibrium conditions can be maintained only by a continuous flow of free energy and matter into and out of the system. Biological systems are prime examples of open systems. Over time, their order and complexity are not only maintained but may actually increase, as in development. Biological systems appear to violate the second law of thermodynamics (their entropy does not increase), but they do so only by infusions of energy directly (plants) or by ingesting energy-rich foods. As Prigogine and Stengers pointed out, this violation is only a local effect; such systems maintain their organizational complexity only by draining the order from some other region of the universe and cycling high-entropy energy back. Prigogine and Stengers named such locally organized structures *dissipative structures* because they maintain equilibrium by drawing energy from a source of high-energy potential, doing work, and dissipating some of this energy, in turn, back to the environment. It is also characteristic of living systems that they cycle energy in a characteristic "squirt" system; energy is delivered in packets to maintain continuous metabolic processes; the importance of this for self-organization is elaborated upon in the next section.

We are interested, then, in a class of systems that meet two criteria: (1) complexity, such that the elements that compose the system can interact in nonlinear and nonhomogeneous ways, and (2) dissipative dynamics, that is, systems that live far from thermodynamic equilibrium. All biological systems meet these criteria, but many other physical and chemical systems do so as well. In the first example of the Belousov-Zhabotinskii reaction, the peculiar mix of chemicals released an energy "boost" that drove the system far from equilibrium. But as the reaction proceeded and the free energy was consumed, the system was overtaken by equilibrium thermodynamics as it went toward maximum stability and disorder—the patterns died out. However, when chemists discovered how to continually infuse new sources of high-negative entropy energy into the reaction by adding more chemicals, the order and pattern continued to emerge and evolve.

In another sense, the special properties of complex, dissipative systems may be thought of as local perturbations in what otherwise would be a thermodynamic universe symmetrical in time and space. These systems break the symmetry by concentrating energy, and thus order, in local pools and eddies. But these local concentrations are maintained only by a continual flux of energy and matter. It is this continual flux that is the wellspring for new forms.

Self-organizing Systems

Open systems where many components are free to relate to one another in nonlinear ways are capable of remarkable properties. When sufficient energy is pumped into these systems, new, ordered structures may spontaneously appear that were not formerly apparent. What started out as an aggregation of molecules or individual parts with no particular or privileged relations may suddenly produce patterns in space and regularities in time. The system may behave in highly complex, although ordered, ways, shifting from one pattern to another, clocking time, resisting perturbations, and generating elaborate structures. These emergent organizations are totally different from the elements that constitute the system, and the patterns cannot be predicted solely from the characteristics of the individual elements.

Above, we described in detail one well-known example, the Belousov-Zabotinskii reaction. The *laser* is another important example; we quote here from Haken (1987), who discovered the laser:

> A laser consists of a rod of laser-active material, i.e., a material that contains atoms that can emit light. Two mirrors at the end-faces of the rod generate a preferential direction in which laser light is eventually emitted. The laser atoms are excited from the outside, perhaps by another lamp. The most interesting feature of the laser is the following: when laser atoms are excited only weakly, each emits an individual light wave with random phase, as in a common lamp. For instance, in a gas-discharge lamp the light field looks very much like "spaghetti." However, as the atoms are increasingly excited, *very suddenly a totally different kind of light is emitted*: a practically infinitely long sinusoidal wave [figure 3.5]. The structural change of the emitted light can be interpreted as follows. In the ordinary lamp, electrons of individual atoms make their optical transitions independently of each other, but in the laser the electrons make their optical transitions cooperatively. To relate this process to self-organization, consider a simple model: Several people stand at a channel filled with water [figure 3.6]. Each one has a bar that can be pushed at will into the water. The action of these people represents the

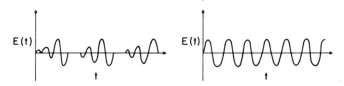

Figure 3.5
Laser light. (From Haken, 1987. Reprinted by permission.)

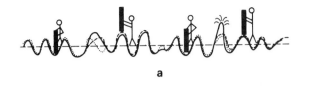

a

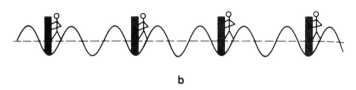

b

Figure. 3.6
Cooperativity produces patterns. (From Haken, 1987. Reprinted by permission.)

behavior of individual atoms, whereas the water represents the behavior of the light field. A situation corresponding to that of the ordinary lamp results when the people push their bars into the water independently of each other: an entirely irregular motion of the water surface is produced. However, if they instead push their bars into the water cooperatively and entirely regularly, i.e., in a well-ordered way, their action is analogous to the activity of laser atoms. Their cooperative activity can be easily brought about if an external boss gives orders to them. But in the laser, there is nobody to give orders. Thus, the regular cooperative behavior of the laser atoms is an act of *self-organization*. (Haken, 1987, pp. 419–420)

In the laser and in the chemical system, changes in certain external conditions that drive the system away from equilibrium—increasing the power of the lamp or the concentration of chemicals—drastically alter the macroscopic state of the system. Whereas before the elements acted independently, now certain configurations or collective actions of the individual elements increase until they appear to dominate and govern the behavior of the system. Haken (1977) refers to these dominant modes as the *order parameters*, which are capable of *slaving* all other modes of the system. The system can be described, therefore, in terms of one- or a few-order parameters, or collective variables, rather than by the individual elements. The order parameter acts to constrain or compress the degrees of freedom available to the elemental components.

It is important to stress again that self-organization in natural systems can only occur when these systems are both complex and open to flux with the environment. A complex, heterogeneous, and noisy system has an enormous amount of potential behavioral variability and a large number of potential cooperative modes. It generates local points of instability, where concentrations of matter and energy can serve as foci for attracting neighboring elements. As the system is driven further from thermodynamic equilibrium, these local asymmetries are amplified, and from this, one mode may arise to act as the order parameter. A homogeneous, symmetrical, and stable system has no such sources for new forms. In self-organization, the system *selects* or is *attracted* to one preferred configuration out of many possible states, but behavioral variability is an essential precursor ("order out of chaos").

We have discussed chemical and physical systems at length because it is perfectly apparent that the dish of chemicals and the light-emitting materials cannot, in any way, contain a prescription beforehand for the patterns they produce. These patterns fall out strictly as a result of the interactions among the elements that compose the system, the constraints on the system, and the energy flux. When these initial conditions are specified, one thing simply leads to another. Elements that were separate now communicate and cooperate. Self-organization is not magic; it occurs because of the inherent nonlinearities in nearly all of our physical and biological universe.

Dynamic Stability and Attractors

When systems self-organize under the influence of an order parameter, they "settle into" one or a few modes of behavior (which themselves may be quite complex) that the system prefers over all the possible modes. In dynamic terminology, this behavioral mode is an *attractor* state, as the system—under certain conditions—has an affinity for that state. Again in dynamic terminology, the system prefers a certain topology in its *state space*.

The state space of a dynamic system is an abstract construct of a space whose coordinates define the components of the system; they define the degrees of freedom of the system's behavior. The coordinates of the abstract state space vary with the context. The behavior of a simple mechanical system such as a pendulum can be described completely in a two-dimensional state space where the coordinates are position and velocity (figure 3.7). As the pendulum swings back and forth, its motion can be plotted on this plane. The motion of an ideal, frictionless pendulum prescribes an orbit or path through the state space that tracks its regular changes of position and velocity. If we add friction to the pendulum, it will eventually come to rest, and its orbit will look like a spiral.

The circular orbit of the frictionless pendulum and the resting point of the pendulum with friction are the *attractors* of this system: a limit cycle attractor and a point attractor. When the pendulum is slightly perturbed, it returns, in time, to its periodic behavior or its resting point. Once the pendulum is given its squirt of energy, these time and space patterns capture all other possible trajectories on the state space, and they represent stable order parameters for the pendulum system.

The state spaces of other complex systems—neural networks, organisms, ecosystems—are abstractions of the possible values of the elements in n-dimensional space, where n is the number of components necessary to characterize the system. For another simplified example, imagine that your state of physical fitness could be completely described by two observables, your heart rate and your body temperature, whose possible values are depicted on a two-dimensional space in figure 3.8. Most of the time, you occupy only a small, preferred part of this hypothetical space, where your normal values of these measurables intersect. Depending on whether we included diurnal fluctuations, your fitness *attractor* would look like a point or a limit cycle. Illness or exercise would shift you temporarily from the most highly preferred region, but your system "wants" to return there and will do so after you stop exercising or when you recover from

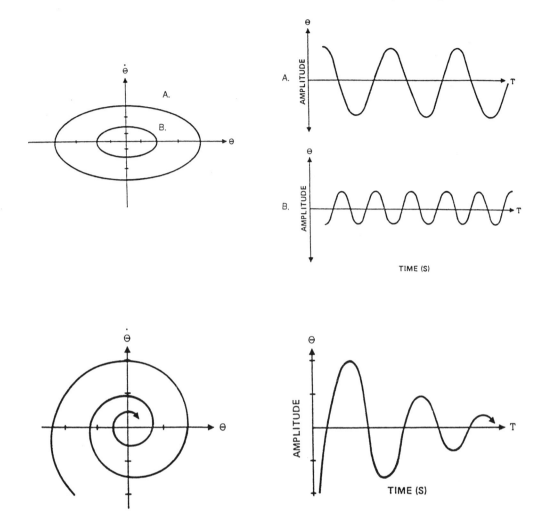

Figure 3.7
The *top panel* shows the motion of two ideal, frictionless pendulums, plotted as the amplitude vs. time on the *right* and on the phase plane (position vs. velocity) on the *left*. Without friction and energy dissipation, the oscillations are sustained indefinitely. In a real pendulum, an occasional energy boost is needed. This is an ideal *limit cycle attractor*. The *bottom panel* depicts a nonconservative or dissipative pendulum, where the amplitude is successively damped down until the pendulum comes to a rest, an example of a *point attractor*.

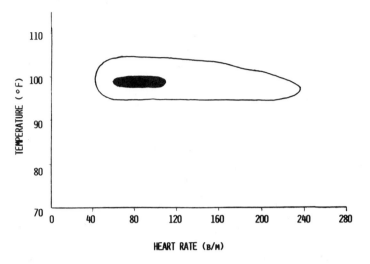

Figure 3.8
Hypothetical "fitness space" of a normal human showing dynamic range of heart rate and temperature. The individual "prefers" to spend time in the dark center portion but is not limited to it. When perturbed, the system normally returns to the center oval. (From Thelen, 1989.)

your infection. You might train extensively and shift the attractor on the state space. Your fitness is thus *dynamically stable*; it is not rigidly fixed on the state space but prefers and is strongly attracted to one region—as long as you remain alive!

The topographical depiction of a dynamic system relies on mapping of the collective variable behavior over time in an appropriate state space that captures the essential compression of the degrees of freedom. For many dynamic systems, the behavior can be described by the two variables, position and velocity, as in the pendulum above. The state space bounded by relevant system variables qualitatively illustrates locations where the system resides and where the trajectories are attracted, as shown in our hypothetical fitness space. Another characterization of attractors is the *return map*, whose power and simplicity were shown by Shaw (1984) in his treatment of the dripping faucet. Shaw measured the time intervals between drops in a dripping faucet and plotted the interval between a drop and its predecessor as a function of the interval between the drop and its successor. If the process were random, these points would be scattered without pattern all over the map. But Shaw found a complex but striking regularity, suggesting that some order underlies this seemingly stochastic process (figure 3.9).

The science of modern nonlinear dynamics has a number of elegant mathematical techniques to characterize attractors such as the dripping faucet, and readers are referred to the references cited earlier for these treatments. Such quantitative modeling is essential to support unequivocally the existence of an attractor and its *dimensionality* (a point attractor has a dimensionality of 1; a cyclic attractor, a dimensionality of 2). This has been done for several biological systems including electroencephalographic (EEG) signals (Rapp, Albano, and Mees, 1988), heart rate rhythms (Goldberger and Rigney, 1988); and motoneuron activity in

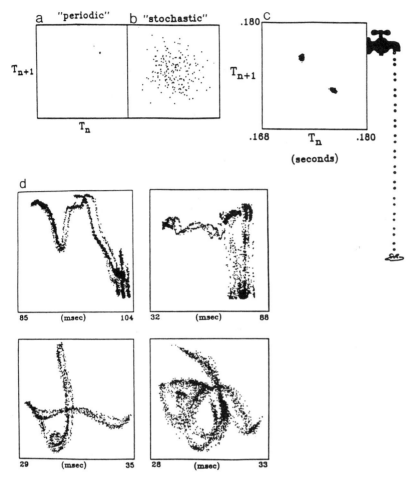

Figure 3.9
Return map of intervals between drips (interval between any two drops plotted against the next interval). *a*, If drips are completely periodic, all points collapse to one place on the space. *b*, If drips were completely random, points would be scattered on the space. *c*, If drips come in pairs, the points collapse to two places on the space. *d*, Actual plots of drips at various flow rates. The pattern is complex, but not random. (From Shaw, 1984. Reprinted by permission.)

sea slugs (Mpitsos, Creech, Cohan, and Mendelson, 1988). We have as yet no developmental data sets with sufficient non-noisy points to satisfy the mathematical requirements for the precise quantification of attractors, although, as we shall see below, this remains an ideal goal for our enterprise.

Point and cyclic attractors are the most simple cases, but as we saw in the example of Shaw's dripping faucet, dynamic systems can generate extraordinarily complex attractors on many different state spaces (figure 3.10; see also Abraham, 1987). Currently, there is intense interest in such *chaotic* or *strange attractors*—a field characterized as growing explosively (Grebogi, Ott, and Yorke, 1987). Chaotic systems look random when they are plotted over time, but they are not. When they are plotted on appropriate state spaces, a highly complex but deterministic pattern emerges, suggesting an underlying global order to the system behavior, but a local unpredictability. Many physical and biological systems are revealing chaotic dynamics; we will return to the important implications of chaotic states for development as we continue.

Several characteristics of attractors, then, are important as a construct in development. First, complex, dynamic systems seek preferred behavioral modes as a function of the interactions of their internal components and their sensitivity to external conditions. The attractor regime is only determined as the system is assembled through the slaving of its order parameter. There are no codes, prescriptions, schemata, or programs orchestrating the nature of the attractor or its trajectory. As we shall see, under different conditions, the components are free to assemble into other stable behavioral modes, and it is indeed this ability of a multicomponent system to "soft-assemble" that both provides the enormous flexibility of biological systems and explains some of the most persistent puzzles of development.

Second, attractors may have varying degrees of stability and instability. It is common to picture an attractor as a ball within a potential well (see figure 3.10).

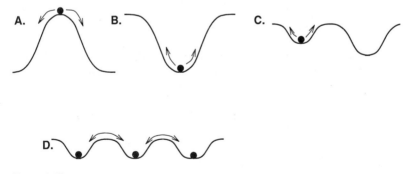

Figure 3.10
Stable and unstable attractors. The stability of the attractor depicted as potential wells. *A*, The ball on the top of the hill has a lot of potential energy, and even a very small push will send it down; it is a repellor. *B*, The ball in the bottom of the steep hill requires a large energy boost to send it over the top. If perturbed, it will quickly return to the bottom. It is a stable attractor. *C*, This is a less stable situation. Relatively small perturbations will push the ball around, although given enough time, it will probably statistically prefer the deeper, left well. *D*, A common behavioral system may have multistability—several quasi-stable options within the attractor basin.

A ball on the top of a potential *hill* has a lot of stored potential energy; with just a very small push, it will roll down the hill. A ball in a deep potential well, in contrast, has very little potential energy and needs a large external boost to change its position. The latter is a very stable attractor; the former is called a repellor, as the system does not want to sit on the hill. A ball in a shallow well is moderately stable, but will respond to a sufficient boost by moving into the neighboring well (while not dwelling very long on the hillock in between).

While some attractor states are so unstable as to almost never be observed, other attractor states are so stable they look like they are inevitable. Because these behavioral states are so reliably seen under certain circumstances, it is easy to believe that they are generated by *hard-wired structures* or *programs* within the system. If the workings of a pendulum were not so transparent, we could easily believe a little clock was hidden somewhere. Very stable attractors take very large pushes to move them from their preferred positions, but they are dynamic and changeable nonetheless. We will argue here that many configurations in action and cognition, and in development, that act like permanent programs or structures are stable attractors whose stability limits may indeed be shifted under appropriate circumstances. That is to say, many mental constructs and movement configurations, object permanence and walking, for example, are attractors of such strength and stability that only the most severe perturbations can disrupt them. They look as though they are wired in. Other abilities—transitive inference, visual illusions, and many sports skills, for example—have attractors whose stability is easily upset by contextual manipulations, lack of practice, or by not paying attention.

Finally, complex systems may have two or more attractors with different basins of attraction coexisting. In this case, the same system may have multistable modes, which are discrete areas in the state space. In the next chapter, we elaborate further the concept of behavior as low-dimensional attractors of varying stability. We then characterize development as the continual stabilization and destabilization, over time, of preferred attractor states.

Phase Shifts: How Dynamic Systems Change States
At this point, we are able to characterize nonequilibrium systems—those whose trajectories in state space converge on a certain limit set, the attractor—in terms of a very general dynamic equation (Haken, 1977):

$$q = N(q, \text{parameters}, \text{noise})$$

In this equation, q is a vector representing the lumping together of the known and relevant subcomponents of the system—its microscopic elements—of potentially very high dimensionality.

Then q, the *behavior* of the system, its trajectory through its state space over time, is in general a nonlinear function N of the vector of the states of the microscopic elements, as well as a number of parameters, which might include environmental factors, and random forces which are not included in q. This equation represents the self-organizing process: in q, the behavior in some attractor regime, the degrees of freedom inherent in q, and the noise are compressed.

Let us go back again to the Belousov-Zhabotinskii reaction, which takes place at room temperature. Imagine, however, that we assemble our components **q** in a very cold chamber, the temperature being a parameter in the equation. As we slowly warm the chamber, we pump thermal energy into the dish of chemicals in a continuous manner proportional to the temperature of the room. For a long time, nothing happens; **q** remains in one attractor in the state space (a point attractor). Then, at a critical temperature, the reaction begins and the spontaneous patterns rotate and change: **q** jumps to a new region of the space and into a more complex attractor regime.

The temperature changes were continuous, but the behavior of the system was dramatically discontinuous. These nonlinearities, or *phase shifts* or *phase transitions*, are highly characteristic of nonequilibrium systems, and are, we argue, the very source of new forms. What is remarkable, and most important for development, is that the parameter change, temperature in this case, was *entirely nonspecific* to **q**. The temperature had no information whatsoever prescribing the nature of the chemical reaction; temperature does not have space, time, or color. The pattern emerged strictly as a function of **N**, the nonlinear dynamics of the system.

In dynamic terminology, temperature here is the control parameter, the parameter to which the collective behavior of the system is sensitive and that moves the system through different collective states. Although we adopt the term *control parameter* here to be consistent with the more general vocabulary, it is an unfortunate term because it invokes control theory and a controller. The control parameter does not control the system in any conventional sense; it is only the variable or parameter that assembles the system in one or another attractor regime *given the states of* **q**.

In biological systems, any number of organismic variables or relevant external boundary conditions can act as control parameters. In photosensitive animals, for example, relative light intensity determines locomotor vectors. At low to moderate intensities, animals may approach the light source, but as the intensity scales up, approach shifts to withdrawal. The light is a nonspecific scalar; the system shifts discontinuously from a point attractor to a point repellor. Energy level is a common control parameter. A well-used, but enlightening example is the gait of horses. As the horse continuously increases its speed, its gait shifts discontinuously from a walk to a trot to a gallop with no stable intermediate pattern. The particular pattern of footfalls acts as a dynamic attractor within a speed range. The preferred gait at any speed level is also the energetically most efficient (McMahon, 1984). Recall that a horse may be trained to perform an unnatural gait, but it is presumably more demanding energetically. In the latter case, the intentional set of the trainer is the control parameter (it imposes constraints on the pattern). The trainer's intentions compete with the natural dynamics of the horse, but the horse's intrinsic dynamics must be very attractive, because it usually takes years to teach a horse a new gait. The Spanish Riding School in Vienna is world-renowned for teaching horses new gait attractors; people pay premium prices to see horses do what does not come naturally.

The concept that a system can assume different collective states through the action of a quite nonspecific control parameter is a powerful challenge to more accepted machine and computer metaphors of biological order. How does the horse switch gaits? Conventionally, one might postulate a neural network or code that switches from one output pattern to another at certain predetermined speed thresholds. Presumably, these thresholds would be structurally encoded in the neural connections and would be anatomically stable and phylogenetically determined. A synergetic view, in contrast, would view the gait as a stable collective variable compressing the possible combinations of the structural components in an energetic and task context that would include not only the intentionality of the horse but the qualities of the support surface, visual information guiding the horse, and so on. Because the gaits are so stable at particular speed ranges, it is tempting to view them as "hard-wired." The neural connections are essential, but the gait patterns are as much a product of the energy and information flowing through the system as of the "hardware" itself. The lesson from chemistry and physics is that self-organization is not mystical; pattern can be generated by a system seeking cooperative stability. Order is not "in there," but is created in the process of the action. Later, we continue this line of reasoning to mental states as well.

Exiling the deus ex machina forever requires abandoning programs and schemata and adopting the concepts of stability and fluctuations. Stability is what defines the collective states of the system and it can be assessed by understanding the dynamics of transitions or phase shifts, when systems lose stability. Fluctuations around stable states are the inevitable accompaniment of complex systems. It is these fluctuations that are the source of new forms in behavior and development and that account for the nonlinearity of much of the natural world.

Fluctuations and Transitions: Unpacking Processes of Change
When we define change as the transition from one stable state or attractor to another, it is important to ask: What is stability? How do we know when a system is stable? Is it stable relative to its state in the next microsecond or to the age of the universe? Recall that even highly attractive states are *dynamically* stable and exhibit fluctuations around their mean state that reflect the noisiness of the components. To discover control parameters we must know transitions; to define transitions we must have a metric to assess the relative stability of our system.

Not all changes in systems are phase shifts. Many phenomena are parametric, that is, variables increase or decrease in a continuous manner. It is common to see systems act parametrically within certain ranges of a control parameter and nonlinearly when certain threshold values are reached. Dynamic theory has, however, specific predictions for the behavior of systems close to true transition points. These predictions are based on the assumption of inherent fluctuations which are the result of the coupled component subsystems. These fluctuations act like continuous perturbations in the form of noise on the collective behavior of the system. Within ranges of the control parameter, the system maintains its preferred behavioral pattern despite the noise. However, at critical points, the system loses its ability to maintain these patterns and the fluctuations become enhanced. At these points, the system is dominated by these fluctuations and may display transient behavior where no stable pattern can be discerned. As the control parameter is continuously scaled, the system then exhibits a new or different pattern with new values of the collective variable. At this point, the fluctuations are again reduced, as the system evolves into a new attractor state.

Figure 3.11 illustrates this phenomenon as a series of potential wells. The deepness of the well indicates the relative stability of the collective variable. The ball normally rests in the well to the left and remains within the well despite the small random fluctuations of the system. However, as the control parameter is scaled, the cooperative interactions of that attractor state become weakened. At the critical point, even small random fluctuations are sufficient to drive the ball out of the well and into a new attractor state. The fluctuations are always there, but the effects of the fluctuations are nonlinear. That is, instability in the system amplifies the fluctuations so that random effects may be manifest. It is at these critical points, therefore, that the system shifts or bifurcates. As we saw in the examples of the laser light and the Belousov-Zhabotinskii reaction, systems produce coherent patterns only in particular values of their control parameters. If the temperature of the solution or the concentration of ions or the energy delivered to the electron beam is too low, the systems are dominated by the random fluctuations of their inherently noisy subelements. Thus, for instance, the concentration of ions in the Belousov-Zhabotinskii reaction varies wildly over time, with no discernible pattern and with a large variability around the mean frequency of oscillation (see figure 3.3). At the critical concentration, however, the system shifts to a patterned oscillation, and the variability around the mean frequency is dramatically reduced.

The measure of relative variability around a mean state, therefore, becomes a potent tool for assessing the stability of a complex system and the states in which it resides. Systems shift into new forms only as the old forms get shaken up by internal perturbations; these are engendered by changes in the values of parameters to which the system is sensitive. As stable dynamic systems approach such transitions, their growing instability should be detectable by increased measures of variability; as they shift into new stable patterns, variability should again be reduced.

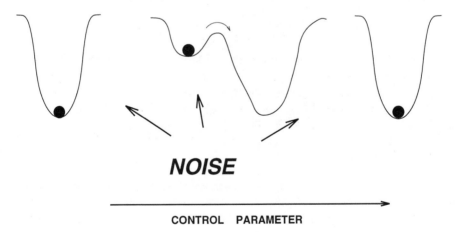

NOISE

CONTROL PARAMETER

Figure 3.11
Phase shifts result from the amplification of normally occurring fluctuations of noise. As the control parameter is scaled up, there are critical values where the internal fluctuations overwhelm the system stability and the system seeks new stable modes.

This prediction was most dramatically demonstrated in a behavioral system by Kelso and his colleagues in a long series of elegant studies and models of human bimanual coordination. In the basic experiment, subjects were asked to move their index fingers under two initial conditions. In the in-phase condition, subjects flexed and extended both digits simultaneously (similar muscles in each hand contracting simultaneously). In the antiphase condition, one finger flexed while the other extended (homologous muscles contracting in alternation). The experimenters systematically increased the pace of the cyclic movements by providing the subjects with a metronome beat. What is remarkable about this paradigm is that when subjects begin their movements antiphase, they spontaneously switch to an in-phase mode at particular, individually reproducible pacing frequencies. They do not switch coordinative patterns when they begin in phase. Two patterns are stable at low frequencies, but the neuromotor system produces only one stable attractor at higher movement frequencies (Kelso, Holt, Rubin, and Kugler, 1981).

Kelso and colleagues have used this deceptively simple model of a discrete phase transition to precisely operationalize predictions of dynamic theory. In particular, they provide compelling confirmation of the loss of system stability as the mechanism underlying the qualitative shift of coordination modes. When subjects began their movements in phase, the phasing between fingers remained steady and the standard deviations around the mean phase were small and constant. However, when the subjects scaled up the cycling frequency of the initially antiphase movements, the fluctuations around the mean increased dramatically before and during the transition to the symmetrical mode. After that transition, the standard deviations quickly decreased to in-phase values (Kelso and Scholz, 1985; Kelso, Scholz, and Schöner, 1986).

Think of both in-phase and antiphase movements as naturally "easy" when they are slow (for anatomical or energetic reasons, or both), much like a particular gait style is associated with a particular locomotor pace in a horse. But for antiphase movements, increasing frequency demands disrupt this natural assembly of the system, and *this disruption can actually be detected* as increased variability as the system wanders from the stable mode as speed is increased. Because, at the transition, the antiphase mode is no longer stable, the system is free to seek (or be bumped) into another, more stable (in-phase) mode. The key here again is the dynamic nature of the assembly from subelements that are themselves noisy. At points in the state space, the noise overwhelms the system coherence, but it also provides the bumps that allow the system to discover its new stable patterns. We will repeatedly emphasize that developing systems must be in this unstable or quasi-stable mode to explore new cooperative patterns (or strategies) and select those that provide a functional match to a task.

That fluctuations are enhanced at state transitions leads to a second powerful prediction for unpacking the processes of change. When an attractor is stable, small perturbations are quickly damped out. In the depiction of the potential well (see figures 3.10 and 3.11), when the ball is pushed up the sides of the well by either its intrinsic noise or by some outside force, it quickly drops back to its strongly attractive point at the bottom of the well. The time it takes for the system to return to the stable state is indeed a measure of the stability of the attractor; strong attractors have very short *local relaxation times*. Remember that as the system approaches a transition, the walls of the potential well flatten out; the ball can be in other states with increasing probability. Likewise, recovery from perturbations will be comparatively delayed; the ball will no longer be so quickly attracted to the local minimum. Indeed, at a critical point, the well may flatten so completely that the ball will fall into a completely new stable attractor, the phase shift. As the point is passed, the relaxation time will again decrease.

Scholz, Kelso, and Schöner (1987) found evidence for critical slowing down in the bimanual finger studies. They perturbed the movements at different frequencies by applying a random, very rapid torque pulse. When the movements were perturbed, the times for the system to recover stable cycles were consistently higher in the antiphase than the in-phase modes (except at very low frequencies), suggesting that the antiphase attractor was not as stable. Most important was that when subjects began antiphase, the recovery to the perturbation was slower as they moved toward their transition frequencies. After transition, recovery was similar to in-phase times. Disintegration of the system coherence was reflected in diminishing strength of the attractor to pull in the trajectories from various regions of the state space. At any measurement instance, therefore, there is a greater probability that the system would reside in some nonpreferred region, reflected in greater variability of the collective variable. At the same time, once the system is perturbed, there is also a higher probability that it will not be in the preferred mode at some subsequent time, $t + 1$.

The Importance of Time Scale Relations

As we shall see in the next chapter, the concept of relative stability of behavioral states is the cornerstone of a dynamic systems approach to development. We have shown here two powerful ways of determining the strength of an attractor: the probability that the system will occupy dense or scattered regions on its state space and the rate at which the trajectories are captured by the attractor. The time scales in which systems evolve toward stability and instability are especially important in ontogenetic considerations. We have discussed thus far recovery from perturbations on a "local" scale, illustrated by pulse perturbations on an ongoing movement. Can we relate these concepts to changes evolving on longer time scales, those of developmental time?

Let us refer back again to the potential well diagram of the finger experiment, where the initial antiphase movements are represented by the more shallow well, and the in-phase movements are represented by the deeper well to the right. The experiments of Kelso et al. increased the control parameter, the cycling frequency, and the instabilities led to the phase transition. Imagine, if you will, the subjects beginning antiphase and continuing to move in this way for a very long time without changing speed. Although the probability is good that they can maintain this antiphase pattern, there is a higher probability that they want to move in-phase. If they move long enough, it becomes increasing likely that their inherent fluctuations will eventually boost the system over the potential hill and into the deeper well. That is, the system will seek global stability, where there is virtually no probability of entering a new regime. Thus, in addition to the local relaxation time, t(rel), the system has a global equilibration time, t(equ). Of course, both the local and global equilibration times must be defined in relation to how long the experimenter observes the system, t(obs); for short observation times, the local minima are stable. (On the other hand, if we watched an organism over a lifetime, the globally stable attractor would be death.) But in the usual observations of real-time and developmental studies, the stability of a local attractor can be defined if:

$$t(rel) \ll t(obs) \ll t(equ)$$

Stable systems return to their minima within the observed time scale, i.e., we would expect to see stable developmental states within the range of our observations and before death! Now, as the system loses stability, we may not see t(rel) within t(obs); i.e., it takes too long for the system to find the local minimum.

These relations depend again, however, on how fast the control parameter is itself changing in time, t(par). With the finger example, the experimenter told the subjects to speed up their fingers within the observation time of the experiment, so that this relation held:

$$t(rel) \ll t(par) \ll t(equ)$$

However, it is conceivable in developmental examples, for instance, for the control parameter to change more slowly than the global equilibration:

$$t(rel) \ll t(equ) \ll t(par)$$

in which case we would see no enhancement of fluctuations because the system would have found global stability before the critical point where the system lost stability. We can imagine that gradual growth changes or long-term practice effects, for example, might act as control parameters whose time scales allow the system to seek global stability without the transient disruption of the current system. On the other hand, there are periods during development when changes are very rapid. There are physical growth spurts during early infancy and early adolescence, for instance. The segregation of the optic tracts leading to binocular acuity apparently occurs within a week or two, at about 3 to 4 months of age (Held, 1985). Synaptic densities in the prefrontal cortex, a primary area for associative memory, increase sharply within a month or two in the second half of the first year (Goldman-Rakic, 1987). Many other, rather sudden changes have been documented, especially in the early years of life. As we shall see in the next chapter, these discernible phase shifts in one component of the behavioral system may act as control parameters for subsequent shifts in other domains. When the time scale relations are appropriate, the loss of system stability that engenders these shifts, measured in the manner described above, become our entries into the developmental process.

A Note on "Noise"

In experimental psychology, "noisy" data are bad data. Noisy data do not produce statistically reliable effects and have to be discarded. Noise can enter behavioral data from several sources. First, there can be systematic or unsystematic errors in the data collection or analysis. This kind of noise is bad from the point of view of dynamics as well; it renders data uninterpretable. However, data can also look noisy because the subjects perform variably on the task. If they perform this way because the task or the instructions are confusing, this also confounds interpretation. Sometimes the experiment and the experimenters are fine, but the subjects still give variable and inconsistent responses. This kind of noise is very informative: it says that the task does not elicit stable performance, that between and within subjects, there is no single attractor. The subjects may be in a state of transition, or there may be several multi- or quasi-stable attractors. When the task demands are not very constraining, subjects may choose among several or many possible responses. This last kind of noise tells us about the task, the subjects, and probably both.

A Further Note on Stability

All of our references to stability should be prefaced with the word "relative." In the most coupled of biological oscillators, such as those seen in the finger experiments above, but also in brain oscillations (see chapter 5), systems are never, ever rigidly synchronized. Rather, sophisticated mathematical and graphical techniques have shown such systems to be only quasi- or intermittently stable (Kelso and DeGuzman, 1991). An elegant example is that of juggling, as described by Beek (1989). Beek found that skilled jugglers, while having to execute highly phase-entrained movements of both hands, stop short of complete phase-locking. Rather, they operate just on the borders of phase-locking, so to speak. This gives them the flexibility to adapt to even the small fluctuations that are inevitable in each catch and throw. To maintain complete phase-locking of components would mean to have exactly reproducible initial conditions at each movement; this is impossible in real-life systems. Interestingly, the more balls the juggler has in the air, the more the juggler modulates his or her movements. As the timing constraints become more severe, so does the complexity, and tight phase-locking limits possibilities for flexible adjustments.

It is important to think of any seemingly stable human thought or action to reside on these cusps of quasi-stability, visiting areas of tight coordination, but also intermittently escaping from them, providing the flexibility to react and assemble new adaptive forms.

Summary

We have, in this chapter, presented a qualitative and nonmathematical introduction to the concepts of nonlinear dynamic systems. We see these concepts as contributing to our study of developmental phenomena in several ways. First, we invoke dynamic systems as a powerful conceptual metaphor to understand the fundamental processes of ontogenetic change. In this endeavor, we are not alone, as the metaphor has been invoked in various guises by many previous theorists. The reincarnation and elaboration of these concepts in one way attests to their intuitive appeal. We show in the bulk of this book how such concepts *explain large and important bodies of data which have heretofore been without theoretical unity.* While these data were, of course, not collected to explicitly test dynamic predictions, they are, conversely, inexplicable by any other competing theoretical interpretation.

Because the principles of dynamic systems are themselves both extremely powerful and extremely general, as a whole the approach may indeed not be empirically unverifiable. Nonetheless, the principles do generate *specific predictions* which can, and have been, confirmed in the developmental literature and in our own work, albeit still in limited and exploratory ways. These confirmations we explain.

Next, we outline empirical strategies that are, at least in principle, capable of generating developmental data that will meet the requirements of a more rigorous dynamic analysis. We do not yet know whether this goal can be achieved, but we are convinced that the developmental data we collect on the way to this ideal goal will advance our understanding of ontogeny in many domains of interest.

Later in this book, we offer a neurologically plausible theory of behavioral development that instantiates dynamic principles in process and mechanism.

Note

1. Readers may also refer to the series by Abraham and Shaw (1984); Barnsley (1988); Devaney (1986); Glass and Mackey (1988); Kelso, Mandell, and Shlesinger (1988); Jackson (1989); Townsend (1992); Grebogi, Ott, and Yorke (1987); Madore and Freedman (1987); Haken (1977, 1985); West and Goldberger (1987); among others.

Chapter 4

Dynamic Principles of Development: Reinterpreting Learning to Walk

In this chapter we return to learning to walk. Recall that we proposed that conventional accounts of locomotor control and development were both impoverished theoretically and unable to explain the data, especially in their rich, flexible, asynchronous, and idiosyncratic aspects. In the last chapter, we set forth a number of principles, derived from synergetics or pattern formation in complex systems, which offer a means for understanding the origins of new forms. Now, we apply those principles directly to development, using as illustrations the puzzles about walking raised in chapter 1.

Several caveats are important before embarking. First, in the last chapter we deliberately used physical examples, such as the Belousov-Zhabotinskii chemical reaction or laser lights, because they are transparent in illustrating pattern formation without a program. In this chapter, we refer to a number of biomechanical influences on the development of locomotion. This can lead to the misconception that dynamic systems may be using a "simple physics model" to represent development (Hofsten, 1989, p. 951). We, of course, do not want to replace the prevailing physical model, the computer, with new physical models, be they chemicals in a dish, dripping faucets, or cloud formation.

First, we reemphasize that dynamic principles are based on thermodynamic realities that describe the way the universe works. These are entirely independent of the level of observation or the particular material instantiation. In our opinion, these principles are only more powerful as they apply to such diverse phenomena as weather and developing organisms. Whether these general principles will be *useful* in understanding development is, however, a relevant and important question, and the one to which this book is addressed.

It may be equally argued that dynamic principles may be of such generality as to be vacuous in development inquiry. It is true that the principles have nothing to say about particular events in particular domains: dynamic theory is uninformed and will not predict when infants begin to talk, for example, or what mechanisms are involved. This is the job of developmental research, and we maintain that no theory that addresses general processes of change can fill in the domain-specific details. By the very nature of development itself—in its contingent, evolving, emergent nature—we will always be required to fill in the story by dint of hard empirical labor.

Then there is the underlying assumption that while the "physical" parts of the body are well, good, and even necessary, the brain, as the problem-solving part of the machinery, requires new categories of explanation. Thus, dynamic systems may be sufficient for movement, but inadequate for plans, intention, and higher-level cognition. The strength of dynamic systems is, in fact, in the principled rejection of such Cartesian dualism. We suggest, and illustrate in this book and the accompanying volume, that dynamic principles may be applied at many levels of analysis of behavioral development, from neural embryology, to what is traditionally considered "pure" cognition, to social interaction. Indeed, we spend considerable effort in this book providing a dynamic interpretation of neural development, which we see as entirely consistent with principles of pattern formation on the behavioral level. Dynamic systems does not exclude the brain, but it does not give it—or the genes—privileged status as the motor for developmental change. Thus, while we use examples primarily from the motor and cognitive domains to illustrate dynamic principles of development, we believe that these principles capture developmental processes at many levels of organization.

Finally, the legitimate objection can be raised that we use dynamic systems only at the level of metaphor. We discuss this issue again when we consider extending dynamics to cognitive development, and in our final chapter. It will suffice at this point for us to defend metaphor as theory on several grounds. First, to date, developmental research has not produced—and may not soon generate—the lengthy and dense data sets of thousands of points necessary for rigorous application of the mathematical formalisms of dynamic theory. Such data sets may be forthcoming for real-time behavior (see, e.g., Robertson, Cohen, and Mayer-Kress, 1993), but are methodologically very difficult over long time spans. Second, even if available, it is questionable whether data collected over an extended time will show the stationarity necessary for application of the classic formalisms (e.g., Schöner and Kelso, 1988; Beek, 1989). But most important, even without formal treatment, concepts of dynamic systems are extraordinarily *useful*. They are useful in explaining data over a wide number of domains and levels, as we show in this and the accompanying volume, and in generating specific predictions about stability and change, variability, and selection. We maintain that these general principles can lead to more precise operational confirmation than conventional and well-accepted developmental constructs such as schemata, knowledge structures, processing capacity, innate principles, skill levels, or stages.

Overview

The view of locomotor development we present here contrasts with traditional neural-maturationist and cognitive accounts. Learning to walk is less a prescribed, logically inevitable process than a confluence of available states within particular contextual opportunities. All normal human infants learn to walk upright because of anatomical and neural elements that have a phylogenetic history; contingent developmental events that have an ontogenetic history; strong motivation to move and to move more efficiently; a shared task environment such as support surfaces, gravity, and things to hold onto; and parenting that facilitates certain sensorimotor configurations. Walking self-organizes under these constraints because nonlinear, complex dynamic systems occupy preferred behavioral states.

In this extended chapter, we present dynamic systems principles of development within the context of early motor development for two reasons. First, the manifest involvement of the physical parts of the system—the body—makes dynamic, multicomponent interactions especially transparent. But even more important are the rich theoretical and empirical applications of dynamic systems to adult motor behavior produced in the last decade. Our first section, therefore, justifies the extension of these real-time adult applications to developmental time scales. In the second section we outline contemporary principles of action, emphasizing the insights of Bernstein and subsequent dynamic action theorists. Next, we apply these real-time principles to the organization of a common infant movement of the legs, kicking. This is followed by the heart of the chapter, the extension of real-time dynamics to the ontogenetic scale and the exposition of a dynamic approach. We apply these principles to developmental changes in kicking patterns, and especially the characteristic instabilities and even regressions during the first year. We then address the question of the entrainment of the organism's intrinsic dynamics to specific tasks, in this case exemplified by early stepping on the treadmill. In the next section, we present a study of the ontogeny of treadmill stepping, explicitly using dynamic principles. Finally, we return to the larger question of learning to walk from a dynamic perspective, and we summarize the chapter by depicting the precursors of walking on an "ontogenetic landscape."

A Note on Time Scales of Emergent Action

Throughout the remainder of this book, we will be using dynamic principles on several interrelated and mutually graded time scales. The first is what we call *real time*—the "here and now"—the seconds and fractions of seconds of immediate behavior. When people have goals, intentions, and tasks, they think, move, and speak. Each act is a new behavioral form: stable and predictable in some of its features, but variable, flexible, and adaptive in each instantiation. When we look at adults doing motor or cognitive tasks under controlled laboratory conditions, in standard environments, we tend to see the stable and predictable features of their behavior. The next step has often been to ascribe this stability to executive agents which encode the details of the action. When subjects are young, unpracticed, or allowed to act more spontaneously and naturally, much of this stability is no longer apparent, or at least the range of variability around a stable mode is greatly expanded. As we illustrate here in locomotion, and subsequently in cognition, even behaviors that look wired in or program-driven can be seen as dynamically emergent: behavior is assembled by the nature of the task, and opportunistically recruits the necessary and available organic components (which themselves have dynamic histories) and environmental support.

The cornerstone of a dynamic theory of development is this emergent nature of behavior assembled in *real time*. We suggest that just as components are free to assemble in response to the rich and varied real-time task environment, they similarly will show dynamic shifts during an *ontogenetic* time scale owing to changes in organic components, task, and environmental support. When an infant sees a toy across the room and intends to move toward it, the form of that locomotion—whether he or she walks or crawls, for example—is a dynamic product of the child's neuromuscular and motivational status, the nature of the support surface, and the location of the toy. With development, the stability of that form may increase (walking) or decrease (crawling), but the dynamic assembly of the behavior remains. These dynamic time scales are completely interwoven. As each action is discovered in real time, it uses components that have a dynamic history. Similarly, as the action is performed, it becomes part of the dynamic history of the organism and contributes to the morphology of future actions. Embedded in these time scales ranging from seconds to weeks, months, and years is the time scale conventionally assigned to *learning* through repetition, reinforcement, observation, or instruction. Thus, in a dynamic view, we can hardly draw distinctions between any of these scales; the line between learning and development is particularly fuzzy. Because dynamic principles of behavior have been best worked out in the area of real-time motor behavior, we begin with this time scale. We hope that the reader will keep in mind that the same principles and processes apply to real and developmental time scales, not only in motor but in other behavioral domains.

Dynamic Principles of Action

Before moving into the developmental time scale, it is instructive to focus on the generation of movement in real time as a dynamic process of emergent form. Recall that in chapter 1 we established two objections to prevailing neurological and cognitive theories of the control and development of locomotion. First, these views were theoretically impoverished because they provided no mechanism for understanding change: how new forms arise in either real or developmental time. And second, they could not account for the observed data.

Two constructs have dominated the study of motor performance. The first, the neurophysiological construct of the central pattern generator (CPG), we reviewed in chapter 1. In experimental psychology, the counterpart to the CPG is the *motor program*. Rosenbaum and Saltzman (1984) define the motor program as follows: "Before the execution of a sequence of voluntary movements, a memory representation for instructions for the entire sequence is thought to be established in the central nervous system" (p. 51). Motor programs are usually hierarchical, with the program itself as the executive at the top of the hierarchy, and to be distinguished from the lower, effector mechanisms that carry out the executive commands. Motor programs are usually studied by chronometric methods, that is, by the dissection of reaction and movement execution times in relation to the elements in and difficulties of a task.

While both constructs have limited application for describing the output of the isolated spinal cord, or for understanding the timing structure of certain human skills, the major failing of these prescriptive theories is their lack of generalizability. Real data from real frogs, chicks, cats, and humans render the construct of the CPG illusory. What is the pure essence of locomotion when its performance, form, and stability are completely at the whim of the age of the animal, its motivation, and the experimental or observational context?

Similarly, the motor program construct has not successfully accounted for the hallmark of human intentional actions: their functional adaptability. If the motor program contains the instructions for the entire sequence of behaviors ahead of time, how can novel and adapted forms be generated? Some movement scientists have attempted to address this fundamental question by proposing generalized motor "schemata," which encode only general movement plans but not specific kinematic details (e.g., Schmidt, 1975). It seems abundantly clear that people moving in the real world must generate plans and intentions and that these must be transmitted to real physical output devices, but again, motor programming theorists have not clearly specified either the nature or origins of such schemata or how they become modified with experience or development.

One important reason that both the CPG and the motor program models fall short of adequate explanation for movement is that they consider movement to be generated by "pure" neural commands. But, as we suggested in chapter 1, the central nervous system (CNS) is not a computer controlling an electronic output device. Rather, the CNS must translate intentions and plans into moving limbs and body segments. The body constitutes a complex linked system, with mass, elastic, energetic, and inertial properties, which has multiple sensory linkages within it and between the organism and the outside world.

The Contributions of Bernstein

The dual problems of the complexity and indeterminacy of the mind-body link were first recognized by the Russian physiologist Nicolas Bernstein, whose work spanned the 1930s through the 1960s. Bernstein's major contribution, *Coordination and Regulation of Movements* was published in English in 1967, but worldwide recognition of his seminal thinking has grown dramatically only in the last decade or so (see Whiting, 1984). Bernstein's many insights are the cornerstone of contemporary movement science. They led directly, through the work of, primarily, Michael Turvey, Scott Kelso, and Peter Kugler (e.g., Kelso, Holt, Kugler, and Turvey, 1980; Kugler, Kelso, and Turvey, 1980), to dynamic perspectives on motor coordination and control, and these real-time applications of dynamic theory are the parents of our developmental theory. Thus, because we can trace the lineage from Bernstein to the present exercise, it is worthwhile to summarize how he revised conceptions of motor organization and control.

Movements occur, according to Bernstein, because of imbalances of forces caused by changes in muscle tension. Nonetheless, these movements cannot reflect a one-to-one relationship between the specific patterns of motor neuron firing, or indeed the forces generated by muscle contraction and the actual movement produced. In other words, it is impossible to map directly muscle activity patterns measured either in the CNS or at the periphery to the actual trajectory of the movement. Why must this be? Imagine lifting your arm to shoulder height and then relaxing your muscles. Then imagine shaking your hand vigorously just at the wrist. The movements you see—your arm drops in the first case, and your lower and upper arm also vibrate in the second instance—are all not controlled by your nervous system. Instead, you also see mechanical consequences of your body as a physical system. As your body parts move, they generate inertial and centripetal forces and are subject to the gravity field. Such forces contribute to all movements *while they are happening* and constitute a continuously changing force field. The same muscle contraction has different consequences on your arm movement when you have lifted it than after it has dropped, and indeed during any part of the trajectory. In addition, muscles and joints themselves have mechanical properties of springiness and tension that depend—but not in a linear way—on how much they are stretched or how stiff you have made your limb.

Thus, during the execution of the movement, the device to be controlled (the limbs and body segments) presents the CNS with a continuously changing biodynamic challenge. How can the CNS coordinate the body parts to produce smooth and functional movements when equivalent muscle contractions have diverse consequences, and conversely, when the same trajectory of movement can be generated from different forces, depending entirely on the movement context? Bernstein asked the question in terms of how the nervous system solved the complex equations of motion needed given the enormous numbers of *degrees of freedom* in the neuromuscular system.

The problem of motor coordination and control identified by Bernstein—how the many and diverse parts of an organism cooperate within a diverse and changing context—is the same problem we must solve to understand the generation of behavior in any realm and in any time scale. Given that the behaving organism is a dynamic creature, acting in an environment that is never exactly the same, how is stable and adaptive behavior produced? How do the many organic (structural, physiological) elements cooperate to respond with functional activity in the physical and social world?

Bernstein's first insight was to conceptualize movements in living organisms as morphologically coherent and holistic forms. He recognized that no action is produced in isolation:

> Studying the biodynamics of movements involved in cutting with a chisel I was able to show that it is impossible to alter selectively any one given detail in this movement without affecting others. If, for example, the trajectory of the elbow is slightly altered, the form of the trajectory of the hammer is also unavoidably changed, as are the relationships between the velocities of the swing and the impact, and between the velocities of the wrist and of the hammer head, and a whole series of other nuances of the movement. . . . Movements react to changes in one single detail with changes in a whole series of others which are sometimes very far removed from the former both in space and in time, and leave untouched such elements as are closely adjacent to the first detail, almost merged with it. In this way *movements are not chains of details but structures which are differentiated into details* [author's emphasis]; they are structurally whole, simultaneously exhibiting a high degree of differentiation of elements and differing in the particular forms of the relationships between these elements. (Bernstein, quoted in Whiting, 1984, p. 179)

Bernstein likewise noted that movement forms are not static, but dynamic. In his terms, "they develop and involute" in relation to their force environment (p. 180). He showed, for example, that in walking, there are complex interactions between the movements of the legs, the center of gravity of the body, and the support surface, and that it is *these interactions themselves* that sculpt the patterns he observed. Although the isolated spinal cord (in animals surgically decerebrated) can produce locomotor-like stepping patterns (presumably from the autonomous activity of the CPG), these efferent impulses alone do not result in the functional and elaborated patterns of normal locomotion. As Bernstein observed:

> The multiplicity of elements interacting regularly with one another and making up a complex and idiosyncratic rhythm of alternation gives the dynamics of each separate step a radically different physiognomy from that which may be observed in the simple stepping reflex in a decerebrate preparation. (Bernstein, quoted in Whiting, 1984, p. 188)

What organizes walking and other movements, by this view, is the relationship between all the elements of the moving segments *and their perception of, and interaction with, the periphery.* The CNS partially solves the degrees of freedom problem by the construction of *synergies of action* that mobilize the heterogeneous but entirely interdependent components. These synergies, in turn, can generate complex and often oscillatory patterns. The indeterminacy of the system, therefore, turns out not be a problem at all, but indeed part of the solution. The system must be, to some degree, indeterminate in order to be sculpted by the dynamic movement context, which includes not only external and internal forces but changes in the goals and intentions of the mover. In the same sense, Greene (1982) pointed out that Bernstein's degrees of freedom may also be recast as degrees of opportunity. That is, the very freedom of the system to assemble and reassemble in response to changing needs is the wellspring for new and adaptive movement forms. If movements, or any behavior, are rigidly programmed, there are no sources of change. We argue below and with many examples in subsequent chapters that it is only when these degrees of freedom are exposed during development by the dissolution of old, rigid forms that the organism is able to explore new, more functional solutions.

The motor system is a particularly instructive entry into a dynamic theory of behavior and development because the cooperativity of the elements is especially transparent. Movement is the final common pathway for all human activity. Functional movement is the melding of the mind and the body and all the components thereof. But equally compelling is the complete and intimate relation between the organism and the physical and informational qualities of the world. The animal must sense, adapt to, and integrate the force and informational fields that surround it in order to move effectively and efficiently. There is no such thing as a "pure" or decontextualized walker. The essence of walking is only in its construction during its execution. Later, we make this claim for all mental activities.

Next we present two examples from real-time actions that illustrate system complexity (multidimensionality), self-organization, and context specificity. Following these examples we begin to extend the concepts to development.

Energetic Aspects of Movement

It is intuitively obvious that motor actions are produced by systems composed of many heterogeneous elements. In principle, no one would deny that walking requires not only a brain, a spinal cord, and peripheral neuromotor and sensory pathways but also bones, joints, muscles, a cardiovascular system, a respiratory apparatus, skin, and so on. Without any of these contributing elements, infants will not walk (and will probably not survive). Many of these contributing elements are not specific to walking, or even to motor behavior, but that does not lessen their importance in the eventual development of this particular ability.

Consider, for example, locomotion as an energetic activity. We know from the work of Alexander (1984), Hildebrand (1989), Taylor (1978), McMahon (1984), and others, that the particular style or gait adopted by terrestrial animals minimizes energy expenditure at the preferred speed of that gait. This means that given the theoretical potential of several modes of coordinating the limbs to provide forward propulsion, only one stable mode emerges for particular speed tasks, and this mode is the most efficient one. Similarly, humans *could* locomote by jumping, hopping, or skipping, but jumping down the street is much more tiring than walking or jogging, even at comparable speeds. Humans certainly try out jumping and other playful forms of locomotion, but settle on walking to accomplish nearly all of their self-propelled travel. (In the reduced gravity of the moon, however, astronauts discovered that jumping was indeed the most efficient locomotor activity [McMahon, 1984]). Likewise, quadrupeds switch to different gait styles at different speeds (walk, trot, gallop), presumably not because these gaits are impossible at nonconventional speeds, but because the system has discovered comfortable modes that are related to respiratory and cardiovascular function as well as many aspects of body scale parameters (Alexander, 1984; McMahon, 1984; Taylor, 1978).

Discussing the role of energetics in movement is not to downplay the role of the CNS in the planning, generation, and monitoring of movement. Rather, we show how even the most general and nondedicated body structures and functions—after all, respiration is not specific to movement—impact on the spatial and temporal characteristics of behavior. There is no information in respiratory demands for coordination, or in pendulum weights. The coordination emerges from all these things within the task.

Self-organization in Real Time: Spontaneous Infant Kicking

A vivid illustration of this inability to separate disembodied instructions—as cognitive structures or neural commands—from the organism acting in dynamic informational and physical fields is provided by Thelen's research on the real-time organization of a common infant movement, kicking. Infants kick their legs in coordinated patterns throughout the first year. They kick when lying on their backs and when held upright, and later when prone or even when sitting in a chair (Thelen, 1979, 1981). Kicking is primarily a manifestation of seemingly nonspecific behavioral arousal; infants kick when happy and excited, but also when fussy or uncomfortable. But infants also appear to "convert" kicking movements into instrumental behaviors, e.g., to shake a toy or mobile attached to the crib (Piaget, 1952; Rovee and Rovee, 1969), or to communicate interest or impatience during a meal (Thelen, 1981).

In the first few months of life, infant kicking appears to be an especially well-coordinated movement, indeed quite distinct from the much less rhythmic and more seemingly random thrashing of the arms. Analysis of the time and space trajectories of the limbs (the *kinematics*) showed that the hip, knee, and ankle joints nearly simultaneously traced a rapid and usually smooth pathway toward the body in flexion, followed by extension, where the leg moved away from the body (figure 4.1). Kicks in one limb often followed each other in rhythmic succession, usually, but not always, alternating with kicks in the other leg. This coordinated movement appeared to be a good candidate for control by a CPG: each leg flexed and extended in alternation, and the oscillation of one leg appeared to be coupled to that of the opposite leg. The duration of the movements was not randomly distributed, but clustered around 300 ms, suggesting a central "timekeeper" metering out neural impulses activating the appropriate muscle groups and creating the cyclic behavior.

Had Thelen and her colleagues discovered a human CPG, which spontaneously produced "pure" oscillatory movement in a one-to-one reflection of "pure" neural oscillations? Was this the privileged and organizing basis of later locomotion? Would understanding the ontogenetic changes in this CPG produce an understanding of how infants learn to walk? (Thelen, Bradshaw, and Ward, 1981) Just as we saw the concept of the CPG falter in the face of the variability and adaptability of walking in frogs, chickens, and cats, it also proved a poor construct to account for the cyclic kicking of young human infants.

The first clue that kicking was a more complex and dynamically assembled behavior came from recording the patterns of muscle contractions underlying kicking using surface electromyography (EMG), which amplifies the minute electrical changes in contracting and relaxing muscle groups. The cornerstone of the CPG concept is that the construction of the spinal neural networks leads to precise alternation between flexor and extensor motoneurons in the limbs (Grillner, 1975, 1980; Pearson and Duysens, 1976). But when Thelen and Fisher (1983) looked at muscle groups in the infants' legs, they did not detect this pattern of alternation, despite the fact that the legs clearly alternated in flexion and extension. What they found instead is that at the initiation of the flexion movement, both the flexors of the joints (primarily the large muscles on the front of the leg) and the extensors (primarily the hamstrings and calf muscles) contracted simultaneously, as shown in figure 4.1. Although quantitative comparisons are difficult to make using surface EMG, it appeared as though the flexor groups contracted more strongly than the extensor groups. Again, this would explain the resulting net flexor movement toward the body even though both flexors and extensors are contracting. (Such co-contractions are very common in immature and unskilled performers.) Equally surprising, they saw little or no muscle contraction at all at the initiation of the extension portion of the kick. They speculated, therefore, that the leg completed the cycle, not because of any preexisting code that told the muscles to extend, but because legs have well-known spring qualities, and are affected by gravity. That is, the elastic potential energy stored by muscles and tendons in the leg during vigorous flexion, combined with the pull of gravity, served to reverse the leg.

Thus, the trajectory and cyclic rhythmicity of kicking and the intrinsic timing of the movement phases could be said to be *dynamically self-organized* (Thelen, Kelso, and Fogel, 1987). These spatiotemporal parameters were the on-line result of cooperative interactions of the neuroskeletal muscular system within particular energetic and environmental constraints. The leg flexed and reversed because of an imbalance of forces, some created by muscle activation and others by physical,

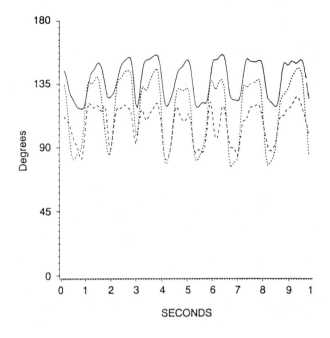

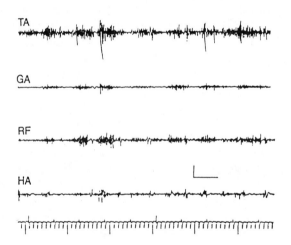

Figure 4.1
Top panel, Rotations of the joints of one leg of a kicking 4-week-old infant showing the rhythmic nature of kicking and coordinated flexions and extensions of the joints. The *solid line* is the hip joint, the *short-dashed line* is the knee joint and the *long-dashed line* is the ankle joint. (Smaller angles are toward flexed joints.) *Bottom panel*, Corresponding EMG of the muscles of the lower leg. (*TA*, tibialis anterior; *GA*, gastrocenemius) and upper leg (*RF*, rectus femoris; *HA*, hamstrings). (From Thelen and Fisher, 1983.)

non-neural sources. The cooperative result—the reduction of the degrees of freedom—was an identifiable topography of movement.

In dynamic terms, we can capture this complex interplay of active and passive forces by looking at the collective variable of the space-time trajectory of kicks on the *phase plane*, which plots the changes in the angular rotation of the joint in question against its velocity. Figure 4.2 shows a sample of kick phase planes from a variety of kicks from infants in different postures and at different ages. The kick portraits on the phase plane show considerable uniformity. The rounded topography of the phase planes indicates that the velocity of the kicks varies smoothly with the excursions of the joint. These phase planes suggest that the leg, in its collective behavior, acts dynamically, like a spring with a mass attached. Recall that when a simple spring with a mass on the end is given an energy impulse (by stretching the spring), the oscillations show a smooth and regular cyclic trajectory on the phase plane (see figure 3.7). Once the burst of energy has been imparted to the spring, the velocity varies smoothly with the position of the spring, with the velocity at zero at the change of direction and highest in the middle of the upward or downward path. Infant kicks also show these characteristic springlike phase planes. This suggests that the neuromuscular apparatus has considerable springlike qualities, which, when given a burst of energy, self-organizes, much like a simple spring, into a smooth trajectory. Heriza (1988) has demonstrated similar organization of the spontaneous kicks of premature infants observed as early as 34 weeks' gestational age. The springlike behavior of infant kicks also explains how regular timing of flexions and extensions (e.g., see Thelen, Bradshaw, and Ward, 1981) can "fall out" without being explicitly planned, just as the excursion time of the spring depends upon its stiffness and mass alone and does not require an explicit clock (see also Thelen, 1991, 1993). (In chapter 9 we again invoke the springlike qualities of the limb when describing how infants learn to reach.)

We can recast these results to be consistent with the principles of complex, dynamic systems. The high dimensionality of infant kicking, which includes not only the structures and processes within the infant but the force fields in which kicking takes place, is condensed to produce a movement of far fewer degrees of freedom, and one that has, in fact, properties of a rather simple mechanical device, a spring. The cyclic trajectories of the movement act like a stable attractor (although this has not been rigorously tested) so that there is topographical similarity in the collective variables of kick displacement vs. velocity from a variety of individual systems and behavioral contexts. When infants are in contexts amenable to them moving their legs, *and* when they pump sufficient energy into their muscles, their legs exhibit a preferred pattern of movement. The anatomy of the leg and the neural wiring permit a wide variety of coordinative possibilities, ranging from simple extensions at the hip with the knee and ankle held stiff (rarely seen in young infants) to the complex timing relations among the joints needed, for example, to tap-dance (never seen in young infants). Given the maturational and energetic status of infants, however, only a few of these possibilities are ever seen, and the springlike kick is by far the most stable, as evidenced by figure 4.2. It is so stable it looks (and was originally interpreted by Thelen!) as if it is hard-wired. But as we have seen, the stability evidenced in the collective variable is produced by the "soft" and context-specific assembly of

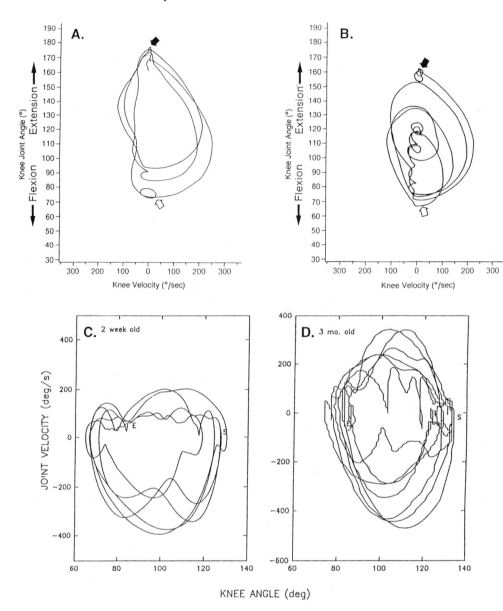

Figure 4.2
Exemplar phase plane representations of kicks of infants of various ages and in different postures. *Top panel,* Knee joint amplitude vs. velocity of supine kicking in (*A*) a premature infant at 40 weeks' gestational age and (*B*) a full-term newborn infant. (From Heriza, 1988.) *Bottom panel,* Knee joint amplitude vs. velocity of vertical kicks in a (*C*) 2-week-old and (*D*) 3-month-old infant. (From Jensen, Thelen, and Ulrich, 1989.)

components which are free to, and do, vary. The attraction of the subsystems to a self-organized pattern, which may be, as we shall see below, variously stable or unstable, is the fundamental premise by which we move our theory to developmental time.

We have pursued this example in considerable detail because it illustrates in a tangible fashion the clear inseparability of the ongoing behavioral stream from the informational and, in this case mundanely physical, aspects of the world in which action and development take place. In addition, we have established two important properties of infant legs, demonstrated in simple, cyclic, and nonintentional movements. The first of these properties is a considerable degree of dynamic self-organization such that the trajectory of the movement was truly emergent—it contained more space-time information than the simple muscle firings that energized the system. This self-organization, we maintain, is an essential feature of behavior of biological systems at any level of organization. It is the feature that gives behavior its rule-based appearance without the need for specific rules. The second important property is the context specificity of this organization. Kicking is not a goal-directed or goal-corrected activity, yet it is organized with respect both to the gravitational field and the internally generated energy pulses that initiate the movement. There is no logical or empirical way to assign priority in the assembly of these movements to *either* the organic components that "belong" to the infant, *or* to the environment in which they are performed. Both determine the collective features of the movement which we call a kick. This simple demonstration of context sensitivity—the openness of the system to the surrounds—is the feature of developing systems that provides the motor and process for change, and we return to this at the end of the chapter. In the next section, in the meantime, we expand the time scale into the developmental domain to illustrate self-organization during development.

Moving Between Time Scales: From Action to Development

In our usual illustrations of self-organizing processes, both in the physical and biological domains, the time scale is that of seconds or minutes. We now wish to introduce and support the claim that similar processes occur over the ontogenetic time scale, which, depending on the species, may be measured in hours, days, weeks, months, or years. Just as the real-time performance is self-assembled with available components within a task and environmental context, new forms arise during development from a similar confluence of the anatomical and physiological elements of the organism within a particular task and energetic context. In our example above, circulatory, neural, and muscular components working within a particular gravitational force field together determined the movement pattern of infant kicking, but no element contained any privileged essence of the kick in iconic detail. Likewise, even in the expanded time scale, no component of the developing organism has the dedicated plan for the outcome state and acts as the executive at the top of a command hierarchy, metering out the markers on a developmental clock. Just as the rhythm and trajectory of a bouncing spring "fell out" of the dynamic interactions of muscles, bones, veins, and nerves and the forces of gravity, so the paced emergence of new behavioral forms "falls out" of the interactions of the contributing resources. How can we span these time scales?

In a dynamic perspective, performance emerges from a confluence of subsystems within a particular task environment. Some patterns of behavior are very stable under particular conditions, and others are unstable, and may be rarely, if ever, seen. An adult person asked to locomote at a comfortable speed on a flat, carpeted surface will produce a highly stable and invariant pattern of movement, measured, for example, by the rotations of his or her limb joints. This will almost certainly involve 180-degree, alternating, phasing of the cycles of the two legs and well-defined periods of single and double support and swing within each limb. As long as the person and the conditions do not change, this pattern will reliably persist. However, if the surface is an icy sidewalk, or the person puts on high-heeled shoes or develops a blister on his or her foot, the characteristic pattern of locomotion may well change. This ability to readjust the pattern in response to intentional, organic, or environmental constraints arises from the previously mentioned ability of subsystems to dynamically assemble.

Infancy and childhood, of course, are times when the subsystems and contexts are changing especially rapidly. Children grow physically, they perceive, act, explore, and accumulate knowledge about the world. Their growth and experiences continually open up new environments for their perceptions and actions. Thus, the real-time assembly of their behavior is a product of subsystems and contexts themselves dynamically changing over a longer time scale.

Of enormous importance to a dynamic account of development is that these subsystems and contexts are changing both asynchronously and nonlinearly. Asynchrony means that not all the components change at the same rate. There are many well-known examples in the literature: the precocity, in humans, for instance, of perceptual over motor systems (the visual system has near-adult capabilities by about 6 months, while motor skill develops over nearly a decade). Perceptual functioning itself does not develop as a piece, but with modality-specific trajectories, and even with asynchronous components within a system. For example, in the infant visual system, stereopsis develops rather rapidly within a period of a week or two in months 3 or 4. Visual acuity has longer, more gradual onset (Held, 1985). Likewise, within the motor system, we can point to the advanced functioning in the newborn of the orofacial nerves and muscles that control sucking compared to those that control head, trunk, and limb movements. Control of head precedes control of trunk; upper limbs precede lower limbs, and so on.

Nonlinearity means that change in subsystems may not be smooth and incremental, but can occur with spurts, plateaus, and even regressions. The subsystems themselves, in dynamic terminology, may undergo phase shifts: sudden, qualitative appearances and disappearances of behavioral forms. Illustrations abound in early development: the onset of babbling, stereopsis, and vocabulary explosions, for example, are rapid and steplike. Of course, other changes, like the acquisition of postural control, are more protracted and gradual.

In a dynamic analysis of developmental process at whatever level and in any domain, we identify a collective variable that expresses the behavioral change over time. This collective variable, by definition, is a compression of these asynchronous and nonlinear subsystems. Over different points in time, the system stability is determined by the cooperative interaction of the subsystems and therefore by the status of the subsystem *at the time the behavior is assembled*. Thus, the time scales are inextricably interwoven: cooperative interactions assembling and disintegrating as environments and tasks change, and as organic subsystems themselves dynamically shift. In no sense are any of the components logically causal in determining the developmental change because all components and context determine the system's product. However, as we note further below, the system may be especially sensitive to particular components or environmental parameters, so that even small changes in those parameters may reverberate into wide and qualitatively distinct system effects. In this developmental model, therefore, there are many potential *control parameters* engendering change, and the task of the developmentalist is to discover these motors of change. Dynamic systems offers, as we also discuss below, principled operational strategies to do this.

Development as Evolving and Dissolving Attractors

A simplified model of dynamic processes of development is offered in figure 4.3. Any behavior of interest, and at any level of analysis, is considered to be the product of parallel, developing, heterogeneous components and subsystems within an environmental and task context. Each of the subsystems itself has a dynamic history, which may be linear or nonlinear. At any point in time, T1, behavior is assembled within the context considering the organic and energetic constraints imposed by the status of the subsystems. Several outcomes are possible. Small changes in critical components may engender wide-ranging phase

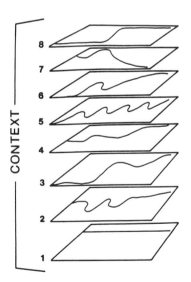

Figure 4.3
Depicting development as parallel developing subsystems, each with its own trajectory. Time is abstractly represented on the *x*-axis; an abstract "quantity" of a contributing subsystem in represented on the *y*-axis. Behavior at any point in time is assembled from these subsystems within a task and environmental context.

shifts, so that at T2, the collective variable may have a different configuration, signaling the appearance of new developmental forms. Alternatively, the collective variable may show more linear and incremental progression as a result of the confluence of organical and environmental effects. Finally, the system may be resilient to changes in the subsystems, so that at T2 no differences in the collective variable are apparent.

In dynamic terminology, then, behavioral development may thus be envisioned as sequences of system *attractors* of varying stability, evolving and dissolving over time. Recall that in any behavior that has a recognizable form, the collective variable resides in only a limited portion of the state space—it does not take on all the potential values of the state space parameters. This means that a nonrandom coordination of the subsystems produces a behavioral outcome which is strongly (or weakly) preferred despite some variability in the initial status of the subsystems. Pattern emerges through the cooperativity of the components alone, and this pattern may dominate over other possible patterns to varying degrees. As we describe later, these notions of evolving and dissolving attractors, representing various states of cohesion of the components, will apply equally well for real-time cognition and new developmental forms.

In the broadest sense, therefore, dynamic systems accounts for the appearance of new forms during development as a series of *phase shifts* engendered by the loss of stability of current forms. These new forms are autonomous solutions to instability in that the system does not know the solutions a priori, but discovers them through the exploration of the space—exploration which is possible, in turn, because the cooperative assembly of components is not rigidly fixed. Constraints in the organism or from the environment may engender novel solutions, which in development may appear as *décalage* ("slippage"), so to speak, in the expected age-appropriate response. That children often show more or less mature performance when the task is even subtly changed attests to their ability to dynamically assemble behavior wholly within a task context. Again, we supply abundant examples in later chapters. The appearance of novel responses is not noise in the system, but a reflection of its relative dynamic status. Under a dynamic view, developmental questions shift from considering behavioral variation as error variance, to using variation as a measure of the relative strength or stability of the attractor state. We should emphasize again here that we refer to real variability in performance, not variability that is a result of measurement error. Although in practice these may be difficult to disentangle, they are theoretically distinct.

A New Role for Variability in Development

Two measures index the stability of the behavioral attractor. First, the *variability* of the collective variable around its mean state measures the strength of the pattern—the degree of coherence of the subsystems. Recall the potential well in figure 3.10. When the well is flattened, the ball is free to visit more regions of the state space than when the well is deep. As the system loses stability, the weaker cooperative bonds are reflected in greater behavioral variability. *This dynamic principle has profound implications for developmental analysis because it raises the status of variability in experimental and observational studies to data rather than noise.* Variability is more than just distracting deviation from an ideal mean performance. It is instead an index of the strength of the behavioral attractor, and because systems are predicted to lose stability during a phase shift, it is an important concomitant of transitions to new forms.

A second indicator of system stability is the resistance of the behavior to perturbation, either encountered in the everyday life of the subject or provided by the experimenter. Again, when the ball is in the deep well (see figure 3.10), it will rapidly rebound from small perturbations and fall into the stable well. In contrast, perturbations when the well is flat will lead the ball to different regions of the space, and perhaps into another, more stable attractor. This means that systems can be more easily pushed around when they are in transition. This principle, too, is a powerful one for development. At times of transition, when attractors are not strongly coherent, small changes in the organism, the task, or the environment can lead to profound reorganizations. This is the source of the well-known décalage effects so common in all aspects of developmental study: even relatively minor and sometimes seemingly unconnected manipulations have a major impact on behavior. Before the transition, and after the behavior is well-established, these same factors do not disrupt ongoing performance.

One example here should suffice. We return to these principles throughout the book because they provide both formidable explanatory power and a theory-based agenda for studying developmental change. Consider here an infant who has recently acquired independent upright stance. We can think of the maintenance of upright balance as a point attractor (with some dispersion, since balance is dynamically stable) in the state space consisting of, for example, the position and velocity of the center of gravity relative to the base of support (see, e.g., Bertenthal, 1990). By a number of dynamic measures, the attractor state of the new stander is less stable than that of a more experienced person. New standers have greater postural sway under normal conditions. When perturbed by visual flow suggesting self-motion in the "moving room" experiment, newly standing infants sway more and fall more often than older children (Lee and Aronson, 1974). Similarly, their stance is easily disrupted by perturbations on a moving platform, either as translational movement or rotation about the ankles (Woollacott, 1990). In addition, stepping forward in the initiation of walking can be envisioned as a perturbation to static upright balance. New walkers sway laterally and often lose their balance as they initiate steps; indeed, steps in new walkers are really controlled falls (Bril and Brenière, 1992).

The unsteady toddler—variable in response and easily put off balance—is a clear and transparent illustration of the (literal) instability of a system in transition. But as in other examples in this chapter, biomechanical instability is both a reality and a metaphor. In toddlers, we can disrupt the balance system coherence by a literal "push," but performance in other domains is also set reeling by pushes imposed by the task or the experimenter at certain sensitive periods, notably transitions. The nature of the push and the response of the system to being pushed are the clues to understanding the emergence of form.

The variability and instability revealed at transitions to new states may be more than noise or epiphenomena in a final, important way. Systems in a single deep well may have limited behavioral options. Thus, behavior may be stable, but inflexible and poorly adapted. The loss of system coherence engendered by changes in subsystems frees up, so to speak, the components to reassemble in new ways. The child may then explore a richer and more varied landscape of possible adaptive solutions and select those patterns that are more efficient, accurate, or better fit their intentional goals. We will later emphasize the critical importance of flexibility to explore many states in the emergence of new forms. The attractor layout of a more skilled child or adult would have multiple regions of stability, representing preferred and well-practiced behavioral configurations. Nonetheless, because even stable forms are dynamically assembled, the system retains global flexibility in the face of unexpected tasks, and sufficient plasticity to reorganize and thus learn new skills.

The data from early leg movements suggest, as we show below, such an ontogenetic sequence, wherein a single, relatively inflexible, attractor pattern dissolves to allow exploration of myriad movement combinations. Through exploration of these movement combinations, several more stable patterns emerge which support stance, locomotion, and other functional activities. (How exploration can lead to adaptive solutions is the subject of the next chapter.) Variability remains the key; a dynamic account replaces notions of inevitable stagelike progressions with probablistic and functionalist selection. Development occurs by the continual dynamic match between the organism and information about the task and the supporting environment.

We now illustrate dynamic principles of development in the leg movements of infants. We show interwoven developmental changes in patterns of movement and function from the stereotyped kicks and steps of the newborn through the refinement of gait in the first few months of walking. Data on prewalking leg movements are from the work of Thelen and her collaborators over the last decade.

Ontogenetic Changes in Infant Leg Movements

In an earlier section, we described the real-time fluidity and context specificity of simple kicks in young infants. If we explain real-time kicks in dynamic terms, we must also account for how the system changes in similar terms. If dynamic principles are truly general they will span time scales. In fact, we suggest that only a dynamic account can explain the enduring puzzles of development we raised in chapters 1 and 2: décalage, heterochrony, and context specificity within global stability of outcome and "staginess."

Consider the developmental course of the coordinative patterns of leg movements during the first year. In figure 4.4, we show schematic profiles of the rates of performance of leg movements in four contexts: (1) when the infant is supine and when the infant is held upright either (2) on a conventional surface or (3) on a moving or stationary treadmill, conditions mentioned in chapter 1, and (4) when the child stands alone unsupported. Note that each of these contextual forms has a different pattern of change. Stepping while held upright, indicated by traces for newborn steps, and stepping with the treadmill stationary, show a low level of performance in the first months, then virtually disappears, and then begins to reappear in months 9 and 10. Kicking while supine becomes increas-

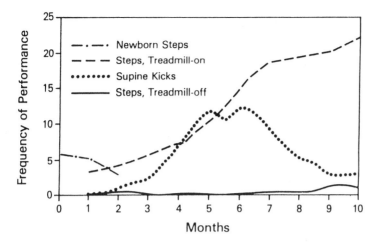

Figure 4.4
Schematic developmental profiles of leg movement types during the first year. (From Thelen, 1989.)

ingly frequent through the first 6 months and then gradually wanes. In contrast, treadmill-elicited stepping continues to increase in frequency until month 10. Independent stepping, in contrast, appears late in the first year and is maintained thereafter. If we accept the proposition that at each point in time the performance and configuration of the leg movements produced is dynamically constructed from available components in a context, we can then ask: What accounts for the time-varying profiles of these actions? Why do forms of movement both appear and disappear? What in infants or in their environment produces new patterns? What are the general and specific processes and agents of change?

The Disappearance of Newborn Stepping

It is clear that, at birth, infants can produce patterned movements of the legs as cyclic kicking and stepping. The neuromotor basis for this pattern generation is likely available much earlier in gestation. Prechtl (1986) reported alternating leg movements in utero by the second trimester, and Heriza (1988) has described kicks in premature infants of 28 weeks' gestational age that are kinematically similar to those of full-term newborns.

The first dramatic developmental transition in this pattern is the apparent loss of the ability to perform stepping movements when infants are held upright. As we discussed in chapter 1, it is unlikely that the reflex or neural substrate for these movements has actually regressed, because leg patterns similar to stepping movements can be elicited in infants in other contexts—supine or underwater, for example. When the stepping pattern is envisioned as the product solely of a dedicated reflex network, this loss is difficult to understand, resulting in ad hoc explanations such as cortical inhibition.

Thelen and Fisher (1982), on the basis of finding kinematic similarity between so-called steps and kicks in the newborn period, speculated that there was something unique in the upright posture that inhibited stepping at about 2 months of age. When they looked beyond presumptive changes in the CNS, they discovered dramatic alterations in body weight and composition that closely paralleled the loss of stepping. That is, infants gain weight rapidly in the first two or three postnatal months. Indeed their weight velocity continues the steep slope characteristic of the last trimester in utero. Most important, this weight gain is primarily subcutaneous fat, necessary for postnatal temperature regulation. Thelen and Fisher proposed that rapidly added, nonmuscle tissue created an additional load on the comparatively weak muscles that would inhibit stepping when the infants were held in the biomechanically more demanding upright posture. In other words, the asynchrony between muscle and fat, two components contributing to the assembly of the step pattern, created an imbalance between the load to be lifted and the energetic plant generating the lift power. The asynchrony was manifest only when the leg movement was dynamically assembled in a particular gravitational context—upright. In dynamic terms, fat deposition acted as the nonspecific control parameter that shifted the pattern from a stable attractor, stepping, to one sufficiently unstable that it was rarely seen.

Thelen and her colleagues supported their hypothesis with several experiments. First, they followed infants at 2, 4, 6, and 8 weeks and compared their step decline with changes in body proportions and arousal (Thelen, Fisher, Ridley-Johnson, and Griffin, 1982). At all ages, arousal correlated with step rate. This makes sense in a dynamic assembly of the step pattern: heightened arousal means more energy delivered to the muscles, and stronger contractions may overcome the biomechanical load of the additional nonmuscle mass. In addition, infants with a more rapid *rate* of weight gain (and increase of leg dimensions) showed a more rapid decline of step performance. No absolute threshold of weight inhibited stepping. Rather, it appeared to be the individual, relative balance of system components. In infants in whom the muscles were rapidly confronted with additional mass, steps declined, of course, to be overcome when arousal was very high.

Thelen and colleagues also manipulated leg mass directly (Thelen, Fisher, and Ridley-Johnson, 1984). In one experiment they supported 6-week-old infants so that their torsos were submerged in a tank of warm water, a manipulation to decrease the load on the legs. In a second experiment they attached weights to the legs of 6-week-old infants, where the weight was calculated to mimic the weight gain between 2 and 6 weeks. As would be predicted by a biodynamic hypothesis of stepping disappearance, infants in the first experiment stepped more and with steps of greater amplitude when their legs were submerged as compared to an out-of-water condition. Similarly, adding weights diminished step rates to those normally seen in older (and heavier) infants (see figure 1.2). These experiments demonstrated that biomechanical factors must be considered along with neural and contextual contributions when explaining losses and gains in motor development.

Several points about these experiments have implications for theory in general. First, these manipulations worked only because the emergent stepping system is assembled dynamically. The system is fluid enough to respond to changes in a particular component—the effective mass of the leg to be lifted. Second, the step attractor must be in a relatively shallow well to respond to such perturbations. Comparable amounts of weight would likely not change the step kinematics of, say, an older child or adult, whose gait is well-practiced and whose muscles are strong and able to compensate for added weight—a much stronger attractor. Finally, we point again to the nonobvious nature of the control parameter in this case. Although neural networks are important contributors to step pattern, they are not the only agents of change. Here changes in the nervous system may well *reflect* and not engender changes at the periphery.

Coordination and Control of Infant Kicking: Dynamic Changes

When infants are placed supine, they perform well-coordinated, cyclic kicking movements from the first days of life. In natural situations, supine kicking (as well as kicking in prone or when seated) increases in frequency throughout the first half of the year and declines when infants begin to sit, stand, crawl, and walk (Thelen, 1979). The intra- and interlimb coordination patterns of kicking— the space and time relations of the movements of the joints of one limb, or of the two limbs—illustrate how behavioral attractors may both evolve and dissolve over ontogenetic time.

Recall that infant kicks in the newborn period are staccato and nearly simultaneous flexions and extensions of the hip, knee, and ankle joints, often occurring in rhythmic succession, and with frequent alterations between the right and left legs (Thelen, Bradshaw, and Ward, 1981; Thelen and Fisher, 1983). We earlier discussed the real-time dynamic organization of infant kicks and suggested that the early configuration was a result of the intrinsic properties of the neuromuscular system in a particular energetic status, specifically, that the leg acted springlike, and that the trajectory and timing could be considered emergent properties of this springlike organization.

In the first month or so, infants kick when they are behaviorally aroused, either when distressed or happily excited (Thelen, 1981). Soon, however, infants begin to use kicks for task-related ends. Piaget (1952) was the first to document the conversion of early spontaneous kicking for intentional ends when he described Lucienne's repeated shaking of her bassinet by kicking. In recent times Carolyn Rovee-Collier and her colleagues have used infants' ability to harness kicking to repeat a pleasurable event to study learning and memory. We discuss this work at length in chapter 7. What is important now is that despite infants' abilities to use kicking intentionally, they are still captive of their dynamics, so to speak. They can alter the frequency and intensity of their kicks, but not the basic movement topography, which is one of alternating or single legs moving and synchronous flexions and extensions of the joints. Infants must escape from the seeming obligatory nature of this coordinative structure to be able to discover and construct limb movements for support, locomotion, and other skills. Again, in dynamic terms, the stable attractor of the early months must lose stability in order for infants to seek new, more adaptive configurations.

Thelen (1985) has documented the process of transition in the supine kicks of infants followed longitudinally from 2 weeks to 10 months. One hallmark of the tight synergy of the early months is the synchronous flexion and extension of all three leg joints: hip, knee, and ankle. This is manifest in pairwise cross-correlations of the angular movements of the joints: joints that flex and extend together show high positive correlations. Naturally, when one joint flexes and the other extends, the correlation is negative, and when there is no coordination, the correlation is zero. Indeed in the first 4 months, all pairwise correlations were positive and high (figure 4.5). There appeared to be a transient uncoupling of this synergy at about 5 months, followed by a return to strong interlimb coupling until about month 8. In the last quarter of the year, this coupling dramatically decreased, leading to strong individual actions of the joints and even out-of-phase coordination of the hip and knee. By this age, infants showed little of the staccato kick of the earlier period, but while supine used the legs in a variety of complex and apparently voluntary patterns. Compare, for instance, exemplar joint angle rotations of 1-month-old infants (see figure 4.1) with those of 10-month old infants (figure 4.6). In the latter, the joints moved more independently,

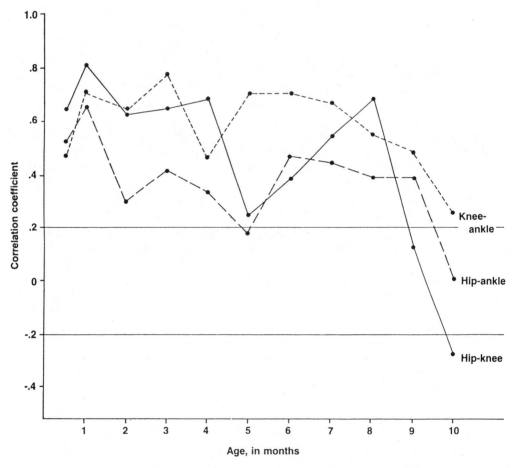

Figure 4.5
Mean pairwise cross-correlations of joint angles during a 10-second segment of spontaneous supine kicking of four infants at 11 ages from 2 weeks to 10 months. Values above and below the *solid horizontal lines* show statistically significant positive and negative correlations, based on 150 joint angle pairs for each correlation. (From Thelen, 1985.)

and in fact, patterns of interjoint coordination were so variable at this age that they could not be easily described.

A similar period of instability marks the development of the coordination *between* the legs in supine kicking. During the first month or so, kicks were predominantly alternating, that is, a kick with one leg was usually followed by a kick with the opposite leg. However, a period of great asymmetry and instability in bilateral leg use followed the newborn period. Between 1 and 5 months, infants were likely to kick with only one leg (Thelen, Ridley-Johnson, and Fisher, 1983). In the Thelen et al. sample cited, the degree of unilaterality and the laterality preference were very unstable during this time, both among infants and between sessions of one infant.

But, as in intralimb coordination, this instability led to new forms of coordination between the legs. Most striking was the appearance of simultaneous or in-phase kicks at about 4 to 6 months. Each of the eight infants studied by Thelen and colleagues showed a dramatic increase in simultaneous kicking after an initial loss of the alternating mode and a period of single-sided kicking. Again, it appeared that infants must free themselves of the stable, almost obligatory, patterns of the newborn period before they can assemble new stable attractor modes.

Human infants begin to use their legs for support and locomotion only in the second half of the year. The data show that the initial attractor state—repetitive, springlike, cyclic, and alternating flexions and extensions—becomes unstable. This *must* happen in order for new patterns of coordination to emerge. Tightly phase-locked patterns of coordination are rigid and afford little opportunity for systems to adapt to even minor changes in task or circumstance. The key to biological coordination may lie in more loosely assembled patterns, which provide both flexibility and richness to assemble and reassemble the components in adaptive modes. We argue in the next chapter that the instabilities associated with transitions in development do indeed provide the organism with a rich landscape of coordinative possibilities, and it is the multimodal exploration of these possibilities that may be an important control parameter for change and the acquisition of functional skills.

In a dynamic view, control of the limbs requires more than the imposition of intentionality. Even young infants can impart some degree of voluntary organization—they can increase the rate and vigor of their kicks, for example. Adapting movements more precisely to specific tasks requires, however, that the organism work within the inherent self-organizing properties of the neuromotor system and the perceptual fields that inform and constrain the task. In the absence of the specific task demands of supine kicking, the inherent organization is springlike and rather rigid. Infants must pull themselves out of this deep attractor well in order to stand, crawl, walk, and climb in natural environments, where movements can be stable but must also be adaptable. At the same time, the intrinsic springiness of the limbs cannot be discarded. Rather, we suggest that the process exploits the self-organizing qualities of the system whenever possible, but again, that the optimal match between these intrinsic dynamics and the demands of the task must be learned through exploration. We see another illustration of this process in chapter 9.

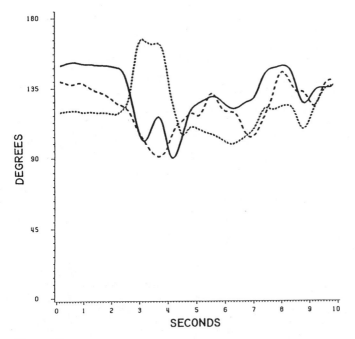

Figure 4.6
Joint angle rotations of two representative 10-month-old infants during 10-second segments of spontaneous supine kicking. The *solid line* is the hip joint, the *short-dashed line* is the knee, and the *long-dashed line* is the ankle. Compare with figure 4.1

Entraining the Intrinsic Dynamics to the Environment: Treadmill-elicited Stepping in Infants

Until now, we have described leg movements in infants under minimal or non-specific task demands. The premier question in motor development is, of course, how infants come to use their bodies to actually do useful and important things in the world. The treadmill stepping task, which we described in chapter 1, provides a window on this process. The treadmill mimics, in a specific way, a perceptual motor action—the dynamic stretching of the leg—that is a normal component of erect locomotion. Thus, we can use the treadmill to study the assembly of a coordinated movement as the intrinsic dynamics of the limbs interacting with an externally imposed and specific task environment. The treadmill paradigm captures and exemplifies the dynamic organization of behavior in both real and developmental time. First we examine "real-time" issues in infant treadmill stepping.

In the initial experiment, Thelen (1986) supported 7-month-old infants on small, motorized treadmills. She found that the treadmill reliably elicited stepping that was kinematically more similar to adult locomotion than any leg movements infants performed without the treadmill. The patterning of rotations of the joints looked more like adult walking than infant stepping (or supine kicking), and most important, on the treadmill infants produced a very stable alternating pattern of the legs. We will use this alternation as the defining collective variable.

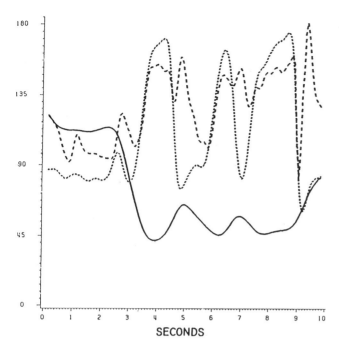

SECONDS

Figure 4.6 (continued)

In real time, treadmill stepping is strong presumptive evidence of the multiply determined nature of locomotor skill. Treadmill stepping is a manifest component of independent walking, yet infants were many months from walking by themselves. The ability to generate a walklike pattern was itself insufficient to produce the functional behavior. Pattern generation is thus logically no more important than any of the other necessary contributors to the final skill such as postural control and leg strength. It is only one element in a complex network of coordinated elements.

Second, treadmill stepping itself is truly an emergent behavior. Recall that the treadmill elicited these more mature kinematic patterns when compared to the spontaneous kicking and stepping *of the same infant at the same test session.* Step patterns thus in no sense "reside" in the infants alone. The infants in this experiment had never encountered a treadmill before, nor, we presume, have treadmills been a part of the normal environment of their evolutionary history. The pattern was a novel form created by the cooperative interaction of the infants' anatomical structures, energetic status, and the mechanical action of the treadmill. While there is no doubt that treadmill stepping shares muscle groups and neural networks with the more commonly seen stepping and kicking behaviors, the particular organization of those subsystems into a dynamic behavior was entirely a function of the particular context.

Finally, the transition from little or no stepping to cyclic and alternating stepping with the treadmill appears to be a characteristic dynamic phase shift from one stable state to another by the action of a control parameter. Several observations allow us to make this suggestion. Without the treadmill, the 7-month-olds stepped very rarely, even when allowed varying amounts of experimenter support, shifted from leg to leg, or encouraged to move by parents and experimenters. (In fact, when infants become excited when they are held upright, at 7 months, they often respond by "bouncing": simultaneous flexions and extensions of the joints without lifting the feet.) Conversely, when the treadmill was turned on, they immediately performed smooth, alternating movements. Once performed, the alternating step pattern was stable, and maintained despite momentary perturbations such as crossing the legs in front, the foot falling off the belts, and so on. Our most dramatic example, of course, of the stability of the pattern is the ability of infants to keep smooth alternations even when their legs are driven by treadmill belts of varying speeds (Thelen, Ulrich, and Niles, 1987).

In dynamic terms, therefore, we can tentatively suggest that the treadmill acted as the real-time control parameter engendering a phase shift between two behavioral modes: no stepping and coordinated stepping. Just as a change in temperature or pressure—relatively nonspecific components in the system—were the agents of change in simple physical systems, here the dynamic, but mechanical action of the treadmill in pulling the leg back resulted in the coalescence of a pattern that was otherwise not seen. Dynamic theory predicts that even small changes in the control parameter can produce qualitative phase shifts. We have not yet explored the detailed dynamics of the treadmill phase shift with parametric scaling of treadmill speeds to determine the critical boundary. However, evidence from Thelen (1986) and Thelen and Ulrich (1991) clearly indicates that stepping performance is much less stable (more variable) at the slow speeds of the treadmill. This suggests that the system prefers to reside (the attractor is more stable) within certain infant-treadmill boundary conditions.

Additional behavioral and neurophysiological evidence supports the suggestion that the mechanical pulling of the legs backward in stance is a control parameter for treadmill stepping. In the first place, the treadmill substitutes for changes in leg dynamics that occur naturally in overground locomotion. As the center of gravity is shifted over the stance leg after the foot touches down, the trailing leg is stretched backward. The stretch is important *energetically* because it imparts the boost used to propel the swing, similar to stretching a spring or providing a squirt of energy to a pendulum. Indeed, the leg swings forward largely as a result of this stored energy and requires little or no additional muscle activation. Recent evidence suggests that this stretch is also important *informationally*. In particular, Pearson, Ramirez, and Jiang (1992) postulate that the unloading of the leg at the end of stance, and as it is maximally stretched, provides the proprioceptive input that triggers the initiation of swing. When these investigators mechanically stretched the ankle extensor muscles in cats whose ankle extensor and knee flexor muscles were surgically isolated, they entrained bilateral locomotor patterning in the knee muscles corresponding to the frequency of their rhythmic stretching of the ankle muscles. This suggests that proprioceptive information about the *biomechanical* status of the legs was being used by the CNS to generate the characteristic muscle patterns seen in mature locomotion. The basic patterning of locomotion is assembled in a dynamic dialogue with the periphery—in this case, with the changing forces and loads generated during the activity.

The dynamic assembly of infant treadmill stepping in real time suggests that this perception-action loop is in place before infants achieve independent walking. The treadmill provides the dynamic biomechanical information to complete the loop and allow the pattern, normally cryptic, to become manifest. That infant treadmill stepping is sensitive to treadmill speed, and to the biomechanical status of the opposite leg, means that this loop is not a simple reflex arc, but a system of continual information and force flow, where the status of the muscles at time 1 is used to adjust their activity at time 2 in the cycle. In addition, particular patterns and frequencies of muscle activity are preferentially performed. The structural and energetic components self-organize into these preferred configurations only in interaction with the entraining task—the movement of the treadmill belts. We suggest below that the components of independent walking self-organize in a similar manner.

The Development of Treadmill Stepping: Mapping the Dynamics of Change

We consider now the assembly of treadmill stepping over a longer time period. By 7 months, infants were adept at maintaining smooth alternating steps. How did they come to acquire this behavior? Is this neuromotor assembly available from birth? If not, what does its developmental course look like? Which of the contributing components acts as the developmental control parameter? How does the system change?

Thelen and Ulrich (1991) used an experimental strategy derived explicitly from dynamic principles to begin to answer these questions. Recall that it is essential to know where the system "lives" in its state space, and the relative stability and instability of the putative attractors. Transitions are marked by instability, reflected in variability around the mean state and an increased sensitivity to perturbation. It is when the system is unstable that components engendering phase shifts can be identified. Thus, the overall strategy for operationalizing dynamic principles for studying development is to identify the *collective variable* and to describe its *attractor states* as they change over time. The point is to discover *phase shifts* where the system assumes new forms and to use the instabilities associated with these transitions to experimentally identify and manipulate the *control parameters* engendering the shift.

The Role of the Individual in a Dynamic Systems Approach

A crucial assumption in a dynamic strategy is that *the individual and his or her behavioral changes over time are the fundamental unit of study.* It is common in developmental studies to compare the performance of groups of subjects at several ages. If reliable differences are found in the mean levels of performance, it is assumed that some type of development has occurred in the measurement interval. The nature of the developmental processes within that interval is less often addressed, but it is legitimate to ask whether all the subjects will have followed the same developmental pathway to their mature performance. Although cross-sectional studies are important and useful for establishing the boundaries of change, dynamic principles suggest that such processes cannot be understood by cross-sectional group comparisons alone. Developmental pathways can only be deconstructed with individual data, collected longitudinally at frequent intervals. The variability in the developmental trajectories suggests the tightness of the constraints on the process. Is this behavior acquired in the same way by all members of the species?

It is the defining feature of dynamic systems that attractors "pull in" trajectories from a variety of initial positions. At the same time, even small differences in the initial conditions can lead to disparate outcomes. Without knowledge of the time course of the behavior, these essential characteristics of the system remain a mystery. Figure 4.7A provides an illustration of the first case. Imagine a behavior that no individual performs at time 1 and that all nondamaged subjects perform at time 5. Now imagine that cross-sectional studies produced data points as illustrated at times 2, 3, and 4. These data points can be connected with a number of different trajectories that all converge at time 5, but which cannot be distinguished from one another in pooled, group data. Indeed, in some individuals, acquisition may be gradual and linear, and in others, nonlinear and even U-shaped. In contrast, figure 4.7B shows a hypothetical behavior where early uniformity is lost, and the mature form is more variable. Again, the dynamics of this transition are obscured by group data. Some subjects may, for example, display dramatic discontinuities and phase shifts due to the cascading effects of initial conditions; others may follow a straight, and somewhat buffered course.

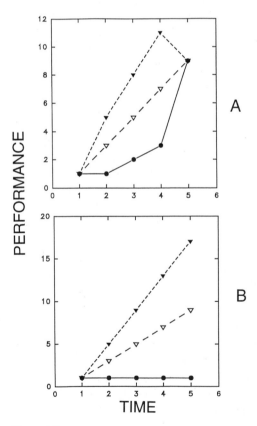

Figure 4.7
Hypothetical developmental trajectories where group data cannot disambiguate the pathways.

Thus, the group data can tell whether there is overall, age-related uniformity of performance, but they cannot reveal transitions or the loss of stability associated with transitions. Groups do not change; individuals do. We are interested in variability as a metric of the stability and instability of specific systems. Therefore, while cross-sectional studies may be necessary to map the boundaries of behavioral change and to assess the stability of behavioral attractors, longitudinal sampling at an appropriately dense time scale is essential to understand the dynamics of this change.

In the next section, we describe Thelen and Ulrich's use of dynamic systems to study treadmill stepping development. Each of the steps is explicitly derived from the principles elaborated in earlier sections.

Operationalizing Dynamic Principles to Understand the Ontogeny of Treadmill Stepping

Identifying the Collective Variable of Interest
In dynamic systems, one or a few variables can be identified that capture the compression of the degrees of freedom in a multidimensional system. In a developmental study, the aim is to describe the behavior of this collective variable over an extended time period of days, weeks, months, or years. Identifying the collective variable in a changing system is not a trivial task. Because the underlying components are themselves nonlinear, and because the organism changes continually in relation to the context, it is difficult to know whether the meaning of any performance parameter remains stationary. This difficulty of choosing age-appropriate tasks has long been recognized by developmentalists, and dynamic systems per se offers no easy solution.

What dynamic systems does suggest is that the collective variable be strictly observable. Constructs such as "attachment" or "information processing capability" are not amenable to a dynamic analysis because their operational instantiations are ambiguous. Collective variables must be clearly quantifiable actions and responses that index the cooperativity of a multidimensional system. These variables may be entirely within the subject as a motor or verbal response or may reflect the subject's interactions with the physical or social world. An example of the former might be a measure of the straightness of a path to a desired goal, or the assignment of a verbal label to a category, and of the latter, the mutual phasing of gaze direction during social interactions.

Thelen and Ulrich (1991) used the phasing of the two limbs as the collective variable to be mapped in their study. Alternation of steps seemed to capture the unique response to the treadmill that was of developmental interest in terms of later locomotion. The action of the treadmill pulls both legs backward. At that point, the infant can make several responses: *no response*, allowing the legs to drag behind; a *single step*, where one leg steps forward and the other drags behind; a *double step*, where one leg takes two successive steps and the other does not respond; or *parallel steps*, where both legs swing forward. Only if they take *alternate steps*, that is, where the step of one leg is followed by a step by the alternate leg, can we be sure that the response was more than a mechanical one. Alternate stepping on the treadmill, as in mature locomotion, requires that one leg be maintained in stance as the other is moved off the ground and forward, and this must involve neural information flow between the legs and their dynamic status. The precision of this alternating response can be quantified by the *relative phasing* of the legs, that is, the point in the cycle of one leg where the opposite leg initiates the cycle. In mature locomotion, the legs are 180 degrees out of phase, or .5 relative phasing.

The treadmill task proved to be especially felicitous for a dynamic analysis because alternating steps was a meaningful collective variable to describe inter-limb coordination, and one that remained stationary over the time course of interest. In addition, pilot studies suggested there would be developmental change in this variable during the period from 1 to 9 months.

Characterizing the Behavioral Attractor States

It is important to understand, before embarking on descriptions of long-term change, the preferred states of the collective variable at particular points in time. Here is where cross-sectional studies are important. Stability can be assessed on a real-time dimension either between individuals, or preferably, within an individual. Within-individual stability may use traditional test-retest situations, within-session variability around mean performance, or manipulations that perturb performance. Behavior that is stable between and within an individual, and to which the system returns when perturbed, acts like a behavioral attractor.

Earlier in this chapter we characterized alternate stepping on the treadmill as a behavioral attractor. At 7 months, infants reliably and consistently performed alternate treadmill steps throughout a range of speeds, although faster speeds seemed to be more strongly preferred. In addition, the behavior was maintained despite the perturbation of the split-belt treadmill. Since stable alternation is also characteristic of independent walking, it seems reasonable to assume that this coordinative solution is highly preferred over other patterns of the two legs moving together.

Describing the Dynamic Trajectory of the Collective Variable

This is the heart of a dynamic approach. Dynamic process accounts require frequent sampling points that will track the state of the collective variable in individual subjects over time. This requires longitudinal study over a time scale that is appropriate to the scale of ontogenetic change. Recall from the previous chapter that in order to assess the true (global) stability of a system, the time scale of observation must be longer than the time scale of the putative phase shift. Thelen and Ulrich knew from pilot studies that treadmill stepping was easily elicited at 7 to 8 months of age, rarely seen at 1 month, and sometimes observed at 3 to 4 months. Thus, the authors decided to map the course of this behavior over the entire time span from 1 to 8 months. This would allow them to identify places in the trajectory where the new form of coordination appeared, where the system gained and lost stability, and thus where the system might be manipulated to uncover control parameters.

Identifying Points of Transition

Transitions are characterized by loss of stability. The study was designed to use variability as an index of stability and instability and not just as noise around mean performance. *Interindividual* variability would be reflected in different developmental trajectories in the onset and stabilization of treadmill stepping. The nature of this variability provides important clues to the control parameters. If all infants were to look quite similar, the behavior would be tightly canalized, and control parameters would be sought in organic conditions and contexts that all the subjects shared in common. On the other hand, variability in the trajectories, which was more likely, provides a kind of "natural experiment" to assess what characteristics of the infants might distinguish their individual developmental profiles and thus be the influential factors engendering the appearance of the coordinated behavior. *Intraindividual* variability is essential for mapping attractor stability, and in this study was measured by variability around mean performance, and by assessing performance on 2 days of testing. Thelen and Ulrich repeated the exact test protocol twice each month within 1 to 3 days. Stability would then be reflected in lower variability in step performance and leg coordination both among steps and between days of testing.

Next, the dynamic map of treadmill stepping was assessed on two time scales. The first, as already mentioned, was the scale of months; how repeatable the infant's performance was from month to month. The second scalar was within age to map the dynamic layout in real time; what were the coordinative responses to changes in speed? What speeds are "preferred" by the system and how do these change with age? These manipulations were inspired by the work on adult bimanual coordination, especially that of Kelso and his colleagues, as described in chapter 3. Recall that Kelso asked subjects to flex and extend fingers or wrists either coordinated in phase or out of phase at different frequencies. In the out-of-phase mode, subjects spontaneously shifted to in phase at critical frequencies that depended on the individual's preferred, or comfortable, oscillation mode. Kelso and colleagues have precisely modeled these phase transitions and their accompanying loss of stability using dynamic principles. Would infants similarly show regions of instability and even phase shift with differing energy delivered to the system? This was tested by providing trials of gradually increasing treadmill speeds.

Finally, the stability of the dynamic trajectory was assessed by introducing two kinds of perturbations. The treadmill speed was increased *within* an ongoing trial. If the alternating state were stable, the infant would be expected to correct and maintain alternation. Second, the experimenters repeated the split-belt challenge, which delivers the strong perturbation of driving each leg at a different speed. Remember that by 7 months, infants compensate with great precision and reliability.

By these various measures, Thelen and Ulrich mapped the course of the emergence of this behavior as changes in the relative stability of the defined coordinative mode. The speed scalars and perturbations allowed them to explore the dynamic landscape of this neuromotor response. No effort was made to assign behavior into idealized stages or structures: the fundamental assumptions are profoundly different. Treadmill stepping does not either "exist" or not, but is probablistically performed under certain defined circumstances. In addition, this approach elevates the status of variability from noise to that of essential data. Individual differences in developmental trajectory provide the descriptive bases for identifying agents of change, and subsequently, for finding a principled basis for experimental interventions.

Alternating Stepping as a Stabilizing Attractor.   What does the overall course of treadmill stepping look like during the first year? In figure 4.8, we show the developmental course of the number of alternating steps for all speeds in the nine subjects, measured at the day of better performance of the two test sessions. Note that the trajectories are similar in showing increases in performance across the months, and most show a period of rather rapid increase. The trajectories differ, however, in the steepness of the slope, and especially in the age at which the increase was manifest. In each infant, treadmill steps also became more sensitive to the speed scalar with age, and by the second half of the first year, all infants consistently showed the highest rate of stepping at a "preferred" speed, which was frequently *not* at the highest speed of the treadmill. This suggests that particular treadmill speeds were optimal in eliciting stepping; in dynamic language, the attractor was the strongest.

Several measures of variability confirmed that alternate treadmill stepping could be envisioned as the emergence of a consistently more stable attractor state.

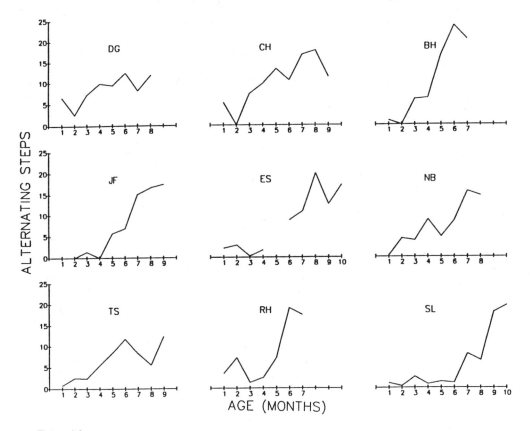

Figure 4.8
Mean number of alternating steps, the collective variable, for nine subjects by age, at all speeds tested. (From Thelen and Ulrich, 1991.)

Remember that infants could perform a variety of step coordination modes, or do nothing at all, as a function of the moving belt. In figure 4.9, we report for individual infants the proportion of the total steps taken each month that were classified as alternating, single, double, or parallel. What stands out is the increasing domination of alternation as the preferred mode, and the concomitant decrease in the other, equally available, ways of moving the two legs. In each infant, there was a highly significant correlation between the number of alternating steps and the total number of steps taken (the two are not necessarily linked.) The individual differences in these data are especially revealing. Contrast, for example, infant CH, whose alternating steps increased most between months 2 and 3, and infant SL, who did not show this increase until after month 6. In CH, the number of alternative coordinations declined dramatically as alternation clicked in, and she performed primarily alternating steps after month 3. SL, however, continued to perform the multiple coordinations (although they were in no sense "obligatory") until after she began to consistently alternate on the treadmill, when the other modes declined. In dynamic terms, the multistable states of single, double, parallel, and alternation were replaced by the singular state of alternation, attractors both dissolving and evolving over the first 8 or 9 months.

Within each infant, the stability of the evolving attractor was also indexed by a measure of the degree of coordination between the legs, or relative phasing. (Recall that 180 degrees out of phase, or .5, is perfect alternation.) Figure 4.10 shows that relative phasing also stabilized in the second half of the year. Here we report relative phasing across all speeds for the subsample of four infants for whom this analysis was completed, and the standard deviations associated with the phasing. Values stabilized between .4 and .5, and the standard deviations also became more consistent.

Next, Thelen and Ulrich found that infants' between-day performance became dramatically more consistent as alternating stepping increased. Figure 4.11 reports the simple metric of the difference between the two performance days plotted with the performance on the better day. Clearly, as overall alternating stepping increased, variability between days decreased. Again contrast the timing of these events between the early stepper, CH, and the much later stepper, SL.

The results on the speed perturbation—increasing the speed in midtrial—were less clearly quantifiable because at early ages infants were less likely to be stepping when the perturbation was introduced, and adjustment was immediate and rapid, even at comparatively young ages. See, for instance, the exemplar plots in figure 4.12, which show infants CH and BH at 3 and 7 months at comparable speeds. In CH at 3 months and BH at 7 months, a parallel swing or stance followed the perturbation, but the infants began alternating in the next phase. In CH at 7 months and BH at 3 months, alternation was not disrupted at all. CH's 7-month trial shows particularly clearly how the infant could continue alternating steps without missing a beat, so to speak.

Finally, performance on the split-belt treadmill confirmed that alternation became an increasingly stable and preferred mode. The split-belt treadmill elicited some alternating steps even in the youngest infants, but performance improved in parallel with the emergence of alternation when the belts were moving at the

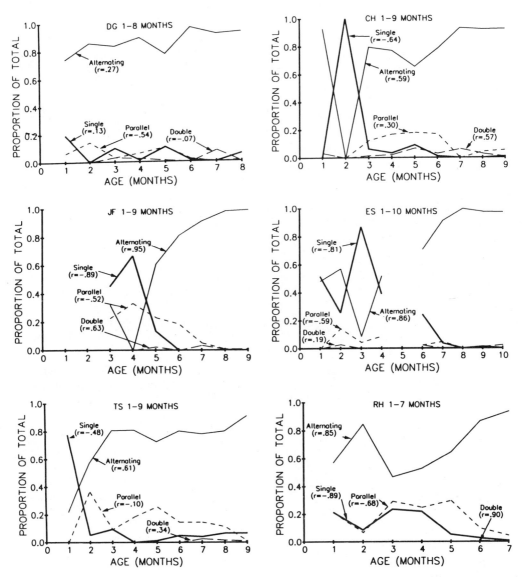

Figure 4.9
Proportion of total number of steps each month that were alternating, single, parallel, or double by individual infant. The *r* values equal the correlation between absolute number of steps taken and the proportion of those steps that were alternating. (From Thelen and Ulrich, 1991.)

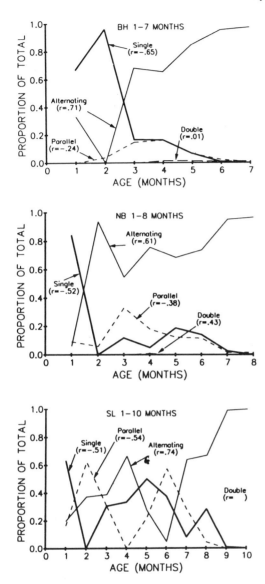

Figure 4.9 (continued)

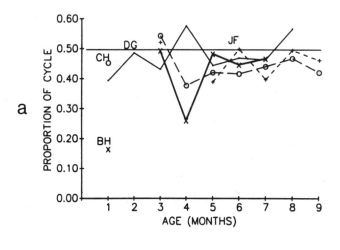

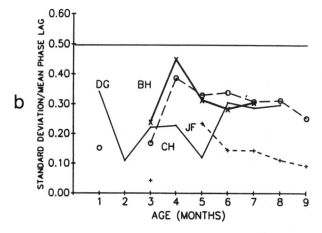

Figure 4.10

a, Mean relative phase lag by infant and age, pooled over speeds. *b*, Standard deviation/mean phase lag. (From Thelen and Ulrich, 1991.)

same speed. Improved performance was indexed both by the overall number of steps on the split-belt treadmill, and by a tighter out-of-phase coordination, measured by relative phase lags, during the second half of the year.

Taken together, these multiple measures provided strong evidence that alternating stepping on a treadmill emerges as a new, stable form of coordination between months 1 and 9. In most infants, the phase shift between the no-stepping or multiple-step mode was relatively dramatic, occurring over a month or two, but others had a more gradual onset. There were significant between-infant differences in the timing of the developmental course, however, suggesting that treadmill stepping was not the result of an autonomous or clocklike, developmental "timer," but rather emerged from the confluence of many components without strong functional constraints. For example, the onset of sucking or smiling is much less variable among infants, reflecting, no doubt, the strong selection pressure on behaviors with obvious physical and social value for survival. If treadmill stepping indexes a neuromuscular pathway that is a normally cryptic component of independent locomotion, there is no obvious value in having the skill accelerated or decelerated as long as it is available concurrently with the other components of mature walking. Since infants normally do not encounter treadmills, the constraints on this behavior can be relatively relaxed and variable. The earlier steppers were at no advantage or disadvantage; all the infants in this study walked without problems within the normal age range.

Exploiting the Instabilities at Transitions to Identify Potential Control Parameters
Having traced the dynamic trajectory of treadmill stepping—its regions of stability and instability—Thelen and Ulrich were now in the position to identify possible control parameters. What were the organic or environmental factors that engendered the shift from no-stepping to multiple-pattern modes of coordination to stable and consistent alternate stepping?

Here the strategy was to map, for each infant, the development of subsystems that could potentially contribute to stepping and to compare these mappings to the ontogenetic profiles of stepping performance. This allowed Thelen and Ulrich to exploit the individual differences in step profiles: changes in potential control parameters must co-occur with changes in the defined collective variable. Remember that this step only isolates potential control parameters as correlating with observed changes in stepping: more conclusive evidence awaits scalar manipulations of the control parameter at times when the system is responsive.

Thelen and Ulrich measured four likely contributors to the shift into stable treadmill stepping: (1) overall rate of general motor maturation from the Bayley Motor Scales, (2) developmental changes in the proportion and composition of the legs (recall that relative chubbiness affected newborn stepping), (3) overall changes in arousal or mood—again, remember that high arousal facilitated leg movements, and (4) specific changes in the predominant postures and movements of the legs, which may indicate relative strength of the muscles of the legs.

There was no relation between individual differences in any of the bodybuild measures or in the infants' arousal levels that predicted the onset of stepping. Infants' relative chubbiness or leanness or limb proportions were not associated with alternate stepping onset. Likewise, all infants were more aroused in the first few months, and arousal during testing did not distinguish early from later steppers.

There was a relation between general motor maturity and treadmill stepping, but only at the extremes. The two infants with the latest onset of treadmill stepping had a comparatively slower rate of motor milestones passed each month, and walked later than the early steppers. The association was weak, however: one infant had an equally slow rate of passed items, but had a stepping onset in the intermediate range. Motor maturity is itself a construct that captures changes in many contributing parts. Thus, it was possible that both the Bayley items and treadmill stepping were influenced by another common factor.

In contrast, the measures of the predominant postures and movements of the legs and feet during the test sessions uncovered a likely control parameter of treadmill stepping onset. Eight of the 17 leg posture variables were moderately correlated with the number of alternate steps over all the trials and ages (table 4.1). Specifically, poor stepping performance was associated with a high degree

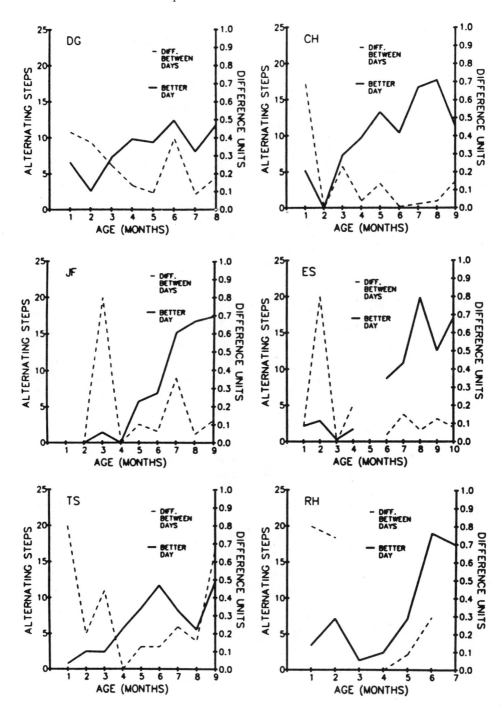

Figure 4.11
Normalized difference (ND) between total number of alternating steps on 2 test days within the same month and the mean number of alternating steps on the better day, plotted by age and subject. ND = |(day 1 − day 2)|/(day 1 + day 2). (From Thelen and Ulrich, 1991.)

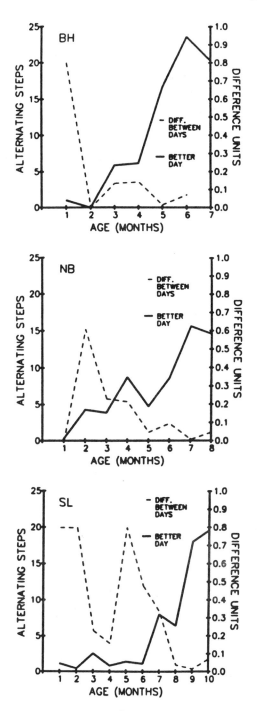

Figure 4.11 (continued)

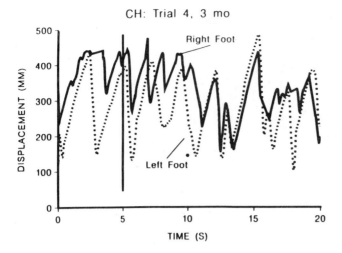

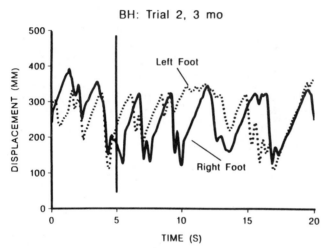

Figure 4.12
Linear displacement of the foot; two trials at each of two ages for two subjects. Increasing displacement values indicate that the foot is moving backward on the treadmill (stance); decreasing values represent the forward swing of the foot. The speed increase was introduced at 5 seconds. (From Thelen and Ulrich, 1991.)

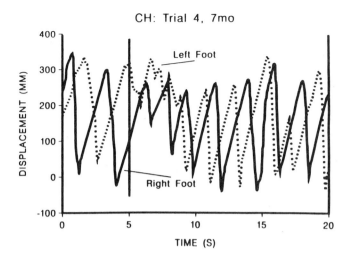

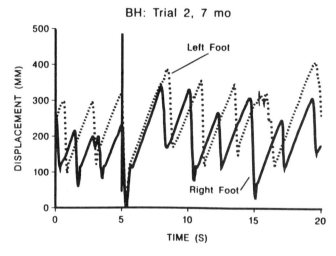

Figure 4.12 (continued)

of flexion both when the belts were moving and the infant was not stepping and during the swing phase when steps were taken. Poor performance was also associated with an inward rotation of the foot. The increase in number of steps correlated with an increase in contacting the belts with a flat foot rather than with the toe; flat-foot contact was, in turn, negatively correlated with a flexed leg posture.

Why was the orientation of the leg and the foot in relation to the treadmill so important in stepping performance? It is likely, as we stated earlier, that alternating steps are elicited when the legs are stretched backward on the moving belts. Two mechanisms are probably involved. When the muscles—primarily the extensor muscles on the back of the legs—are stretched, they store energy like a spring. As the leg is fully stretched, this potential energy is used to swing the leg forward. There are also receptors in the muscles that are sensitive to the

Table 4.1
Leg posture variables showing moderate correlations with total number of treadmill steps and their intercorrelations

| | Leg Posture Variable | | | | | | | | Number of |
	1	2	3	4	5	6	7	8	Steps
Legs high flexed									
1. When not sleeping		.38	.19	.29	.04	−.33	.05	−.29	−.50
2. In swing phase			.23	.12	.09	−.35	.02	−.18	−.26
Foot orientation inward									
3. In swing				.68	.01	−.13	−.05	−.18	−.26
4. In baseline					−.09	−.14	.01	−.30	−.29
Foot contact at touchdown									
5. On toes						−.75	.52	−.53	−.46
6. Flat							−.33	.48	.45
Foot contact in stance									
7. On toes								−.86	−.43
8. Flat									.60

From Thelen and Ulrich (1991).

unloading of the leg—when the weight is shifted at the initiation of the swing—and that convey information about the load status between the two legs to control their mutual phasing. Thus, the two features of treadmill stepping, the swing of the leg forward and the alternation, are dependent on the leg being properly stretched back by the treadmill.

Imagine, again, that infants' legs are like springs with masses, and that the relative tightness or springiness of the spring can vary. If the tension of the spring is too loose, the treadmill will not impart sufficient stretch to overcome the inertia of the leg and it will not swing forward. Similarly, if the spring is too tightly coiled, the treadmill will not impart enough pull to stretch it. In neither case will the stretch receptors be sufficiently activated to initiate reciprocal phasing. Newborn infants have a characteristic flexor bias in their limbs; legs and arms are held tightly to the body. (This flexor bias is probably partially a result of the tightly packed fetal position.) The limbs are relaxed only over many months, and indeed extensor strength in the legs lags behind flexor strength throughout the first year. Highly flexed infants, and those that did not have sufficient extensor strength to put their flat foot on the belt, did less well in treadmill stepping than those whose postures indicated more extensor dominance.

Thus, the relative flexor (very tight) or extensor (more loose) tendencies of the legs, in this case as indexed by several postural characteristics, acted as the control parameter to engender the shift into stable alternate stepping. As a control parameter, flexor tone constrained the interacting elements, but did not prescribe the outcome in a privileged way. Refer to figure 4.13, which presents the measured variables as a layered, multilevel system. The figure compares two infants with somewhat different step-onset patterns: DG, who stepped even at month 1 and who had reached stable performance by month 5, and JF, who performed few steps until month 5 and increased thereafter. Their development is plotted as a function of a number of measured variables. Note the dramatic differences between these infants in the foot and leg posture variables. DG had no inward or outward rotation of the feet and a strong proportion of low flexions (extended legs) from the earliest months, while these optimal stepping postures developed much later for JF. Both infants were relatively chubby (which may work against early stepping) but note DG's high arousal level in the first month compared to JF, which may have facilitated stepping. In sum, this depiction illustrates the multiple, interacting components, all of which contribute to the behavioral performance, and some of which may be critical in the developmental process.

Thelen and Ulrich proposed that the developmental control parameter in treadmill stepping was a change in the flexor-extensor balance of the leg muscles. Ongoing studies in several non-normal groups of infants provide support for this conclusion. Ulrich, Ulrich, and Collier (1992) tested a sample of Down syndrome infants on the treadmill. These infants are characteristically hypotonic (low muscle tone or "floppy") and show delayed motor milestones. They found comparatively delayed onset of treadmill stepping as well, suggesting that these infants lacked sufficient muscle tension to benefit from the stretch of the treadmill action. In addition, Davis (1991) tested a group of premature infants during their first year. These infants, remarkably, showed *improved* performance on the treadmill at 1-month corrected age compared with full-term infants. How can this be, given that this group is generally believed to be at risk for motor disabilities? The explanation implicates peripheral and not central factors. Heriza (1988) discovered that premature infants with 6 weeks or more experience out of utero were distinctly more extensor-dominant in kicking than infants of comparable gestational age. This was most likely due to the premature infants' additional time released from the confines of the uterine space and exposed to the extensor influence of gravity. It may also be that comparatively more experience in an extended posture and in gravity also facilitated a muscle tension balance more amenable to being stretched on the treadmill, accounting for the improved performance in Davis's premature sample.

The emergence of coordinated treadmill stepping must be a multidetermined process. While it seems likely that the pathways essential for treadmill-stepping pattern production can function by 1 month of age, central neural pattern generation is likely *not* the developmental control parameter in this case. Rather, the behavior itself emerges only when the central elements cooperate with the effectors—the muscles, joints, tendons—in the appropriate physical context. Treadmill stepping requires muscles that can be stretched to detect and respond to the treadmill just as much as neural pathways that transmit the sensory and motor signals.

To this point, however, the identification of a potential control parameter has been strictly correlational. More rigorous characterization requires experimental manipulation, which is the next step in a dynamic strategy.

Manipulating the Putative Control Parameters to Experimentally Generate Phase Transitions

In dynamic systems terms, points of transition allow the experimenter to test potential control parameters. When systems are stable and unchanging, they resist perturbation: the ball is in a deep well. Small nudges only displace the ball momentarily; a strong push is required for the ball to escape. When systems are

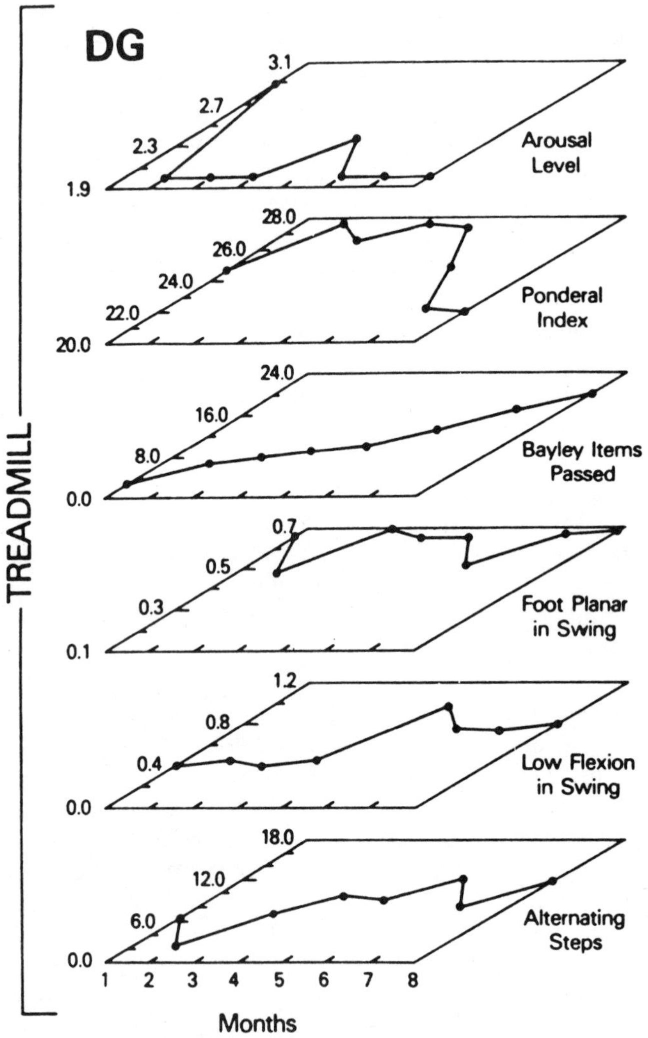

Figure 4.13
The development of alternating treadmill steps depicted as parallel developmental trajectories of related subsystems. (From Thelen and Ulrich, 1991.)

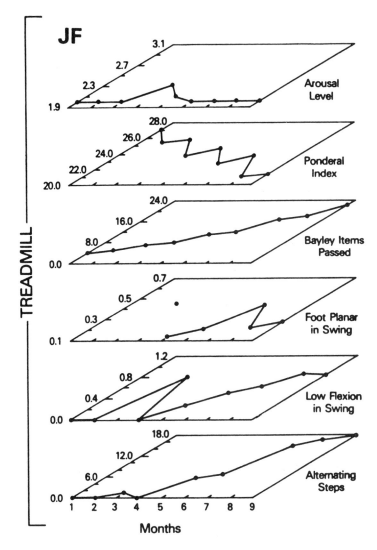

Figure 4.13 (continued)

undergoing phase shifts, however, their components are more loosely interwoven. Relatively small perturbations will suffice to push the ball out of the shallow potential well.

Developmental researchers have always exploited this characteristic of systems in transition to design experiments and interventions that move systems around in their developmental landscapes. Much applied developmental research is devoted to discovering the optimal time for a specific intervention—the time when the organism is most receptive to supplemental education, physical therapy, emotional counseling, and so on. If the infant, child, or family is developmentally unprepared, the intervention is useless. Conversely, if the undesirable behavior is already firmly entrenched, intervention may do no good, or change may require a relatively massive program.

This is also akin to the concept of *sensitive periods* (Hinde, 1961); the earlier term was "critical period" (Lorenz, 1937; Gottlieb, 1961). During ontogeny there are times when the organism responds to particular environmental inputs while at other times it is relatively resistant to those same stimuli. Traditionally, sensitive periods were believed to be rather rigid and maturationally defined, but contemporary researchers have adopted a more dynamic view (Bateson, 1987; Gottlieb, 1991).

Developmental control parameters can be tested by providing specific interventions that the researchers have reason to believe engender long-range behavioral change. For ethical reasons, these are usually enrichments. A now-classic experiment of this type relevant to the current topic is Zelazo, Zelazo, and Kolb's (1972) experiment providing infants with practice in newborn stepping through a time when the response undergoes rapid diminution in frequency. In dynamic terms, Zelazo et al. made the assumption that some effects of practice (although the specific effects are in dispute; e.g., see Thelen, 1984) were acting as a control parameter that could shift the unstable system, in this case to overcome whatever components led to performance decrements.

More common than long-term interventions are what Vygotsky (1962) called *microgenesis* experiments (see, e.g., Kuhn and Phelps, 1982; Siegler and Jenkins, 1989). These are attempts to mimic developmental changes by manipulating the putative control parameters over a shorter time span to attempt to push the child into more or less mature performance. An example, again in the realm of newborn stepping, is Thelen, Fisher, and Ridley-Johnson's (1984) test of their hypothesis that the rapid deposition of subcutaneous fat in the legs depressed step performance. They reasoned that if added weight suppressed steps over a developmental time span—the developmental control parameter—then manipulations of the control parameter in real time should shift the system in the predicted direction. Indeed, decreasing the mechanical load by submerging the legs increased stepping, while adding weights to the infants' legs diminished their steps.

The microgenesis experiment of Thelen et al. worked because the infant stepping system was sufficiently unstable to be measurably affected by changes in the effective mass of the legs. Dynamic theory predicts that once strength and the stepping pattern are well established, comparable manipulations would have little effect. For example, adults would overcome similar leg weights and continue to walk unperturbed, and stepping would not be dependent on submersion. Only because weight gain is rapid and muscle strength is not synchronously developing in infants do we see the phenomenon of behavioral loss in the first few months. While systems are fluid, they are free to autonomously seek new places in their space, and they do so when any of the subcomponents are experimentally changed. When they are more tightly bound, they still may change, but they require significantly larger perturbations.

These studies are also suggestive of a strong experiential component to the development of leg motor patterns. Since changes from flexor to extensor dominance are *time-out-of-utero–* rather than *gestational age–*dependent, the neuromuscular system must be responding to the experience of moving in a gravitational field. Thus, our control parameter question can be recast at another level. If the shift from flexor dominance engenders stepping on the treadmill, what are the developmental processes working to change predominant muscle tone? In the next chapter we make the case that it is primarily the intermodal consequences of continual experience in the world that causes development to happen. In this case, as muscles are stretched by movement and by gravity, they become stronger, more flexible, and increasingly calibrated to perception in the cause of function. Since infants never encounter treadmills in their daily lives, it is likely that performance on the treadmill is aided by nonspecific experiences of moving the legs, which through the resulting changes in muscles, tendons, and the neural pathway provide the organic context for the action of the treadmill.

A dynamic context for the treadmill phenomenon suggests a more rigorous test of a putative developmental control parameter. Before describing this experiment, it is useful to introduce the adult experiment upon which it is modeled. Recall that Kelso and his colleagues discovered two regions of stability in the bimanual coordination of finger flexing and extending: an *in-phase* attractor, where both fingers flex and extend simultaneously and which is stable at all cycle frequencies, and an *antiphase* attractor, where flexion in the left finger alternates with extension in the right. The antiphase attractor is stable at low frequencies, but as subjects scaled up the frequency of movements, they spontaneously shifted to the in-phase pattern.

Subsequently, Zanone and Kelso (1991) asked how these stable patterns would be affected by *learning* to perform a *novel* coordinative goal, in particular a 90-degree relative phase, wherein the left finger lags with respect to the right finger by a quarter of a cycle. In most untrained subjects, this pattern is in many ways analogous to a developmental process, in which practice in the task is the control parameter. Subjects practiced this novel pattern, with each finger synchronized to an appropriately timed light diode, for 15 trials per day over 5 consecutive days. To assess the relative stability of the old and new coordinative attractors as a function of practice of the novel form, Zanone and Kelso administered a scalar probe before, after, and during the practice. This probe sampled the possible coordinative patterns systematically by requiring subjects to execute finger movements with relative phases starting at 0 degrees and progressively increasing by steps of 15 degrees to 180 degrees, or antiphase. In other words, the probe asked: What coordination patterns would subjects perform as they were required to move away from the stable and preferred movement patterns and as they practiced the novel task?

Figure 4.14 captures the rich and dynamic portrait of the learning process. The figure plots for two subjects the successive four probes per practice day. Each point, labeled *A* through *O*, is the mean response produced at the required relative phase as it is scaled from 0 to 180 degrees. If the subjects were able to reproduce perfectly all the requested relative phasing, then the 13 mean values (the scalar probes) would be equally spaced on the *y*-axis and no stronger coordinative attractor would exist. Therefore, a cluster of several neighboring means reflects the presence of an attractor at this value, and their density around a given value indexes the strength of the attractor. Thus, the attractors are dynamically mapped on two time scales of the probe scaling and of learning over 5 days.

The main feature of this representation is that, independent of the subject's initial dynamics, the 90-degree attractor is progressively discovered, "sucking

Subject TM

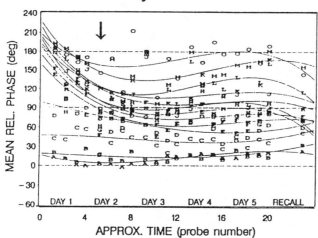

Subject MS

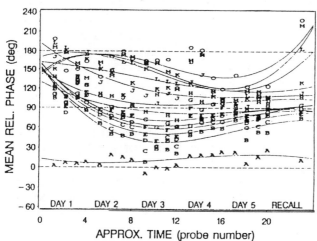

Figure 4.14
Change of performance on the finger coordination task with practice for two subjects. The *top solid curves* plot the mean intratrial relative phase as a function of the practice trials. The *lower dashed curves* display the corresponding standard deviation. (From Zanone and Kelso, 1991. Reprinted with permission.)

in," so to speak, other relative phase patterns into its basin of attraction. It is of interest that the majority of the curves come from the initial 180-degree attractor, which is less stable than the 0-degree pattern. In the subject MS, for example (*bottom panel*), the 180-degree pattern is totally lost, and all required phases between 30 and 180 degrees are attracted to the newly learned 90-degree pattern. The probe shows how practice has disrupted the initial stable attractors, allowing the subjects to explore many coordinative regions and the system to "settle" on the solution demanded by the experimental task.

The Thelen and Ulrich study (1991) revealed similar real- and developmental-time dynamics for infant treadmill stepping. In real time, the alternating pattern attractor was more stable at faster, rather than slower, treadmill speeds. In developmental time, alternation as a pattern stabilized after months 4 or 5 in most infants, replacing the several step patterns (single, double, parallel) which were equally likely in the earlier months. In addition, step rate became increasingly responsive to the imposed speed scalar. Thus, in the early months, treadmill stepping was in a nonstable transition state and should be sensitive to manipulations of a control parameter. Would specific or nonspecific training in this skill condense and accelerate the discovery of the alternating attractor, much as the Zanone and Kelso experiment allowed adults to find a new coordinative solution to meet the task demands?

Recently Vereijken and Thelen (Vereijken, 1993; Vereijken and Thelen, 1993) have tested the effects of training on treadmill dynamics. They provided daily practice sessions for 1 month on the treadmill for 3-month-old infants whose step performance was unstable and for 7-month-old infants who were stable alternating steppers. Half of the young infants were trained at a slow speed and half at the faster speed known to be optimal at older ages. The 7-month-olds received training at only the less stable slower speed. Control infants received either no at-home training or an equal time spent standing upright with the treadmill turned off. The changing layout of their step pattern attractor was assessed twice each week, using a speed scalar like the one used by Thelen and Ulrich.

The changing attractor strengths as a function of training are shown in figure 4.15, with the depth of the wells representing the relative proportion of each of the step types before and after the month's training (Vereijken, 1993). At the top of the figure are the two 3-month experimental infants trained at fast and slow speeds. These infants showed strong training effects toward alternating stepping from initial single and double steps. They also increased dramatically in their overall number of steps compared with the control infants, which is not shown in this figure. The 7-month-old infants, who were presumably already stable, demonstrated little effects of training, either in frequency of stepping or relative coordination, as expected. What was especially interesting, however, was the group trained by standing on a nonmoving treadmill. These infants had a big increase in the proportion of parallel steps, suggesting that treadmill training specifically enhanced the alternating neuromotor pattern, while standing alone facilitated moving both legs in parallel when the treadmill was turned on. Analysis of the patterns of coordination in the weeks during training will reveal individual responses to training over time.

Stability of stepping patterns

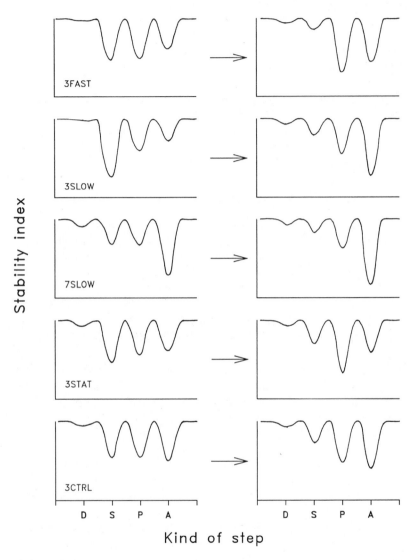

Figure 4.15
Stability map of stepping patterns as a function of training on moving and stationary treadmills. Depth of the wells indicates relative proportion of steps. Experimental groups: *3FAST*, 3-month-olds trained at fast speed; *3SLOW*, 3-month-olds trained at slow speeds; *7SLOW*, 7-month-olds trained at slow speeds; *3STAT*, 3-month-olds trained by standing on stationary treadmill; *3CTRL*, 3-month-olds given no daily training. Kinds of steps: *D*, double; *S*, single; *P*, parallel; *A*, alternating.

Integrating Dynamic Accounts at Many Levels of Analysis

The final principle in a dynamic strategy is both the most important and most difficult to achieve operationally. So far, we have used dynamics to characterize behavior, and specifically the patterns of leg movements of infants as they evolve during the first year. These behavioral dynamics are supported by, and reside in, the dynamics of the many contributing subsystems. For example, we might study the developmental changes in muscle physiology as a dynamic system, considering the contractile properties of the muscle, and the changes in the cellular membrane dynamics, neuromuscular junctions, and so on. These changes are part and parcel of the behavioral dynamics; they are not more or less fundamental or causal, but they must be consistent. That is, without efficient transmission at the neuromuscular junction, we would not expect infants to develop sufficient strength and rapid responses to maintain upright posture. But it is equally likely that efforts to stand and support the weight facilitate efficient transition. The integration, therefore, spans both *levels of analysis* and *levels of time*, a point we will repeatedly stress in the remainder of the book. In the following chapters, we attempt to show how behavioral dynamics can be meshed with brain dynamics over both levels and scales.

A Dynamic Account of Learning to Walk: The Ontogenetic Landscape

We conclude this extended chapter by returning to the more general problem of learning to walk which we posed in chapter 1. Recall that traditional accounts of locomotor development are essentially single-causal. Although theorists like McGraw and neurophysiologists like Forssberg have recognized that locomotion requires postural control, strength, and so on, they ascribe the engines of developmental change to central neural structures, whose autonomous maturation results in functional locomotion from earlier poorly coordinated and controlled movements. We showed how any single-causal model was deficient in accounting for the modular, heterochronic, context-dependent, and multidimensional nature of locomotor development, not only in human infants but in other vertebrates as well. We subsequently argued that development in the cognitive realm was equally ill served by models which ignore the richness and nonlinearity of process.

How, then, can we conceptualize the process of learning to walk from a dynamic framework that will capture the continuity that must underlie all ontogeny just as it does justice to development's stagelike characteristics? Can a dynamic systems perspective capture both the grand sweep and the messy details under the same principles? Are we closer to understanding what makes locomotor development happen?

Human infants, like all biological organisms, are maintained by a flux of energy. Through their metabolic processes they draw energy from a high potential source—their food—and use it to do work—move—and to generate heat. Like other dynamic systems, the flow of energy through the multiple, interacting components of the body produces one or many self-organized equilibrium points or attractors, whose form and stability depend upon the system's constraints. In newborn and young infants, one of the stable attractors is the pattern of cyclic kicking. Within certain energetic states, presumably regulated through the nervous system, and within the constraints of the muscles, tendons, bones, and circulatory and nervous systems within a gravitational field, kicks self-organize with springlike properties. Later, with the additional energetic and informational constraints of the treadmill, another attractor cycle emerges, which similarly condenses into a low-dimensional dynamic, the multiple contributing elements. These attractors, which are assembled from continuous elements, act like singularities in the developmental state space—stages, when the conditions are so defined. But also, because behavioral attractors are always softly assembled from the interactions of their component elements, and are always in open energy exchange with the surrounds, changes in either the components or in the context may influence the patterns that emerge and their stability. Thus, the development of locomotion must be seen as the successive stabilization and destabilization of attractors as the contributing components and the constraining contexts themselves change. The addition of new behavioral forms or the deletion of old ones provides a matrix of new contexts and challenges, which in turn requires the discovery of new stable solutions.

A new way of describing locomotor development, therefore, is as multiple and changing points of attraction, which coalesce and dissolve with time. One way to visualize this process is with an *ontogenetic landscape* for locomotion created by Michael Muchisky, Lisa Gershkoff-Stowe, Emily Cole, and Esther Thelen (1993). Figure 4.16 is an adaptation of C.H. Waddington's (1956) famous *epigenetic landscape* (figure 4.17). Waddington initially used the epigenetic landscape to depict the process of *canalization*, or the increasing differentiation of tissues and organs during embryogenesis, but it has since become a powerful metaphor for all developmental processes. Waddington was primarily concerned with the central question of how, despite variations in genetic inheritance and environmental conditions, developmental processes produced stable, species-typical phenotypes. (This is the same question we posed in the Introduction: How does global order arise from local variability?) Waddington believed that development was genetically buffered, depicted by the ball rolling into progressively deepening valleys in the landscape as time progressed. Thus, once developmental processes started, they became increasingly more stable, more protected from random noise, and more differentiated.

In our dynamic landscape (see figure 4.16) we see development as not just progression toward increasing stability (nor do we assume that the control parameters are ultimately genetic), but as a series of *changes* of relative stability and instability. The landscape is thus a series of potential wells, as introduced in chapter 3, where the steepness of the walls of the well indicate the amount of "push" the system needs to escape that attractor. Likewise, the relative width of the valley indicates the variability inherent in that attractor space. A well could be steep and narrow, specifying few, highly stable behavioral choices. The well might, in turn, have steep walls but a flat floor if there are several stable choices but no preference among them. Additionally, there could be multistable possibilities with several small hillocks in the valley suggesting that the system may move among a number of possible attractors. The locomotor landscape incorporates all of these topographies. During development the hills and valleys both deepen and become more shallow as preferred states emerge and disappear.

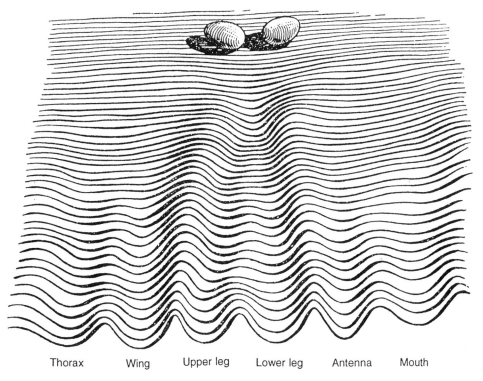

Thorax   Wing   Upper leg   Lower leg   Antenna   Mouth

Figure 4.16
Waddington's epigenetic landscape as he originally applied it to tissue differentiation in *Drosophila*. As development proceeds, the initial undifferentiated embryo becomes canalized into more specific body tissues and organs. (From Waddington, 1956. Reprinted by permission.)

The ontogenetic landscape for locomotion begins with the prenatal period, depicted at the top of the landscape by relatively flat terrain, suggesting few strong movement attractors. In fact, there may be very constrained and rigid motor patterns; research on prenatal movement has identified a number of movement types but there is no information on their variability or stability. We do know that at birth, and likely some months before (Heriza, 1988), infants have a number of stereotyped and stable leg movement patterns: in particular, alternating kicking and stepping, and the ability to entrain to the treadmill. These are depicted by narrow wells. Note that both the categories of "kicking" and "stepping" have separate wells, with the different types of each movement as subvalleys separated by the hill representing the postural constraints. Parallel and single kicking are initially more shallow wells and only deepen after alternate kicking is well established.

The disappearance of newborn stepping and the continuing ability of infants to step on the treadmill is seen as the gradual flattening and merging of the newborn attractor with the treadmill valley. Without the treadmill, stepping is no longer a preferred state. Likewise, the gradual decrease of kicking over the first year is reflected in the flattening of those hills. Kicking is still possible, but

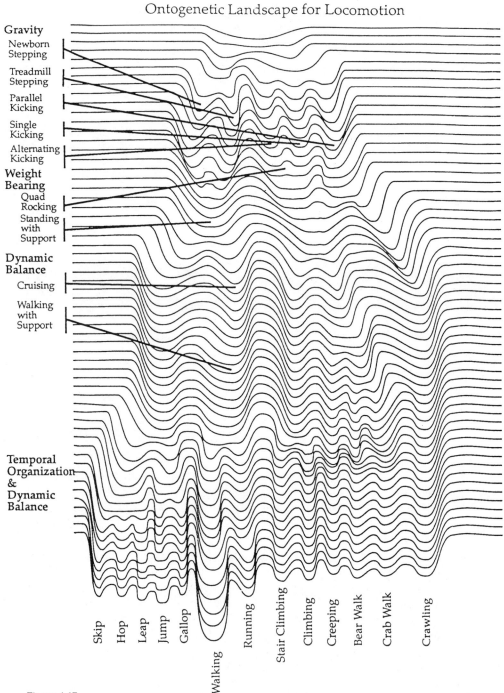

Figure 4.17
Ontogenetic landscape for locomotion. (From Muchisky, Gershkoff-Stowe, Cole, and Thelen, 1993.)

not likely. The primary task for this first period of kicking and stepping is to maintain movement against gravity.

The second task is adding weightbearing to the gravitational task. Here we see a large relatively flat landscape as infants explore the multiple configurations of postural support, quadruped or standing with support. These are depicted as evolving from and using elements of the earlier leg movements, but without highly specific task demands, not producing very rigid or stable configurations.

The addition of dynamic balance forces the system into more confined attractor spaces, although at first infants explore many corners of the landscape—sometimes exceeding their limits and falling, for example, into discrete locomotor forms. Walking, of course, becomes the preferred attractor, selected from the other possible ways of locomoting. It is energetically and dynamically stable and automatic for most locomotor tasks. As a deep attractor, it "sucks in" other organizations of the system. Adults will try to walk bipedally before they resort to crawling! However, infants learn other configurations, possibly less stable, but available for certain intentional tasks. They may skip, hop, or gallop for play or exercise, or climb, creep, or crawl on difficult terrain. In each case, the configuration is sufficiently stable to be reliably recalled and performed, yet flexible enough to meet changing task demands.

In the next several chapters, we build a case for calling these evolving and dissolving attractor valleys a type of *perceptual category*, wherein the movement configuration is selected, stored, and retrieved by the very same processes as other mental categories. To understand how we make that claim, we must first explore the dynamics of another level, that of neural development.

PART II

Seeking Mechanisms of Change

Chapter 5

Dynamics of Neural Organization and Development

In the previous chapter we formulated both a set of very general principles for understanding development and an operational strategy for studying development based on dynamic theory. We then applied the principles and strategies to the particular case of learning to walk. We derived these principles and strategies quite explicitly from *synergetics*, the theory of pattern formation in complex systems associated most closely with Haken and his followers. Key concepts are compression of the degrees of freedom of a complex, multicomponent system into dynamic patterns that can be expressed as a collective variable, behavioral attractors of varying and changing stabilities, which can be operationally defined, and the appearance of new forms as phase shifts. The approach emphasized the importance of transitions as windows into developmental process and the identification of control parameters moving the organism into new developmental phases. We proposed that the phenomenon of learning to walk could only be understood in dynamic terms, and will make a similar claim for the phenomena of cognitive development.

In characterizing development at the level of general synergetic principles, we have accomplished several goals. First, we have shown how new forms of behavior can arise during development in a self-organizing manner, consistent with universal laws of physics, and without invoking homunculi or other internal or external "knowers" of the end-state. Second, we have articulated principles of sufficient generality to apply to time-dependent systems regardless of the particular organism or the specific behavior of interest. Third, although these principles are very general, they generate specific predictions about stability and change, which can provide a theoretical rationale for experimental manipulations. And finally, dynamic principles erase the gap between real-time assembly of behavior and its assembly over ontogenetic time, an issue not usually addressed in traditional theories.

At this level, these principles are clear about the general processes of change through the loss of stability of coherent dynamic organization, but completely uninformed about the more precise mechanisms of changing attractor stability. In this chapter, we attempt to add a more specific mechanism to the process of development. In doing so, we also build a conceptual framework for linking our earlier chapters on the development of motor processes to the rest of the book dealing with cognition. We do this by showing that cognition emerges in development through repeated cycles of perception-action-perception, and that the processes that build stable, adaptive movement are the same that build stable, adaptive cognition. As we stated earlier, our view has a distinct Piagetian flavor in giving primacy to active, repetitive perception and movement, and the ability of the system to self-equilibrate. We differ, however, in our fundamental view of mental activity as a dynamic assembly rather than a hierarchy of structures, and in seeing the process of development as one of selection rather than construction.

Explanation and Mechanism

What do we seek when we talk about mechanism? Mechanistic explanations can be at many levels. For example, by discovering that the deposition of body fat acts as a control parameter in the disappearance of newborn stepping, we have supplied a mechanism of change. It is valid to ask, of course, what physiological or nutritional processes accelerate the deposition of fat, and some may want to pursue mechanism at that level as well. The search for mechanism is often interpreted as reductionist, but there is no reason to assume that body fat is somehow a more basic (and therefore more real) explanation than one at any other level. In a dynamic view, changes in body fat are coequal with changes in neurotransmitter efficiency, for example, as both must contribute to the behavioral changes we observe. Indeed, the ultimate goal would be to integrate these multilevel processes and understand their mutual interactions. For example, it is at least conceivable that body fat deposition augments neurotransmitter efficiency by increasing the biomechanical demands on the muscles of the legs, thus increasing motoneuron recruitment and firing rate. Explanation, therefore, requires that we tease apart these reciprocal interactions.

While mechanisms of change for mental processes most certainly do involve changes in neurotransmission, satisfactory explanations need not reside only at this level. Nonetheless, we strongly believe that explanations at every level must be consistent and ultimately reconcilable. At a minimum, the dynamics of the behavioral phenomena must be consistent with the dynamics of the neural phenomena. Likewise, while a theory of behavioral development need not address the developmental neurophysiology of the brain, it is immeasurably strengthened by being informed by and coherent with what is known in that discipline.

In considering mechanisms for early development, we have been strongly influenced by the work of Gerald Edelman, especially his theory of neuronal group selection (TNGS), which he has elaborated in a series of three books (1987, 1988, 1989). While Edelman's theory is speculative in some respects, it is also, in our opinion, the first attempt to integrate contemporary neuroanatomy, neuroembryology, and developmental psychology in a cohesive and plausible fashion. The theory is entirely consistent with the synergetic principles we have elaborated thus far, but adds mechanism because it instantiates change processes at several levels of analysis. TNGS manifests dynamic principles and processes at the molecular level during the early phases of embryology in the establishment of primary cellular morphology, at the neuronal level during the emergence of primary neuroanatomy, and at the behavioral level in the formation of perception-action categories. We will use Edelman to support our contentions that (1) during development, behavior is *selected* from a wider universe of possibilities rather than imposed; (2) dynamic perception-action mappings are primary in early life; (3) multimodal exploration is a key process for acquiring new forms; and (4) creation and exploitation of variability are key elements in the process. Thus, TNGS adds to our understanding of the origins of behavior because it builds this mechanistic bridge between the traditional poles of development: innate vs. acquired, learning vs. maturation, evolution vs. development, genes vs. environment.

Dynamic Organization of the Brain

In chapter 4, we set the stage for studying the *development* of motor processes by examining how actions were assembled in real time. A strength of dynamic systems is recognition of the continuity between real- and developmental time scales: the same principles of self-organization, task assembly, and nonlinearity apply to both, for example, how an adult grabs a cup of coffee and how an infant learns to reach for a cup. Before considering TNGS as a theory of the developing brain, we also want to link the time scales between real-time brain function and its ontogeny. The link again is dynamic systems and especially recent work that goes beyond the microscopic views of individual neurons, membranes, and transmitters, to a more macroscopic picture of the brain as a dynamic collective. What this work shows is that the brain works in a holistic, plastic, self-organizing fashion, with structural boundaries that are less-fixed than previously thought, and where collectives of neurons exhibit many dynamic properties, including phase entrainment and chaos. Although there are, as yet, no comparable developmental experiments, understanding these properties of the adult brain makes TNGS more plausible.

Dynamics of Perception: Olfaction in the Rabbit

The most complete, and remarkable, picture of the dynamic functioning of the brain comes from the studies of Walter J. Freeman and his colleagues at Berkeley. (We base this account on Freeman, 1981, 1987, 1991; Freeman and Skarda, 1985; and Skarda and Freeman, 1981, 1987a,b). Freeman has been concerned over the last 30 years with the neurophysiology of perception: How does the brain recognize and give meaning to events in the world accurately and quickly, even when the stimuli are complex and appear in different contexts? This question is of fundamental developmental importance.

Rather than focusing only on the properties of single neurons, Freeman has looked at the cooperative behavior of millions of neurons spread throughout the brain. He has discovered that perception can only be understood as patterns generated at this macroscopic level. In addition, he has found evidence of chaos in cooperative brain activity—chaos that, he believes, underlies the ability of the brain to produce novel and flexible responses. Later, we also speculate on the role of chaos in the generation of new ontogenetic forms.

Freeman has based his conclusions on his studies of olfaction, primarily in rabbits trained to recognize several different odorants. While the rabbits were sniffing, the investigators recorded electroencephalograms (EEGs) simultaneously from 60 to 64 sites covering a large part of the surface of the olfactory bulb. The tracing from each EEG site reflected the excitation not of a single neuron but of pools of thousands of neurons just below the EEG electrode. When the rabbit sniffed a familiar scent, with each inhalation the usual oscillations seen in the EEG became more regular, and returned to a more disordered state with an exhalation. Elaborate computer analysis of the data allowed Freeman to tease out patterns of collective behavior of all the recording sites from the complex background activity. What he found was that the identity of an odorant was carried not in any single neuron or group of neurons, nor even in the shape of the EEG waves, but in the spatial pattern of the amplitude of the waves across the entire olfactory bulb. The perceptual information was indeed "mapped" in terms of wave amplitude much like a contour diagram in a topographic map of a geographic area (figure 5.1). Each time the rabbit sniffed the same odorant under the same conditions, it produced the same global map, even though the dominant frequency of the EEG waves might be different.

Olfactory perception in the rabbit acts like a dynamic system in several important ways. First, the spatial map that emerged with each familiar sniff self-organized not just in response to the odor itself but in a complex context that included the rabbit's training and arousal state. The amplitude maps, for example, changed strikingly with the reinforcement associated with that scent, and even more dramatically with the rabbit's reinforcement history with other smells as well. For example, rabbits were conditioned to associate the scent of sawdust with a particular reinforcement, and they produced a characteristic sawdust contour map. When, however, they were taught to recognize the odor of banana, a new sawdust plot emerged along with a characteristic banana map.

This can only happen if sawdust is represented in the bulb not as a fixed structure or schema but as a dynamic assembly that is always a function of global activity. This means that neurons that participate in sawdust are also affected by the history of neurons encoding banana, and that this history has preeminence over a static representation of the stimulus. Freeman postulated that groups of mutually excited neurons he calls the *nerve cell assembly* participate in the global pattern and are such a repository of past association (Freeman's nerve cell assem-

Figure 5.1
Contour plots of the spatial patterns of EEG amplitudes across the cortex of the rabbit olfactory bulb. The contour plot on the *left* emerged consistently from bulbar EEGs of a rabbit that had been conditioned to associate the scent of sawdust with a particular reinforcement. After the animal learned to recognize the smell of banana (*middle*), however, reexposure to sawdust led to the emergence of a new sawdust plot. Freeman (1991) concludes that the bulbar activity is dominated more by experience than by stimuli; otherwise sawdust would always give rise to the same plot. (From Freeman, 1991. Reprinted with permission.)

blies are similar, but not identical, to Edelman's neuronal groups, also discussed below). Nerve cell assemblies are groups of interconnected neurons whose synapses become mutually and simultaneously strengthened by input neurons during learning (so-called Hebbian synapses). In this way, experience selects a certain pattern of cell connections, selectively strengthened for a particular odorant. But because the connections are widely distributed, when any subset of neurons receives familiar input, the entire assembly rapidly responds. Also, because the neurons of the olfactory system are richly interconnected, other sources of input, in addition to the odor itself, impact upon the response. Freeman found that general arousal "primes" the olfactory response. When the rabbit is hungry, for example, the general level of raised arousal lowers the threshold and the rabbit responds more strongly to the odor. In addition, input to the network itself increases its sensitivity, so that as excitatory input from only one part of the network spreads, it releases collective activity in an increasingly stronger fashion, leading to an explosion of collective activity. This clear nonlinearity of response— a small input is enormously amplified—is, of course, another hallmark of dynamic systems.

Dynamic processes also are essential in the next step of the perceptual process, how the information from the olfactory bulb is recognized by the higher brain centers—the olfactory cortex. Like the networks within the bulb, the bulb and the cortex are massively interconnected, so that each cortical cell receives input from thousands of bulbar neurons. When the patterned signal is transmitted from the bulb, every recipient neuron picks up a share of that signal. Although the cortical cells are continually activated, the odor signal can be distinguished from the background signal because it is more coherent. The cortical cells, in turn, generate a similar collective burst.

Freeman believes, however, that it is the particular chaotic nature of the ongoing activity in these structures that allows extremely rapid and precise recognition of these messages, which, you recall, are patterned only in their collective activity. Again, with complex computer simulations and elaborate three-dimensional phase portrait plots, Freeman produced evidence of chaos—activity that looks random but is not—in the activity of the bulb and the olfactory cortex. The shapes of the plots represent chaotic attractors, or the behavior the system settles into when under the influence of a particular odorant. In Freeman's words:

> The images suggest that an act of perception consists of an explosive leap of the dynamic system from the "basin" of one chaotic attractor to another; the basin of an attractor is the set of initial conditions from which the system goes into a particular behavior. The bottom of a bowl would be the basin of attraction for a ball placed anywhere along the sides of the bowl. In our experiments, the basin for each attractor would be defined by the receptor neurons that were activated during training to form the nerve cell assembly.
>
> We think the olfactory bulb and cortex maintain many chaotic attractors, one for each odorant an animal or human being can discriminate. *Whenever an odorant becomes meaningful in some way, another attractor is added, and all the others undergo slight modification* [emphasis added]. (Freeman, 1991, pp. 85–86)

Freeman further believes that chaos is the source of novel activity patterns, which are crucial to adding new nerve cell assemblies. It is this diversity of activity that provides the "trials" of trial-and-error problem solving. We also will argue that the process of exploration and selection is the major pathway for developmental change. Thus, controlled variability stands as the source of new forms in both real and ontogenetic time.

We end this section with a second extended quote by Freeman, again because of the striking convergence between his dynamics of perception and the ontogeny of cognition and action:

> I begin to envision the general dynamics of perception. The brain seeks information, mainly by directing an individual to look, listen, and sniff. The search results from self-organizing activity in the limbic system . . . which funnels a search command to the motor systems. As the motor command is transmitted, the limbic system issues what is called a reafference message, alerting all the sensory systems to prepare to respond to new information.
>
> And respond they do, with every neuron in a given region participating in a collective activity—a burst. Synchronous activity in each system is then transmitted back to the limbic system, where it combines with similarly generated output to form a gestalt. Then, within a fraction of a second, another search for information is demanded, and the sensory systems are prepared again by reafference.
>
> Consciousness may well be the subjective experience of this recursive process of motor command, reafference, and perception. If so, it enables the brain to plan and prepare for each subsequent action on the basis of past action, sensory input and perceptual synthesis. In short, an act of perception is not the copying of an incoming stimulus. *It is a step in a trajectory by which brains grow, reorganize themselves and reach into their environment to change it to their own advantage* [emphasis added]. [Freeman, 1991, p. 85]

Dynamics of Movement: Neural Control of Reaching

A second area where real-time brain dynamics can inform our developmental story is in the cortical control of movement. Here we report primarily on the work of Apostolos Georgopoulos and his colleagues (1990, 1991; reviewed in Georgopoulos, 1986, 1988) who have recorded from multiple sites in the motor and premotor cortex of the behaving monkey. In a series of important experiments, Georgopoulos and his colleagues trained monkeys to reach for targets in certain two- and three-dimensional spatial locations. At the same time, they recorded continuously from single cells in the brain areas of interest. Their major finding was that in both motor and premotor cortex, the activity of single cells changed in an orderly manner with the direction of the movement in space. Thus, for any given cell, activity was highest in a preferred direction and decreased when the arm moved away from that preferred direction. Note that the cells responded to the actual direction of the arm movement, not the absolute direction of the target. However, within the recorded area, different cells exhibited different preferred directions, distributed around the three-dimensional space of the possible target directions. What this showed was that any single cell participates in movement in various directions *and* that movement in any particular direction involves activity of a population of cells.

The question arose, therefore, about how a particular and unique direction of movement could be generated from these populations of cells. Georgopoulos and colleagues suggested that the cells worked in concert to generate a motor command by contributing to an overall population vector of activity delimiting the final movement direction. That is, each cell, broadly tuned to prefer a certain direction "voted" by changing activity a certain amount. The monkey moves in the direction determined by the vector sum of the individual directional preferences. Thus, the final direction is an ensemble product of the dynamic assembly of many individual contributing neurons—a process that is similar in both premotor and motor cortex. What is especially remarkable is that Georgopoulos and his colleagues could use these population vectors to predict the direction of movement when neural activity was recorded before movement actually began, that is, after the time the monkey saw the target, but before it actually began to move (figure 5.2, Georgopoulos, Kettner, and Schwartz, 1988). It is also relevant to our discussion of the Edelman model below, that population coding appears

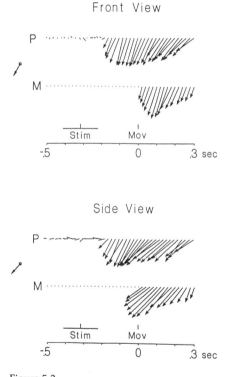

Figure 5.2
Predicting the direction of reaching movement by the population vectors of directionally specific cortical neurons in monkeys. Front and side views of time series of population (*P*) and movement (*M*) vectors are shown (normalized to maximum values). Note that at the onset of the target light (*Stim*), the population vectors point in the direction of the movement 160 ms before the onset of movement. (From Georgopoulos, Kettner, and Schwartz, 1988. Reprinted with permission.)

to occur simultaneously in many cortical layers and that there is enormous overlap in the connectivity between motor cortex and the motoneuron pools in the spinal cord. For example, spinal interneurons involved in reaching receive inputs from a number of supraspinal sources and in turn project to a variety of cortical and subcortical brain structures.

There are two major points, therefore, from this work on the neurophysiology of reaching. First, in concert with the Freeman work discussed previously, representations of action (like those of perception) are encoded not in fixed structures or topographies but in populations of activity, which emerge within a specific task context. While a particular neuron is preferentially tuned, the system only responds to patterns of neurons acting cooperatively. The origins and stability of individually tuned neurons, or of the population patterns they create, are not known in the reaching system, but in concert with the plasticity work we discuss next, it is likely that these are functionally established. The second point to be learned from this work is the overdetermined and overlapping connectivity in the reaching pathways. The functional significance of these pathways and their developmental importance are becoming increasingly apparent, as we discuss after the next section.

Dynamics of Change: Experience-driven Plasticity in the Adult Brain
Since Penfield's discovery that the sensory and motor functions of the body surfaces and parts are topographically mapped on the cerebral cortex, it has been enchanting to imagine that a clever homunculus resides in the brain, whose anatomy both represented and controlled the larger versions to which he or she was attached (figure 5.3, Penfield and Rasmussen, 1957, reprinted in Jeannerod, 1985). Since then, neurophysiologists have tacitly assumed both that these neatly ordered representations were established in early life by the anatomical maturation of the nervous system and that they were functionally static thereafter (Merzenich, Allard, and Jenkins, 1990).[1] Thus, the discoveries in the last decade of Merzenich and Kaas (1991) and their colleagues of experience-driven reorganization of skin sensory maps in adult monkey cortex has forced a drastic reexamination of those beliefs. Subsequently, investigators have found similar reorganization for somatic senses in subcortical areas and in the visual, auditory, and motor cortices in monkeys, and in other mammals (Kaas, 1991). The basic experimental procedure has been to carefully map the topography of the sensory or motor responses in accessible areas of the brain, to change the nature of the input to the map through functional means, or by altering the neural input directly, and then to remap the same individual after a varying period of time. These demonstrations of adult plasticity are very important for understanding development because first, they are additional confirmation that brain representations—even those which are "geographically" located—are dynamic processes and not fixed structures, and second, because they illuminate the very processes by which skill may be acquired in both developing and mature animals.

The experiments warrant reporting in some detail. Merzenich and his group at the University of California at San Francisco have concentrated their efforts on the primary somatosensory cortex (S-I) of New World monkeys, who have relatively unfissured brains with a clear somatotopic representation of their articulated and sensitive hands. Extensive electrophysiological mapping of the

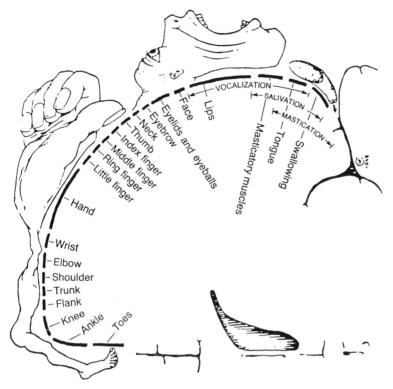

Figure 5.3
Topographical representations of the movements produced in humans by electrical stimulation of the motor cortex. In Penfield and Rasmussen's (1957) drawing, the "homunculus" is represented on a schematic vertical slice of the brain at the level of the frontal cortex. Different amounts of cortical area are devoted to different body parts, with the hands and face relatively more important.

cortical surface revealed a number of common features among individual monkeys. For example, the fingers were represented in accurate topographic order, that is, the ends of the fingers were near the border of the area, followed by the middle segments, followed by the proximal segments, and ordered from the lateral to the medial parts of the hand (figure 5.4). The dorsal surface of the hand was represented much more sparsely than the palmer surface, and the representations of each digit were abruptly separated from one another. In contrast to the ordered positioning of the topographic areas, their shapes and sizes varied substantially among individuals, including the proportion of area devoted to any one part of the hand, the detailed topographic relationships, and the completeness of the representations of the dorsal hand surface. The researchers hypothesized that the details of the cortical maps reflected the monkeys' use of their hands over their lifetimes (Jenkins, Merzenich, and Recanzone, 1990). Presumably, commonalities in the maps resulted from the ways all monkeys use their hands similarly, while the individual differences are the result of their idiosyncratic experiences.

The plasticity of these maps in the face of differing inputs was demonstrated in a number of ways. The experimenters surgically amputated one or two digits.

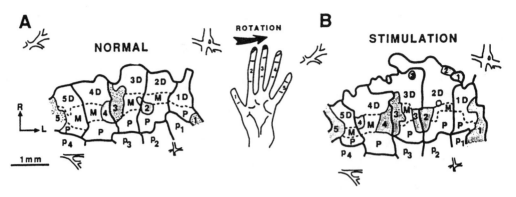

Figure 5.4
A, Mapping of the hand representation in cortical area 3b of the owl monkey before differential stimulation. *B*, Representation of the same area after 109 days of daily stimulation of digits 2 and 3 (and occasionally the tip of digit 4) for about 1½ hours a day. Note the enlarged representation of the stimulated digits. (From Jenkins, Merzenich, and Recanzone, 1990. Reprinted with permission.)

After amputation, the representations of the adjacent digits and of the palm expanded to occupy the topographic areas of the cortex formerly represented by the amputated digits. Sharp new discontinuous borders were formed, and new boundaries appeared between digits that were previously not adjacent (figure 5.5). The boundaries between the digits cannot be anatomically fixed and rigid, therefore, but must be continually dynamically established and maintained through function.

In a second series of experiments, the Merzenich group functionally fused the fingers of adult monkeys by suturing together the skin of two adjacent fingers while maintaining the normal nerve endings. After several months, when the monkeys were using the fused fingers as they would a single digit, their brains were remapped. In this case, the discontinuities between the mapped fingers were abolished (see figure 5.5) and the receptive fields overlapped. Remarkably, when the digits were subsequently surgically separated again, their distinctive boundaries returned.

Finally, these investigators were able to demonstrate cortical reorganization strictly as a function of the normal use of the fingers. Monkeys were trained to obtain a food reward by contacting a device that stimulated only the tips of one or two fingers. As a result of the thousands of discrete stimulations on their fingertips, the monkeys developed greatly enlarged representations in the somatosensory cortex of the digits involved (see figure 5.4). When the training stopped, the distorted representations returned to normal. These and other experiments reveal, in the words of Merzenich et al. (1990), that *"the specific details of cortical 'representations'—of the distributed, selective responses of cortical neurons—are established and are continually remodelled BY OUR EXPERIENCES throughout life"* (p.195) [emphasis in original].

How does experience lead to spatial "representation" of function? These experiments make clear that somatotopic organization cannot be the result of a direct anatomical map from hand to brain. Rather, it must be the *temporal structure* of experience—the strengthening of connections by temporally coincident acti-

A   Normal

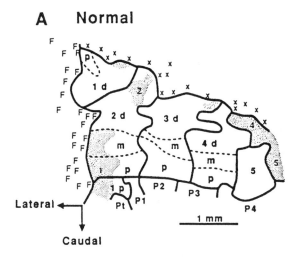

B
62 days after digit 3 amputation

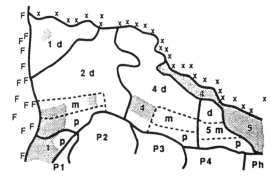

Figure 5.5
Representation of the hand surfaces within and adjacent to cortical area 3b in the owl monkey. Receptive field located on the face are indicated by an *F*. Sites at which neurons were driven by deep but not cutaneous receptor inputs are marked by an *x*. The large numbers 1 to 5 indicate the digits; *d*, *m*, and *p* are distal, middle, and proximal phalanges, respectively. *A*, Representation before amputation. *B*, 62 days after amputation of digit 3 in the same adult. Note that the former representations of digit 3 are now occupied by expanded representations of adjacent digits 2 and 4. (From Jenkins, Merzenich, and Recanzone, 1990. Reprinted by permission.)

vation—that allows the fine, dynamic mapping to emerge and to change. As Merzenich et al. (1990) emphasize, *"cortical areas spatially map TEMPORAL continua"* (p. 195) [emphasis in original]. How this temporal coding may operate is illustrated with studies of the visual cortex, as described in the next section.

Time-locked Dynamic Processes in the Visual Cortex
Elegant evidence of the primacy of temporal coding comes from the recent discovery of *functionally related* time-correlated activity in spatially distant cortical sites. There has been a persistent problem with all Hebbian, neuronal assembly-type theories of brain function. If representation of perceptual features is embedded in the relative strengthening of groups of neurons, then what happens with processing of complex scenes that activate many closely related assemblies? How can the system avoid the false conjunctions of features and thus generate unique categories?

The solution again appears to be distinctive coding in the *temporal* domain, and indeed Singer and his colleagues have found compelling evidence for such coding in the visual cortex (Engel, König, Kreiter, Schillen, and Singer, 1992; Singer, 1986, 1990; Singer, Artola, Engel, König, Kreiter, Löwel, and Schillen, 1993; Singer, Gray, Engel, König, Artola, and Bröcher, 1990). Recall that in each of the examples of real-time brain dynamics we discussed above, the basis of featural or performance coherence was the *time-locked* nature of the signal in populations or groups of neurons. Singer and his colleagues discovered that, in the cat visual cortex, stimuli induced synchronous oscillations of neural activity in spatially separate fields. These oscillations were recurrent synchronous bursts of neuronal groups, within a rather broad frequency range. A single stimulus figure seen by the cat elicited coherent bursting not only in groups of cells separated by more than 7 mm in the same field but also, remarkably, in both right and left hemispheres. The oscillations were synchronized with a zero phase lag; anatomical evidence indicated that this precise timing was not a result of common input, but rather came from parallel, corticocortical connections. Moreover, and most important for our developmental story, is that this coherence was stimulus-specific. As is well known, cells in the cat visual cortex respond preferentially to stimuli (in this case light bars) of different orientations and directions of movement. These researchers showed that in area 17, nonoverlapping receptive fields oscillated synchronously if they were activated by a single continuous stimulus, the light bar moving in one direction. However, the same fields fired in an uncorrelated fashion if the light bars were moving in opposite directions, thus violating the time-locked nature of the activation patterns (Engel et al., 1992). This is illustrated in Figure 5.6.

Taken in total these are important results for several reasons. First, they provide compelling support for the dynamic and self-organizing nature of mental activity—that categories of perception and action are assembled from multiple brain sites and interconnections on the basis primarily of temporal and not spatial codes. Second, they suggest a mechanism whereby both flexibility and uniqueness can coexist. Although cell groups coexist and overlap, their activity can be recognized as distinct because of a unique temporal code. At the same time, the same cell or group of cells may participate in different assemblies by changing their temporal relationships, providing a mechanism for both the extreme context

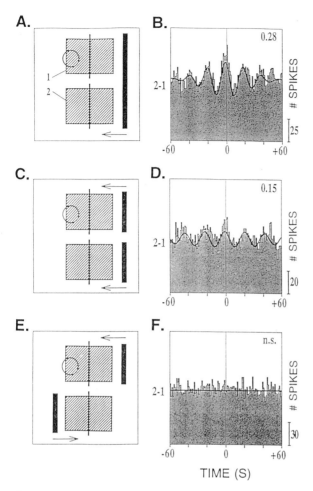

Figure 5.6
How long-range synchronization of neural oscillators is influenced by global stimulus coherence. Multiunit activity was recorded in two sites separated by 7 mm in area 17 of the cat visual cortex. The two cell groups preferred vertical orientations in the visual field. *A, C,* and *E* are schematic plots of the receptive fields under three different stimulus conditions. In *A* a long continuous bar moves across both fields, in *B* two independent light bars move in the same direction, and in *C* two bars move in opposite directions. The *circle* represents the center of the visual field, and the *thick line* drawn across each receptive field indicates the preferred orientation. *B, D,* and *F* show the respective crosscorrelograms obtained with each stimulus condition. (The crosscorrelogram is a measure of the phase entrainment of the oscillations of the neurons in the two groups.) With the long light bar, the two oscillatory responses were synchronized, as indicated by the strong modulation of the crosscorrelogram with alternating peaks and troughs (*B*). With the continuity of the stimulus weaker, the synchronization became weaker (*D*). Synchrony disappeared when the bars were not moving coherently (*F*). (From Engel, König, Kreiter, Schillen, and Singer, 1992. Reprinted with permission.)

sensitivity of perceptual responses and their gestalt character. Finally, the oscillatory nature of these synchronous responses is further evidence of the dynamic nature of all brain processes. As Engel et al. (1992) suggest, there are many advantages to synchronization through coupled oscillators that are not too tightly phased-locked, a general principle of biological organization that we discussed in chapter 4.

How does function—the varied and continual acting on and perceiving of the world—become topographically encoded in the brain? How, in turn, does that stored experience direct and refine our further actions? The common theme that emerges from these macroscopic studies of the brain is *time:* it is the temporal pattern and contiguity of the input—the smells, the sights, the sounds, the sensations in the skin and of movement—that become mapped into the spatial domain of attractor maps that emerge in real time and become "stored" as more permanent patterns over longer time. Similarly, it is the simultaneous assembly of a functionally related population of neurons that translates into the spatial domain of a movement direction. The picture is much different from that offered by the symbol-system view of the brain. This traditional cognitive view sees the brain as a storage bank of a large number of computer programs: stored symbols manipulated according to a predetermined logical hierarchy. The dynamic physical and biological systems we described in chapter 3 are better metaphors: systems where spatiotemporal patterns are self-assembled from large, often heterogeneous groups of elements and where "hard wiring" is replaced with patterns of varying degrees of stability. But most important, the dynamic characterization of brain function provides us with a mechanism for understanding where the stable, stored features of behavior *come from,* the enduring question in development.

Following Merzenich, Edelman, and others, we argue that it is this temporal association of perception and action that lays the foundation for behavioral development and, it is likely, for all other aspects of changing skill. To continue this argument, however, and extend it into the ontogenetic time scale, we shift now to Edelman's full theory, which spans embryology, neuroembryology, and the postnatal development of brain and behavior.

The Theory of Neuronal Group Selection

The great strength of Edelman's synthesis is a coherent, process-oriented account of behavioral development from the embryo onward. The overall theme is the *epigenetic* nature of the entire developmental process. Epigenesis means that development enfolds in a contingent and historical fashion. At both the cellular level and higher, events that lead to increased complexity and diversity of structures and functions are all dependent upon events that preceded them. This means that both in the formation of the primary anatomical structures of the nervous system and in the functionally imposed maps that are later etched by experience, developing systems exhibit properties that are emergent from their interactions and not dependent on preexisting codes. Edelman emphasizes *selection* as the primary developmental mechanism: while epigenetic processes produce brain structures that are modally similar in all members of a species, these same processes also produce—through selection—enormous individual variability at the level of anatomical connectivity of the individual neurons and groups. Selection also occurs postnatally as experience selects among neuronal groups by specifically strengthening those connections whose activities are correlated with functional behavior. As we explain below, it is the temporal coherence of sensory and motor signals that acts as the selective process.

What Edelman has done, and what we summarize here, is to provide a neural account of the more macroscropic dynamic principles of behavioral development to which we devote most of this book. As we move through his argument, we will continue to point out the parallels between these levels of analysis. To understand his account of neural ontogeny, however, the reader must first be familiar with what Edelman considers to be the fundamental psychological task of development: the perceptual categorization of the world. We introduce the important issue of categorization here and expand our discussion more fully in the next chapter.

Perceptual Categorization and the Origins of Behavior
The primitive in all behavior and mental functioning is categorization. Intelligent behavior requires in some manner the comparison of ongoing perceptual activity to past activity. For example, if an organism has acted to avoid danger (or secure food) in the context of a specific pattern of sensory activation, then patterns of activation that have sufficient overlap with the original experience will lead to a similar response. The *generalization* of behavior demonstrates the existence of a perceptual category. Now, for students of conceptual development, generalizations of behaviors from one time to another barely skim the theoretical complexity of human concepts and the knowledge that allows people to say such things as, "A whale looks like a fish but it isn't one really." We address this link between categories and higher concepts more fully in the next chapter. Suffice it to say now that we believe that Edelman's theory of neuronal group selection can be usefully applied to the problem of categorization at the multiple levels of categorization that are inherent in intelligent behavior. In this section, we introduce Edelman's theory by using the terms *categories* and *categorization* as Edelman defined them.

Edelman's use of the concept of categories is simpler even than response generalization because it involves no external response at all. Indeed, Edelman's concept of category centers on the core meaning of concept that transcends the specific categories, perception, action, and knowledge. Edelman defines *perception* as the "discrimination of an object or an event through one or more sensory modalities, separating them [sic] from the background or from other objects or events" (1987, p. 26). *Perceptual categorization*, then, "is a process by which an individual may treat nonidentical objects or events as equivalent" (p. 26). However, for Edelman the equivalence emerges in the mapping between two disjunctive processes. The category *is* the mapping and it need not be between an object and a response nor lead to a positive or negative consequence. In Edelman's view, categories emerge from the dynamic interaction of groups of neurons; the mappings—the categories—self-organize through their reciprocal interaction with one another.

Perceptual categorization viewed in this way, in Edelman's way, is the essential developmental core because there are no immutable categories in the world which tell animals what things are and how they must act in relation to them. The solutions to the problems of perceptual taxonomies can only be broadly anticipated by phylogenetic adaptation. The crucial details must be acquired by individuals within their lifetimes. The individuals' discovered solutions to this problem are in turn determined by their own ecological niche and their particular functional adaptation to that niche. Thus, for each organism, categories are relative and not immutable, nor are they veridical descriptions of an abstract physical world. Although the world contains information for the organism, the information is always in relation to the organism's past and current functioning in the world. The problem for the developing nervous system, then, is to make sense of the world with sufficient specificity to know how to correctly act within an information-rich environment, and at the same time, be able to generalize broadly to recognize novel objects, even from very few instances of that category.

There is continuing active debate about the nature of the information in the world (e.g., Gibson, 1979) or how specifically the organism has been prepared by phylogeny to form perceptual categories (e.g., Spelke, 1988; Marler, 1991). Nonetheless, we fully agree with Edelman that perceptual categorization, as broadly defined to include perception of self-movement as well as signals from outside the individual, forms the base of cognition and action. It is essential to remember, however, that at both the neural level and the behavioral level that we describe, *these categories are dynamic entities.* They are entirely dependent on cues, contexts, and salience, and on the dynamic history and the current state of the animal. Some categories may be very stable, easily called forth, and not easily changed. Others may be far more mutable, their attractor basins easily moved by new perceptual information. The diverse and overlapping nature of the neuroanatomy, as we describe below, insures that no two category recollections are assembled in exactly the same way: this flexibility is the essential source of both generalization and novel forms of cognition and action.

Development by Selection
It is our central theme that perceptual categories are dynamically established in ontogeny and maintained in daily use by the process of *selection.* In classic Darwinian theory, natural selection works because natural populations are always genetically (and phenotypically) diverse. At the species level, adaptation to an environment, and to a changing environment, is possible because there is sufficient heritable diversity in the population to produce differential reproduction. As many have recognized, this diversity is manifested in the behavior of organisms as well as their anatomy and physiology. In dynamic systems terms, natural selection creates attractor basins in the population's n-dimensional state space. That is, in the hypothetical state space bounded by any number of species characteristics, the real population only occupies particular regions, as only certain constellations of attributes will occur together. But these basins are not fixed. Just as the maps created by odorants in the rabbit olfactory bulb responded dynamically to the cumulative history of the rabbit's experience with smells, the attractor maps of a population are dynamically altered with changes in the environment. On the ontogenetic time scale, a similar dynamic is envisioned: imagine that a newborn animal has a large, but not infinite, potential state space for any set of attributes. With development, the attractor basins will shift to more

functionally specific sites on that space. The sites emerge by selection, as the animal perceives the world and produces actions on it. Depending on the particular behavioral collections, the basins may be more or less stable. For motor actions, for example, the basins for walking are quite stable and only disrupted by injury or prolonged inactivity, while those for playing the piano have to be maintained by continual practice, practice being the repeated cycle of action and perception that selects the musically correct sequences and pressures of the fingers.

As in traditional Darwinian theory, a selectionist view of development requires a source of diversity and variability from which adaptive patterns can be chosen. If development is seen primarily as a hierarchical accretion of more complex structures, then variability and diversity are viewed only as "noise" in the system, much as noise in a telephone circuit detracts from the signal in the point-to-point wiring. Individual differences are deviations from modal performances. If variability among individuals is high, we cannot detect group differences, and we will conclude that our hypothesized effect does not exist. This mode of thinking, and its operationalization in experimental design, works against detecting selectionist processes because we do not consider variability *in and of itself* as important. A dynamic view of development, in sharp contrast, considers the origins and functions of variability as absolutely central for understanding change. Variability is the very source of new adaptive forms in ontogeny and in real time, just as it is in phylogenetic time. Variability is revealed when systems are in transition, and when they undergo these shifts, the system is free to explore new and more adaptive associations and configurations. Individual differences reveal the range of possible state spaces the system can occupy and the range of possible trajectories between stable attractor states. Individual similarities, in turn, tell us about the constraints and limitations of that space and how different individuals may have converged on the same selected solutions. Individual pathways toward similar performance describe the ways the components can be assembled and the dynamics of how the space can be explored. We specifically use these ideas of variability and similarities among individuals in subsequent chapters to show how developmental trajectories can be mapped and how the interacting forces that constitute a developmental system can be revealed.

While we retain the classic Darwinian emphasis on variability as the source of new forms, we also agree with the post-Darwinian thinkers (e.g., Gould and Lewontin, 1979) who eschew the notion that selection produces a series of "optimal" fits between organism and environment. We believe that in development, as in evolution, change consists of successive "make do" solutions that work, given abilities, goals, and history of the organism at the time. We like the analogy put forth by Varela, Thompson, and Rosch (1992) and first used by Edelman and Gall (1979) in reference to antibody production:

> John needs a suit. In a fully symbolic and representational world, he goes to his tailor who measures him and produces a nice suit according to the exact specifications of his measurements. There is, however, another obvious possibility, one that does not demand so much from the environment. John goes to several department stores and chooses a suit that fits well from among the various ones available. Although these do not suit him exactly

they are good enough, and he chooses the optimal one for fit and taste. Here we have a good selectionist alternative that uses some optimal criteria of fitness. The analogy admits, however, further refinement. John, like any human being, cannot buy a suit in isolation from the rest of what goes on in his life. In buying a suit, he considers how his looks will affect the response of his boss at work, the response of his girl friend, and he may also be concerned with political and economic factors. Indeed, the very decision to buy a suit is not given from the outset as a problem, but is constituted by the global situation of his life. His final choice has the form of satisfying some very loose constraints (e.g., being well dressed) but does not have the form of a fit—even less so of an optimal fit—to any of these constraints (p. 194)

The analogy is especially appropriate: organisms are active seekers of solutions, they have biases and goals, they try out various alternatives, and the fit is *ad hoc* rather than prescribed. They do not build suits from various assorted collections of sleeves, pockets, zippers, and buttons but select the best one of the current lot that does the job. Development may involve being a better shopper—remembering what sizes come closest, discriminating colors and fabrics, and shopping more efficiently—but along the way, there are many suits that will do just fine. Again, the key is having a diversity of choices.

The Anatomical Bases and Functions of Neural Diversity

We saw in earlier sections that perception and action are represented in the central nervous system (CNS) by the dynamic patterns generated by large populations of interconnected neurons. These patterns may have stable features over time scales ranging from fractions of a second to much longer, but they were always a function of the historical and current context of the activity and the current state of the organism. In the case of rabbit olfaction, Freeman has suggested that patterns of odor recognition are selected from a chaotic background of neural activity—activity that was highly complex and diverse, but not infinitely so. In each of the cases, sniffing, reaching, and finger use, the distributed nature of the representations depends entirely on highly interconnected networks of neurons within each area of the brain and in the links among them. A diverse and overlapping anatomical structure is also an essential feature of selectionist theories of neurological and behavioral development. In the next sections, therefore, we first summarize Edelman's argument for the anatomical substrate for neuronal selection. We then follow with an outline of how these structures emerge dynamically during embryology. The concluding section describes how such neural architecture functions in behavioral development.

The first part of Edelman's theory is concerned with the nature of diversity in the nervous system. Neural diversity is the cornerstone of the theory because without it, the nervous system could not acquire and modify perceptual categories to be both specific and general. What, then, is neural diversity? How does it originate? Why is neural diversity important? We address these questions in turn.

Variability in the Structure of the Nervous System
In animals with complex nervous systems, anatomists can recognize and name various nuclei, tracts, layers, fissures, circuits, and other morphologically distinct areas that are common to all members of that species. Over many years, neuroanatomists and physiologists have traced the elaborate connectivities of the brain through these anatomically defined circuits. One interpretation of the gross neuroanatomy is that the CNS is wired much like a complex telephone exchange, with point-to-point wiring, in which neural signals are processed like telephone messages through various relays and way stations, undergoing transformations along the way. This anatomical view, in turn, supports computer-based models of the brain where symbols are manipulated by algorithmic rules.

A step down from the gross anatomy of the brain a very different picture emerges. Edelman points out (table 5.1) that the nervous system is indeed

Table 5.1
Sites and Levels of Neuronal Variation

A. Variation in genetic traits and developmental primary processes: cell division, migration, adhesion, differentiation, and death

B. Variation in cell morphology
   1. Cell shape and size
   2. Dendritic and axonal arborizations
      a. Spatial distribution
      b. Branching order
      c. Length of branches
      d. Number of spines

C. Variation in connection patterns
   1. Number of inputs and outputs
   2. Connection order with other neutrons
   3. Local vs. long-range connections
   4. Degree of overlap of arbors

D. Variation in cytoarchitectonics
   1. Number or density of cells
   2. Thickness of individual cortical layers
   3. Relative thickness of supragranular, infragranular, and granular layers
   4. Position of somata
   5. Variation in columns
   6. Variation in strips or patches of terminations
   7. Variations in anisotropy of fibers

E. Variation in transmitters
   1. Between cells in a population
   2. Between cells at different times

F. Variation in dynamic response
   1. In synaptic chemistry and size of synapse
   2. In electrical properties
   3. In excitatory/inhibitory ratios and locations of these synapses
   4. In short- and long-term synaptic alteration
   5. In metabolic state

G. Variation in neuronal transport

H. Variation in interactions with glia

From Edelmen (1987) with permission.

extremely variable at many levels, from the size and shapes of the cells and their processes, to the number, type, and degree of connections, to the grouping of cells into larger layers, columns, patches, and fibers, and even to the electrical and chemical communications between the neurons.   But two particular properties of local complexity and variability have fundamental importance in the acquisition of perceptual categorization: degeneracy and reentrant structures. Because these are somewhat difficult concepts and new ones in psychology, we elaborate further.

The notion of *degeneracy* in neural structure means that any single function can be carried out by more than one configuration of neuronal signals. At the same time, a single group of neurons can participate in several functional relations. Recall that in the account of the rabbit olfactory bulb, Freeman postulated the necessity of groups of neurons acting together whose synaptic strengths are modified by the associations of the odor and the reinforcement. This is similar to Edelman's definition of a neuronal group: "a collection of cells of similar or variant types, ranging in number from hundreds to thousands, that are closely connected in their intrinsic circuitry and whose mutual dynamic interaction may be further enhanced by increases in synaptic efficiency" (1987, pp. 46–47).

Edelman maintains that vast collections of such neuronal groups are laid down in early development and constitute a "primary repertoire." From this diverse primary repertoire certain synapses, or patterns of connectivity, become strengthened with experience. Now the nervous system must be prepared to interpret both a wide range of sensory signals *and* to recognize *specific* signals in an accurate manner. If the connections in the neuronal groups are broadly strengthened, i.e., if the stimuli excite many groups at the same time, the system will respond to a wide class of stimuli, but not in a distinctive manner. For example, all round, small objects would be recognized, but not apples from oranges. Conversely, if only a very narrow class of groups is strengthened, the brain might respond to highly specific stimuli, but be unable to generalize. Here, for instance, it would know only red apples in a particular orientation, but not apples in general. So in order for these neuronal groups to make sense out of the stream of signals from the periphery, the primary repertoire must be degenerate—sufficiently overlapping so that stimuli impinging on only part of the network would invoke a generalized response, but not so broad as to exclude highly specific properties. The anatomical connections must insure that the system is "tuned somewhere between the extremes of absolute specificity and complete range" (1987, p. 56). Degeneracy in this form is a necessary condition for TNGS to work, as Edelman has shown in various simulations of such distributed networks. Because any neuronal group can participate in several functions at the same time that a particular function can be executed by more than one set of neuronal groups, there is both variability and flexibility for the selection of perceptual categories. Our picture of this process of experience-driven clumping and pruning may be made clearer by imagining an alternative: development proceeding by the establishment of highly specific wiring pathways, much like an electrician wires a house or a technician builds a switchboard. (The difficulty with the latter explanation is, of course, that the electrician or the technician needs a highly specific blueprint; the origin of the developmental "blueprint" remains the central unsolved logical problem.)

The actual anatomical bases for neural degeneracy, according to Edelman, are likely in the highly branched connections between neurons in and between many different regions of the nervous system. Arbors of individual neurons often branch over whole areas of the brain or spinal cord, insuring that the output of a single cell is widely distributed to a network of other neurons. When these branches are multiplied by millions of neurons, the result is a vast network of variant interconnections. The dynamic, emergent functioning of the rabbit olfactory bulb and the monkey somatosensory and motor cortices, which we described above, could only be accomplished with such widely distributed groups. This makes groups and populations of neurons, not single cells, the operational units.

The second characteristic of CNS organization that is essential to Edelman's developmental story is *reentry*, or the anatomical interrelating of several or many simultaneous perceptual and motor representations. Reentry is necessary to account for the *coordination* of responses across several sensory modalities. When a person experiences an apple—and immediately categorizes it as such—the experience is visual, but also invokes the smell of the apple, its taste, its feel, its heft, and a constellation of sensations and movements associated with various actions upon the apple—slicing it, eating it, making applesauce, and so on. The experience of any set of objects or events is nearly always multimodal—even simple looking involves eye movements and their perceptual consequences. If the responses to perceptual information of many types are to hang together, then information reaching the different collections of neuronal groups must be correlated. The basis for the correlation, as we introduced above, must be the temporal contiguity of the incoming signals. As we bite into the apple, the feel of crispness against our teeth and the fibers in our mouth, the tart and sweet taste, the distinctive smell, and the movements of chewing are always perfectly correlated throughout the course of the event. This perfect temporal association of multimodal information is perhaps the only perceptual invariant that spans all ages, contexts, and modalities. We believe, with Edelman, that this correlation is the primary link between the mind and the world.

How, then, does the nervous system compute these massive, dynamic correlations, given the complex interconnectivities and variability of its structure? *Reentry* is the important neural requirement: to carry out perceptual categorization dynamically, i.e., by an uninstructed system, "two independent abstracting networks must work simultaneously (and disjunctively) in response to a stimulus and then interact by reentry to provide some abstract higher-order linkage of their representations" (1987, p. 61).

Consider a very simplified example of how a reentrant network can perform classification with a *classification couple*, as indicated in figure 5.7. For the sake of illustration, let us imagine that the input to the couple arises from biting into the aforementioned apple. One classification couple might receive a pattern of neural firing from the somatosensory neurons in the skin and the lining of the mouth which detect the mechanical deformations of biting and chewing. As you bite and chew, your skin receptors detect a particular space and time distribution of stimulation, which is abstractly represented at this first step. The second feature detector abstracts the pattern of, say, the impulses from the taste buds or the olfactory neurons, which are excited specifically to the characteristics of apple in a dynamic fashion similar to what Freeman described in the rabbit. These patterns

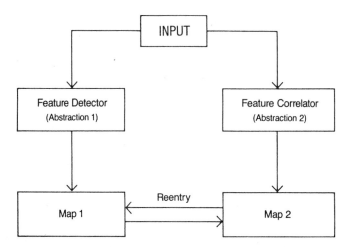

Figure 5.7
A classification couple operating through reentry in real time. The stimulus input is independently sampled by two different networks, one of which carries out feature detection and the other, feature correlation. Selected mapped responses at higher levels are related through reentry by reciprocally arranged connections between mapped areas. (From Edelman, 1987. Reprinted with permission.)

are transmitted independently to sets of degenerate maps, which are, in turn, anatomically connected to one another so that their input can be reciprocally regulated. The input to the two feature detectors must be correlated in real time; the neurons indicating downward pressure of the jaw and those coding a particularly strong sensation of apple taste as the apple is crushed in the teeth must have an invariant and self-consistent real-world relation. Because the two maps are interconnected, they form a network between them that links the patterns detected originally by separate sensory systems.

Now recall that connections among groups of neurons are selectively strengthened by their repeated function. As you continue to bite and chew the apple, similar, but not identical patterns are reiteratively generated in the haptic and olfactory or taste maps *and in their mutual, self-consistent interconnections,* which must have this invariant relation because of their perfect real temporal association. This process *selects,* therefore, groups of synapses strengthened by their association in the real world, and detected through signals from the two coherent modalities. This selection is the basis of perceptual categorization, as categories of objects and actions "fall out" of their correlated features. Thus, through perception of the object through various senses and our perception of our own actions on the object, we establish a long-lasting—but dynamic—association in memory of a category of perception and action related to eating apples. Because the networks are degenerate, the category may be invoked through many pathways—the sight of the apple alone may invoke associations of also consuming it. And most important for development—we return to this point later—these degenerate and reentrant connections allow for the emergence of new associative functions not present in either set of the original groups.

Another anatomical requirement of TNGS is that the nervous system have reentrant networks both locally within areas and at long distances between nuclei. This is needed to maintain feature correlations at all the levels of CNS processing. Consider again the neural patterns coding the sight, feel, and taste of apples relayed from the periphery to the higher cortical centers. How does the nervous system keep track of the temporal simultaneity of the information from various modalities? If these multilevel networks were not in place, representations from each modality would need to be serially marked, like the lines of a computer program, for the system to keep track of what follows what as processing proceeds. However, if the CNS has reentrant connections at all the levels, then internal categories can be generated simultaneously in a parallel manner and separate time-and-place markers for the signals are not needed as they pass along the networks. Reentry at all levels allows for a continual spatio-temporal representation of the sensory input.

Edelman maintains that the anatomical evidence that the nervous system is built to form categories in such a manner is compelling. The visual system provides an excellent example of the multiple, parallel, and highly interconnected nature of the brain. It was earlier believed that visual information was processed by two pathways: a subcortical pathway from the retina through the colliculus, and the primary pathway through the lateral geniculate nuclei to the visual cortex. Recent evidence, however, points to several related streams of visual cortical processing, all of which are intimately related to the corresponding control of eye movements. In figure 5.8 (provided by Peter Schiller; see Schiller, 1986, 1993; Felleman and Van Essen, 1991), we reproduce a schematic representation of a model of oculomotor control in primates, which clearly shows the interrelated, reentrant nature of the pathways between and within nuclei and brain areas. Note, for example, the connections to the superior colliculus (SC), which include not only a direct pathway from the retina but also reentrant pathways from the primary visual cortex, middle temporal area, and frontal eye field pathways, all of which process different types of visual information. In addition, the superior colliculus receives inhibitory influence from the substantia nigra through the basal ganglia. Thus, both the eye (and head) movements generated by the basal ganglia and the input received through the eye in parallel channels are multiply and continuously linked and correlated. Johnson (1990; Morton and Johnson, 1991) provides an excellent model of how the development of these neuroanatomical pathways is related to the development of visual attention and face recognition in infants.

The Creation of Diversity in Neuroembryology

Having established that diversity in the form of degenerate and reentrant networks is an essential precondition for behavioral development through a selective process, Edelman proceeds to show how basic embryological processes—as dynamic systems—create that variability. The question is how the fundamental, species-specific elements of the neuroanatomy, what Edelman calls the primary repertoire, is laid down as the basis for experience-driven perceptual categorization.

Development of the Primary Repertoire

As stated earlier, epigenesis is the theme that unites developmental processes across the life span. From the time of fertilization, ontogeny is contingent and

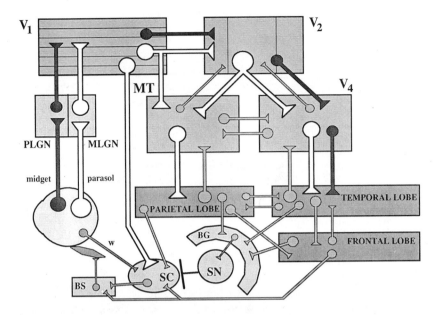

Figure 5.8
Major pathways involved in the generation of visually guided saccadic eye movements. Depicted are three pathways that originate in the retina in the midget, parasol, and w-like (*w*) retinal ganglion cells. The midget cells project to the parvocellular (*PLGN*) and the parasol cells to the magnocellular (*MLGN*) portions of the lateral geniculate nucleus. These two systems remain separate as they project to the striate cortex (V1). Both the midget and parasol systems project to areas V2 and V4. However, cells projecting from the striate cortex to the superior colliculus (*SC*) and to the middle temporal area (*MT*), either directly or via area V2, are driven predominantly by the parasol system. The visual cortical areas are extensively interconnected, even more so than indicated. Not shown are extensive feedback connections from extrastriate cortex to the striate cortex and projections from the striate cortex back to the lateral geniculate nucleus. The extrastriate areas and the parietal, temporal, and frontal lobes make extensive connections with both the superior colliculus and the basal ganglia (*BG*). The substantia nigra (*SN*) has a major inhibitory influence on the superior colliculus. The other inputs to the superior colliculus, including the direct retinal projection from the w-like cells, make mostly excitatory connections with this structure. The brain stem (*BS*) receives extensive projections from both the frontal lobe and the superior colliculus. The abducens, trochlear, and oculomotor nuclei in the brain stem contain the cells that form the final common path to the eye muscles to produce the eye movements. For a more detailed description of the subdivisions and connections of the visual system see Felleman and Van Essen, 1991. (Courtesy of Peter Schiller.)

emergent. While processes are bounded by genetic constraints, the local morphogenetic details cannot be encoded specifically in the genes, but arise from milieu-dependent and contextual events. This interplay between genetic and epigenetic processes extends to the most "biological" level of development—early embryogenesis. We summarize here Edelman's account of embryogenesis and the formation of the primary neural repertoire for two reasons. First, because developmental psychologists may be less familiar with contemporary neuroembryology, it is important to emphasize the continuity of dynamic process from the earliest stages. And second, and most important, we believe that this account (and the work of Edelman and the many others on which it is based) renders forever meaningless the perennial developmental dichotomies of nature vs. nurture or genetics vs. environment.

Dynamic Processes in the Early Embryo
According to Edelman, the basic developmental question in embryology is the emergence of *form*. (In that behavior is time-dependent form, we can pose all of behavioral development as a similar fundamental problem.) Specifically, Edelman asks, how does the genetic code, which is essentially one-dimensional—a string of chemicals—specify a three-dimensional animal? Edelman reminds us that the great triumph of molecular biology, the unlocking of the structure and coding of DNA, while answering the question of how traits are *transmitted*, does not itself tell us how genes *determine* traits. Consider that all animals begin as a single cell, with mammals having about 10^5 genes. At maturity, the animal will have 10^{11} cells, with 200 tissue types, 10^9 physiological control loops, and in humans, 10^{15} synapses in the brain. The scale and complexity of the mature animal far exceeds the scale of the DNA code, and indeed there is no relation between the DNA content of the genome and the complexity of the species (Edelman, 1988, p.12). Thus, while guided by the genes, complexity of form must arise *during development* in self-organizing fashion: the genes cannot store the information on the time and space position of each cell of each animal.

How can this happen? During embryogenesis, cells divide, they change character, they move, and they organize into larger collectives of tissues, organs, and organ systems. Embryologists have focused on these cell and tissue dynamics themselves as a source of order and complexity, in particular on how cells cooperate to mutually influence each other to form patterns. Just as in the classic physical dynamic systems that we described in chapter 3, patterns emerge from the collective influence of systems with many potentially independent elements, under general constraints. The role of the genes can be loosely compared to the nonspecific control parameters in these physical systems. Thus, while pressure and temperature, for example, are crucial determinants of the nature of the patterns in the Belousov-Zhabotinskii chemical reaction, or in the patterns of flow in a pipe, they themselves do not specify the local details of the patterns. (This analogy is only partially correct, however, because the genetic control parameters regulate development in a continually interactive manner, with cycles of mutual influence between the genes and the rest of the cell.)

Edelman proposes several *primary processes of development*, depicted in figure 5.9. Cell division, cell motion, and cell death are the *driving force processes*, while cell adhesion and differentiation are the *regulatory processes*. During development

Primary Process of Development

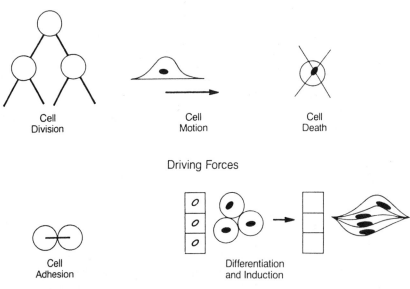

Cell
Division

Cell
Motion

Cell
Death

Driving Forces

Cell
Adhesion

Differentiation
and Induction

Regulatory Processes

Figure 5.9

Cartoons of the primary processes of development. The "driving force" processes—cell division, cell motions, and cell death—are regulated by adhesion and differentiation events. The key event is milieu-dependent differentiation or embryonic induction, which occurs not between single cells but between different cell collectives. (From Edelman, 1987. Reprinted by permission.)

these processes sometimes work independently and sometimes interactively, the first processes changing the number and location of the cells, leading to changes in the mechanical properties of the embryo, and the second leading to different types of interactions between cells. Overall, early embryogenesis is marked by what is known as *induction,* where cells of different histories are brought together and where their new locations, in turn, lead to changes in their gene expressions. Thus, fundamental cellular changes are signaled from cell surfaces in interaction with other cells. As stated by Edelman,

> It appears likely that induction involves signaling from the cell surface to the nucleus of the induced cells in a tissue. Induction occurs in general not between single cells but rather between cells in groups or cell collectives, as we will call such groups. (1988, p. 18).

Not only is the timing of induction dependent on the nature of the surrounding tissues but crucially on the *location* of those tissues. The ability of cells to detect and react to location is what Edelman calls their *topobiological potency; topobiology* is his term for place-dependent interactions. For example, in the embryo, *gastrulation* is the transformation of the first sheet of similar cells (the blastula) into the structure with a primitive neural tube and the three primary germ layers, ectoderm, mesoderm, and endoderm—the sources of future tissues and organs. The cells in the blastula do not have equal potential to migrate to produce these layers; only those in particular positions do so, and they only have this potential at specific points in time. Any particular cell may act as an inducer of say, the neural tube, not by its individual characteristics, but only as it acts in relation to its neighbors and in the historical context of that group of cells. Moreover, the processes of cell division, and especially cell motion and cell death, are not exactly or deterministically controlled, but are rather stochastic processes. According to Edelman:

> These observations have provided us with a basis for a hypothesis on the evolutionary selection of regulative properties of cells in a neighborhood: while the location of a cell within a particular *collective* in a certain period of time is important, its *exact* location in that collective does not in general appear to be critical. As long as there is a sufficient number of cells of similar histories, the death of a particular cell would not alter the fate of adjoining cells. (1988, p. 24)

> The pathways of induction and determination involve a historical series of milieu dependent gene expressions that are coupled to those mechanical and mechanochemical events that actually govern the achievement of form and pattern. At any one time, there is an interplay between the place, scale, and size of bordering collectives, and various inductive molecular signals not only maintain the pattern so far established but also transform it into a new pattern. (1988, p. 26)

The theme of development from these earliest stages to the acquisition of complex human cognition is the emergence of pattern and form. As we introduced in the first chapters of this book, accounts of development must explain two seemingly contradictory tendencies. At the macroscopic level, there is great uniformity and regularity in developmental outcome: striking species similarities in the precise events that create a human embryo and fetus from the fertilized egg, and striking convergences in normal humans on how they act, think, and communicate. At the same time, we see at the "local" level diversity, indeterminacy, and the emergence of pattern from seemingly uninstructed precursors; no one cell contains the code for neural tube induction, and no one neuron or even brain nucleus determines patterns of perception and action.

It is in the embryological events that lead to the primary neural repertoire that these tendencies can be resolved mechanistically. That is, in proposing molecular mechanisms that control the spatial and temporal dynamics of early morphogenesis, Edelman attempts to link gene products—the source of the heritable similarities among members of a species—and the emergent patterns which detail complexity and diversity not specifically coded within the genes per se. By then showing how this primary repertoire anticipates and is molded by experience within the world, Edelman bridges the gap between the diversity and similarity of structure and its counterparts in function.

The Role of the Cell Surface in Morphogenesis

Edelman sees the cell surface as playing a key role in the cell interactions that result in evolving form during embryogenesis. The cell surface is important because that is where the essential communication between cells is mediated, where the cell receives signals from the environment, and because the cell surface (a two-dimensional sheet) reflects and responds to all other morphological changes resulting from cell shape, division, and migration. In particular, the cell surface has been found to be a complex layer with receptors to a wide variety of molecules, where local phase transitions can result from mechanical as well as chemical changes within and outside of the cell. The surface thus responds to internal events: chemical changes in the cell cytoplasm lead to alterations in the structure of proteins and produce corresponding changes in cell shape, rigidity, and mobility. For example, the chemical events of fertilization set in motion a structural polarity in the egg that determines the fate of subsequent cell divisions. Likewise, the cell surface responds to mechanical and chemical influences from its neighboring cells and adjusts its own properties in response. These reciprocal mechanicochemical interactions between cells are the immediate cause of the unfolding structural complexity of the embryo through cell migration and condensation, cell division, and cell death.

The driving forces at the cell surface are mediated, according to Edelman, through a series of specific molecules which change the nature of the adhesion of cell surfaces to one another. These molecules, so-called cell adhesion molecules (CAMs), are, in turn, specific gene products that act as the translators between the regulatory genes and their three-dimensional developmental manifestations. The CAMs link cells into collectives—different CAMs specifying differential cell borders. The binding properties of the cells linked by these different CAMs are controlled by the cells themselves through signals exchanged between collectives. As cells bind into these various and specific collectives, the binding itself changes the form of the cell, inducing changes of gene expression by signaling back to the genome. Thus, an interactive cycle is established where the alteration of CAM binding alters morphology, and where changes in morphology alter CAM expression. This cycle is depicted schematically in figure 5.10.

Readers are referred to Edelman's *Neural Darwinism* (1987) and *Topobiology* (1988) for the details of this process. For our purposes, the CAM cycle illustrates a number of principles supporting a dynamic theory of development. First, while the process is under ultimate genetic control, it is also historical and contingent, with gene expression not autonomously regulated, but acting in response to morphological events outside of the nucleus and even outside of the cell. Once the CAM is expressed, a series of changes cascade from that initial event. Because of this contingent, cascading effect, *variability* at the local level is inevitably introduced. As in other dynamic systems, this process illustrates significant nonlinearity: there are likely only a small number of different CAMs that can be expressed at different times during early ontogeny. Yet, through their differential expression, and the contingent nature of the succeeding morphological and chemical events, the expression of these specific molecules at particular times leads to large changes downstream, so to speak. Because there is no one-to-one correspondence between the chemical messages and the fate of any particular cell, the products of CAM-regulated morphogenesis are statistical, rather than strictly determined. CAMs modulate rather than control specifically because the locus of control resides both in the messages from the genes and in the emergent patterns created through those messages.

A   CAM Cycle

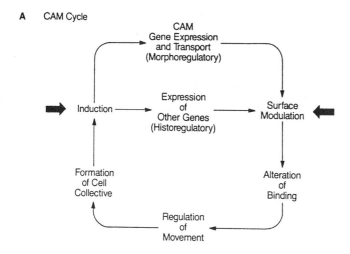

B   Epigenetic Sequences

Development:

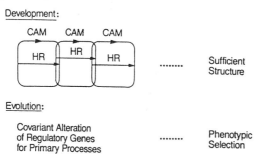

Evolution:

Covariant Alteration
of Regulatory Genes   ········   Phenotypic
for Primary Processes   Selection

Figure 5.10

A cell adhesion molecule (*CAM*) regulatory cycle in an epigenetic sequence. Early induction signals (*heavy arrows at left*) lead to CAM gene expression. Surface modulation alters the binding rates of cells. This regulates morphogenetic movements, which in turn affect embryonic induction or milieu-dependent differentiation. The inductive agents can again affect CAM genes expression as well as expression of other genes for specific tissues. The *heavy arrows at left* and *right* refer to candidate signals for initiation of induction that are still unknown. These signals could result from global surface modulation as a result of CAM binding or from release of morphogens affecting induction, or from both; in any case a mechanicochemical link between gene expression and morphogenesis is provided by the cycle. (From Edelman, 1987. Reprinted by permission.)

In the early development of the nervous system, therefore, emerging specificity of pattern and place is a product of a relatively small number of CAM molecules expressed differentially and at different times in the developmental sequence in a dynamic fashion. As development proceeds, as Edelman states:

> An extraordinarily large number of neural patterns can result from the functions of a relatively small number of CAMs of different specificities under the influence of five or six surface modulation mechanisms. The early regulation of CAM genes with subsequent and relatively independent expression of cell differentiation under control of historegulatory genes, as is seen in the CAM cycle, could lead to a virtually unlimited set of patterns. Diversity in these patterns would originate from the *obligate local fluctuations in modulation mechanisms.* [emphasis added] (1987, p. 102)

The theme of "obligate local fluctuations" reoccurs, as we have seen, in our accounts of all dynamic systems, both physical and biological. These local fluctuations and the resulting sensitivity to initial conditions mean that the exact nature of the resulting local diversity cannot be predicted. This "noise," however, is also the ultimate source of new and emergent patterns because it provides the variability and flexibility necessary to generate new combinations upon which selection can work. However, just as physical dynamic systems are globally deterministic, Edelman's regulator hypothesis also is consistent with the regional consistency of neural patterns seen within a particular species. That is, by the genetic regulation of CAM expression, insured through phylogenetic selection, the process is kept on course, and the local variability is generated within global consistency. The result of early neurogenesis, therefore, is both a modal and species-constant neural architecture and, at the more microscopic level, a system of enormous three-dimensional variability in the number and connectivity of the neurons.

Cellular Processes of Neural Development

The specific cellular processes involved in the development of the nervous system continue this theme of both global ordering in the tracts, layers, and nuclei, and local obligate variability. In particular, following the synthesis of Cowan (1978), Edelman describes the following phases of neurogenesis:

> *1. Cell proliferation.* Cell proliferation in the CNS occurs in an orderly sequence in time and space, and appears to be independent of either afferent or efferent connections. Most cell proliferation is completed by late embryonic life. In contrast, cells in the peripheral nervous system proliferate in response to input.
> *2. Cell migration.* Different factors determine cell movement and the growth of axonal connections. Cell migration appears to be directed by glial cells, likely through interactions with CAM expressions.
> *3. Cell aggregation.* Cells appear to aggregate by similar mechanisms as those of migration: epigenetic processes involving the CAM modulation of cell surfaces.
> *4. Neural differentiation.* Two processes are at work: the overall shape of the neuron appears to be genetically determined. The distribution and nature

of the branching of the arbors (axons and dendrites), in contrast, depend upon input—the onset of activity, type of channels, nature of the synaptic transmission, and so on.

5. *Cell death.* Up to 70% of cells die in certain areas during development, often in a very short time. There is considerable evidence that cell survival and death are experience-dependent (see also Greenough, Black, and Wallace, 1987). Since differential cell survival depends upon its particular innervation pattern, this process cannot be preprogrammed and thus must have stochastic and dynamic qualities.

6. *Formation of connections.* The formation and stabilization of neural connections, according to Edelman, "*depends upon a complex set of cooperative and competitive mechanisms that are dynamic and also to some extent stochastic in their actions* [Edelman's emphasis]" (1987, p. 115). These processes, which lead to topographically ordered structures with appropriate connections, occur both independently and sometimes in concert—e.g., differentiation may occur at the same time as migration and death. Taken as a whole, they suggest that neural specificity is not predetermined: genetic processes provide only the broad outlines. Rather, at the neural level, specificity arises through selection and competition among dynamic systems. We agree with Edelman that a similar process occurs ontogenetically at the behavioral level.

The Relation between Neurogenesis, Mapping, and Behavior: Moving to Perception and Action

We have established that dynamic processes in the embryo set neurogenesis in motion and that epigenetic interactions between the genome and cell populations lead to the formation of the primary neural architecture. We have further considered Edelman's hypothesis that specificity of neural structure—the formation of functionally related groups of neurons into maps—is likely largely experience-driven, probably in a manner consistent with the map formation revealed in adult cortical plasticity. There is considerable developmental evidence for the crucial role of experience in postnatal brain development, especially in the visual cortex (for reviews, see Huttenlocher, 1990; Frégnac and Imbert, 1984; Greenough, Black, and Wallace, 1987; Merzenich, Allard, and Jenkins, 1990; Gottlieb, 1991a,b; Movshon and Van Sluyters, 1981; Singer, 1990). The role of experience in the development of binocular connections is especially well worked-out (e.g., Weisel and Hubel, 1965) and is consistent with the picture of time-locked activation as the selective agent for establishing the coherent functioning of the two eyes. That is, binocular activity only occurs when the image between the eyes is optimally matched; if the experimenters give divergent information to the two eyes, correct connections do not develop. Most important for our further developmental story is the discovery that movement—the control of behavior—plays an essential role in establishing ocular dominance. Signals from the retina are not enough; if kittens are paralyzed or anesthetized when exposed to visual patterns, or when the visual signals are not usable to control behavior, they do not lead to changes in cortical function (Singer, 1990).

In the next chapters, we again follow Edelman's theory to link neural development to the fundamental processes of postnatal behavioral development and the question of perceptual categorization. An attractive feature of Edelman's theoretical synthesis is his consideration of the fundamental importance of movement in the development of mental behavior. Since our main objective in writing this book was to integrate the development of action and cognition within a single theoretical framework, we have found this aspect of his theory particularly instructive. The key notion here is that the global functions of categorization—memory, learning, and performance—arise dynamically from the reentrant mapping of motor activity along with sensory information from many modalities. More specifically, in early development, movement and sensory signals are completely coupled and act together to form the global maps that are the basis of further development—a notion that is born out not only in the neurophysiology of visual development but in behavioral studies of infants as well. Before applying these ideas to specific aspects of early development—walking, reaching, object knowledge, and language—we consider the theoretical status of categories, and the link—via the Edelman theory—between global dynamics and neural dynamics in development.

Note

1. Recently, the whole concept of somatotopy has come under question. Movements thought to be controlled by a localized area in the primary motor cortex (M1) may well involve widely distributed neurons. Schieber and Hibbard (1993) reported that when monkeys were trained to move different fingers, single M1 neurons were active with movements of different fingers. At the same time, neuronal populations that were activated by different fingers were highly overlapping. These authors concluded that "Control of any finger movement thus appears to utilize a population of neurons distributed throughout the M1 hand area rather than a somatotopically segregated population" (p. 489).

Chapter 6

Categories and Dynamic Knowledge

A central concern of developmental psychology is how humans get to know things, things about their bodies and their social and physical environments, and eventually about themselves, self-awareness and self-concept. In this chapter, we establish a theoretical link between the dynamics of pattern formation which concerned us in the first part of the book, the neural substrate of behavioral development as suggested by Edelman's theory of neuronal group selection (TNGS), and the emergence of knowledge for thought and action. In particular, we emphasize how perception, action, and cognition are rooted in the same dynamic processes of pattern formation: patterns that are reflections of the experiences of acting in and perceiving the world. The common process is the multimodal mapping of experience by a brain genetically wired to benefit from the time-linked properties of the input. TNGS provides the embryological and anatomical evidence for such a developmental story.

A key concept in this chapter is categorization. We explore more deeply the concepts of perceptual categorization, show how categories can arise autonomously without a specific teacher, and then, using TNGS, discuss in a general way how perception-action categories in early infancy form the basis of mental life. In the next chapter, we present empirical evidence from infant perceptual, motor, and memory development that fits the theoretical ideas we begin to pursue in this chapter.

Philosophy versus Biology

Traditional developmental psychology, following the lead of Piaget and other structuralists, views the ontogeny of mental life as the progressive construction of ever more elaborated knowledge structures. Because Piaget's roots are so deeply in philosophy, and because he was primarily interested in the structure of logical knowledge, his legacy is a view of the mind as a logical device that mirrors the logic of the world. And although Piaget himself saw the process of this construction as dynamic, the acquisitions themselves are *things*—entities in the mind that perform logical operations of varying sophistication. As things, they can be represented by logical formalisms, with the implication that the brain manipulates these formalisms in the same manner as the logician.

From the principles of complex pattern formation and Edelman's TNGS, we consider the operations of the mind as those of a dynamic system. Critical to understanding how a fluid, dynamic assembly of neurons can make sense of the world is the ability of the mind to form *categories*, that is, to recognize that events or objects that are not identical may have equivalent meaning. Without this ability, there is no basis for mental operations of any kind, either for thought or for action. Category formation is the primitive of mental life; the ontogeny of category formation is the basis for behavioral development.

Philosophical Categories

In the traditional reasoning of philosophy, *categories* are different from *concepts*. In such a view, the category is the *extension* of a concept, that is, the category is all the true members of a category that exist in the world. The concept is the *intensional* definition of a category; it is the mental event—the internal representation that enables the individual to determine the category membership of objects in the world. In this *objectivist* philosophy, concepts *represent* an external reality—an external set of "true" categories that exist independently of the minds that create them. In this almost Platonistic view of categories, the mind's job is not so much to construct categories but to discover them (e.g., see Ghiselin, 1969; Gelman and Coley, 1991; Markman, 1989; Carey, 1985; Keil, 1989). Even Piaget, a developmental constructivist who believed that conceptual structure developed in and from the child's action on the world, adhered to the objectivist view of what these "constructed" concepts were. According to Piaget, development consists of building an internal model of external reality—a model that with development becomes increasingly *correct*. Correctness is defined by the enduring physical structure of the world and logic.

In the objectivist view, the mind represents external reality by structuring a set of symbols so that the symbols are in correspondence with the structure of external reality. For theorists who study categories from this point of view, the critical issue is how concepts *represent* reality, not how concepts are used in particular tasks, not how they make *contact* with reality as it happens. Indeed, the developmental story for Piaget and others (see Smith and Heise, 1992, for review) is a story of moving away from here-and-now reality to sterile concepts that transcend momentary tasks and contexts. Therefore, debates in the literature on categorization principally concern the structure of internal representations, not so much the correspondence of the mental state to any external or ecological reality or the processes through which internal structures are connected to specific real-time experiences. In the debates about the details of these internal representations of external reality, there have been periods of considerable consensus, but there has been little progress on the nature of these representations.

The starting point in the traditional debate about concept structure is the classic view borrowed directly from predicate logic: an object is an instance of a particular category if and only if it possesses a set of defining features. By this view our internal representation of a category, our concept, is a definition that specifies the necessary and sufficient features to be a member of a category. This classic view came to be rejected as a psychological theory, however, because it seemed impossible to discover the necessary and sufficient properties for any category and because human category judgments are often graded—not all or none. By the classic definition, any object that meets the definition of a category is a member and all objects that meet that definition are equally good members. But this classic definition hit a psychological roadblock when Rosch (1973) showed that people judge some members of a category to be better instances of that category than other members. For example, a robin is a better instance of the category bird than is a bluejay. Concepts—our internal representations—do not operate like logical definitions. In light of these (and other similar sorts of results), the classic view of categories was replaced by the probabilistic view.

In the probabilistic view, categories are defined by a set of features none of which is criterial. Rather, an object is a member of a category *to the degree* that it possesses a number of characteristic features. But the probablistic view also had problems. Even the graded structure of individual categories is a highly variable experimental effect. Whether an individual judges robins to be the better (and more rapidly recognized) bird depends on context and the individual's knowledge (Johnson, 1992). Moreover, graded category structures turn up even when, at first glance, the defining characteristics seem unequivocal. The concept of *triangle*, for example, seems to have a classic definition; ordinary people know the necessary and sufficient property (a closed object with three sides) which makes an object a triangle. Yet the same people who will maintain that being a triangle is a yes or no logical matter also judge equilateral triangles to be better triangles than all others and even recognize equilateral triangles more rapidly than other triangles (Armstrong, Gleitman, and Gleitman, 1983).

Categories with classically logical definitions are not the only ones that ought not to show a graded structure but do. For example, the category "all the things on my desk at this very moment" has an extension, but it has no stable internal representation. If graded structure in judgments of category membership—if the greater birdness of robins over hawks—is an inherent property of stable represented category structures, then ad hoc categories such as "all the things on my desk at this very moment" should not show a graded structure in people's judgments of category membership. But Barsalou (1987) has shown that special-purpose categories—categories created on the fly to fit some task—show standard "graded-structure" effects. For example, we might create a category of "all the things on my desk that can be used to pound a nail," yet, on viewing the desk, shift the defining characteristics of heavy, graspable objects to exclude those made of glass—the paperweight, for instance. We have no stable "thinglike" concept that is our internal representation, our set model of an objective reality, for "all the things on my desk that can be used to pound a nail." Thus graded effects with ad hoc categories have led some (Medin and Ortony, 1989) to conclude that graded structure is an unreliable aspect of human *performance* that might have little to do with people's internal representations of external realities.

The probabilistic view of concepts has also come under attack because people have intuitions about how they determine category membership that seems decidedly not probabilistic. When people introspect on category structure, they act as if categories are organized like classically defined logical classes. People seem to believe that there are definitions, that there are specific properties that are essential to category membership. For example, people will maintain that an object is a skunk if its mother is a skunk regardless of what it looks like (e.g., Keil, 1989). The object in question might be blue, bald, earless, and three times the size of all known skunks, but it does not matter; if its mother and father are skunks, people maintain that the object in question is also a skunk. The essential property here is one of causal relations—parenthood—and is not perceptual (parenthood cannot be seen or felt). Peoples' intuitions about what properties are criterial for category membership usually do not concern the kind of properties used to perceptually recognize objects; that is, when people talk about what properties really make skunks, they rarely talk about the properties they use in determining whether an object crossing one's path is a skunk or not.

These studies of people's intuitions about category structure have led some theorists (Keil, 1989; Gelman and Markman, 1987; but see Gelman and Medin, 1993) to suggest that the perceptual procedures through which we recognize objects are not part (or not central parts) of our concepts. By this view, what objects look, sound, and feel like have little to do with what they *really* are, or have little to do with our internal representations of what they really are (e.g., Medin and Ortony, 1989; Gelman and Markman, 1987; Mandler, Bauer, and McDonough, 1990; Keil, 1981; see Smith and Heise, 1992, and Jones and Smith, 1993, for further discussion of these issues).

Thus in the objectivist approach to categories we have circled from classic definitions back to classic definitions, gaining only the idea that the perceptual processes used to recognize and interact with objects (performance) and the processes that lead to the rampant graded judgments in human categorization are not core parts of represented concepts. In our minds, objectivist theorists have dismissed on logical grounds the very richness, diversity, and adaptability of human thought. How can perception and the processes through which we make category judgments not be central to psychological explanations of human categorization? Perception can be outside the study of concepts and categories only *if* mind is viewed as representing reality instead of contacting it, if knowledge exists outside of performance, and if the dynamic of knowledge acquisition is divorced from the processes of its storage and use.

Biological Categories
The philosophically rarefied approach makes no sense to us. We want to understand the form and function of our continuous contact with the world. Minds do not just represent the world, they live in and are part of physical reality, a reality of the embodied self and the material world. In our view, there is no need to argue about whether perceptual properties, essential properties, or graded structures are what concepts are really about. Instead, we ought to recognize and embrace the real diversity that is human category behavior. The graded structures, the intuitions, and the perceptual recognition of objects may all be manifestations of a system of essentially disjunctive, degenerate, and thereby creative processes. Perception, action, and cognition are thus assembled under a single dynamic from a high-dimensional substrate, whose noisiness, variability, and sensitivity to initial conditions provide not only the flexibility we observe in human cognition but also its source of new forms. The objectivist reality of world-in-the-mind ignores the biological reality of organism-in-the-world.

Starting from a very different perspective, Lakoff (1987a) has also argued for a rejection of the philosophical *objectivist* approach to cognition. Using linguistic phenomena as his base, he argues that cognition is not an internal representation of external reality:

> Conceptual categories are, on the whole, very different from what the objectivist view requires of them. That evidence suggests a very different view, not only of categories, but of human reason in general:

• Thought is *embodied,* that is, the structures used to put together our conceptual systems grow out of bodily experience and make sense in terms of it; moreover, the core of our conceptual system is directly grounded in perception, body movement, and experience of a physical and social character.

• Thought is *imaginative,* in that those concepts which are not directly grounded in experience employ metaphor, metonymy, and mental imagery—all of which go beyond the . . . *representation* of external reality.

• Thought has *gestalt* properties and is thus not atomistic; concepts have an overall structure that goes beyond merely putting together conceptual "building blocks" by general rules.

• Thought has an *ecological structure.* The efficiency of cognitive processing, as in learning and memory, depends on the overall structure of the conceptual system and on what the concepts mean. Thought is thus more than just the mechanical manipulation of abstract symbols. . . .

• Human reason is not an instantiation of transcendental reason; it grows out of the nature of the organism and all that contributes to its individual and collective experience: its genetic inheritance, the nature of the environment it lives in, the way it functions in that environment, the nature of its social functioning, and the like. (Lakoff, 1987b, pp. xiv–xv)

Lakoff argues for the embodied and creative as opposed to the representing, nature of human categories because, in Edelman's terms, human categories are degenerate; they are composed of multiple disjunctive solutions that are jointly creative. In Lakoff's terms, categories are organized by clusters of "cognitive models" which do not cohere into a single logical whole but which are generative and imaginative.

Lakoff's (1987a) analysis of the concept of mother illustrates the potentially degenerate nature of human concepts. According to Lakoff, there is no single coherent idea of mother, no definition, no one procedure for determining what a mother really is. The concept of mother, like all other concepts, is inherently degenerate. Specifically, by Lakoff's linguistic analysis, we possess the following multiple models of *mother.*

• The birth model: the person giving birth is the *mother.*
• The genetic model: the female who contributed the genetic material is the *mother.*
• The nurturance model: the female adult who nurtures and raises a child is the *mother* of that child.
• The marital model: the wife of the father is the *mother.*
• The genealogical model: the closest female ancestor is the *mother.*

According to Lakoff, all these are our concept of "mother." Ordinary people, like philosophers, may have *intuitions* that categories have essential properties and like philosophers often try to argue that there is a single definition of what a *real* mother is. But try as we and the philosophers might, the above examples suggest that one cannot pick one definition as the *true* definition of what a mother is. This example suggests that there is no single truth out there to be discovered.

As the following sentences indicate, there is more than one criterion for 'real' motherhood:

I was adopted and I don't know who my real mother is.

I am not a nurturant person, so I don't think I could ever be a real mother to any child.

My real mother died when I was in embryo, and I was frozen and later implanted in the womb of the woman who gave birth to me.

I had a genetic mother who contributed the egg that was planted in the womb of my real mother, who gave birth to me and raised me.

By genetic engineering, the genes in the egg my father's sperm fertilized were spliced together from genes in the eggs of twenty different women. I wouldn't call any of them my real mother. My real mother is the woman who bore and raised me, even though I don't have any single genetic mother.

In short, more than one of these models contributes to the characterization of a *real mother,* and any one of them may be absent from such a characterization. (Lakoff, 1987b, p. 68)

The fact that we understand all these sentences shows that our psychology contains all these understandings and definitions of mother. These are overlapping but degenerate models. They do not cohere into a single definition of *mother.* As Lakoff wrote, it would be bizarre for someone to say: "I have four real mothers: the woman who contributed my genes, the woman who gave birth to me, the woman who raised me, and my father's current wife" (Lakoff, 1987b, p. 87).

These multiple models of *mother* are not a special case brought forth by contemporary pressures of novel birth technology and changing family structures. Lakoff has analyzed the degeneracy of a variety of categories—the Japanese *hon,* the Dyirbal classifier system, the concepts of *lust* and *over* in English, to name a few. All of these are made up of overlapping but inconsistent multiple meanings. In being so, they are also essentially creative. The sentences, "Necessity can be the *mother* of invention," and, "We all want our boyfriends to *mother* us," *imaginatively* use different aspects of the same incoherent concept of mother. Imagination and creativity require variability; they are examples of the inherent instability of biological categorization.

Lakoff's insights are troubling if we seek a single, coherent, objectivist definition of categories—one in which represented entities are mapped by truth-conditional statements to the reality of the world. These insights are not troubling if we view categories as embodied—living—processes that are creative because they emerge from the interactions of multiple disjunctive glosses on the same reality. These insights are not troubling if we view our multiple understandings of *mother* with all their subtle and perfectly apt nuances as the products of a dynamic system that leaps from the basin of one attractor to that of another (Freeman, 1991), as an ensemble product of dynamic assembly (Georgopoulus, 1986, 1988, 1990), as not fixed and rigid but continuously dynamically established and maintained by function (Merzenich, Allard, and Jenkins, 1990).

Categories that Teach Themselves—A Computer Model

If an abstract logical structure is not built into the brain, how do people acquire the ability to divide the world up into knowable chunks? Into, for example, multiple senses of *mother?* How can the neural anatomy we described in the previous chapter—overlapping, reentrant, overspecified, variable, and degenerate—support and maintain the mind, which at the same time is logical and subtle, computational and contextual? Most important, what are the processes and mechanisms that allow meaning to be assigned to the multiple and continuous sensations of everyday life without the benefit of a homunculus—a prior knower already established and suggesting the answers?

In this section, we consider a simple case of category learning—a demonstration proof provided by Reeke and Edelman (1984) of the learning of categories of alphabetic letters. This demonstration shows that categories *can* self-organize through multimodal correlations in real time. (In the next chapter we review evidence of such multimodal mapping in human infants.) Such demonstration proofs through computer simulations are important because they affirm the *plausibility* of the neuronal processes suggested by TNGS by instantiating them in purely observable and transparent mechanisms.

Recall that Edelman makes five central claims about the origin of categories: (a) the system is degenerate—there are multiple disjunctive processes that operate over the same input in real time; (b) categories develop from the reentrant mapping of these disjunctive samples of the perceptual space; (c) the mapping is accomplished through the real-time correlations that exist across the independent samples; (d) the reentrant maps are activity-dependent—what we perceive depends in precise time-locked fashion on what we do; and (e) there is always variability in the system. The variability is anatomical, owing to the high connectivity in the system, and dynamic. The dynamic variability is a result of intrinsic continuous activity in the central nervous system (CNS) and the continuous and changing nature of the input, which insures that the system is never in the same state twice.

Reeke and Edelman used these assumptions to design a computer simulation of the learning of a category—in this case, the letter A. The device's task was to learn alphabetic letter categories *from the mere experience of them.* The learning of letter categories without explicit training is a powerful demonstration proof of the strength of these ideas. Alphabetic letters are typically viewed as *quintessentially arbitrary* categories because they are strictly a cultural construction. We have no specially evolved devices for recognizing As as A, Bs as B, and Cs as C. Nonetheless, we get to be very good at it and as adults, can recognize all the items in figure 6.1 as As.

A straightforward assumption of how we learn letter categories is that we are explicitly taught what scribbles are instances of which letter category and which are not. The idea of the explicit teaching of categories dominates models of adult category learning (e.g., Nosofsky, 1986). Of course, letter categories are not truly arbitrary. Letter systems are constrained and maintained by the manual processes we use to write them, the visual processes we use to perceive them, and the memorial processes we use to remember them. Reeke and Edelman show how the confluence of these constraints is sufficient in and of itself for the emergence

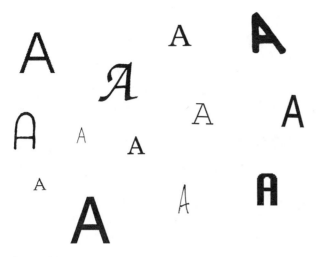

Figure 6.1
A variety of recognizable As.

of letter categories. Reeke and Edelman's device learns As, Bs, and so on all by itself—just from looking at and acting on specific instances.

Figure 6.2 provides a schematic illustration of their category generating device. The key component that makes self-organizing categories possible in Reeke and Edelman's model is the proposal of two *degenerate* and *disjunctive* sets of processes that simultaneously process the same physical stimulus. One set of processes illustrated on the left of the figure is feature analysis. In a manner similar to standard feature recognition models, angle, line, curve, and orientation detectors are excited by corresponding patterns of stimulation. A second set of processes illustrated on the right of the figure is the *activity* of tracing the letter; these tracing movements provide information about global shape. Thus, this model does not choose between an analytic and a global approach to letter recognition but posits instead both kinds of processes. The system is therefore *degenerate* in that there are redundant processes applied to the same task. Moreover, the two processes are *disjunctive:* they are separate and independent; one is not built out of the other. But this is not mere dual process theory. The power is in the coupling of the two independent processes in real time. At the same time that the feature analyzer is analyzing features, the shape tracer is extracting a global description. The outputs of these two heterogeneous processes—at every step in real time——are mapped to each other.

In Reeke and Edelman's device, there are actually three mappings being accomplished simultaneously in real time. One mapping—the feature analysis map—maps the input letter to a list of features. The second mapping—the tracing map—maps the input letter to the action sequences of a continuous tracing of the letter. The third mapping is the reentrant map; it maps the two representations to each other in real time. The new idea of the model is this: the two independent mappings of the stimulus to internal processes take *qualitatively different* glosses on the perceptual information and by being correlated in real time, they educate each other. Self-education is achieved by two further pro-

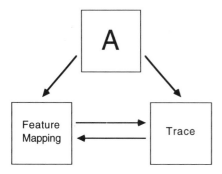

Figure 6.2
A schematic illustration of Reeke and Edelman's model.

cesses: (a) the tracer seeks and moves in the direction of activity (this bias is a motivational *value*) and (b) selectionist processes that retain active connections. By this model, we learn to recognize As and Bs through the correlations that exist between *time-linked* independent samples of a single stimulus.

Reeke and Edelman showed that this device could learn and generalize letter categories. The device *teaches itself* to recognize letters without making any externally evaluated responses. No one needs to tell it that all As are As for it to discover the similarities that exist between As. The intelligence of the device is in the simultaneous self-organizing activity of the three maps; the intelligence is in the pattern of activity of the whole.

Reeke and Edelman's implementation of interacting disjunctive samples in letter recognition is a demonstration model; it shows that this kind of self-organizing category learning is possible—even with artifactual categories such as letters. If people *actually* learned letters the way that Reeke and Edelman's model suggests, then experimental studies of letter recognition should show results that sometimes look like an independent feature analysis and sometimes like a global extraction of the relational features between parts.

A further prediction of Reeke and Edelman's model is that the relational analyses dependent on the dynamic experience of letter tracings will influence feature analysis. That is, the letter categories—the features we use to recognize letters—depend precisely on the motor movements involved in tracing them (or writing them). The implication is that if we all wrote individual letters from right to left instead of from left to right, *we would accept different physical stimuli as instances of the letter A*. This prediction is supported by data. Freyd (1983) taught adults to recognize new letter-like characters by having them watch a letter being drawn. Subjects watched characters drawn by one of two drawing methods. Figure 6.3 illustrates a character and the two drawing methods. Although the drawing methods differed, the final static characters that resulted from the drawing in the two conditions were identical. After training with one drawing method, subjects were presented with *static* representations and asked whether or not they were instances of the modeled character. Some of these test characters were "sloppily" drawn versions of the modeled character.

Freyd found that subjects were reliably faster at recognizing static characters distorted in a manner consistent with the drawing method they observed during

DRAWING METHODS

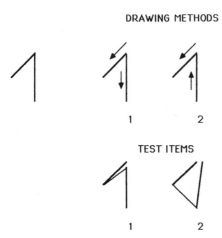

1   2

TEST ITEMS

1   2

Figure 6.3
Illustration of two drawing techniques and two test items used by Freyd (1983).

training than they were at recognizing equally distorted characters that were inconsistent with the observed drawing method. For example, subjects who observed drawing method 1 during training recognized test item 1 more rapidly than test item 2, whereas subjects who watched drawing method 2 during training recognized test item 2 more rapidly than test item 1. In brief, the static visual features that mattered for category membership were influenced by dynamic information about how those features were made in real time. This is precisely the sort of result expected by Reeke and Edelman's model. The procedures for recognizing category members presumably developed from the real-time interactions of the processes involved in the extraction of static features and the visual tracing of the form as the subject watched the experimenter draw.

The success of Reeke and Edelman's model suggests the following about categories. First, categories *self-organize*. The model learns merely by perceptually exploring the world. There is neither a template for the category in the world nor a template for the category in the head. Development can happen in an organized way all on its own with neither an external teacher nor a blueprint for the developmental outcome. The dichotomy we are usually offered between innate or arbitrary categories is a false one. Categories—developmental outcomes—need not be innate or arbitrary. Rather, they may be constrained by the time-locked interactions of multiple processes that converge on the same stimulus.

Second, in Reeke and Edelman's model, there are no represented concepts stored in particular locations. Learning the category A does not consist of learning a definition of A. There is no set concept, no intensional definition, of the letter A stored anywhere. Recognizing the letter A does not consist of making contact with ("accessing") an icon of A. As in connectionist models of cognition generally and in the olfactory bulb of rats, as described by Freeman, categories are bursts of mutually reinforcing and synchronized activity. And because they emerge in the context of ongoing activity, they are inherently variable.

Third, the idea of degenerate disjunctive sampling implies that there is no single, more fundamental answer to the question of how we recognize an instance of a category. In Reeke and Edelman's model, the letter A is neither its features nor its tracing. It is neither of these, but both of these, and more than these.

We believe that these ideas form a basis for explaining category development and that they provide a biologically plausible interpretation of dynamic representations. We develop these ideas by considering the perceptual origins of one of the most fundamental of all categories—that of object. We show how these ideas may be used to understand developmental change by reinterpreting data on how infants come to perceive the world as made up of individuated objects that are distinct from one another. In this extension of TNGS to developmental data, we make explicit our proposals about the nature of dynamic representation: how such representations may form, how they work, and how they are the basis for a new—more organic and biological—view of cognition.

Developing Definitions of Objects

As with much that is important in development, the phenomenon of interest was first identified by Piaget in his observations of his own children as infants. Piaget (1955) observed that a young baby's visual tracking of an object or an older baby's reach for an object could be disrupted by placing the object on top of or behind another object. According to Piaget, an object such as the ball in figure 6.4 becomes functionally invisible for young infants—ceases to exist as a separate object—when it is placed on top of another object. For Piaget, an understanding that objects are bounded and exist independently of our experience of them is a *cognitive* construction built out of perceiving and acting.

Piaget's observation that two objects cease to be perceived as two independent objects when one is laid on top of the other contrasts with the Gestalt psychologists' ideas that the parsing of a visual scene into objects is controlled by innate "laws." These laws—good continuation, closure, proximity—concerned the static properties of visual displays. Current research in computational vision and scene analysis (Marr, 1982), though differing in major aspects from the Gestalt approach, takes a similar view and attempts to define objects in terms of the static properties of their edges and discontinuities in textures.

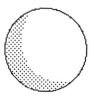 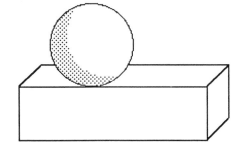

Figure 6.4
Young infants fail to recognize a ball as an individual entity when it is placed on top of another object.

Spelke and her colleagues have shown that Piaget was developmentally more correct than the Gestalt psychologists. Young infants do not use static properties to segregate objects. Young infants do not, for example, perceive figure 6.5A as more like figure 6.5B rather than like figure 6.5C. The use of gestalt properties and procedures for segmenting static visual scenes into objects is developmentally late (see Spelke, 1990, for a review): gestalt properties *begin* to be used to define objects between 7 and 30 months of age (e.g., Kellman and Spelke, 1983; Kellman, Spelke, and Short, 1986; Schmidt, Spelke, and LaMorte, 1986). Use of gestalt properties to segregate one object from another is a *product* of development.

The Importance of Motion
Spelke's research has also caused her to reject Piaget's proposal that infants perceive objects as unbounded and discontinuous in space and time. Spelke's research shows that babies do not perceive objects as bounded and unitary through space and time because she has additional evidence that shows that young infants do perceive separate objects as separate *if the objects move independently relative to one another.* Kellman and Spelke's (1983) first experiment in this long and elegant series provides an illustration of the findings and the experimental procedures. In that experiment, 4-month-olds were habituated to an object whose top and bottom were visible but whose center was occluded by a nearer object. The object—a rod behind a box—is illustrated in figure 6.6. Babies were habituated to the display and then shown two test displays. Babies should look longest at whatever test display they perceive as most different from the habituating display: the whole rod or the broken rod.

Kellman and Spelke investigated various habituation displays: the rod moved; the block moved; the rod and box moved independently; the rod and block moved together; no movement. The test displays consisted of a single rod or the two pieces of a rod, and across experiments these test displays either oscillated or were stationary. The question was whether the baby perceived a single unitary rod or two rod pieces as more different from the habituating event. The results were clear: broken rods were perceived as different and unitary rods as similar only when test objects moved and only when the ends of the habituation rod had moved in common translation behind the occluder. Early in development, the boundary of an object—whether there is one object or two—is defined by motion.

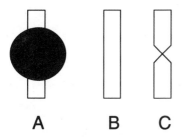

A   B   C

Figure 6.5
Adults perceive *B* as more like *A* than *C*; infants do not.

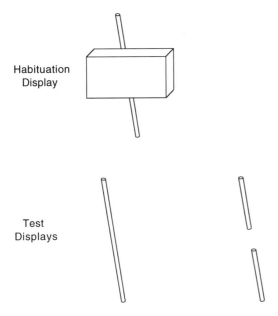

Figure 6.6
Habituation and test displays used by Kellman and Spelke.

Further studies indicate that static cues to object boundaries—cues such as relative size or color and texture differences—play little role in young babies' definition of the rod as unitary or disjoint. In one sense, this is surprising, as infants at this age readily perceive sizes, colors, and texture differences (see Aslin and Smith, 1988). However, Kellman and Spelke's results clearly indicate that babies do not initially use these perceptually available static properties to define separate objects.

Spelke (1990) suggested that the developmentally early dynamic cues to object segregation might themselves be innate. The evidence does not demand this conclusion. The dynamic cues—the cues that arrive from moving objects (and moving perceivers)—may be no more innate than are topographical maps in the somatosensory cortex. The dynamic cues that initially segregate objects for babies may themselves emerge in the time-locked cross-correlations of edges, textures, and motions. Just as Reeke and Edelman's device discovered categories of letters from time-locked mappings between perception and action, so may the baby discover individuated moving objects. And once discovered, this developmental change may drive others—like the discovery of static cues to object segregation.

A Dynamic Systems Account
We offer here a dynamic systems account of the perceptual definition of objects. We believe that our proposed system for the emergence of object segregation, though far too simple, may nonetheless capture the key elements of how development goes forward. We propose specifically that object segregation develops in the interaction of two disjunctive perceptual systems—a "what" system and a "where" system. The what mechanisms are concerned with categorizing and

identifying objects and make use of the static properties of objects—edges and colors and shapes. The where mechanisms *situate* perception and make use of movement generated and dynamic information in visual displays. We propose that the what and the where systems interact as illustrated in figure 6.7 to create the perception of distinct objects. We suggest that a device such as that in figure 6.7 learns to segregate objects through three time-locked and interacting maps. One mapping—the what map—maps textures and edges from the visual input to levels of activity in a population of units. The second mapping—the where map—maps movement in the physical word to the activity level of the second group of units. The third mapping is the reentrant map; it maps the activity levels of the what and where systems onto each other.

The neural event behind seeing an object move unfolds in time. We portray the temporal course of that neural event by plotting the activity of the what system against the activity of the other in a state space. The state space in figure 6.8 contains all the possible combinations of joint activity of the what and where systems. Thus for any given perceptual event, points can be located in the space that indicate the joint activity of the two systems at a moment in time. Those "moment-in-time" points form a line that grows *in one direction* in time—a trajectory in time as in figure 6.8a. If we have a repeating event such as Kellman and Spelke used, our trajectory of neural events in the state space repeatedly travels over a similar path that may, if it is a repeating event, yield a repeating pattern of activity, as in figure 6.8b.

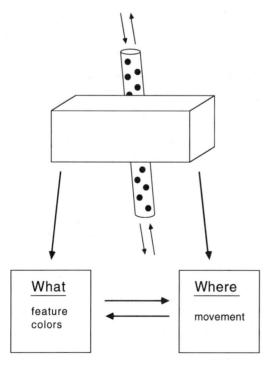

Figure 6.7
Coupled *what* and *where* mechanisms in a dynamic systems account of Kellman and Spelke's results.

a

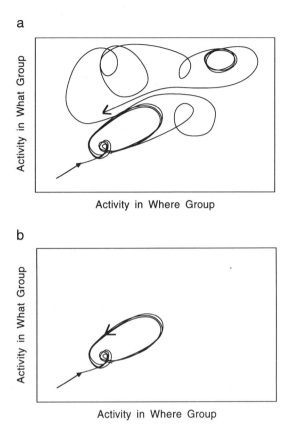

Activity in What Group

Activity in Where Group

b

Activity in What Group

Activity in Where Group

Figure 6.8
Theoretical trajectories of internal activity in the coupled what and where systems.

Consistent with the evidence on neural processes reviewed in chapter 5, we propose that the activity of the what and where systems are continuous, that there are no discrete processing steps. The where system, for example, does not collect sensory data, process it, and then output some finished product in quantum steps. Rather, each system is made up of a population of neurons and the activity of the group as a whole is continuous. These systems are also always active; they do not shut off. There is *continuously* and *always* a path of joint activity of the what and where systems being traced through the state space. Given an awake organism with open eyes, this path of activity depends on two maps from the physical stimulus to the systems and the reentrant map. What is needed to start the process going is minimal. The infant needs only to look, to have a preference (a motivational value) for watching things rather than not and for watching complex or moving things rather than blank walls. They need not have preexisting "knowledge" of what properties define and delimit objects. In this continuous activity of an awake and looking infant, then, regular *organized* paths through the state space will emerge *because* of the inherent properties of the neural systems and the world: (a) the activity of the two heterogeneous systems is time-locked, (b) the objects and the actions of organisms are constrained by the laws of physics, and (c) at each moment in time, the activity level of each system is determined by the physical stimulus, its own just-preceding activity, and the just-preceding activity of the other system.

From the continuous experience of looking at the world, there will emerge densely pathed regions of the state space and sparsely pathed regions. Portions of the continuous trajectory of experience will occur again and again such that in some regions of the state space, paths will repeatedly fall on top of each other. These repeated portions of the continuous trajectory of experience are represented by overlapping darker lines in figure 6.8b. By simple Hebbian notions of increasing strength of connections in all three mappings with joint activity, paths that are commonly repeated will become attractors—stimuli and actions that formerly gave rise to close but distinct patterns of activity will now yield a single trajectory. These attractor trajectories enable the system to generalize from past experiences and to make predictions about the future.

We propose that in Kellman and Spelke's experiment and others like it, the habituation phase sets up an attracting trajectory. The repeated experience of seeing a single rod move behind the occluding box, for example, causes a pattern of joint activity between the what and where systems that repeats itself. A particular path is repeatedly traced in the state space. This trajectory embodies a set of expectations that can be violated. We propose that surprise (i.e., increased looking) results when subsequent events generate a trajectory that initially falls on—is captured by—the attractor, but then veers unexpectedly away. Surprise would not result from test events that generate trajectories that fall on the attractor trajectory or from experiences that generate trajectories far removed in the state space. It is the violation of an expectancy that generates surprise.

These ideas may be used to explain the results in Kellman and Spelke's experiment as follows: During the habituation phase, infants in the uniform movement condition watch the two rod ends move in unison back and forth behind the occluding block. This activity sets up an attracting trajectory based on the joint interactions of the what system activity determined by textures and edges and the where system activity determined by the motion of edges. When the infants are presented with the moving complete rod in a test condition, the pattern of joint activity of the what and where systems is close to, falls on, or is captured by the attracting trajectory, and the infant shows no surprise. However, when the infants are presented with the broken rod moving back and forth in that test condition, the pattern of joint neural activity falls near or on the attracting trajectory but then violates its course. We offer an illustration of these ideas in figure 6.9. Shown here is the state space made up of all possible combinations of activation in the what and where systems. The thick line trajectory represents the recurring pattern of activity in the what and where systems engendered by the habituating event in Kellman and Spelke's experiment. The dashed line represents the test event of a moving solid rod and the thin line represents the test event of two moving half-rods. The trajectory of activity for the solid rod falls on a major portion of the habituating trajectory and therefore this event is not surprising. In contrast, the trajectory of the broken rod repeatedly overlaps and then moves far from the habituating trajectory—an event that violates expectancies and thus generates interest.

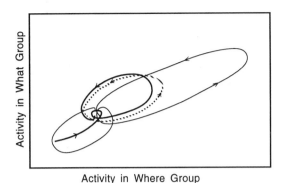

Activity in Where Group

Figure 6.9
Hypothetical trajectories of internal activity in Kellman and Spelke's task. Thick, habituation; dashed, solid rod; thin, half-rods.

This account is, of course, wholly fictional and begs the question of *why* the solid rod generates a trajectory that is more similar to the habituating trajectory than the broken rod. Why and how should uniform movement of the rod ends behind the occluding block generate a trajectory that is violated by the trajectory of broken rod ends moving in the same path without an occluding block, but that is not violated by a solid moving rod? The answer to this question requires specific investigations of the mechanisms of the hypothesized heterogeneous systems. We present this account here for two reasons. First, it introduces the idea about knowledge as trajectories of time-locked heterogeneous patterns of activity that we will use in more detailed and testable accounts of developmental phenomena in chapters 8 and 10. Second, it shows how knowledge can be something other than a thing—something other than a static, objectivist, mental model of the external world. Indeed, although we have no empirical evidence or computational simulation of the plausibility of our "account" of Kellman and Spelke's findings, we nonetheless believe that our account offers a better explanation than any current account. Our explanation gives meaning to the word "notion" in traditional accounts, such as: Infants have the "notion that the environment is composed of things that are coherent, that move as units independently of each other, and that tend to persist, maintaining their coherence and boundaries as they move" (Kellman and Spelke, 1983, p. 521).

Our account also offers an understanding of how knowledge can be locally specific and contextually sensitive. Our account denies the competence-performance distinction. A pertinent question in the objectivist-based cognitive development is whether the infants in Kellman and Spelke's experiments can be said to know anything general about the coherence of parts that move in time-locked unison. In this objectivist condition, our account might be seen as a denial that the infants have the central idea of unitary objects as "maintaining their coherence and boundaries as they move." In our account, the infants' behavior in the experiments depended on the trajectories set up by the specific habituating experience. Are we suggesting, then, that infants do not *really know* that independently moving objects are independent, that they lack a generalized competence, and that they only "know" that objects in this experiment that move independently are independent? Is the surprise shown by infants in Kellman and Spelke's experiment a demonstration of only context-specific knowledge? This question makes no sense in a dynamic systems framework: competence *is* context-specific knowledge. In order to behave adaptively in the world, the infant (indeed, the child and the adult) needs to form on-line expectations about specific object events—about rods moving behind blocks, about rolling balls, about stacked blocks and how they will fall, about walking dogs whose legs move independently. Whatever children "know" about objects, it does them little good if that knowledge cannot make contact with and be made manifest in the here and now—in the specifics of the task at hand. The infants in Kellman and Spelke's experiment are competent and the same confluence of processes that set up their expectations about rods will set up task-specific competencies in other contexts when there are other kinds of objects and motions.

Our account also offers insights into the developmental origins of knowledge about objects. Spelke (1990) has suggested that infants have an innate understanding of objects. Thus, in her account the habituating experience does not make knowledge but instead makes contact with preexisting abstract ideas about what makes an object an object. We *are not* suggesting in our account that the expectations are *solely* dependent on the experimental experience. Rather, in our account, the behavior of the infants reveals both the preexperimental history and context-specific expectations. The very question of whether the trajectories are *solely* set up in the experiment during habituation or whether they reflect generalized "preexperimental" knowledge is not sensible in our dynamics systems view of development. History always matters—in every percept, action, and concept. The infants in Kellman and Spelke's experiments were 4-month-olds. Process trajectories—the joint activity of the two hypothesized heterogeneous processes—have been ongoing continuously since birth. Because of the structure of the world, and the reentrant mapping, deep attractors have been forming. These attractors *are* expectations and an understanding of how the world works. But this understanding can be engaged and realized only through real—context-specific—experience. The shape of the perhaps transient attracting trajectory that is set up during habituation will depend both on what is happening in real time and the *life* history of the organism.

We illustrate these ideas in figure 6.10 which shows a series of evolving attractors in an infant's state space with continuous experience. The contour of the state space—attracting regions (or valleys) that shape neighboring patterns of activity—is illustrated by thicker darker lines. The top panel shows the state space at some early point in history. The middle panel shows the state space at some later point in the history of the infant, say at 4 months of age. The pattern of internal activity in time represented by the darker path has been experienced often. Because of the reentrant mapping and learning between the what and where systems, this region constitutes an attractor. If at this point, the infant is a subject in Spelke and Kellman's experiment, the experiences in that experiment will (as do all experiences) trace a path through that space as in the bottom panel. The location and shape of that path will depend on the topology of the state space at that point in time—on the history of the infant. Specifically, the trajectory of activity at that point in time, regardless of where in the state space it starts, will be pulled toward the attracting trajectory. The *repeated* exposure to the

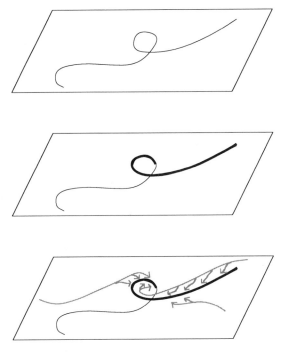

Figure 6.10
Evolving attractors with experience.

habituating event will cause the path that is the habituation experience to be expected. A *transient* region of attraction will be formed that constitutes the specific expectations about these specific rod ends and the occluding box. In this account, real time, context-specific behavior, generalized knowledge, and competence are all one. This is a view profoundly different from that of objectivist cognitive psychology.

Figure 6.10 illustrates how specific experiences are interpreted by past experience: the pattern of activity in neural processes depends on the life history of the organism. Figure 6.10 also illustrates how knowledge grows out of specific experiences: the topology of the state space depends on the specific patterns of activity that emerge in real time. From these ideas, we can see how changes over the developmental time scale will emerge. With the continuous experience of perceiving and acting, deep and stable attractors will emerge in the landscape of the state space and these deep and stable attractors will affect the paths caused by other experiences. More specifically, some attractors are deep and stable enough that they will cause many experiences to yield *the same mental event*. They will constitute *generalized predictions* about the world. In other words, they will perform the functions generally ascribed to conceptual knowledge.

Consider the three objects in figure 6.11. Early in development, when these objects move in the same way, back and forth in space, each may generate distinct patterns of activity—distinct trajectories of internal activity because of their different properties and the different internal states of the organism at the start of the experience. But with continued experience of the motion of these symmetrical

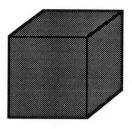 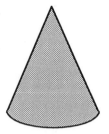 

Figure 6.11
Three solid objects.

and uniformly colored forms, a single deep attractor may develop that captures
the formerly distinct and variable process trajectories and makes them one stable
mental event, a mental event that embodies and is the idea of a unitary and
bounded object.

Repeated experiences of symmetrical and uniformly textured unitary objects
moving as wholes will cause one attractor to form. Repeated experiences of
objects with irregular shapes and discontinuous textures that move independently will form another—distinct—attractor to form. These distinct attracting
patterns of joint activity in the what and where systems will enable static cues
for object segregation to emerge *because* the attracting trajectories are the expected
course of perceptual experience. A "snapshot" experience of a single bounded
form will give rise to a joint pattern of activity in the two systems—a pattern of
activity that is a small portion of the trajectory for unitary objects. Because of
reentrant mapping, the static snapshot of a symmetrical, uniformly textured
object will not give rise to a punctate burst of activity. Rather, a brief portion of
joint activity that falls on an attractor will *generate* further activity along that
attracting trajectory.

Dynamic processes thus do not enable organisms to predict future events in
the same way that propositional representations do. Internal dynamic trajectories
of activity do not change by induction; they are not internal hypotheses that are
confirmed or rejected. There is only process—only activity. Patterns of repeated
activity over time become stable attractors. Thus, particular configurations of
activity at one moment in time generate future activity. These ideas provide a
process account of what J. J. Gibson meant when he argued that we *see* the back
of a sphere when we look at its front.

Cognitive Momentum
Our idea that static perceptual events generate the neural activity associated with
dynamic events is related to Freyd's (1983, 1992) idea of *cognitive momentum*. As
in our account of how static cues give rise (in older infants and adults) to
perceptually segregated objects, Freyd argues that people do *not infer* dynamic
information from pictures but rather directly perceive it. In the first study of
cognitive momentum, Freyd and Finke (1984) presented adults with static displays such as those shown in figure 6.12. Each picture in the sequence was
presented for a very brief period of time and the subject's task was to judge
whether the last picture was the same or different from the preceding one. The

Sequence A: Coherent

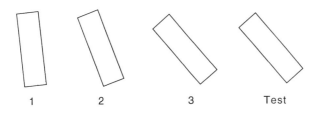

1   2   3   Test

Sequence B: Incoherent

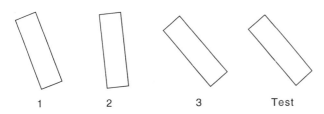

1   2   3   Test

Figure 6.12
Coherent and incoherent series in the experiments by Freyd and Finke (1984).

first three pictures in sequence A set up a coherent rate of rotation; the first three pictures in sequence B do not. The subject's task was to judge whether the final bar was the same or different. Freyd and Finke found that subjects were less successful in judging a different orientation to be different when it was in the direction of implicit motion in a coherent sequence. We explain these results by proposing that the coherent rate of rotation is coherent precisely because a near-uniform rate of change has been experienced many times before. Thus the trajectory of internal activity that constitutes the subjective experience of coherent rotation generates—predicts—a course of action that continues beyond the final bar. When subjects are asked whether the test bar is the same or different, they reply based on whether there is deviation from the current state of activity at the sight of the test bar. There is no deviation when the test bar is where it is expected to be from continuous coherent rotation.

Cognitive momentum fits with a picture of cognition as changes in activity over time. When a sequence of perceptual events (or even a single static event) starts a trajectory of interacting internal processes, the trace of that trajectory is maintained for a period of time, giving us a "perception of the future" in the sense of building expectation. Notice that we have here prediction about novel events without representation—without putting static symbolic entities in the head that *stand for* something in the world.

What Is a Category?

There are many results in the literature that do not fit well together in the traditional objectivist view of concepts and categories. In this traditional view, concepts are symbolic structures that endure, that transcend specific experience, and that interpret and make sense of experience. But this idea of concepts as representations does not fit well with the diversity of human categorization behavior—with the fact people maintain that objects are triangles if and only if they are closed figures with three sides, yet judge equilateral triangles to be better triangles than other triangles; with the fact that people do not recognize blue, hairless animals as skunks, but will judge such an animal to be a real skunk if its mother is a skunk; with the fact that people create novel categories to fit specific tasks; nor does it fit with the multiple meanings of mother. As Jones and Smith (1993) point out there are two possible kinds of responses to this diversity in human category judgment. One response—the one that seems to dominate discussions in the current literature—is to try to decide which aspects of human category judgment are about the structure of represented categories and which are about something else (performance as opposed to competence). The other response in the face of a theory that cannot handle the data in all its diversity is to conclude that the theory is fundamentally wrong—that categorization is not governed by enduring abstract structures that transcend specific experiences. Represented concepts do not exist.

We believe that our account of how infants perceptually segregate objects—the ideas of dynamic representations and time-locked and reentrant maps—forms a basis for a new *biological* theory of categories—a theory in which diversity and context specificity is the fundamental core of knowing. In this view, knowledge is not a symbolic representation of external reality. There is no sense in asking if categories are structured by criterial properties or by essential properties or by graded structures or by perception. There is no sense to this question because the behaviors that suggest criterial properties, essential properties, and graded structures are all temporally specific manifestations of interacting processes. They are the behavioral and context-specific products of the activity of knowing, not the structural components of knowledge. The intelligent diversity and context specificity of knowing is to be expected if categories are like the categories of A formed by Reeke and Edelman's device and if categories are like infants' concepts of object in our account. In these accounts a category is created in context in a trajectory of internal activity in time. The trajectory *always* is a complex product of the immediate context, the just prior internal activity, and the history of reentrant mappings between the heterogeneous processes that make up the system.

This is a radical reinterpretation of concepts. In the traditional objectivist view, concepts are to knowing what central pattern generations (CPGs) are to walking: they are enduring structures that interpret and direct behavior. In the traditional view, the infant sees one object on top of another, as in figure 6.4, and this perception accesses a concept—a knowledge structure—which then *interprets* and gives meaning to the perception. In the present view, perceptions are not interpreted and given meaning by anything. Meaning is emergent in perceiving and acting in specific contexts and in a history of perceiving and acting in contexts.

Development as the Dynamic Selection of Categories

The ideas offered in this chapter form a link between the ideas of dynamic pattern formation outlined in chapter 3, dynamic neural organization as discussed in chapter 5, and a new theory of development that we present and explore in various domains in the following chapters. Our proposals about dynamic representation and categories in this chapter derive principally from TNGS—the ideas of time-locked reentrant maps—that make and make manifest knowledge. We build on these specific ideas in subsequent chapters to consider developmental phenomena as diverse as memory, transversing slopes, word knowledge, reaching, and the A-not-B error. But before proceeding, we shall attempt to make clearer the link between these ideas and those of previous chapters, that is, the relation between dynamic category formation in TNGS, dynamic systems, and what we are learning about the neuroanatomical and physiological data on the developing and adult brain. In our view, all these ideas meld together well to present a picture of development as dynamic pattern formation.

In particular, we see perceptual categories as the cornerstone of cognitive development and as a specific case of pattern formation. The task facing newborn infants is to reduce the degrees of freedom at many levels. Infants must reduce the degrees of freedom of the external world—the potentially indeterminate nature of the stimuli—by forming perceptual categories. They must do the same for their internal worlds—the equally indeterminate nature of the multiple joints and muscles—by seeking patterns of motor coordination and control. At the same time, and most important, they must match their internal dynamics to those of the world around them. That is, they must make their perceptual categories and their action categories congruent to function in flexible, adaptive ways. However, in our dynamic approach, perception, action, and cognition are not disjoint, but part of a singular process.

Thus, we believe that whether we call it pattern formation, coordination, or category acquisition, we are referring to the same dynamic processes whereby complex, heterogeneous elements self-organize to produce coherence in time and space. Dynamic patterns can be fleeting or very stable, but most important, they are *time-dependent* and seamless. By "time-dependent" we mean that each event in brain and body has not only a here and now but also a history and an effect on the future. By "seamless" we mean that these time domains are themselves without interruption. The stuff of development is the dynamics of perception, action, and cognition in real time. What the infant sees, thinks, and does in the present provides the aliment for what the child is in the future, just as what the child did in the past is the substrate for how she or he sees, thinks, and acts right now. Thus, we can envision the neuronal processes postulated by TNGS as a specific form of dynamic pattern formation, with the patterns being the categories of perception and action that form the developmental core of higher mental functions and the patterns of thought that become increasingly complex and generalized throughout infancy and childhood.

Recall from chapter 5 that the epigenetic processes of neuroembryology created a primary neural repertoire of globally similar, but locally highly variant tracts which provide the gross connectivity between all areas of the developing brain, the spinal cord, and the peripheral neurons. We argue in subsequent chapters that even at birth this primary repertoire is capable of generating simple perceptual and motor patterns. That is, given the anatomy and physiology of newborns and particular patterns of sensory stimuli, they will exhibit certain preferred behavioral configurations that can be characterized as attractors of varying stability. Thus, even at birth, each real-time action is a result of an epigenetic history, and surely, by its very performance, sets a metric on the future.

Recall also that the distinguishing characteristic of the primary repertoire is its degenerate and reentrant structure. Again, degeneracy means the brain wiring is so overlapping that any single function can be carried out by more than one pattern of neuronal connections *and* that a single group of neurons can participate in more than one function. Reentry is also crucial; it means that two or more abstracting networks are working disjunctively to process the same stimuli. We saw that a critical element in the disjunctive input was that it was time-locked, that is, that the multimodal sampling of the same event must be correlated in time. This, again, will be a critical feature for early perception-action categories. Finally, we note that the early CNS comes with the requisite variability in its exuberant connectivity to be the basis of the selection and pruning that constitute developmental change.

We agree with Edelman that this functional anatomy and the ability of the system to dynamically self-organize are sufficient to start the process of categorization—understanding the world. Indeed, detailed "knowledge" or a wise knower need not be postulated, even for some of the seemingly sophisticated cognitive abilities of young infants. What we suggest is that from the very first, the infant is a continuous, active dynamic system, whose activity constitutes the stuff of development. Consider even the most simple of newborn activities: looking and moving the head and neck. Even the irregular eye movements and slow imprecise tracking of newborns provide time-locked, reentrant information that links visual input with proprioception from muscles of head, neck, and eyes, and mechanoreceptors in the stretched skin. In Edelman's terms, these are disjunctive samplings of the same events which form categories through the distinctive wiring in the brain. Figure 6.13 is Edelman's cartoon of the basic neuronal units that allow independent sampling to form categories: the classification couple. The minimal unit consists of two functionally different maps connected by reentry as in the device that recognizes A in figure 6.2 or in our proposed account of how infants perceive objects as in figure 6.6, or the couple that exists between the visual systems and the mechanoreceptors that respond to eye movement. The units in these classification couples are functionally distinct. However, the mutual connections of the couple allow for relations between them to be built. The key is that certain mutually overlapping connections are excited and strengthened by stimuli that are time-locked together. So imagine the newborn tracking with the eyes and moving the head ever so slightly in the same direction. Features of the tracked object which enter into map 1 are correlated with the features of neck movement, independently sampled by map 2. The fibers that connect the two maps "map the maps," so to speak. Events that are correlated in the world, such as moving the neck and keeping an object in view, selectively strengthen certain synaptic pathways and couple them into a kind of sensorimotor classification—a useful one for keeping track of things.

But remember that even this simple act has multiple sampling possibilities, and indeed the massive connectivity of the brain means that such selective strengthening is going on over all modalities and *in continuous time*. This is reflected in the *global mapping* of sensory input and movement that indeed involves the entire brain, as diagrammed by Edelman in figure 6.13. Multiple

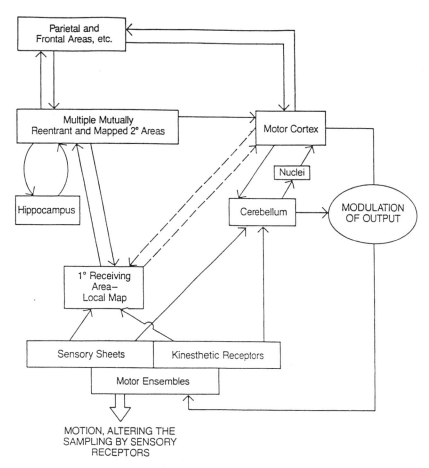

Figure 6.13
Illustration of the massive coupling and connectivity of heterogeneous structures in the brain from Edelman (1987).

classification couples are connected by reentry such that the multiple signals that are picked up from the world and from self-movement lead, in concert with other areas of the brain, to subsequent movement (as spontaneous or goal-directed action). This movement, in turn, alters the sensory information picked up, and so on. The entire process, therefore, is dynamic and seamless. Each time the newborn moves and sees, the system is changed as certain connections grow stronger and persist and others weaken and even die.

How, it may be asked, can such an undirected process lead to developmental change that is progressively more adaptive? How does the system know what is appropriate behavior (i.e., following the object in view)? It is necessary to postulate some very general biases that are the heritage of natural selection. Edelman calls these biases "value." For example, one general value must be to keep moving objects in view. Others might include grasping objects with the hand or mouth for feeding and other exploratory functions. Values, Edelman believes, are exhibited in the parts of the brain—hypothalamus, midbrain, and other limbic structures—involved with basic survival functions such as heartbeat, breathing, feeding, sexual responses, and so on. However, value does not create categorization, which must have experience-based selective strengthening of neuronal groups, but acts as a higher-level driving force maintaining the essential functions of life. Further, these values are not "constraints" in the standard sense of developmental theory in that they do not constrain the organism from acting in certain ways. Rather, values are more like "prods" that start activity and thus self-organizational processes.

To take our example further, a "value" such as maintaining a level of neural activation creates the simple goal of keeping interesting objects in sight. This in turn may create the conditions necessary for emergent perceptual categorization. By visually tracking moving objects, infants link the seen external world with a particular felt movement. In doing so, they map the correlated features of the objects in view—edges that move together, for example. This mapping in turn creates the opportunity for other mappings, each based on the time-dependent reentrant interactions of neuronal groups. For example, the colinear and rigid movement of edges for solid objects vs. the independent movements and changing edges for nonsolid objects may create the perception-action categories solid vs. nonsolid objects—categories that have been proposed to be part of the ontological basis for a conceptual growth (Soja, Carey, and Spelke, 1991). A simple value of starting the system off with a goal of maintaining neural activity, along with the neural organization, sets off a pattern of here-and-now experiences that *create*, not prescribe, conceptual primitives. We will pursue these ideas more fully in the chapters that follow, and we especially discuss *value* in chapter 11. In the next chapter, we consider evidence that infants do form reentrant maps in their time-locked multimodal experiences of events.

Chapter 7

The Dynamics of Selection in Human Infants

In the last chapter, we characterized the process of neuronal group selection as a specific instance of dynamic pattern formation, with perceptual-motor categories as the attractors that emerge from infants' ongoing, but uninstructed, interactions with the world. Critical to the mechanism of dynamic category formation is the degenerate structure of the central nervous system (CNS) and its properties of reentry, where experience from perceiving and acting is independently but simultaneously processed in highly overlapping maps. In this chapter, we make these claims more concrete. First, we show that multimodal mapping may be a primitive in early infancy; evidence shows that such reentry is part of infants' early intrinsic dynamics. Second, we discuss the importance of movement in the acquisition of dynamic perception-action categories. Third, we discuss the role of memory in the emergence of dynamic category formation. Here again, we emphasize the continuity of time scales between real time and developmental dynamics. This chapter introduces themes we explore more fully in chapter 8. In particular, we build the foundation for understanding the central dual nature of development: its global coherence and its pervasive local sensitivity. Finally, we present recent empirical evidence that integrates these themes.

The Unity of Perception

The central idea of the last two chapters is that infants discover action and object categories through the cross-correlation of multimodal experiences. The disjunctive, heterogeneous experiences of hearing and seeing and feeling and moving are all time-locked and change together as the infants' activity, state, and actions change. We proposed that infants discover the *category-relevant* properties of objects and events—invariant cues to shape, color, and texture across changes in lighting, perspective, and distance—through their multimodal and activity-dependent experiences of objects. Likewise, they discover patterns of coordination that provide functional actions through movement and its perceptual consequences. These ideas turn the usual developmental stories backward: multimodal correspondences are the *cause* of development rather than a *product* of development.

There is a long and time-honored tradition in psychology and the neurosciences to consider the nervous system as a modular, information-processing machine. Since Johannes Müller, for instance, it has been clear that the brain specifically and separately organizes each sensory modality. Likewise, in the shadow of Sherrington (1906), psychologists and neurophysiologists have drawn a clear distinction between sensory and motor pathways and between central and peripheral processes. This modularity of anatomy and function is both intuitive and a commonplace. What we see, we see; what we hear, we hear. Actions are either reflexive and involuntary, or intentional and planned. In the primary organization of the mammalian brain, sensory information is transmitted along parallel, modality-specific, "labeled lines" (Mountcastle, 1980). The CNS is hierarchically organized, starting with the spinal system and going up to the neocortex. Reflexes result when information from the periphery is sent centrally and responses are channeled outward without conscious awareness; voluntary movements originate in the cortex (see Reed, 1982, for discussion).

This intuitive view of modular functioning is contradicted by our psychological reality. If the primary organization is of qualitatively separate experiences, how are our perceptions made unitary? How are the sight, sound, and feel of an experience coordinated? How does experience, in turn, gain meaning if its parts are disparate? At a higher level, how does a modular system create such multisensory experiences as images and metaphor?

The traditional neurophysiological solution to the unity of experience, called *the binding problem* by Damasio (1989), has been to assume that there must be in the brain specific localities where the diverse sensory streams are merged and integrated—the association areas in the cortex. Association areas were presumed to be the final resting place of percepts, which as they cascaded up from the receptors through the higher structures of the brain would become increasingly more abstracted and representational. Anatomically, perceptual processing moved serially from the primary sensory areas to the anterior temporal and frontal regions, where the sensory modalities would be combined.

The developmental solution, as offered by Piaget, to these disparities between anatomy and reality was the active *construction* of coordination, coordination among sensory modalities, between perception and action, and between the sensorimotor associations and higher, more abstract forms of human reason. Piaget (1952) began his developmental theory assuming that the sensory modalities were distinct and separate, and that reflexes formed the cornerstone of later motor function. The task for infants, therefore, was to gradually put together these multiple modes of experience, to match eye with hand, to link the hand and the mouth, and to coordinate seeing and hearing. But Piaget is clear in stating that the first acquired adaptations of the infant are *within* modality and only later *between* modalities.

For example, in Piaget's (1952) account, reaching and grasping build from the individual elementary reflexes of grasping, sucking, and looking. For prehension, "The *first stage* is that of *impulsive movements* and of *pure reflex*, where the newborn moves hands spontaneously and reflexively" (p. 89). According to Piaget, "The *second stage* is that of *the first circular reactions related to hand movements, prior to any actual coordination between prehension and sucking or vision*" (p. 90). In the second stage, the infant moves for the sake of moving itself, but the movements begin to be repeated and seem to begin to be oriented and accommodated to the grasped objects. Only by the third stage are the hand movements linked functionally to other modalities: "During the *third stage* notable progress is revealed: henceforth there is *coordination between prehension and sucking*" (p. 99). Looking is gradually brought in during the fourth and fifth stages: first by grasping only when both the hand and object are in view, and finally by grasping the seen object without the need to also see the hands. Thus, Piaget's account fits the traditional neurophysiological view. Knowledge must be constructed from the assimilation of the separate perceptual streams, presumably embodied in the later-maturing association areas of frontal cortex.

As we also discussed in chapter 5, recent neurophysiology and developmental studies have turned this eminently plausible view on its head. There is now grave doubt that the primary developmental task is this construction of an integrated reality from distinct and modular cores of functioning. A strict constructionist view has been undermined by studies that show vast and previously unimagined networks of interconnections both within and among anatomically distinct areas. There is the primary sensory organization of separate modalities and separate channels of processing within modalities, for example, for color, form, and motion in the visual system. But this organization is only *half* the story. Beyond these channels, the evidence shows many types of rich interconnectivity, as we reviewed in chapter 5. First, there is early separation and divergence of sensory information into several functional areas. These connections are divergent, one-to-many, parallel, and sequential (Damasio, 1989). Second, fibers projecting backward to the feeding area—Edelman's reentry—affect processing in a retroactive manner and, through cross-projections to the same level, form local networks or patterns. Third, there is strong evidence of convergence of the sensory information downstream: multiple areas where projections from the visual, auditory, and somatosensory cortices converge. Finally, these convergent areas themselves project back into the sensory cortices, again feeding the convergent information back into divergent areas. The important point is that there is *no* evidence for a localized "association area" anywhere in the brain where perceptual binding occurs. Damasio asks, "Which area or set of areas could possibly function as a fully encompassing and single convergence region, based on what is currently known about neural connectivity?" And he answers, "None" (1989, pp. 35–36). Likewise, Ettlinger and Wilson conclude, ". . . no region exists for the storage of multimodal representations, and that CMP [cross-modal performance] is achieved by direct communication between the within-modal systems" (1990, p. 185).

This direct communication has recently been confirmed by electrophysiological recording. Recall that in chapter 5 we described patterns of synchronous oscillations of neural firing in the visual cortex. Recently, investigators have reported synchronized oscillatory activity similar to that described by Singer and his colleagues in the cat visual cortex in the somatosensory *and* motor areas of the awake, behaving monkey (Murthy and Fetz, 1991). This confirms a suggestion made by Ettlinger and Wilson (1990), that cross-modal performance involves neither special areas in the brain nor unique mechanisms. Rather, cross-modal performance reflects the same processes as those producing association of features within a modality.

Indeed, some of the neural structures showing intersensory integration are subcortical, early maturing, and phylogenetically old. In their elegant book, *The Merging of the Senses*, Stein and Meredith (1993) build a compelling case for sensory convergence as a fundamental and enduring characteristic of animal nervous systems, universal in all phyla, and occurring at many levels of the neuraxis.

They focus specifically on the superior colliculus, a midbrain structure widely studied for its role in visual processing. What is less well known about the structure is that a very large proportion of the neurons are responsive not only to visual input, but to auditory and somatosensory input as well. Indeed, there are strong correspondences between the topographic maps of these modalities, which share a common coordinate system of "multisensory space" as shown in figure 7.1. These authors further suggest that motor responses are similarly integrated to produce a "multisensory-multimotor map" (p. 115). The maps are so multiply degenerate and reentrant that inputs from each modality are processed both in parallel and convergently. For instance, at the same time that visual inputs are processed unimodally, "a core of multisensory-multimotor neurons initiates movements via a common circuit" (p. 116).

From their experiments on cats, Stein and Meredith found that the multimodal inputs interact in the superior colliculus in interesting and nonlinear ways. Specifically, inputs that are close to each other in spatial receptive fields and are temporally continuous (within a range appropriate to capture the differing transmissions of the various senses) act to enhance neuronal responses. But the enhancement is a function of the stimulus intensities and is greatest at low intensities. This means that multimodal information is most potent when the individual sensory information is least effective. When stimuli from a single modality are very strong, there is little functional advantage to be gained from amplification. In situations, however, where important stimuli are hard to detect, the multimodal enhancement is more critical. As every bird-watcher knows, a

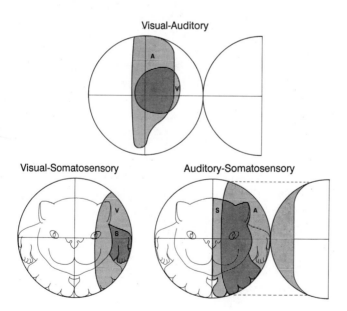

Figure 7.1
Spatial alignment of receptive fields in multisensory neurons. Note the overlapping visual (*V*) and auditory (*A*) (*top*); visual and somatosensory (*S*) (*bottom left*); and auditory and somatosensory (*bottom right*) receptive fields in three typical bimodal neurons. (From Stein and Meredith, 1993. Reprinted with permission.)

flash of a tail or a snatch of a song may be individually ambiguous, but when experienced together, may be sufficient for identifying the hidden culprit.

Below we present behavioral evidence that suggests that such multisensory integration is not only ubiquitous in the brain, but widespread and not solely the province of late-maturing association areas. As a consequence of the neuroanatomy, sensory *integration* may be the primitive. The developmental task may not be to construct, but to *select* from all the possible multimodal associations those that represent persistent real-life correlations of perception and action in the world.

Intermodal Integration in Infants

Consistent with the neuroanatomy and neurophysiology, there is compelling behavioral evidence of strong intermodal linkages in newborns and young infants, long before the gradual process of assimilation and accommodation posited by Piaget would allow these coordinations to develop. First, there is sparse, but provocative evidence of a kind of unity of the senses in the newborn. For example, newborns visually orient to the spatial location of a heard sound (Mendelson and Haith, 1976). Brightness and loudness summate in producing neonate arousal (Lewkowicz and Turkewitz, 1980). Turkewitz and colleagues have proposed that it is the *intensity* of the stimuli, the simple "how much," not the qualitative aspects, that is the basis of the unity (Turkewitz, Birch, Moreau, Levy, and Cornwell, 1966; Turkewitz, Gardner, and Lewkowicz, 1984).

The evidence for cross-modal performance in infants after the newborn stage is considerable (see reviews by Rose and Ruff, 1987; Meltzoff, 1990; Spelke, 1984). By 1 month, infants match the oral feel and sight of textured pacifiers (Meltzoff and Borton, 1979) and show oral-visual transfer also with rigid and elastic cylinders (Gibson and Walker, 1984). Four-month-olds prefer to watch complex visual events that dynamically match an ongoing complex auditory event (Spelke, 1976, 1979). At the same age, infants matched by preferential looking rings moving in rigid or flexible fashion with similar rings they have explored haptically (Streri and Pecheux, 1986). Many experiments have shown that infants can match temporal and spatiotemporal qualities of stimuli heard and seen: puppets and sounds (Spelke, 1979), sponges and blocks and their sounds (Bahrick, 1983), speech sounds and lip movements (Kuhl and Meltzoff, 1982). There are many examples of cross-modal performance throughout infancy: clearly, intersensory interactions are the norm during the first year. The neuroanatomy and recent neurophysiology support this primacy of cross-modal functioning.

In sum, then, there are two truths about the organization system. First are the separate qualitatively di   physical world that are the separate modalities. Second, up and down the system, at all levels of complexity, and from the beginning of development, are the multiple interactions between these parallel and disjunctive processing systems. The developmental significance lies in the two truths considered jointly. The engine behind development must be the reciprocal education of the heterogeneous yet continuously interacting systems, and the generation of new forms made possible by the self-organizing dynamics of such a system.

Viewed in this way, what does it mean when we show that an infant is capable of detecting a cross-modal equivalence? Typically, to demonstrate cross-modal performance experimentally, infants are first familiarized with a stimulus in one modality, or they are trained to make a response to a particular object in one modality. They are then tested with a different modality alone to see if they can recognize the object or event or respond as they have been trained. If they can, we assume they have transferred information gained in one modality to another. A second way of testing cross-modal performance is to allow infants to explore an object in one modality while simultaneously having to choose that object or a different one in another modality. (Will the infant choose to look at an object that looks the same as the object they are exploring haptically?) Again, a match must mean transfer of information.

What do such results mean? One possible meaning of these results is that there is a link between one modality and another that existed prior to the experiment. For example, the finding that only after oral exposure to a bumpy pacifier do 1-month-old infants prefer to look at a matching shape shows that pathways must exist which transfer experience in the tactile realm into visual fields (Meltzoff and Borton, 1979; see also Meltzoff, 1990). We believe that the neurophysiology strongly supports such a contention. Infants do not have to build these linkages, they are general and pervasive, although demonstrating them behaviorally in very young infants may be very difficult.

However, the developmental significance may be far more than that intersensory coordination exists. Indeed we believe that what we are observing in experiments is the very *mechanism* of development—not a product, but the process through which intelligent commerce with the world is selected and maintained. In our view, what experimental tests of cross-modal performance do is reveal how perception-action categories—the fundamental stuff of cognitive development—are selected in real time. Recall that in each case, infants are given time to explore the properties of the stimulus object, by looking, by mouthing, by feeling, by listening. As was demonstrated in the cat visual cortex, *within* modality, coherent features of stimuli such as common movement, edges, contours, pitch changes, and so on set up correlated activity in groups of neurons. This time-locked pattern establishes an experience-based basin of attraction, the dynamic emergence of a neuronal group. In a single modality such as the visual cortex, the neuronal group associates common features detected visually. But because the neuroanatomy provides for vast interconnectivity, coherent patterns of firing will also be established in distant fields, including those associated with other modalities. Thus, what the experimental manipulation does is to create those dynamic attractor basins in real time through the infants' exploration of and familiarization with the stimuli. During this time infants learn about the cross-modal properties of objects the same way they learn about their intramodal properties. Cross-modal matching is intrinsic to infants in that the primary neural repertoire supports these linkages. It also makes sense that we might detect some global transfer of stimulus properties even in very young infants, and thus it is entirely plausible that early matches might be on nonspecific stimulus characteristics such as relative intensity.

But most important is that this real-time process of familiarization and categorization created in the experimental situation mimics infants' own experience in the real world. Infants receive massive amounts of multimodal sensory correlation continually, literally every waking hour. Every time someone speaks or touches an infant, or the infant shakes and looks at a rattle, the infant receives time-locked multimodal sensations. According to the theory of neuronal group selection (TNGS), cross-modal features that are continually and reliably associated in the real world will become stable and persistent basins of attraction. Through exposure to real correlated events in the world, some of these global mappings will be selectively strengthened. Those that are not reliably time-locked will not be linked.

Thus, events that are disjoint in the experimental situation, for example, sounds not correlated with visual events, are surprising to infants because they have become accustomed to matches between the stimuli, either in the familiarization period or *through real-life experience*. Categories of multimodal matches that have been experienced more frequently, and in more varied situations, should have stronger attractor basins. Predictably, therefore, matches that infants have been observing for themselves for some period of time in their daily life would be especially easy to capture experimentally. For example, by 4 months, infants are very good at recognizing the match between heard speech and seen facial movements (Kuhl and Meltzoff, 1982). Although we know very little about the developmental course of this ability, by 4 months, infants have been exposed to probably several hundred hours of watching a close-by face speak. Other matches, for example, between object shape detected visually and haptically, occur many months later, presumably because infants have had less experience making the manual-visual maps (Bushnell & Boudreau, 1993).

The critical importance of this is the complete continuity between time scales of learning in the experimental situation, and what infants pick up in the real world. The process by which infants come to expect features to be associated in a familiarity procedure is the same as that by which they acquire long-term "knowledge" in many modalities—through the strengthening and remembering of associated features. Thus, intermodal matching is not just a competency that infants have in varying degrees at particular ages. Rather, it is a revelation of the most fundamental developmental process, and provides a window to the nature of change. In this and subsequent chapters we reinterpret several lines of infant research from this dynamic perspective.

Movement as Perception: The Critical Role of Movement in Development

Self-produced movement plays a critical role in Edelman's selective theory of development. Recall that the sensory sheets providing the disjunctive sampling of events (touch, vision, audition, etc.) enter the first reentrant mapping area *along with the kinesthetic sensations produced by self-movement* (see figure 6.13). In other words, *movement must itself be considered a perceptual system*. The sensation of movement is as time-locked with one external stimuli as the properties of the external stimuli are time-locked with one another. Note that movement in this case includes not only large limb and trunk movements associated with locomotion and manipulation but also head and neck movements, and most significantly, eye movements. Indeed in experiments with cat visual development that we cited in chapter 5, proprioception from the muscles that control the movements in the eyes—that allow both eyes to align and focus on the same object—were absolutely critical in creating binocular coherence in the visual cortex (Singer, 1990). As we discuss below, behavioral evidence suggests a similar motor requirement for human binocular vision.

This view of movement as perception is very different from the traditional view of afference and efference, where behavior is triggered and guided by objects and events external to the actor, and where input can be neatly separated from output. Indeed, we may not be overstating the case when we say that if movement is another form of perception, there is little or no learning or development that is strictly within modality. Consider any type of familiarization or exploration occurring during real-life looking or playing, or during a cross-modal experiment. Whether the stimuli are presented visually, haptically, or through hearing, there is always associated movement of the eyes, hands and arms, and head and neck (Gibson, 1988). These motor signals are part of the reentrant package that is correlated in time with the disjoint signals from the explored object or event. Thus, even in the most seemingly "pure" presentation of a visual stimulus, the edges, colors, and motion of the scene are joined by precise and always synchronous activation of eye movement detectors as well.

We believe that correlated movement is important *and perhaps critical* in establishing dynamic categories. By the tenets of TNGS, it is the conjoining of the correlated multiple inputs that allows the selective strengthening of groups to occur without specific instruction. Thus, it seems likely that the more modalities from which time-locked information is received, the stronger the correlations and the more quickly and efficiently the associations will be made. The potency of movement may help explain the powerful learning and memory effects of experiments using contingent foot kicking (e.g., Rovee and Rovee, 1969; Bahrick and Watson, 1985). Although this seems intuitively correct, we know of no direct experimental tests of this in human infants. Indeed, most natural situations for learning are richly multimodal and involve much associated movement.

Movement plays another critical role in learning and development by selection. It is movement that provides the dynamic sampling of the stimulus attributes (Bushnell and Boudreau, 1993). Infants cannot explore contours, edges, backs of objects, sources of sounds, textures, weights, and surfaces without some means of dynamically sampling the stimulus array. They must move—their eyes, their heads, their hands, the soles of their feet—to provide the same "takes" on the objects and events, and on their own activities within the stimulus array. From a Gibsonian perspective, movement is what allows discrimination and discovery of the invariants in the environment—the common and correlated properties of flow, movement, edges, textures—that are necessary for adaptive actions. However, it is not just *moving* that is important. Recall that in the classic Held and Hein (1963) experiment, passive movement was not effective for the development of normal visual functioning in kittens; the key was self-motion, and presumably the perception unique to self-motion. We discuss below the critical role of self-movement in human infant development.

If disjoint sampling is the process by which categories are selected, movement—action of the infant within the environment—must be considered the common primitive of cognitive development, and may well be the dynamic control parameter in the emergence of many early skills. If self-produced movement is critical, then dynamic category formation—the infant's basic organization of the world—must be paced and constrained by the ability to produce and control that movement. Without the ability to control the two eyes, binocular convergence and its associated mapping in the visual cortex is impossible. Without control of the head, it is difficult to localize sound; without the ability to move the hands and arms, infants cannot effectively explore the haptic properties of objects; without the ability to locomote, there is no way to understand that an object is the same from the back.

At the same time that these motor skills are critical for understanding, the increased perceptual specificity learned through movement also contributes to more accurate and efficient actions. Thus, as objects are explored haptically and their qualities categorized, motor actions can be adapted to account for these qualities. Infants learn that heavy objects require more limb stiffness, and that small objects require a more accurate approach to grasp.

Finally, in the sense that movement is perception, then motor categories, that is, general types of responses that are both stable and flexible, may be acquired by the same processes as other categories of the world. As infants learn about the properties of cups—that they hold liquid, afford drinking from and putting small objects into, are graspable by the handle or with two hands—they also learn dynamically the appropriate motor responses by which to accomplish these actions. That is, they learn that putting things into cups requires stabilizing the cup with one hand, or that grasping the cup by the handle requires a precision grip. These functionally adaptive actions must be dynamically stored and recalled so that the actions can match the task at hand—reach for reachable things, walk over walkable surfaces, and so on. Again, in Gibsonian terms, infants must learn the *affordances* of the environment, the match between their own abilities and the qualities of the world that support action within it (Gibson, 1988; Adolph, Eppler, and Gibson, 1993b).

The Central Role of Movement in the Development of Perception and Cognition

Just as there is ample evidence of the primacy of multimodal mapping in early development, there is also abundant support for the premise of TNGS that self-produced motion provides critical input for the formation of dynamic categories. (Readers are referred to several reviews on this theme, including Adolph, Eppler, and Gibson, 1993b; Bushnell and Boudreau, 1993; Bertenthal and Campos, 1990; Bertenthal, Campos, and Barrett, 1984; Fogel, 1993; Gibson, 1988; Lockman, 1990).[1]

Self-produced Locomotion
The most dramatic example of the cascading and emergent effects of movement on development are the major perceptual, cognitive, and social changes engendered by acquiring self-locomotion. As argued by Bertenthal et al. (1984; see also Bertenthal and Campos, 1990), self-locomotion serves as the setting event, or in our dynamic terms, the control parameter, for a variety of changes in other domains of functioning. For example, at 6½ months of age locomoting infants (those who could crawl themselves or move in a wheeled walker) explored more, increased their attention to the environment, and even spent more time social-

izing with other people in the room than the infants who just sat on the floor and did not move (Gustafson, 1984). Locomoting, but not prelocomoting infants showed evidence of fear on the visual cliff. But the most direct and compelling link between self-movement and cognition comes from the demonstrated effect of locomotion on spatial abilities. Bertenthal et al. (1984) tested three groups of infants in a spatial orientation task. The three groups included infants who could crawl, infants who could not crawl, but who had extensive experience in a walker, and infants who could neither crawl nor had walker experience. The task involved training infants to anticipate an interesting event in one location and then rotating them to the other side of the room. Infants with crawling and walker experience looked in anticipation to the trained location, even though it was in an opposite direction in relation to their bodies, while those without self-locomotion continued to turn the same way in relation to their own body. That is, if the original direction of the object was to the left, nonlocomoting infants continued to turn to their left. Clearly, some aspect of locomotor experience facilitated a new dynamic categorization of space ("pay attention to landmarks that specify fixed locations even if you are yourself moving") that could not be mapped without the concurrent experience of movement.

What does the experience of moving provide? An intriguing clue comes from a study by Kermoian and Campos (1988) who showed that while nonlocomoting infants with walker experience and crawlers both performed better on the A-not-B task than nonlocomoting infants, not all prone progression was equally effective. Indeed, infants who were belly crawlers, those who did not lift their bellies as did hands-and-knees creepers, but dragged them along, were no better than nonlocomoting infants, no matter how long they crawled. Belly crawlers have to expend a lot of energy, and in addition, they have their heads and faces close to the floor. They may not be able to pay attention to their spatial surrounds and thus will not get the varied experience of viewing spatial locations as they move. The *mechanism* for the locomotor effect is not mysterious. If the ability to represent spatial locations independent from the self depends on sampling the correlated attributes of that location with self-position, then infants must track the location. If their heads are buried in the carpet, they cannot do this. Such an explanation is consistent with the direct behavioral evidence of visual tracking given below.

Many other elegant experiments have confirmed that self-locomotion acts as a control parameter in the shift from so-called egocentric to landmark coding (see reviews by Acredelo, 1985, 1988) both for visual search and for reaching toward hidden objects. We return to this literature in chapter 10, when we consider the search for a hidden object task indexed by the so-called A-not-B error. One particular experiment is relevant at this point in our argument, however. We have introduced the notion that experience—both in the short-time scale of learning through exploration and familiarization, and in the long-time scale of developmental change—sets up a dynamic category, an attractor in the space of possible perceptual correlations, that persists over a time scale that is directly related to the strength of the mutually activated neural groups. We have argued that in the case of cross-modal performance this learning in one modality (plus movement!) entraps, so to speak, correlated activation in the other modalities, and that we are experimentally demonstrating, therefore, a process that is repeated over many experiences over a longer time scale. In dynamic terms, we are engendering a phase shift from one stable mode to another by manipulating control parameters to which the system is sensitive.

A perfect example of this microgenesis process involving movement as a perceptual modality comes from Acredolo, Adams, and Goodwyn (1984) who showed that self-movement improved spatial performance even within the time scale of the experiment. They presented infants with a large Plexiglas box with two wells at the center in which toys could be hidden (figure 7.2). The front wall of the box had an opening through which the infants could reach and recover the toys. The infant was seated facing the wall opposite the opening, which was removed so the infant could still retrieve the toy during a series of training trials. Once the infant had successfully retrieved the toy a number of times, that wall was replaced, and the object again hidden. One group of infants were encouraged to move by themselves to the opened wall, and the second group were carried upright by their parent at the same height to the open wall. Thus, the independent variable was simply whether they got to the appropriate wall by themselves or were moved passively.

At 12 months, infants who moved independently were clearly better at recovering the toy, which required that they reach in an opposite direction from their original reach. And most important, the infants in the active condition were also more likely to keep their eyes on the target well as they moved. By 18 months, in contrast, these same infants were accurate in both active and passive condi-

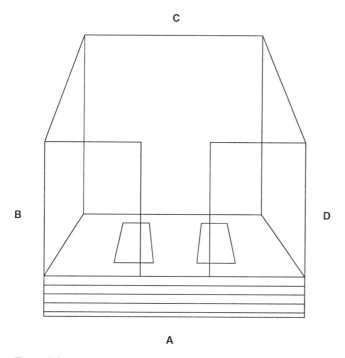

Figure 7.2
Experimental box used to test the role of active locomotion vs. passive transport in infants' abilities to recover the toy through an opening. Wall A is the front wall; C is the back wall. (From Acredolo, Adams, and Goodwyn, 1984. Reprinted with permission.)

tions, and no longer visually tracked the well of interest. In a second experiment, these authors showed that the visual tracking was indeed important. When they replaced the transparent walls of the box with opaque ones, performance in the locomotor condition declined. Again, at 18 months, infants remembered the location in both active and passive conditions despite the opaque walls.

What is happening in this experiment? The repeated familiarization of the spatial location of the hidden toy through looking and reaching must establish a set of expectations through the correlated activity of the neural groups. When infants were passively moved, no new location–movement categories were established. However, in the locomoting infants, who must already have discovered that moving requires keeping your eye on the target, the visual component provided a disjoint, but continuous and correlated take on the same spatial location. Movement thus provided the dynamic sampling of the stimulus attributes time-locked with the perception of movement—a combination that allowed this shift even within the time scale of the experimental manipulation. Without self-produced locomotion, spatial coding remained egocentric in this novel environment. Note also that by 18 months, these infants could remember the correct well without movement and visual tracking. In the intervening 6 months, experience moving and finding objects selected a higher-order category, a representation of the space independent of the self.

We can also cast this experiment directly into the more general dynamic terms we introduced in the first section of this book. Infants younger than about 8 months of age cannot remember the target location after spatial dislocation under any circumstances. They persevere in their motor-response habits set up by the training trials, and indeed, as we argue further below, by their expectations built up by their real-world experiences. After 18 months, they respond nonegocentrically in almost all circumstances. In the transition between one stable attractor and the second stable mode of performance, spatial coding is highly variable, and depends entirely on the nature of training trials, test context (home or in the laboratory, familiar or unfamiliar tester), time delays, and so on (Acredolo, 1985). Thus, in this time of transition, when the components of the system are fluid, performance is affected greatly by even small changes in the infant or the context. When the patterns of response are stable, these contextual manipulations are ineffective. No amount of contextual support can make very young infants notice the location of an object when they have been rotated in respect to that location. Likewise, in the second half of the second year, they are not fooled by their own ego-motion. The attractors in both cases are deep and narrow. Only when they are in the broad plateau between the stable patterns can we perform the experiment of Acredolo et al. Important for our consideration of mechanism, however, is that these authors manipulated a putative control parameter in real time—self-produced locomotion—and mimicked the effect of this control parameter in engendering developmental change.

Other Motor Skills as Control Parameters
The onset of independent locomotion is a dramatic developmental milestone, with broad and far-reaching consequences. But other, more subtle and gradual motor skills may be equally powerful as engines of cognitive change. Bushnell and Boudreau (1993) point out two such instances: the motor component of

haptic perception and that of visual depth perception. In both cases, they found a high correspondence between unfolding perceptual abilities and the acquisition of particular motor patterns.

According to Bushnell and Boudreau's review of the literature, infants acquire the ability to haptically detect various object properties asynchronously. Although the literature is incomplete, they suggest that infants are haptically sensitive first to size or volume, around 3 months, followed at 6 months by texture, temperature, and hardness. Only at 6 to 9 months are they able to distinguish objects by weight, and not until the last part of the first year is configurational shape relevant. What is required to detect object properties haptically? From studies in adults, investigators have identified particular patterns of exploratory hand movements that seem to maximize the sensory information gained by haptic exploration. For example, if texture is relevant, adults use a lateral rubbing movement, but if asked about object weight, adults use a hefting motion. In terms of the neuronal assumptions of TNGS, we might say that certain hand movements optimize the dynamic sampling of the correlated stimulus attributes: What is the coherent pattern of haptic stimulation and associated movement proprioception that will provide the most relevant information? Clearly, only rubbing an object does not activate the joint and muscle stretch receptors that are sensitive to loads on the limb, while hefting does not create a pattern of sensory stimulation on the hand associated with velvet vs. Velcro. If there are indeed optimal patterns of haptic exploration, then infants would not differentiate well in that modality if they lacked the motor control to produce those patterns.

This seems to be the case, at least at a correlational level. From birth until about 3 months, infants mostly just grasp and clutch objects and perform "kneading"-type movements of their fingers. This might be sufficient to detect temperature, size, and hardness, although there are scant experimental results at these ages. At about 4 months, infants begin a much more diverse group of movements, often rhythmic in nature, including scratching, rubbing, waving, banging, squeezing, poking, and passing objects from hand to hand. These are most often unimanual, and would be appropriate for detecting texture and weight. Finally, the detection of configurational shape requires the cooperative use of two hands, which does not develop until late in the first year. In principle, there should be no reason why shape is a later haptic percept than, say, hardness, and indeed, shape may be distinguished visually before it is detected haptically. Thus, it may be the motor limitations on the exploratory movements are indeed the control parameters (Gibson, 1988), again supporting the critical importance of repeated, disjunctive sampling of the stimulus attributes in dynamic category formation.

The second example, the development of visual depth perception, concerns the ability to perceive the world in three dimensions using two eyes (and a two-dimensional retina). There are conventionally three ways in which cues for depth may be picked up, and in his extended and elegant work, Yonas (e.g., Yonas and Granrud, 1985) has shown that these ways do not develop synchronously. First comes sensitivity to kinetic cues, that is, patterns of optical expansion and contraction and motion parallax. Because kinetic cues are equally present whether the object or the observer is moving, movements of the head can provide information about depth. However, the observer must "know" whether his or her head or the scene is actually moving, and this requires control of the head. Thus, control of the head, one of the first motor skills mastered by infants, is a control parameter for using kinetic depth cues. Indeed, such depth sensitivity is evidenced by 3-month-olds, an age by which head control is excellent.

The second cue for depth is binocular information. This relies on having two eyes, both of which sample the three-dimensional scene simultaneously, but where the images fall on different points on the two retinas. It is the comparison of the images on the two retinas that allows us to judge the three-dimensional distance of the target. However, it is essential that when the eyes are surveying the scene, the two eyes move perfectly together to provide consistent information about the distance of the object to both eyes together. This capability—ocular vergence—develops slowly over the first 3 to 4 months of age, and is believed to be a critical contributor to binocular vision, which appears at 4 to 5 months. This finding accords with the animal visual system studies that indicate that correlated input from eye muscles is critical in binocular mapping in the brain.

The third type of depth cues are static monocular cues, which include information available to the retina of a single eye. These include relative size, texture gradients, familiarity, shading, perspective, and other "pictorial" cues. These kinds of cues provide information about depth only when combined with other information. For example, to assume depth from relative size, one has to "know" that closer images appear larger. These cues are effective relatively later in infancy, around 5 to 7 months, and remarkably at about the same range of ages for the various cues. Bushnell and Boudreau offer a motor interpretation of these findings, that is, that these cues for three-dimensional invariants must be learned through some amount of object manipulation, especially as objects are held, looked at, and rotated. This ability first emerges at 4 to 5 months. In other words, the active exploration of the object provides information about real size and shape as objects are moved within the visual field, information sufficient for infants to form more general dynamic categories about the invariants of form as distance from the eye changes.

Development in the Absence of a Perceptual Modality

If the tenets of TNGS are correct, and development of higher-order abilities is based on early dynamic perceptual categorization of multimodal input, then there ought to be dramatic and informative consequences on development if one or more of those modalities are deficient or absent. Because in the last section we have emphasized movement as a critical perceptual input, we report here several recent studies of locomotion and spatial abilities in infants with either vision or movement impairment.

What happens to infants' reasoning about space if they do not locomote? Bertenthal et al. (1984) reported on an orthopedically handicapped infant, who because of two dislocated hips wore a full-body cast until she was 7½ months old and a lighter cast for another month. At 8½ months, she was allowed to crawl and quickly mastered this skill. These authors tested her once a month from age 6 to 10 months on the spatial orientation task we described earlier. Tests at months 6, 7, and 8 showed this infant to have high levels of egocentric responses, but this level dropped dramatically at the 9-month visit, just weeks after she began crawling.

An even more robust confirmation of locomotion as a control parameter in spatial cognition comes from a recent study of seven infants who had delayed locomotion because of meningomyelocele, and who functioned normally in other tests of cognitive functioning (Telzrow, Campos, Kermoian, and Bertenthal, 1992). These infants were tested monthly with two tasks, a hidden object task and a task of following the experimenter's point and gaze. The infants began to crawl at different ages, ranging from 8½ to 13½ months. Nonetheless, there was a dramatic improvement in performance on the object search task in five of the seven infants after the onset of locomotion (whatever the age), and an equally convincing increase in following the point and gaze associated with this milestone. This is especially strong evidence against a strictly maturational hypothesis for hidden search behavior because the infants' performances shifted on both tasks, not as a function of age, but of skill.

Recall that we suggested earlier that perception and action formed an inseparable loop, where improvements in perceptual capabilities may be paced by movement, but that motor skills were also facilitated by concurrent improvements in perception. Intriguing evidence of this loop and the dynamic assembly of skill (a theme we address further in chapter 9) comes from Bigelow's (1992) study of three blind infants. Bigelow tracked these infants from before the onset of crawling until they walked alone. As is well known, blind infants are significantly delayed in locomotor milestones, despite having no motor handicaps. Bigelow tested them monthly with tasks designed to elicit their understanding of object permanence—that is, whether they could locate by reaching toys that either sounded or were silent as they moved in increasingly complex locations away from the infants' bodies. Bigelow found that the emergence of locomotor skills was related to infants' performance on the object permanence task despite considerable differences in age when the tasks were mastered. For example, the infants showed the highest-level performance, that is, tracking a sounding toy or accurately localizing it after it had been displaced, just before or at the time of independent walking, which varied from 17 to 36 months.

Bigelow concluded that for these blind children there was a "sustained relationship between advancement in locomotive skills and object knowledge" (p. 186), but that the relation may not be the same as that in sighted children. In children with normal vision, locomotion provides the setting event which changes infants' attentional relation with objects in the world. In blind children, object knowledge through other modalities may indeed be the setting event for locomotion. The reasoning is thus: sighted children learn of the independent existence of objects in space by just looking and moving their heads and eyes. Thus, the motivation to move forward to capture the items exists long before the motor subsystems support independent locomotion. As was first suggested by Fraiberg (1977), blind children must establish the existence of objects distant from themselves, and the objects' locations, through manual and auditory search and mapping. For them, the motivation to move forward emerges only after these spatial and cognitive relations develop. Although postural and muscle strength may be appropriate for locomotion, motivation acts as the developmental control parameter.

The evidence from blind children is especially cogent confirmation of the dynamic assembly of locomotor skills (Thelen, 1986) and indeed the mutual interaction of the heterogeneous components of the system (see figure 4.4). Development does not proceed as the inevitable consequence of genetic time-tables pacing brain maturation, but as a series of contingencies and tasks. When infants are blocked from learning about the world in one modality, the system is capable of substituting other modalities. When this happens, we see reorganization of subsequent skill development in a manner appropriate to the task at hand. What counts is not a species-typical pattern, but the individual infant's continual problem solving, given his or her current status and the preceding history. Blind infants confront a different task for understanding object permanence and must recruit a different configuration of components to accomplish this task. These patterns, in turn, impose further constraints on subsequent task solutions. The developmental landscape we built in chapter 4 is one each infant constructs epigenetically and contingently. There exist many potential furrows in the state space, and the selection of one pathway over another is through individual experience, whether infants are handicapped or not. We develop this theme further in chapter 9.

Dynamic Memory: From Learning to Development

According to our dynamic view, and consistent with the tenets of TNGS, behavioral development is engendered through the processes of *learning and remembering* in concert with certain tasks or value states. Unfortunately, learning and remembering have been vastly understudied in the infancy period, so that while we know much about the *outcomes* of these processes in terms of behavioral performance, we are not so well informed about the dynamics of the processes themselves. What do infants remember? How do they learn and how do learning and remembering themselves change with age? In the traditional information processing approach, the conclusion is often that infants and children become better information processors with age, that they can handle more information, process it more quickly, and do more things at the same time. While these statements are undoubtedly true, information processing ability is sometimes used as an *explanation for* developmental change. But where do these abilities come from? Does information become more efficiently handled simply as a matter of brain growth? If so, how does that explain the rich, diverse, and nonlinear path of behavioral change?

Although process accounts of infant learning and memory are sparse, the richest source of our understanding comes from a remarkable series of programmatic studies by Carolyn Rovee-Collier and her colleagues. Before interpreting this work in terms of dynamic category formation, we want to review the status of learning and memory in TNGS. Again, we emphasize our assumption of the continuity of time scales, that is, that the dynamics of change in real time are seamless and integral with the dynamics of change over developmental time.

In chapter 4, we described an experiment by Zanone and Kelso (1991), in which adult subjects practiced a novel perceptual motor mapping—learning a new phase relation between the rhythmic movements of the fingers of both hands. Recall that subjects, through exploration and matching of their individual intrinsic dynamics to the task, discovered or selected stable patterns, indicating attractive regions in the state space. As the days of practice progressed, individuals discovered *and remembered* coordination patterns that fit the task, while forgetting less-adaptive solutions.

How did they learn and how did they remember? According to the principles of TNGS we presented in chapter 5, under the goal of matching their finger movements to the pacing of the metronome, subjects repeatedly mapped their felt movements to the beats they heard. Neuronal networks whose dynamics matched the to-be-learned phasing were selectively strengthened through the reentrant and degenerate global mappings. Thus, the 90-degree pattern became a perception-action category dynamically selected through the subjects' repeated exploration.

According to Edelman, the memory of such a match is a kind of recategorization, "the specific enhancement of a previously established ability to categorize" (1992, p. 102). He continues:

> This kind of memory emerges as a population property from continual dynamic changes in the synaptic populations within global mappings— changes that allow a categorization to occur in the first place. Alterations in the synaptic strengths of groups in a global mapping provide the biochemical basis of memory. (p. 102)

Here again we see the continuity of time scales:

> Since perceptual categories are not immutable and are altered by the ongoing behavior of the animal, memory in this view results from a process of continual recategorization. By its nature, memory is procedural and involves continual motor activity and repeated rehearsal in different contexts. Because of the new associations arising in these contexts, because of changing inputs and stimuli, and because different combinations of neuronal groups can give rise to similar output, a given categorical response in memory can be achieved in several ways. (p. 102)

Thus, remembering is not rigid or fixed, but highly dependent on the whole context of the current situation and the history of the remembered category. Each memory is dynamically constructed from many, but not all, of the previously facilitated connections, and as a dynamic attractor may also "pull in" associations not previously included in that dynamic category. Because the perceptual categories are themselves probablistic and context-bound, so are the memories that are based on these categories themselves fluid and inexact. Memory works not as a digital symbol-manipulating machine, but as a dynamic system.

What we suggest in the examples in the rest of this section, and in our later discussion of the A-not-B error, is that during infancy, memory can be particularly context-bound. Because infants' experience acting and thinking in many different contexts—a necessity for moving from perceptual categories to higher level concepts—is limited primarily by their motor skills, what infants remember should be tied closely to the perceptual-motor situation in which the associations were established. This context defines the initial attractor, and the system will be stuck in that attractor—a motor-experience habit, so to speak—until new mappings can be established through different "takes" on the situation. Thus, the onset of a new motor skill acts as a control parameter: it shakes up the stable system, it provides the needed variability, the quasi-stability that allows the system to explore new ways of grouping the components. With this freedom from context-boundedness, this system can acquire enough disjunctive input to recategorize, to form higher-level concepts and access memories from both convergent and divergent pathways.

Most important, however, the theory predicts that perceptual categories and recategorizations (memories and concepts) should be most easily established in modalities where the opportunity for exploration exists, as exploration provides the rich, disjunctive mappings that facilitate the formation and stabilizing of neuronal groups. This means that in any experimental situation where perceptual-motor "knowledge" is assessed, infants will demonstrate a more sophisticated understanding in domains where they have had the opportunity to make these multimodal maps *and* where the experimental situation particularly taps their previous experience. In other words, what any test of infant ability taps is not just current knowledge, but the strength of the attractor formed by the infants' previous opportunities to explore and form perceptual categories and higher-level categorizations. These are individually acquired and reflect absolutely infants' interactions in the world, minute by minute and day by day.

It is just because knowledge is dynamically acquired, stored, and retrieved that we see the pervasive messiness we described in chapter 2—décalage, context specificity, precocity, and seeming gaps between competence and performance. This messiness reflects the sometimes predictable and sometimes nonsystematic encounters between infants, who differ in their capabilities, and their environments, which differ in their opportunities. It explains why infants "know" certain properties about objects very early in life and are resistantly stupid about other, equally defining properties of objects quite late in infancy. It explains why some multimodal matching tasks are easy while others take many more months to acquire, and why some associations may never be learned at all. And it explains why, as we discuss below, younger infants can remember some things better than older ones, why memories can become attached to peculiar situations, and why memory development appears to have a particular nonlinear character.

Experimental Studies of Infant Learning and Memory
It is not an understatement to say that most of what we know about infant memory comes from a long and highly systematic series of studies conducted by Rovee-Collier and her associates (see Rovee-Collier and Gekoski, 1979; Rovee-Collier and Hayne, 1987; Rovee-Collier, 1990, for reviews). What makes these studies so unique and informative is that Rovee-Collier has used the same robust behavioral phenomenon—infant conjugate reinforcement—to explore the conditions of learning, remembering, and forgetting in infants at 3 and 6 months of age. The training and testing are deceptively simple. Infants are placed on their backs (3-month-olds), or in a soft sling (6-month-olds) and their ankles are attached by a ribbon to a mobile which is suspended overhead. As the infants kick their feet, at first spontaneously, they activate the mobile. Within a few minutes, they learn the contingency between their foot kicks and the jiggling of the mobile, which presents interesting sights and sounds. The mobile responds conjugately to the infants' actions: the more they kick and the more vigorously

they move, the more motion and sound they produce. In this situation, infants increase their kicking to above the baseline spontaneous level measured when they simply looked at a nonmoving mobile. Infants can then be tested for how much they remember about the training situation, by counting foot kicks in the same or a different situation at various times subsequent to the original training. The experiments can vary not only the times of retesting but the qualities of the mobile, immediate context, time of day, etc. In addition, Rovee-Collier and associates have effectively used a "reminder" condition, where infants are placed in the training situation and shown the moving mobile, but where the infant does not actually produce mobile movements with self-generated foot kicks.

Before reinterpreting the results of these many experiments, we must comment on how rich and appropriate the training task is in terms of the dynamic principles of TNGS. The mobile is a complex, but above all, *moving* visual and sounding display, where looking and listening provides the infant with many correlated examples of coherent object properties from different takes. But most important, the infants themselves are moving contingently with the mobile; the faster and harder they kick, the more vigorously the mobile will jiggle. Thus, the experimental training procedure provides an unusually complex, diverse, and repeated, *yet perfectly time-locked* set of inputs—visual, auditory, tactile, and proprioceptive. In turn, the contingent control of the mobile is highly reinforcing. Infants remain intensely engaged in the task, often smile and laugh, and become angry when the contingency is removed. Mobile jiggling is associated with high positive value. It is difficult to imagine many other naturally occurring circumstances where 3-month-olds (who are not good at either locomotion or manipulation) could so easily fulfill the optimal conditions for categorization and learning.

Placed in these highly facilitative conditions, 3-month-old infants show remarkable memory capabilities over very long times—producing kicks at a high level more than a week after their training (Fagen and Rovee-Collier, 1983). With more time, they forgot the training and responded at baseline levels by 2 weeks after training.

What infants remembered was not a general impression of the task, however, but was highly specifically tied to the original training context. Both the features of the mobile and of the rest of the training environment mattered greatly in what infants remembered and how they forgot. For example, both 2- and 3-month-olds tested at 24 hours after training performed better than baseline only when the test mobile was virtually identical to the original training mobile. Even when one or two items on the mobile were changed, infants forgot their training completely. Likewise, even these young infants encoded and remembered specific details of their environment of training. When trained and tested with the same distinctive cloth "bumper" on the crib, they remembered the task a week later. When the bumper was changed for the test, however, infants could not recall training even after only 3 days. Recall that without the distinctive bumper change, forgetting occurred gradually over 2 weeks. Even more remarkable was that if infants were tested *with a different bumper within 24 hours of training*, the change of context did *not* disrupt performance (Butler and Rovee-Collier, 1989).

How to interpret these puzzling results? Under the favorable conditions of this experiment, even very young infants not only quickly learned the contingent relation between their actions and interesting events, they remembered this relation in a highly specific and context-dependent and nonlinear way. Presumably the highly salient training situation creates dynamic categories which capture both the specific details of the mobile, the movement producing the interesting effect, and the context of training. We have depicted this process in an ontogenetic landscape seen in figure 7.3. As usual, the depth and steepness of the valleys indicate the attractor strength. A strong attractor produces stable behavior that is not easily disrupted. When trained in a familiar, nondistinctive context, infants pay little attention to the familiar context and the context attractor is not very strong, as depicted in figure 7.3A. However, the distinctive context—a surprise—captures attention and creates a new, associated attractor. But because the infants' attention is directed toward the mobile itself, and the activity of the mobile provides so many disjoint takes on the experience, let us further assume that the perceptual categories of the mobile are always stronger than, but associated with, those of the bumper. While the multimodal maps of this experience are very strong (within 24 hours) and the attractor basins are deep, the infant can retrieve details of the mobile and its associated kicking without "pulling in"

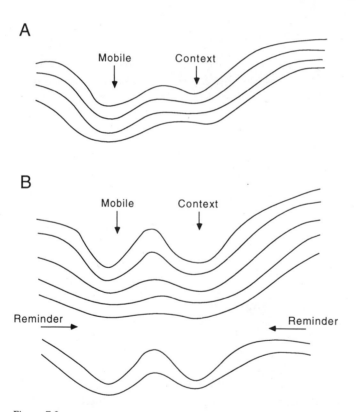

Figure 7.3
Landscape of context effects on remembering mobile reinforcement. *A,* When the context is familiar, the infant pays little attention to it and the attractor basin of the mobile dominates. *B,* When context is salient, the infant forms two associated attractors, which are separately retrievable initially, but become more closely associated with time. After time, visual reminder of either the training mobile or the context reactivates memories of both the mobile and the context.

the nearby context attractor, as in the top of the landscape of figure 7.3B. However, as the attractor basin flattens and widens somewhat with time, the mobile-kicking association becomes more linked and tied to the context attractor.

No one remembers his or her infancy. What happens to the memories of events early in life? Does the "forgetting" how to activate the mobile reveal infants' poor capacities for memory storage, which faded after 2 weeks? Remarkably, Rovee-Collier and her associates have demonstrated that infants store memories for a long time, but need appropriate activation cues in order to retrieve them. These cues need not be an exact replicate of the entire situation of training, but only salient parts of the training environment. Thus, infants who see the mobile, or the distinctive bumper in which training takes place, recall the motor training completely, even after 2 weeks, when unreminded forgetting is nearly complete. In terms of our landscape, either a view of the mobile or of the distinctive context is sufficient to reactivate the network through its high degenerative and reentrant connections, and again form a more stable performance attractor (see figure 7.3B). In other words, the kicking memory is so closely categorized with the visual memory of the training site that the action is remembered only through activation of the visual trace. Paradoxically, although infants become less disrupted by novel mobile elements as time passes, the reminder mobile in the reactivation task—when forgetting was nearly complete—needs to be a replicate of the original training mobile (Rovee-Collier, Griesler, and Early, 1985). This is especially intriguing given that if infants were trained with a novel crib bumper—a distinctive context—seeing the bumper alone, *without the mobile*, also effectively reminded the babies of the kicking contingency 2 weeks after the original test event. However, the presence of the training mobile in the reminder could override a change of context.

There are a number of important implications from these training and reminder studies in 3-month-olds. First, forgetting in infants, as in adults, may be a problem not so much of memory storage as one of retrieval. Infants can remember a few minutes of an interesting situation many weeks later when given sufficient facilitating memory support. (We are reminded of the uncomfortably common situation at professional meetings of greeting a familiar face and not being able to recall the person's name. However, even a small cue in the conversation can trigger the name memory, and a host of other details.) Second, and most relevant to our dynamic view, is the complex interplay between the focal and contextual retrieval cues. Rovee-Collier and her associates (Rovee-Collier and Hayne, 1987; Butler and Rovee-Collier, 1989) interpret this as reflecting a hierarchical gating structure for retrieval cues. Recall that infants generalize to novel mobiles if trained in a neutral context, but once the distinctive context is present, novelty in the mobile disrupts performance. They suggest that contextual retrieval cues are exploited hierarchically:

> We propose that infants use information in the proximal context as their primary source of retrieval cues if that information is unambiguous. If it is ambiguous, then they use more distal contextual information. If distal cues match attributes in the memory representation, then infants turn again to the proximal context; if it is also the same, then retrieval is initiated; if it is different then retrieval is not initiated. If, however, the distal contextual

cues do not match the attributes in the memory representation, then memory processing is terminated at that point. Thus, we assign to the distal context an initial gating function for retrieval: in addition, we see that the distal context disambiguates proximal contextual information that is "fuzzy," enhancing its discriminability. (Rovee-Collier and Hayne, 1987, pp. 219–220)

A dynamic account can explain both remembering and reminding without putting an "if-then" logical machine into the infant's head. Again, the focal object, the mobile, with its salient colors, shapes, movements, noises, all contingently linked to vigorous leg movements, forms an initial strong perceptual-motor attractor category which indeed broadens and becomes "fuzzier" with the passage of time. Since the neutral or familiar stimulus is much less salient than the mobile, it does not capture the infant's attention and contributes only a shallow well in the attractor basin. Under these circumstances, and when the original trace is fuzzy, novelty in the mobile reminder is not sufficient to attract the rest of the training cues, including the motor memory. However, when the training context is also salient and nearby, interacting attractor wells are created, a context reminder generates sufficient activation to pull in the more proximal, mobile connections as well. However, if the reminder context is different from the training context, there are no necessary connections between the context and the original mobile attractor trace, and mutually activated networks are insufficient to link the two events. The process need not be either logical or hierarchical, but depends entirely on the strength of the original training, that is, the salience and correspondence of the mobile and the context, and the time-dependent trajectory of the weakening of the original neuronal group connections.

Given that remembering in 3-month-olds is so tied to the training context, how can infants ever learn to generalize—to realize that all mobiles afford kicking, or that rattles afford shaking, bottles sucking, and so on? Exactly as would be predicted by TGNS, the key appears to be in increasing the variability, in the multiple takes of situations, that allows the common features to be successively selected and recategorized. Three-month-old infants trained with the same mobile for two daily sessions did not respond to a novel mobile 24 hours later. However, infants trained with a *novel* mobile in each daily session generalized their kicking rate to another novel mobile the next day (Fagen, Morrongiello, Rovee-Collier, and Gekoski, 1984). Rovee-Collier and her associates interpret these, and other supporting results, as the infants having learned the *category* "mobile-to-be-kicked," which was more general than the specific cues of the individual training mobiles. Indeed, once infants had been trained on several mobiles, novel mobiles were equally effective as reminders to alleviate forgetting, although without this variable training, infants discriminate even small differences between training and test mobiles and do not kick at training rates. Indeed, whether a novel mobile is considered part of the training category "mobile-to-be-kicked" depends on the physical and functional characteristics of that mobile, the similarity of the context between the test and exemplar situations, and the time between training and test (Greco, Hayne, and Rovee-Collier, 1990).

Again, these dynamics can be summarized in a landscape (figure 7.4). Imagine that training on one mobile creates a basin and that training on the second mobile

Training with several mobiles

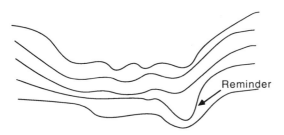

Figure 7.4
Landscape of generalization when trained with different mobiles. The attractor basin has many overlapping valleys. Reminder with novel mobile activates some common features and pulls in nearby attractor wells.

creates another basin, but with many overlapping areas in the state space. These overlaps are created because, although some features differ, the two training situations will activate many common and degenerate perceptual neural groups. Indeed, it is this wider overlap that allows a basin to emerge from the training session that can be activated by more general features of "mobiles-to-be-kicked" than the more steep and deep attractor of single-mobile training. Thus, when the infant is either tested or reminded by a third novel mobile, the shared features of the category are sufficient to activate the entire perceptual-motor group, and training kicking rates emerge. Training from many exemplars allows recognition and recall from many entries. As we shall see in the next section and succeeding chapters, such an account explains the tight contextual memory of other early skills, and their subsequent generalization to novel events and encounters.

This account of memory supports our process account of décalage. Events in the real world that naturally provide many disjoint, repeated takes allow early recategorization and generalization. A principle salient activity for young infants is moving their eyes and head and looking at objects and events around them, an action they repeat many, many times and in many different contexts. This time-locked activity forms memory attractors of the correlated features of events and objects that are broad and allow entry from many different stimulus characteristics. Infants come to expect, for example, that there is a category of events whose edges move together. They learn this quickly in an experimental situation and are surprised when their expectations are violated. Categories that are associated with more complex motor skills such as reaching and locomotion are more specifically tied to the gradually improving skills. Thus, infants first may remember responses only when their postural or situational context reminds them of their real-life "training" situation. Only when the motor skill itself is sufficiently established to provide the multiple takes to effectively recategorize, do they respond to more general situations. Because of the cyclic nature of action and perception, improved motor skill also allows infants to become better perceptual learners. Increased perceptual discrimination, in turn, increases the multiple takes of objects and events, which further enhances the process of recategorization and makes memory more general. Because infants' skills and opportunities in the real world interact in a nonlinear and asynchronous manner, at the performance level, this process looks like striking décalage, not only between domains but even within spheres of functioning.

Developmental Changes in Memory

How then, do developing perceptual and motor skills change the dynamics of memory? Can we see effects of the infants' own abilities and experiences on what they remember and how they remember it? Here we turn the usual developmental story around; conventionally, memory capacity is believed to increase autonomously as the brain "matures." As memory increases, so does the complexity of the resulting cognitive skills. While a better memory can certainly lead to more complex behavior, we may also ask: What constitutes a better memory? By what processes does memory capacity improve? Here again, we invoke the dynamic and interactive processes of TNGS.

A recent series of experiments on 6-month-olds by Rovee-Collier and her associates is especially enlightening. Recall that in 3-month-old infants, a change of context did not disrupt retention of the mobile training situation after 1 day, but did so after 3 days. For 3-month-olds, the training context was important, but especially when it was distinctive and when the mobile context was somewhat fuzzy. Surprisingly, the context effect was even stronger in 6-month-old infants. At this age, reminders were not effective in retrieval unless the infants had been trained, reminded, and tested in the same, highly distinct context (Boller, Rovee-Collier, Borovsky, O'Connor, and Shyi, 1990). Even 1 day after training, a change in context disrupted retention, and when infants were reminded with the original mobile, they did not retain training if the reminding condition was different (Borovsky and Rovee-Collier, 1990). Like the younger infants, 6-month-olds were able to form categories of "mobiles-to-be-kicked" when trained on several novel mobiles and to transfer this category learning to a novel test mobile a day later. However, the context of testing needed to be the same. This context specificity was retained over a long time period—reactivation of the forgotten memory required the training context (Shields and Rovee-Collier, 1992).

The 6-month-olds' increased attention to context seems counterintuitive at first. Why should memories become increasingly tied to training situation with age, given that it would seem to be more adaptive to ignore the context and generalize the mobile category itself? Borovsky and Rovee-Collier (1990) speculate that it is infants' "progressive expansion of the range of focal attention" (p. 1580) over the first half of the year that matters. Young infants only pay attention to the mobile itself and are not as concerned with the characteristics of the crib or playpen, room setting, and so on. But as infants pay attention to a wider range of places and events around them, the same contextual cues become encoded along with the salient training experience. Although Borovsky and Rovee-Collier envision these other more remote contexts as acting as "attention gates" that must be detected before the target stimulus can be retrieved, we suggest that they provide an even richer set of associated activations that form with the associations of the target mobile. This means that the attractor may well be even deeper and more stable than when the contextual cues were more weakly associated with the target cues. In other words, the older infants are "cementing" their memories of the mobile with those of other salient parts of the context, and changes in either the mobile itself or in the training context are highly disruptive for retrieval. The components of the memory are tightly linked, but not broadly associated with varying contexts, and thus cannot be retrieved with more general access cues.

There are a number of important implications from the results on 6-month-olds. First, as Borovsky and Rovee-Collier (1990) suggest, it is intriguing that infants would be paying more attention to their surroundings just as they are about to embark on independent locomotion. Thus, it looks as if this expansion of visual attention and the consequent encoding into memory of distal places and events set the stage for learning landmarks. It is important for infants first to understand what happens where, so that they may remember locations as they move about. But these results also explain why infants' spatial knowledge is so egocentric before they embark on independent locomotion, as their memories are quite specifically tied to the place where they learned the activity. As we shall see, this context specificity of action is not age-specific, but appears to be a function of the infants' own activity status. Infants need to generate their own repeated, reentrant information—at whatever age—to provide the multiple takes on the events in the world.

Finally, Rovee-Collier's work as a whole is compelling evidence for the dynamic nature of early cognition. Categories—the foundations of knowledge—emerge from infants' ongoing activities and encounters with the world. As infants' act and perceive, remember and forget, they select those associations in the world that naturally cohere. Their categories are informed by their experiences, which are naturally variable, and thus provide the messy, rich, redundant information from which neural selection can act.

These experiments on learning to kick a mobile reveal how infants acquire fundamental knowledge about the world. As Piaget suggested, this knowledge is inextricably tied up with action. Movement is not incidental to learning, but part of the perceptual package that is the basis of categorization and recategorization. What infants know and what they remember is of a piece with what they see, hear, and feel. However, in contrast to Piaget, we believe that knowledge is not constructed from the successive integration of separate modalities or from the elaboration of structures which contain general knowledge schemata. Rather, what infants know and how they act are selected continuously and dynamically from what they encounter and how they act. Sensory integration is the primitive, not the derived, state, and knowledge is limited not primarily by deficits in storage but in the ability to adequately sample and thus categorize the world.

In the next chapter, we see that this dynamic process applies to early learning in other domains.

Note

1. Credit for recognizing the central importance of self-activity in the development of cognition must go to Piaget, of course. However, as we discussed earlier, Piaget considered movement to originate as separate from the other sensory systems, primarily in the form of unguided reflexes, and that action served to bring together the disparate systems to allow for adaptive behavior.

PART III

Dynamics and the Origins of Knowledge

Chapter 8

The Context-Specific Origin of Knowledge

In the last chapter, we argued that categories emerge in and from infants' ongoing activities. Being in the world—acting, perceiving, remembering—*selects* associations and relationships that cohere. We found support for these ideas in Rovee-Collier's findings about infant memory. In this chapter, we consider three more lines of research: (1) studies of infants' locomotion over sloping surfaces, (2) studies of infants' perceptions of possible and impossible events, and (3) studies of children's novel word interpretations. All three lines of research can be understood in terms of a developmental process that accrues over and in real-time activities, in behavior that contains *at one and the same time* the history of the organism, the here and now, and the future. We show in this chapter how these ideas have radical consequences for how we understand development and how we study it.

Global Structure–Local Variability: The Integration of Time Scales

There are, for any behavior, two perspectives. There is, first, the *view from above.* As we discussed in chapters 1 and 2, what we see when we look at behavior with our lowest level of magnification is a global structure that inheres in and across individual acts. Thus, when cats walk, they walk in the same general way with alternating limbs regardless of the terrain. When we reach for the coffee cup, we perform the same general act. Each time we understand the word *mother*—in the sentence *That is my mother there* and in the sentence *What an odd mother Bill has*—we understand a common meaning. There is a global structure to cat walks, to reaches for coffee cups, and to word meanings. Part of the job of developmental psychology is to explain where this global order comes from and how it changes with development.

But there is also the second perspective on behavior. There is the *view from below.* From here behavior looks messy, fluid, and highly context-dependent. When we turn up the magnification of the microscope, we see that individual cat walks are nothing at all alike. They involve different patterns of muscle activity tightly tied to the nature of the terrain—different patterns, very different details, for going up hills and down hills and around obstacles in the path. When we turn up the microscope, we see that each individual reach for the coffee cup is not the same: it is sometimes fast, sometimes slow, and sometimes we bobble it and spill coffee all over our desk. When we turn up the microscope, even the meanings of words appear messy and fluid; *mother*, as we discussed in chapter 6, means many different things. When we look closely at behavior, we see lots of local variability. No two acts are ever exactly alike. Developmental psychology has also to explain the local adaptability of individual acts—how the global structure is made to fit the task at hand.

This second problem, the one of explaining how behavior is fit to specific task contexts, has not received much attention in traditional psychology. Moreover, the problem of local variability has been considered separate from and secondary to the problem of explaining the global structure. Traditional approaches explain the global order of behavior by postulating an underlying order—a central pattern generator (CPG) for cat walking, a motor plan for cup reaches, an essence for word meanings. In traditional static-structure approaches, the reasons all instances of cat walking (or cup reaches or understandings of a word) are globally similar to one another is because they share a common underlying structure. This constant underlying structure is accessed and directs individual acts.

This form of explanation leaves unexplained the local details of individual acts—"their fit" to the specific context. In leaving unexplained how the global details are fit to the task at hand, the global structure is left unexplained as well. We can see this by rethinking about an idea we rejected in chapter 1, that quadruped walking in cats is controlled by a CPG. We rejected the idea of a CPG because a CPG alone is not enough to explain cat walking. Real cats walk backward, over obstacles, with casts, uphill and down. The global structure of cat walking is present in all these cases but the variability between these individual contexts is enormous. Indeed, as we discussed in chapter 1, these various actions require fundamentally different patterns of muscle firing to maintain the alternating pattern of walking. Yet the presumptive CPG is a supposed constant. If the CPG outputs a constant fixed pattern, then it *cannot be the sole cause* of the similar structure of walking backward, forward, and with a cast. If a CPG exists, then there must be other processes that make walking happen in qualitatively similar yet appropriately different ways in all these contexts. By not explaining how the global order is realized amid the local details, there is a failure to explain the global order itself.

Dynamic systems explains both the global order and the local details. The global order and the local variability are *the same thing;* they are inextricably tied together in a way that confers a special status on context—on the role of the immediate here and now. Context—the here and now—matters in three ways. First, context *makes* the global order. The global order is a history of perceiving and acting in specific contexts; it is through repeated here-and-now experiences that the global order is developed. Second, context *selects* the global order such that we can perform qualitatively different acts. For example, depending on the terrain, we can sometimes walk, sometimes slide, and sometimes stand still. Third, context *adapts* the global order; it fits the history of past here and nows to the task at hand. Context makes, selects, and adapts knowledge in our dynamic systems theory because knowledge is only made manifest in a real-time task. The global order is the pattern of the real-time activity of time-locked and reentrant systems—a pattern of activity that includes the sensory input of the moment, the preceding activity, and the history of activity. Since the global order is made by and made manifest in the details of the here and now, it is most fundamentally always context-dependent.

This view suggests a particular developmental direction. Early in development, patterns of behavior should be closely tied to the specifics of experience, to the details of the task contexts in which it is emerging. Continued activity, perceiving and acting in and thereby exploring additional contexts, will lead to two kinds of changes: (a) the selection of associations that inhere across the most diverse contexts and (b) the selection of details that cause the system to reorganize—to jump between—global structures. With development—with the continued exploration of perceiving and acting—the global structure will become both more general—more seemingly removed from the here and now—and more highly differentiated and distinguishing of different classes of context. In the vocabulary of dynamic systems, continued reentrant mappings between the systems that comprise perceiving and acting will cause deep attractors to form. These deep attractors embody the global structure: the knowledge. These attractors, however, are not things; they are trajectories of activity of neuronal groups through time—trajectories built through the reentrant mapping of heterogeneous systems. In the activity of these neuronal groups, the here and now is always of a piece with the past.

We begin our consideration of the pivotal role of context—the here and now—in the development of knowledge by showing how knowledge in one domain, that of self-locomotion on sloping surfaces, is formed in a highly context-specific way. We then show how infants' abstract ideas about the physical laws of the universe may be understood in terms of evolving event trajectories—abstract knowledge that is made by and made manifest in context-specific experience. Finally, we consider developmental evidence about children's novel word interpretations. We show how patterns of activity become increasingly differentiated and how context comes increasingly to shift the system from one global order to another.

Learning About Slopes

How do humans solve the cat walking problem? How do we learn to move effectively on flat land, up slopes, down slopes? How do we discover what our bodies can and cannot do on different terrains? Karen Adolph and her colleagues (Adolph, Eppler, and Gibson, 1993a,b) are discovering that we learn it task by task, context by context, with little initial transfer from one form of locomotion (crawling) to another (walking). The pattern of development being uncovered in this research looks just like Rovee-Collier's findings on the context-specific nature of infant memories. It looks as one would expect it to look if knowledge is built through the time-locked interactions of perceiving and acting in particular contexts.

Working within a Gibsonian affordance framework, Adolph and her colleagues have been asking how crawling and walking infants perceive the "fit" between their abilities and the steepness of slopes. Placed at the top or bottom of an inclined plane, do infants recognize slopes that are too steep to traverse safely—without falling—and do they adjust their behavior accordingly? Classic work on infant perception suggests that they should. Readers will recall the classic visual cliff experiments: crawling babies avoid crossing a visually specified vertical drop-off, even though the cliff is covered with Plexiglas and has a rigid surface that can be detected haptically (Gibson and Walk, 1960). If crawling infants' perfor-mance on the visual cliff signals a general competence, a knowledge structure about depths and their consequences, then one might expect this knowledge structure to show itself when the infant is faced not with a cliff but with a steep incline as shown in figure 8.1. It does not, however.

Before turning to the data, it is important to acknowledge three potentially critical ways that the slope experiments of Adolph and colleagues differ from the visual cliff experiments. First, whereas infants commonly encounter vertical drop-offs in beds, sofas, chairs, and stairs, they do not so regularly encounter sloping surfaces. Traversing inclined planes is a relatively novel task. Second, in the slope experiments, there was no conflict between perceptual modalities. Haptic and visual information were congruent and veridically specified the de-gree of slope. Third, infants were tested both ascending and descending slopes. Ascent and descent create different biomechanical challenges; they are, in their local details, very different tasks.

In their first experiments, Adolph, Eppler, and Gibson (1993a) tested 14-month-old toddlers and 8½-month-old crawlers on an apparatus whose sloping surface could be varied to be 10, 20, 30, or 40 degrees. Infants were encouraged to walk or crawl both up and down the slopes. Remarkably, both crawlers and walkers attempted to go up every slope, usually without any hesitation or exploration of the slope with their hands or feet. They often fell or lost postural control on the steeper slopes, but continued to climb. Falling forward while walking or crawling

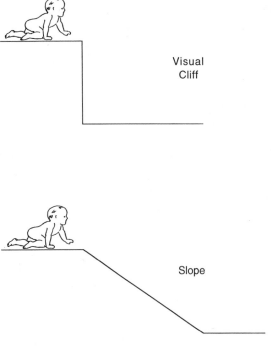

Figure 8.1
The different perceptual motor tasks presented by a visual cliff versus a slope.

uphill has relatively mild consequences—infants can catch their short fall with their hands.

Descending a hill, however, is biomechanically challenging. Falling has severe consequences. In this downhill task, walkers and crawlers differed dramatically. Walkers were very cautious, and as the slopes became steeper—at 20, 30, and 40 degrees—they hesitated, explored, and either refused or, most often, changed their mode of locomotion from walking to sliding, backing down, etc. Crawlers, in contrast, plunged headfirst down the slopes, as if they could not detect the consequences. Most of the infants attempted to crawl down 10- and 20-degree slopes, even though many fell. Many still tried the steeper slopes, and they nearly always fell. And a considerable proportion of the crawlers seemed oblivious even to steep drop-offs and plunged down these slopes to a certain fall. This reckless behavior of crawlers on the edge of slopes contrasts sharply with crawlers on the edge of a cliff; crawlers always avoid the visual cliff.

Why these striking differences between walkers and crawlers on slopes? Were walkers just generally smarter because they were 6 months older, and therefore figured out the danger of falling downhill? This is not likely because crawlers of the same age and locomotor abilities as those plunging down slopes *could* detect the vertical drop of the visual cliff and actively avoided it. We have here a dramatic example of décalage in the classic sense—the crawlers show they know the consequences of heights and falling for cliffs but they seem not to know the consequences of heights and falling for slopes. Perhaps, one might argue, crawlers are insensitive to the visual properties of the slopes. This is also not likely because even though crawlers overestimated their abilities to descend, they did hesitate more on the steeper slopes and explored them more before attempting descent.

Another possibility and one that is supported by the subsequent findings of Adolph et al. is that the crawlers could detect the slopes, but they did not know what slopes meant. They could not *match their own locomotor abilities* to the demands of going up or going down slopes (Adolph et al., 1993b). For ascent, the consequences of this inability to match locomotor skill and task were minimal, but on descent, poor matches between skill and task led to real losses of posture. Walkers, in contrast to crawlers, were able to match their skills to the task at hand. They knew they could walk up shallow and steep slopes, could walk down shallow slopes, but could not walk down steep slopes. Evidence for such a matching process in the walkers is also supported by the finding that skilled walkers, as indexed by increasing step length, attempted to descend steeper slopes. No relation between crawling skill and attempts was clearly demarcated in the crawlers.

In a second experiment, Adolph (1993) used smaller increments of slope and varied the slope order to detect the precision with which walkers were able to match their perceptions of "walkability" with their actual performance. Did walkers always succeed without falling *if* they attempted a slope? Adolph found that, indeed, walking infants were very accurate at making the match between their own skills and the properties of the slopes. Especially on the descending trials, where the consequences of falling were more severe, infants made very few errors. They recognized a stable steepness threshold; when the slopes were shallower than their individual threshold, they walked down without falling.

When the slopes were steeper, they did not walk, but found alternative means of descent. These walking infants, unlike the crawlers, know precisely the boundary between what can be walked and what cannot.

By what processes do infants come to make such specific matches between their evolving motor and perceptual skills? Findings from a longitudinal study indicate that the locomotor consequences of slopes are learned (Adolph, 1993). Adolph followed individual infants from early crawling through initial walking to proficient walking. This longitudinal approach reveals a developmental trajectory built on context-specific experience that is not obvious in the cross-sectional data.

The longitudinal data indicate that when infants first crawl, they plunge head-first down slopes of any steepness, seemingly with reckless abandon. If they notice that their arms collapse under them, it does not inhibit their further downward attempts. (Note that in all these studies, the experimenters carefully "catch" the infants!) Gradually, however, over months of crawling experience, these same infants—now proficient crawlers and through their experience in the longitudinal study, crawlers with regular experiences on slopes—do become more cautious as the steepness of the hills increases, and eventually they show strong indications—by hesitation, exploration, refusal, and finding alternative modes of transport—that they recognize that slopes may lead to falling. From these results, we know that it is not walking alone that can teach the infants about the consequences of slopes nor does knowing about slopes depend on reaching some magical point in maturation.

But what do these now proficient crawlers know about slopes? Does the knowledge that they can go down shallow slopes but not steep ones generalize when they stand up and walk? The answer to this second question is a resounding no; their knowledge *does not* generalize. When crawlers become walkers, they have to learn about slopes all over again. Adolph found that 10 of 15 just-newly walking infants plunged without hesitation down all the steep slopes, just as they did when they first encountered them as crawlers. Among the other subjects, some infants made many mistakes, walking over slopes and stumbling, although a few were overly cautious and did not walk down even very shallow slopes they might have managed. In some infants, the transition between crawling knowledge and walking knowledge was dramatic even within a session. Placed on hands and knees at the top of a steep slope, the infants would hesitate and explore, but not descend and fall. Stood up immediately thereafter, the infants plunged headfirst over, as though they had become instantly ignorant of slopeness. Understanding returned when they were put in the crawling position again. Several persistent new toddlers, when positioned on hands and knees at the top of the hill, immediately stood up by themselves—the more grown-up posture—and just as quickly flung themselves headfirst down the steep hill. Knowing about slopes is for early walkers task-specific. All the infants, of course, relearned rather quickly over the next weeks and months of walking to adjust their attempts to their increasing levels of skill in balance and control.

This remarkable décalage is compelling evidence against domain-general knowledge structures and eloquently supports the dynamic account of learning and memory we outlined in the previous chapter. In dynamic terms, we can explain infants' behavior on slopes as an interaction between their accumulated experience perceiving and acting, the relative novelty and familiarity of the testing procedure, and the relevance of the test situation in helping infants retrieve a perception-action category. We explain the developmental progression as follows: as infants begin to crawl they are, as Rovee-Collier's work shows, likely to be attending and encoding their surrounds. When infants begin to crawl, their "surrounds" are almost always flat surfaces and with some frequency, they will approach head-on vertical drops between flat surfaces. It is unlikely they will approach head-on inclined planes. If action memories are highly activity- and context-specific, as in the mobile experiments, then general categories discovered about vertical drops would not easily generalize to slopes. In other words, the attractor formed by the match—*crawl on flat–hesitate on visually detected vertical drop*—would not be activated by a slope. The contents of here-and-now experience, of being on and looking down a slope, would not be enough of a "reminder" of the history of accumulated here-and-now experiences with vertical drops for that knowledge to generalize. In other words, the novel event of a slope is not linked to the well-stabilized attractor.

We illustrate this developmental set of affairs in figure 8.2. Shown is a theoretical state space like those we drew for the perceptual segregation of objects in chapter 6. The theoretical space is defined by two complex and *time-locked* systems: perception and action. Using the same ideas of the theory of neuronal group selection (TNGS) that Reeke and Edelman used to build a device that recognized letters, and the same ideas we used to explain the development of static cues to object perception from dynamic ones, we proposed that through reentrant maps built through the time-locked perceptions and felt movements of crawling on flat surfaces, a complex and deep attractor would emerge. This hypothetical attractor, shown in figure 8.2, represents the crawling infant's accumulated experiences and sets of expectations given certain combinations of visual events and felt movements. Portions of this complex attractor thus correspond to the sequence of time-locked perceptions and actions that are coming up to a visual cliff and backing away. Adolph's data suggest that the visual events of looking down an incline are far from those that occur when infants look down a visual cliff; when the young crawler is placed on the slope he is far from the attractor that is knowledge of cliffs. Presumably, months of crawling and ex-

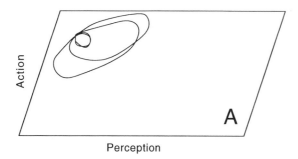

Figure 8.2
Hypothetical attractor for crawling in the state space of self-locomotion tasks. The letter *A* denotes the distant region of the state space that the infant places him or herself once standing and walking.

ploring the reactions of the body to a variety of situations would widen the attractor basin and enrich the linkages, as the perception-action category of "crawlable on" becomes more generalized. In our view, this is what is happening in the longitudinal studies as infants repeatedly experience going up and down slopes in the laboratory and as they encounter diverse surfaces in the world.

With the transition to independent standing, however, and a whole new set of haptic, proprioceptive, and visual associations, there is little or weak connection to the crawling-based attractor, which is nested in the particular posture and movement of crawling and a particular view of the world from on all fours. Before infants have good locomotor skills and are able to sample the environment widely, their memories are tightly context-bound. In this case it is the posture context that determines both the infants' perceptual view of the world and felt movements. As infants practice their skills they put themselves in new postural contexts—in new regions of the state space—a point A, perhaps, in figure 8.2. Infants explore these new regions by perceiving and acting in new postural contexts and in so doing they develop deeper and broader attractors, attractors that embody more generally accessible categories. Thus, it may be that with sufficient exploration of a variety of postures and a variety of terrains, that knowledge about slopes and other kinds of deviations from flat surfaces become general. At some point, children might have general ideas that going down slopes are tricky–walking, crawling, or jumping.

We believe that these experiments on learning to descend a slope reveal fundamental truths about the nature of our knowledge of the world. First, knowledge is inextricably tied up with action. Movement is not incidental to learning, but part of the perceptual package that is the basis of categorization and recategorization. What infants know and what they remember is one with what they see, hear, and feel. Second, knowledge is not constructed from the successive integration of separate modalities or elaboration of structures that contain general knowledge schemata. Rather, what infants know and how they act are selected continuously and dynamically from what they encounter and how they act. Knowledge has its origins in the real-time details of the here and now and that fact is evidenced in the context specificity of early knowledge.

Knowing What Is Possible

In our dynamic systems view, knowledge does not *just* have its origins in the specifics of the here and now. It is always of a piece with both the present and past because knowledge is a trajectory of activity that depends on both the past and the current. Embracing this idea makes many classic themes—and current arguments against them—moot. One such debate that can be retired concerns the traditional idea that the direction of cognitive development is away from perceiving and acting in the here and now and toward abstract ideas that exist apart from immediate experience. Are infants tied to the here and now as Piaget (1952), Vygotsky (1986), and Werner (1957) would have it? Is development *away from perception* as Flavell (1970), Wohlwill (1962), Bruner and Olver (1963), and, more recently, Gentner (1989) and Keil (1989) suggest? Or are infants' rational Kantians with very abstract knowledge structures that do not derive from, but preexist, and are used to interpret immediate experience, as Baillargeon (1991), Spelke (1990), and Fodor (1975) maintain?

There is a shared assumption on both sides of this debate which, we believe, is fundamentally wrong. The shared assumption is that what is intelligent is the global structure and not the local variability that sets each individual act in its context. This assumption makes sense in the terms of the traditional claim of a developmental trend from an understanding stuck in the here and now to one based on symbolic structures. Because development is directional and older children are more intelligent than younger children, contacting immediate reality is seen as *less intelligent* and immature. Abstract thought stripped of the distinctive details of authentic experience is seen as intelligent and mature. Both sides of the debate share this view that abstract, context-free knowledge is more intelligent than richly detailed, context-specific knowledge. What is under contention is only the issue of whether infants are "just as smart as adults" and also have abstract ideas. In our view, the founding assumption is wrong. We show this by considering research on infants' perceptions of certain events as "possible" or "impossible," research that led Spelke to conclude:

> I believe that humans begin life with a conception of material objects. That conception leads infants to perceive certain objects as unitary and bounded. That conception also leads infants to perceive an object as persisting when it moves and changes in certain ways, and to predict whether it will persist over future transformations. (1985, p. 89)

Possible and Impossible Events

In their studies of infants' "conceptions" of the world Spelke (1990) and Baillargeon (Baillargeon, Spelke, and Wasserman, 1985; Baillargeon, 1987a,b; Baillargeon, 1991) have studied what infants know to be possible and impossible using habituation and familiarization procedures. The logic of the procedure is as follows: infants are presented with a specific instantiation of some physical "law" and familiarized with that instantiating event. They are then presented with one of two novel test events. The two test events are designed to segregate the details of here-and-now perceiving and transcendent abstract ideas. Thus, the *possible* event has new perceptual features but instantiates the same abstract physical law. The *impossible* event is deemed (by introspection) to be similar to the possible event in here-and-now details but to violate the physical law. Results from a variety of experiments have shown that in this paradigm, infants look more at the impossible than the possible event, suggesting that they perceive it as novel, odd, and perhaps impossible. We will consider one such study in some detail.

Baillargeon (1986) showed 6- and 8-month-old infants a habituating (or familiarization) event in which a toy cart rolled down an inclined plane and behind a screen. The sequence of continuous actions that comprised the familiarization event are shown in figure 8.3. First the infants saw the static display, then they saw the screen lifted showing the track behind it, and then they saw the cart roll down the incline, behind the screen, and then out from behind the screen. Infants repeatedly watched this habituating event until their total looking time was 50% of that on the initial habituating trials. On average, the infants watched the

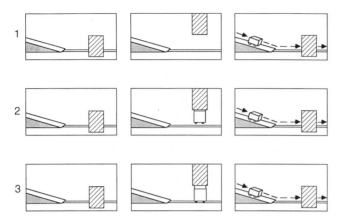

Figure 8.3
Baillargeon's task: *1*, habituation event; *2*, possible event; *3*, impossible event. (Redrawn from Baillargeon, 1986.)

habituating event eight times before being presented with possible or impossible test trials.

The possible event is illustrated in the second row of panels in figure 8.3. This event begins with the static display that is identical to the habituating event. The screen is then lifted revealing a box that is *behind* the track. The screen is replaced and the cart is rolled down the incline following the track behind the screen and then out again.

The impossible event is illustrated in the third row of panels in figure 8.3. Again, the impossible event begins with a static display that is identical to the habituating event. But when the screen is lifted, it reveals a box *sitting on* the track. Nonetheless, when the screen is replaced and the cart is rolled down the incline, it passes behind the screen and out again. This is an impossible event if the box is still on the track blocking the path of the cart.

In this study infants looked at the impossible event more than the possible event, implying that they saw them as different and saw the impossible event as more different from the habituating event than the possible event. These results suggest to some that the infant possesses abstract ideas about what objects in general can and cannot do. Thus, Baillargeon concluded that:

> infants understood (1) the box continued to exist in its same location after it was occluded by the screen; (2) the car continued to exist, and pursued its trajectory, after it disappeared behind the screen; and (3) the car could not roll through the space occupied by the box. (1986, p. 37)

If infants know all these things, we might wonder why a habituating event was needed at all? If infants truly possess abstract knowledge structures, shouldn't they show more surprise at the impossible event than the possible one—even without experiencing the prior habituating event? The answer is no, because even in static-structure theories of mind there has to be some way to connect represented abstract structures to the here and now. Intelligence does one no good if it cannot make contact with ongoing reality. By the knowledge-as-represented-structure view, the habituation event is needed to call up the requisite knowledge structures and enable infants to ignore the local details that are irrelevant to this abstract knowledge. Thus, if infants had been shown merely the possible event or the impossible event with no prior habituating event, both events would have been sufficiently novel across so many dimensions—the particular objects, sitting before a screen in a laboratory, the moving hand—that the abstract peculiarity of the impossible event for the infant might not have been measurable. The repeated exposure to the habituating event activated the relevant abstract knowledge structures and also stripped away the details irrelevant to that abstract knowledge. The habituation event enabled the infant to compare the test events not to the unique details of the habituating event but to their conception of the continued and bounded existence of objects in space and time. In brief, the knowledge revealed is preexisting knowledge and the only role of immediate experience is to activate what is already known.

We offer here a radically different view of the role of the habituating experience and the context-specific details of the events—in which those details both make and make manifest infants' knowledge and expectations about the objects they are perceiving. As a preliminary caveat, we make no claims that this proposal is accurate in its details, but we believe that it is accurate in its large claims. Our point is to show in a concrete way how abstract ideas are emergent in dynamic representations—in a way that integrates developmental history and real time.

The central idea of our proposal is similar to our account of object segregation in chapter 6. We propose that during the habituation phase of the experiment, processes that interact—"reenter"—create an attracting trajectory. This attracting trajectory constitutes a prediction from any point along that trajectory about what will happen next. To make these ideas concrete and transparent, we offer a detailed reaccounting of the cart-box results. We suggest that the beginning of the impossible event is prematurely captured by the end of the habituating trajectory and thus the prediction of "what should happen next" is strongly violated.

Knowing Carts Can't Go Through Boxes

Our account of the cart-box results is again based on the interaction of what and where visual systems as illustrated in figure 8.4. We propose that performance *and* development are generated through three simultaneous mappings happening continuously in real time: (a) a mapping from the stimulus event to the what system that is activated by the static visual properties (color, shape, etc.) of such things as carts, screens, and boxes; (b) a mapping from the stimulus event to a where system that processes the spatial location at which stimulus motion occurs; and (c) a mapping between the what and where systems such that the processing in any one system at time $t + 1$ is determined by the stimulus event, the activity of that system at the just-preceding time t, *and* the activity of the other system at the just-preceding time t.

For purposes of explication, we employ very simple characterizations of the activity of the what and where systems. For the what system we assume three general levels of activity—one for each of the three key objects. Specifically, we propose that in the what system, there is a different global activity level for each

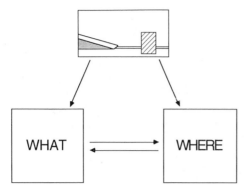

Figure 8.4
Coupled what and where analyzers.

1	3	6	10	15	21	28	35	42
2	5	9	14	20	27	34	41	48
4	8	13	19	26	33	40	47	53
7	12	18	25	32	39	46	52	57
11	17	24	31	38	45	51	56	60
16	23	30	37	44	50	55	59	62
22	29	36	43	49	54	58	61	63

Figure 8.5
Activation levels in the where system associated with movement in space. The numbers in outline denote the spatial positions at which movement occurred in the habituation event.

of the central objects in the event—an activity level of 3 for the cart, 5 for the box, and 10 for the screen. These quantities of activation were picked unsystematically except that since the box is more similar to the cart than to the screen in Baillargeon's experiment, we retained this similarity in the activation levels. We propose that in the where system, global activity is a function of location in the two-dimensional plane of the visual field. The scheme we used to generate activity levels corresponding to locations is also illustrated in figure 8.5, and in this scheme, nearer locations cause similar activity levels. Some "landmarks" in this space are these: 2 denotes the starting position of the cart, 31 the bottom of the inclined plane, and 62 the right-hand side of the screen. The only critical assumption in the mapping of location to activity level in the where system is that the activity in each system reflects the object at which a change (e.g., a movement) occurs or the location at which movement occurs. One further assumption is that the infant looks at moving events; looking at movement is the value in this system.

As events unfold in the experiment, the what system's activity at each point in time will be determined by the sensory input about the object, its past activity, and the level of activity of the where system. However, to make matters simpler, we assume that the dominant force on each system's activity level is the current—the here-and-now—sensory input. If this is so, then as the habituation event unfolds and as the activity shifts from that caused by one moving object to another, the temporal sequence of the what system's activity levels will be (roughly) *10* (the screen), *3, 3, 3, 3* (the cart), *10* (the screen as the cart moves behind it), *3, 3, 3, 3* (as the cart emerges). The activity level in the where system will change as a function of the location of movement. Using the scheme given in the figure, its temporal sequence of activity levels will be (roughly) *49* (the location of the screen), *2* (the location of the cart at the top of the plane), *8, 18, 31, 49* (the location of the screen), *50, 55, 59, 60*.

Critical to this process of emergent knowledge in the act of perceiving is the time-locked character of the activity levels in the what and where systems. Together, the what and where systems trace a trajectory through time of internal mental activity. This trajectory for one complete habituating event is shown in the top panel of figure 8.6. Point *1* indicates the starting point of the trajectory—the joint activity in the two systems as the habituating event begins (the screen at location *49*). Point *2* indicates a subsequent aspect of the event. This trajectory is thus *not the trajectory of the cart in the world* or an internal model of that physical trajectory. The trajectory illustrated is the trajectory of internal mental processes *through time*, processes which do not look like and do not model the external events. However, as this pattern of activity levels is repeatedly evoked by the repeated experience of the habituating event, it will become an attractor. It will increasingly attract "nearby" patterns of activity. And it will embody a set of expectations and knowledge; stimulus events that trace small regions on the trajectory will come to increasingly project continuing activity further along on the trajectory. We propose that this is the situation of the infant at the end of the habituating period.

What should happen at this point if the infant is presented with a slightly different event, such as the possible or impossible habituating event? What should happen depends on whether the now-formed attracting trajectory captures the activity level of the two processes and the region in which capture occurs. If the test event is *very* different, it should not be captured and one might expect that infants' behavior to a radically different test event would not be measurably different from their reaction to such an event without the prior experience of the habituating event. If the process trajectory of the test event is very similar to the process trajectory of the habituating event, then the test event will be mentally the same event as the habituation event. The infants' reaction to the test would be comparable to their reaction to the habituating event. In contrast, *infants' behavior would be most dramatically affected when the test event starts a pattern of activity that is captured by a region of the attracting trajectory and then violates the projected course.*

Given these assumptions, we generate Baillargeon's results when we plot possible- and impossible-event trajectories. The trajectory for the possible event is shown in figure 8.6B along with the thicker (and attracting) habituation trajectory. The possible-event trajectory deviates substantially from the habituating-event trajectory at the beginning, but then falls directly on top of it. Specifically, the temporal sequence of activity levels of the what system in the possible test event is as follows: *10* (the screen), *5* (the box), *10* (the screen), *3* (the cart), *3, 3,*

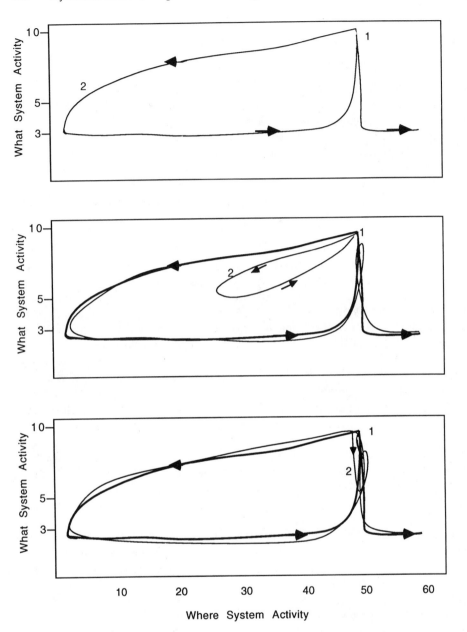

Figure 8.6
Trajectories through time of activity in the what and where systems during (*top*) the Habituation event; (*middle*) the Possible event; and (*bottom*) the Impossible event. 1 denotes the state of the system when the screen is lifted. (The events are shown in the middle panels in figure 8.3.)

3, 10 (the screen), *3, 3, 3, 3.* The temporal sequence of activity levels of the where system is: *49* (location of the screen), *26* (location of the box), *49, 2, 8, 31, 49, 50, 55, 59, 60.* The trajectory in the middle panel of figure 8.6 results from plotting the activity of each system as a function of the other through time. As is apparent, the possible test event veers off from the attracting trajectory at the beginning (when the box is revealed behind the track). This portion of the possible-event trajectory is sufficiently far from the habituating-event trajectory that it may be unlikely to be captured. When the screen is replaced, however, the possible event's unfolding activity levels fall directly on top of the attracting trajectory. By our analysis, this is an event that should be mildly interesting to infants at the beginning, but then completely predictable.

By introspection and intuition, the impossible test event is very much like the possible event. However, the process trajectory of the impossible event and its relation to the habituating event trajectory is radically different from the possible event. Critically, the emerging trajectory at the *beginning* of the impossible event falls *on (or very near) the end of* the attracting trajectory, but then veers off from that course. This is the situation in which surprise and increased looking are expected. Specifically, using the same scheme from which we developed the habituating- and possible-event trajectories, the temporal sequence of activity levels of the what system in the impossible event is *10, 5, 10, 3, 3, 3, 3, 10, 3, 3, 3, 3* and the temporal sequence of activity levels for the where system is *49, 44* (location of box on track), *49, 2, 8, 18, 31, 49* (location of screen), *50, 55, 59, 60.* The resulting trajectory of process in time is shown in the bottom panel of figure 8.6. Note how the very beginning of the impossible-event trajectory (the portion in which the box is being revealed on the track) lies very close to the end of the attracting trajectory. If the impossible-event trajectory is captured by the attracting trajectory, the processes will move in that direction for a bit, but then will shift abruptly to a quite different pattern given sensory input that substantially differs from the "expected" conclusion of the habituating event. Thus infants show surprise to the impossible event because it violates their expectations— expectations derived from immediate experience. In this account, the habituating event does not access preexisting knowledge and make it available to the here and now; it makes knowledge. Infants are not surprised because their abstract understanding of objects is violated but because their very specific expectations about this cart on this track. The system is intelligent precisely because it can form on-line very specific expectations about particular objects.

Thus, we propose that infants' knowledge about carts and boxes should be context-specific as are their memories for mobiles and knowledge about slopes. The here and now will matter because it assembles the knowledge. What infants know about carts and boxes at *any particular moment in time* depends on the history of experiences contained in acts of perceiving and activating. And thus infants' understanding of impossible and possible events should be contained in the specifics of how they got that knowledge. If the habituating event sets up specific expectations that are violated in the impossible test event, then changes between the habituating event and the test events that significantly alter the overlap of the internal central activity should alter the results. This is important: the claim of context dependency does not mean that just *any* change should matter, nor should all changes matter equally.

Indeed, the empirical determination of which contexts matter and how they matter is the central research question in a dynamic systems theory of development. In this view, the infants' knowledge is a manifestation in time of (a) the *intrinsic dynamics* of the system—the heterogeneous groups of processes in the brain and the history of system and (b) the *forces*—i.e., the sensory input of the here and now—that influence the system. The goal of empirical research is to specify the internal dynamics, the forces, and the manner of their interaction. The empirical strategy consists of perturbing the system—manipulating context—and studying the response of the system. This is, of course, the opposite empirical approach to a competence model of cognition, and at present the relevant data, data on how specific contextual factors influence infants' perception of possible and impossible events, have not been collected.

We can make empirical predictions, however, based on the account we have offered of infants' understanding of the events. We suggest that the contextual factors that matter most are those that significantly alter the pattern of perceiving and acting. For example, changes in the infant's posture, from upright to prone, or a 90-degree rotation of the event might significantly alter the outcome of Baillargeon's experiment. Certainly, by our specific account, if infants watched the habituating event sitting up and then saw the test events while lying on the stomach, it would be surprising if either test event would be "similar" to the habituating event. The what–where trajectory of a habituating event seen from one angle might well fall far in the state space from the what-where trajectory of test events watched from another angle. On the other hand, we might predict from our account that some changes in the static properties of the individual objects—their color or shape, for instance—might matter little if changed between the habituating and test events. The contextual factors that should matter most are those that significantly alter the pattern of perceiving and acting. Static changes in cart color or shape, for example, are unlikely to significantly alter *the global order of looking in certain places and seeing certain sights*. The global order of looking and seeing is the attracting trajectory of the habituating event and it is this global order that needs to be reinstantiated by the here and now of a test event for that test event to be perceived as "like" the habituating event. Changes in static properties might not alter the what–where trajectory much, whereas changes in posture and position might. These are testable predictions worthy of empirical scrutiny.

Does our proposal that specific experiences set up specific expectations mean, then, that infants do not have abstract knowledge of the continuing permanence of objects—that they *just have context-specific expectations* and don't really know anything general about objects? We are not comfortable with this question. It is an old question based on old assumptions that we reject. Experiments such as Baillargeon's neither reveal underlying competence nor can they be dismissed as "merely" about context-specific and nongeneralizable expectations. They are, instead, experiments on microgeneses—experiments that make use of, and thereby reveal, the same developmental processes that actually transform 6-month-olds into 8-month-olds into 24-month-olds. Those processes are the reentrant mappings of heterogeneous systems in the time-locked activities of perceiving and acting. Thus, as the repeated experiences of the particular habituating event used by Baillargeon set up an attractor that embodies expectations about the objects in the habituating event and influences the perception and expectations about objects in the similar test events, so will the infant's continuous real-world experiences of objects set up attractors that capture and influence the perception and expectations about increasingly diverse object events.

We can illustrate these ideas about the influence of history on perceiving and acting in terms of the changing landscape of the state space as illustrated in figure 8.7. In these landscapes, we represent the potential for change from any given location in the landscape by the hills and valleys in their terrain. At any given moment (t) in time, the system's activity is one point in this space. The direction of change and the speed of change in the activity (what the system's activity is at t + 1) will depend on the forces operating on the system (the sensory input—the here and now) and the system's location in the terrain. Change will be faster from unstable states to stable states, moving from hills to valleys. The hills and valleys thus reflect the intrinsic dynamics of the system.

The top landscape in figure 8.7 might represent the intrinsic dynamics at birth; the hills and valleys are determined by genetic structure and prenatal experience. When external forces perceiving and acting in real time drive the internal activity, the resulting trajectory of activity, as shown at bottom, will be determined both by the shape of the landscape and by the forces.

The shape of the landscape, however, is not a developmental constant. Perceiving and acting will trace, as illustrated in figure 8.7, repeating process trajectories through the space. As process trajectories are continually traced through the state space, new hills and valleys will form, as shown in figure 8.8. Once hills and valleys have formed, the process trajectory of perceiving and acting

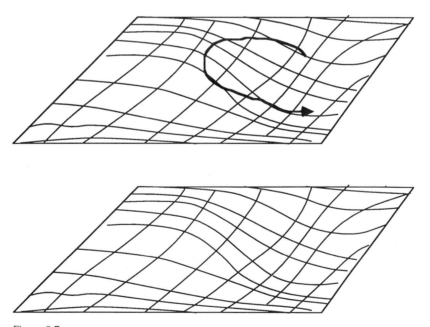

Figure 8.7
Top, A state-space landscape reflecting the history of the system. *Bottom,* A trajectory of internal activity in time in some specific task.

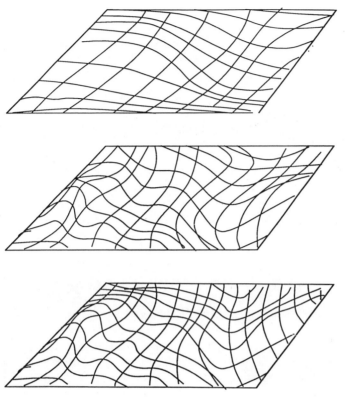

Figure 8.8
From top to bottom, Changes in the state-space landscape as function of activity.

will, if it comes close to the valleys in the state space, be pulled toward them. The history will influence the pattern of activity in the coupled systems—the activity that is knowing. With increasing experience, deeper valleys and steeper hills will form that influence what is perceived, known, and expected at any moment in real time. Thus, real experiences like Baillargeon's habituating event— but each with its own unique details—will have an aggregate effect of forming a deep and broad attractor that will influence the understanding of subsequent specific events. We might call this broad and deep attractor abstract knowledge about the continuous and bounded nature of objects. But it is abstract knowledge that emerges and is uniquely realized in the detailed activity of perceiving and acting in real time. Thus in this view, intelligence is neither more nor less tied to the here and now when the landscape is flat than when it is hilly.

From the results of this one experiment by Baillargeon, we have no way of knowing whether the "landscape" in which the events are understood is flat or hilly. The infants' surprise at the impossible event could be generated by an attractor set up by the habituating event in a flat terrain or it could be generated by an attractor set up by the habituating event and shaped by a history of perceiving objects as bounded and permanent. We can distinguish these two possibilities only by attempting to perturb infants' perception of possible and impossible events to see how stable it is. If the perception of impossible and possible events is easily disrupted by shifts in body posture or by the specific details of objects and timing of events, if it is highly dependent on the specifics of the here-and-now experience, then the attractor is shallow. If impossible events are easily made to be as expected as possible events, if Baillargeon's impossible event were made the habituating event instead of the test event, then infants' expectations in these experiments would seem to be narrowly context-specific and not yet influenced by deep attractors formed by and through diverse experiences of perceiving and acting on objects. These are empirical questions that need to be answered. They are not, however, questions that are likely to be asked when the experimental goals are demonstrations of competence.

Developing Multiple Attractors

The picture of development in figure 8.8 of an evolving attractor that becomes deeper and broader, embodying more and more abstract knowledge by capturing more and more diverse instances, is only one way that development may go. Development may also consist of developing deeper and *narrower* attractors. This pattern of development is seen in a further set of experiments by Baillargeon (see Baillargeon, 1987a,b, 1992): infants' perception of impossible and possible rotation events.

In this series of experiments, Baillargeon habituated babies to a screen that rotated back and forth through a 180-degree arc as shown in figure 8.9. In the test events, a box was added to the scene. In the possible event, the screen rotated until it hit the box—112 degrees—and then it stopped. There were three impossible events, all of which presented a screen that seemed to pass through the box, rotating either 135 degrees (the mild violation in figure 8.9), 157 degrees (the severe violation), or 180 degrees. Surprise was related both to the degree of dissimilarity of the test events from the possible event and age: 4½-month-old infants showed surprise for only the most extreme violation (180 degrees) and 6½-month-old infants showed surprise for the second two most extreme items (157 and 180 degrees). What mattered was the similarity of the test event to the possible one and *not its physical "impossibility"* as predicted by our view that the habituating experience sets up an attracting trajectory. The younger infants required a greater dissimilarity than older babies because the lifelong experiences of older babies with events like the habituating event shaped a tighter and deeper attractor. Thus, for younger infants, the habituating event may have set up a broad and relatively shallow attractor; the internal trajectories of perceiving a screen pass through a considerable portion of the box in the impossible events are close enough to this habituating attractor to be pulled in. But with development, with perceiving various screens not passing through boxes in the world, the landscape into which the habituating event falls is different. The attractor developed by repeatedly perceiving the habituating event falls in between well-developed and deep attractors. Small shifts in the perceptual particulars of the event—a box in the way—will cause the evolving trajectory to shift abruptly from the habituating attractor to another, and surprise and increased looking will result.

To summarize, the shape of development emerges from infants' continual perception and action in the world. Early in development, knowledge is like the

Habituation Event

Mild Violation

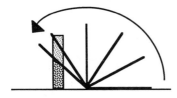

Severe Violation

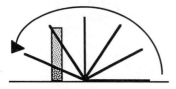

Figure 8.9
Habituation and test events from Baillargeon (1992).

rolling hills of Ohio. The valleys, broad basins of expectations, pull in and shape the real-time trajectories of perceiving and acting. In these broad valleys, specific tasks set up transient attractors—expectations about the specific course of events in the present task that are influenced by and influence the developing shape of the terrain. With increasing experience in perceiving and acting, the terrain will become increasingly like West Virginia —deep narrow valleys separated by steep ridges. The narrow valleys constitute deep attractors and well-articulated and differentiated kinds of knowledge—knowledge about what kinds of similarities and differences between events matter—knowledge, for example, that an adjacent box does not matter for how far a screen can rotate but that a box directly behind the screen does matter. The role of context—of the here and now—is both to make the valleys and the ridges *and* to place immediate experience in the landscape.

These ideas suggest a new approach to the experimental study of development—one that will take the "magic" out of demonstrations of infant competence and begin to make scientific sense of the truly amazing things that are infants' and adults' minds. Consider one further remarkable demonstration of infant competence in 5½-month-olds. Baillargeon and Graber (1987) presented infants with the two possible events shown in figure 8.10 and then the possible and impossible test events also shown in the figure. In the possible familiarization events, a short or tall rabbit passed behind a screen and then reappeared on the

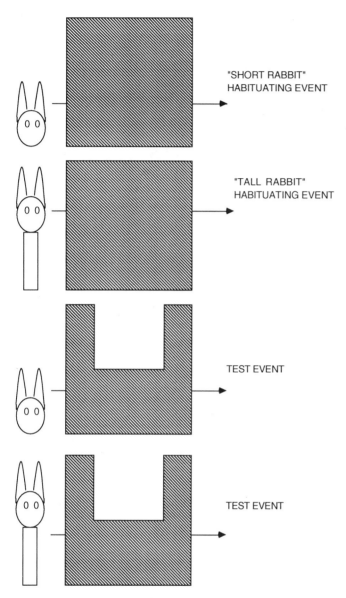

Figure 8.10
The events in Baillargeon and Graber's (1987) experiment.

other side. In the test events, the rabbit passed behind a screen with a window in it—one too high for the short rabbit to be seen behind it but high enough for the tall rabbit to be seen as it passed by the window. The short rabbit's traversal constituted the possible event: it was not (and should not have been) seen in the window. The tall rabbit's traversal constituted the impossible event: it was not *and it should have been* seen in the window. Baillargeon and Graber found that the babies looked more at this impossible test event than at the possible test event. This suggested to the researchers that infants could make inferences about relative height, and thus were surprised at the rabbit's failure to appear in the window. The authors concluded that

> by 5.5 months of age, infants represent the height of occluded objects and use this information to predict the outcome of simple physical events involving these objects. These results point to the remarkable and hitherto largely unsuspected physical reasoning abilities in young infants. Clearly, one important task facing cognitive developmentalists in the future is that of describing (a) the nature of young infants' physical knowledge and the processes by which they acquire it and (b) the nature of infants' physical reasoning abilities and the processes by which these develop. (1987, pp. 391–392)

We suspect that infants' uncanny ability to expect the tall rabbit to appear in the window, and not the short one, is explainable, again, in terms of the pattern of looking and perceiving—the what–where trajectory set up by the familiarization events and not by physical reasoning abilities and inferences. Our ideas, however, constitute a proposal for accomplishing exactly what Baillargeon and Graber call for: a description of infants' knowledge about objects, how it develops, and how it is *used in context*. The repeated demonstrations of remarkably sensible behaviors of infants in contexts as diverse as rolling carts, rotating screens, and traveling rabbits tell us that intelligence fits the context. In our view, it fits the context because it is the here-and-now product of the history of the organism, the just-preceding internal state, and the sensory input.

Jumping Between Global Structures: Novel Word Interpretations

Recent findings about children's novel word interpretations offer a third illustration of the central role of context in developing knowledge. Between the ages of 18 months and 6 years, children acquire, on average, nine new words a day (Templin, 1957). In order to acquire so many words so fast, children must learn individual words from hearing them used in context. Studies of novel word interpretation investigate just how children might accomplish this task by presenting very young children with a novel word in context and then asking what— from that one experience—the children think the word means. Many of these studies have concentrated on children's interpretations of novel count nouns as they apply to concrete objects. *Count nouns* refer to individuated entities that can be counted (one dog, two houses) and contrast with mass nouns that refer to aggregates (sand, sugar, water). Studies of novel word interpretation show that when young children (and adults) hear a novel count noun used to refer to a novel object, they interpret the noun as referring to a category organized by shape (e.g., see Landau, Smith, and Jones, 1988; Jones, Smith, and Landau, 1993; Smith, Jones, and Landau, 1992). The typical study in this line of research consists of presenting children with a novel three-dimensional exemplar object, giving it a novel name and then asking what other objects are called by this name. In the original study, Landau et al. (1988) found that children as young as 24 months interpreted the novel noun as referring to objects that were the same shape as the exemplar. The magnitude of this effect was quite dramatic. For example, given a 2-in. wooden object that was called "a dax," the children called sponges, wire screens, and objects over 100 times larger than the original "daxes" as long as these objects were the same shape as the exemplar dax.

Most important, this shape bias is specific to the context of *naming objects;* it is the task of *naming* that organizes children's attention to shape. We can see this context dependency by comparing children's performances in the naming task with their performance in a control task in which the children were simply asked whether one object "was like" another object. In this control task (using the very same stimuli), children did not attend to the shapes of the objects more than to their textures or sizes. Indeed, these similarity judgments were controlled by the magnitude of overall difference with no one dimension showing precedence. Landau et al. (1988) found that naming recruited attention to shape in both the 24- and 36-month-old children. But the effect, and particularly the difference between the naming task and the similarity judgment task, was most marked in the 36-month-olds.

Subsequent studies have shown that the shape bias in naming changes with development, becoming more robust, more specific to count nouns, and less exclusive in children's novel word interpretations (see Jones and Smith, 1993, for a review). We can summarize the developmental trend by plotting children's attention to shape as a function of age in different task contexts as in figure 8.11.

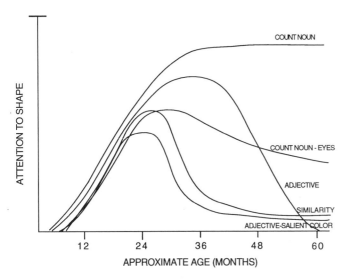

Figure 8.11
The developmental trend in attention to shape in different novel word interpretation tasks.

Consider, first, the developmental function labeled *count noun*. This function summarizes results in a variety of experiments in the task in which subjects are shown a novel object, it is labeled by a novel count noun, and the children are asked what objects are instances of that lexical category. The results suggest that selective attention to shape in this context grows between 18 and 24 months and becomes asymptotic just before the 36-month mark. The finding that the shape bias *emerged* between 18 and 24 months was discovered by Jones, Smith, Landau, and Gershkoff-Stowe (1992). Thus, in the task context of interpreting a novel count noun, selective attention to shape appears to increase with development and in young children is specifically related to the number of count nouns in the productive vocabulary. They found that a shape bias in interpreting novel count nouns emerged in individual children when they possessed more than 50 object names in their productive vocabularies.

Now consider the function in the figure labeled *similarity*. This result summarizes findings in studies in which the child is shown a novel exemplar object, it is *not* named, and the child is asked which other objects are like the exemplar. In this task children older than 30 months do not selectively attend to shape. Jones et al. (1992), however, found that in very young children the task of judging the similarity of two objects, like the task of interpreting a novel count noun, resulted in attention to shape, and this attention to shape in both the "alike" and "noun" task increased with the number of words produced by individual children. Their results indicated that for a brief period following its appearance, the shape bias is not specifically lexical. In the course of learning object names, attention to shape increases in both naming and nonnaming contexts. Results reported by Landau et al. (1988), however, indicate that the shape bias rapidly becomes specific to novel word interpretations. Thus, the shape bias appears to grow as a function of early word learning, to initially influence attention in both novel word interpretation tasks and nonword tasks, but to become differentiated and specific to novel word interpretation tasks with further development.

With development, the shape bias also becomes specific to specific kinds of novel words. In figure 8.11, consider the two functions labeled *adjective*. In two studies, Smith et al. (1992) and Landau et al. (1993), examined 3- to 5-year-olds' interpretations of novel count nouns and novel adjectives. In these studies, the children were shown a novel object and it was either named with a novel count noun (e.g., *This is a dax.*) or described with a novel adjective (e.g., *This is a riff one.*). Three-year-old children attended to shape; they interpreted the novel word as referring to objects with the same shape in both these task contexts. However, older children, 5-year-olds, attended to different dimensions when interpreting novel adjectives and novel nouns. Specifically, novel adjectives appeared to direct attention away from shape.

Words, however, are not the only factors that matter in these tasks. The power of words depends on the stimuli. This fact is illustrated in figure 8.11 by comparing the function labeled *adjective* with the one labeled *adjective-salient color*. Smith et al. (1992) showed that whether adjectives recruited attention to shape depended on how salient the other dimensions were for younger (36-month-old) children. Finally, consider the function labeled *count-noun eyes*. Jones et al. (1991) found that 24- and 36-month old children interpreted novel names for objects with and without eyes in fundamentally different ways, attending to shape *and texture* when the objects had eyes and to shape alone when these same objects did not have eyes.

What we see, all told, in the developmental trend depicted in figure 8.11 is a marvelous emergence of context specificity in which children seem to bring everything they know—whatever they know—to bear on their interpretation of a novel word. Different contexts—linguistic contexts, task contexts, and stimulus contexts—work together to organize children's attention to objects in different ways that adaptively fit the different contexts. These data suggest an emerging developmental landscape like that pictured in figure 8.12. Early in development, as children acquire their first few words, there is an increased attention to shape— an attractor that reflects the fact that children's first words are dominated by categories of concrete objects (e.g., *dog, car, chair*) that are well organized by shape. This forming shape attractor is initially broad; it pulls attention in the direction of shape in a wide variety of contexts, including nonword contexts. But as children learn more and more words and more and more kinds of categories, attention to different object properties becomes linked to different contexts. Multiple attractors close together in the landscape emerge so that with small variations in context—a change from a novel noun to a novel object or from an object with eyes to one without eyes—the system may "jump" from one highly organized pattern of attending to another.

The role of context in causing the system to jump between equally highly organized modes of attending is seen clearly in a study on 36-month-olds' interpretations of novel adjectives and novel count nouns (Smith et al., 1992). Examples of the stimuli are shown in figure 8.13. In one condition the exemplar was an inverted letter U painted with green, white, and red "camouflage." The test objects matched the exemplar either in color or shape. In the second condition, the exemplar was a wooden W covered in silver and gold glitter. Some test objects matched the exemplar in shape but not in the glitter coloring and other test objects matched the exemplar in glitter coloring but not in shape. Different

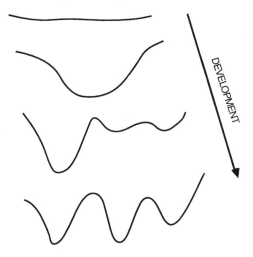

Figure 8.12
The changing landscape and emerging attractors in novel word interpretation tasks.

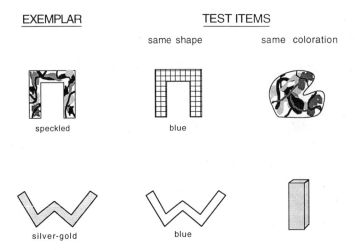

EXEMPLAR   TEST ITEMS

same shape   same coloration

speckled   blue

silver-gold   blue

Figure 8.13
Examples of stimuli in the Smith, Jones and Landau (1992) experiment.

children made yes or no judgments about individual test stimuli in three different linguistic contexts with each set of stimuli. In the control task, they were asked if each test object was "like" the exemplar; in the count noun task, they were told the exemplar was "a dax" and they were asked if each test object was also "a dax"; in the adjective condition, they were told that the exemplar was "a dax one" and they were asked if each test object was also "a dax one." The children were also tested in two lighting contexts. The matte-camouflage stimuli were presented and the questions asked in a room with normal illumination. The glitter stimuli, in contrast, were presented in a dark mock cave with a beam of light centered from above so that the glitter exemplar and the test objects with glitter sparkled and glowed.

We can represent children's performances in this experiment in terms of their position in a state space such as that shown at the top of figure 8.14. On the x axis is the number of yeses to the test items that were the same color as the exemplar; on the y axis is the number of yeses to the test items that were the same shape as the exemplars. Thus, a child's performance in a specific context can be located by a point in the state space. And the individual performances of a group of children can be illustrated by a scatterplot, as in figure 8.14.

We can use these scatterplots as an index of the developmental landscape. One measure of the shape of the attractor landscape is provided by the location of children's performances; thus in figure 8.14, 12 of the 15 children said yes to the same shape items but no to same color items when asked if the items were "a dax." A second relevant clue to the landscape is the variability of children—how diverse the performances of individual children are. If all children do the *very same thing in a particular context*, then a deep narrow attractor given that context is suggested. If, however, the between-subject variability is very high, then, at best, a broad shallow attractor is suggested.

Smith (1992, 1994) developed an algorithm to look at the location and spread of children's data as a measure of the developmental landscape. This algorithm

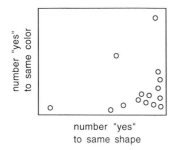

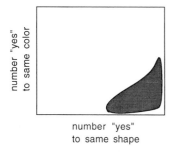

Figure 8.14

Top, Scatterplot of individual children's performances in attending to shape in a novel word interpretation task; *Bottom*, Performance area in which 80% of the children's performances fall.

finds a *performance area* in the state space in which 80% of the children fall. The outcome of this algorithm is illustrated by the shaded areas in the state space at the bottom of figure 8.14. The algorithm works as follows. A scatterplot of individual children's performances in the state space is made. The location of the modal response is found; then the outer boundary of the performance area is found by moving out from the mode in the direction of the greatest number of subjects until there is a gap (defined by a proportion of the space). At this gap a boundary point is located. This procedure is repeated by starting again at the mode and working out, until 80% of all subjects are found and the boundary of the performance area is defined. The locations of these performance areas thus illustrate the character of children's judgments. If a performance area in one context falls in the upper right of the space, then children attended to both color and shape (said yes to everything). If it falls in the upper-left corner, children attended to color. If falls in the lower-right corner, children attended to shape. If it falls in the bottom lower-left corner, it again indicates attention to both color and shape but the rejection of all items, regardless of how they differ from the exemplar, as being "like" or labeled by the same word as the exemplar. The size of the performance area indicates the shape of the developmental landscape. Does it contain a narrow and deep valley indicating that all performances are highly similar or is it a broad plain indicating that individuals are scattered widely?

Figure 8.15 shows these performance areas in the three linguistic and two stimulus conditions of the Smith et al. (1992) experiments. There were sixteen

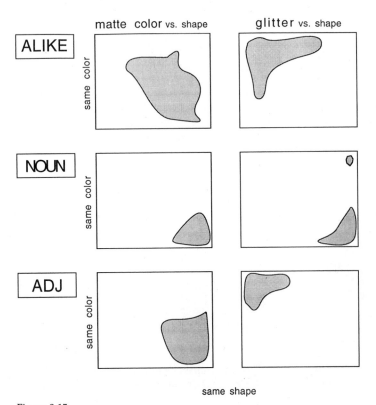

Figure 8.15
Changing performance areas as a function of task, Alike, Noun, or Adjective, in the two stimulus conditions of matte color or glitter.

36-month-old children in each condition, so the size of the performance area directly reflects the diversity of individual performances. First, look at the top of figure 8.15, which illustrates the children's performances in the alike linguistic context in which children were simply asked whether each test object was like the exemplar. As is apparent, with nonglittering stimuli in normal lighting conditions, the children attend to shape and color, and given the wide performance area, it is apparent that the children do not agree among themselves as to the best solution to this task. Some said the same-color test objects were like the exemplar, some said the same-shape test objects were like the exemplar, and some said both kinds of test objects were like the exemplar. With the glitter stimuli, however, the children attended principally to glitter. They said test objects with glitter were *like* the exemplar, although some children also said that test items that were the same shape as the exemplar were like it.

Second, look at the remarkably different pattern of performance in the count noun condition—the condition in which the exemplar was named "a dax." Here virtually all children attend to shape—with both nonglitter and glittering stimuli. The *task of interpreting a novel count noun* clearly causes a deep shape attractor to form. There is very little variability among children. They all say that test objects that are the same shape as the exemplar have the same name. This noun-shape bias is apparently a very strong attractor that persists even when given a sparkling and glowing, glittery exemplar. The increased salience of color from the nonglitter to glitter conditions barely alters the shape and breadth of the performance area, although we do see in the glitter condition a hint of a second area of attraction beginning to be formed with increased salience of color.

Third, look at the bottom of figure 8.15, which shows the patterns of performance in the adjective condition—the condition in which the exemplar was called "a dax one" and children were asked if each test object was also "a dax one." As can be seen, in this linguistic context, the two stimulus conditions have dramatically different effects. Under normal lighting and with nonglittering colors, a novel adjective—like a novel noun—pulls attention to shape. The size of the performance area suggests that the shape attractor is not as narrow in the context of a novel adjective as in the context of a novel noun, but still the pull on attention is toward shape and away from the glitter color. But given a glittery, glowing exemplar, a novel adjective pulls attention to glitter. The attractor basin has moved to the upper left of the state space. What we see here is a clear example of a bifurcation; from a single attractor basin for count nouns, there emerge two distinct, tight attractor basins for adjectives. There is a nonlinear interaction of the syntactic form class of the words (nouns vs. adjectives) and the task- and object-specific saliences of the object properties.

These results and other evidence on the developing complexity and context specificity of the shape bias conforms wholly to the idea that the global structure of behavior is assembled in the here and now and contradicts the idea that the global structure of behavior derives from a constant internal structure that exists apart from the here and now. Quite simply, the complex context-dependent variability of children's novel word interpretations are too systematic to be noise and too complicated to be a structure in the head. Rather, children's novel word interpretations seem truly assembled in context through the interaction of knowledge about words, knowledge about syntactic form classes, knowledge about specific properties (e.g., eyes), and context-specific forces like lighting and glitter. All these forces—and probably more—push and pull on the child's attention to object properties. But all these degrees of freedom are compressed in the child to yield in each act of attention an organized whole that, with repeated acts of hearing words and figuring out their meaning, becomes exquisitely sensitive to context. In richly detailed experiences of the here and now, highly organized pulls on attention develop that reflect the accrued wisdom of all those past individual acts of word interpretation.

We can clearly see in these data the three critical roles—making, selecting, and adapting—that context plays in developing knowledge. First, the learning of words in specific contexts drives development; it is the accumulated effects through time of individual acts of novel word interpretations that make the attractors form. Second, it is the here-and-now context that interacts in nonlinear ways with the system as a whole to select qualitatively different global structures. It is the here and now that places the individual in a particular location in the landscape. Third, the details of the here and now are always part of the pattern, and thus the system can act adaptively by doing what it has never done before— in the creative synergy of the history of the system and in the immediate context in the activity of perceiving and acting. It is because the here and now is integral to the knowledge made manifest that children can show such a tightly organized and distinct global order in their interpretation of novel nouns and novel adjectives in the odd context of glittering Ws in mock caves with beams of light. Where is the intelligence here? It is not in context-free rules and abstract representations. Intelligence lies in our activity in authentic reality.

Context and Competence

In traditional cognitive psychology, knowledge is a mental *thing*, like an encyclopedia on the shelf. When faced with a task, one pulls the appropriate volume off the shelf and then brings that information to bear on the task at hand. This traditional framework is replete with dualities: structure vs. process, long-term memory vs. working memory, competence vs. performance. Our view of knowledge as dynamic activity does away with all these theoretical dichotomies and by doing away with all these dichotomies, we solve two fundamental problems. First, we solve the problem of how there is both global structure and local adaptability. Global structure adapts to the local context because it is manifestation of both the intrinsic dynamics of the system and the local details of the here and now. Second, we solve the problem of how developmental time emerges in real time. In our view there is only one time dimension. There is not one time dimension that matters for act-to-act variability and another for developmental change. Rather, developmental time is the accrual of real-time events.

In solving these problems, we also provide a new perspective on intelligence and direction of development. Intelligence does *not* mean less dependence on the here and now. Intelligence does *not* mean dependence on the same rigid structures across task contexts. Intelligence means the ability to adapt, to fit behavior and cognition to the changing context. A smart system seems unlikely to ever do exactly the same thing twice. Rather, a smart system would shift its behavior slightly to fit the nuances of the particular context or would shift radically—jump to an all-new state—if the situation demanded it. Our dynamic system is inherently smart. Because its activity is *always* dependent on the here and now, the just-previous activity, and the history of the system as a whole, it will always incorporate—always bend—to the demands of both history and immediate experience. Our dynamic system is a system always on the move.

Kelso, Scholz, and Schöner (1986) suggested that an intelligent dynamic system is one that is always on the move and that lives on the edge of multiple attractors. Such a system could move in and out of *almost* stable states of dramatically different kinds with small amounts of energy—with small forces. The older child's interpretation of novel words in contexts appears to be such a system. If we think of the stimulus context as the force that pushes the system about in the attractor landscape, then only small forces—"a dax" vs. "a dax one"—are needed to push the system from one organized state to a very different one. However, as Kelso argues, it would not be an intelligent or healthy system if these forces could push the system into very deep and narrow attractors. An attractor that is too deep means that the system would stay stuck in that state unless perturbed greatly. A system that did only one thing would not be intelligent. It would not be useful to the acquisition of novel words—given the variety of kinds of meanings—if children *always* attended rigidly to shape and only shape. Rather, an intelligent system is one that lives on the edge of many close attractors—dipping in along the side of an attractor and out again, perhaps never falling all the way to the bottom.

We believe these ideas that we have developed in these eight chapters make for a new developmental psychology. In the next two chapters, we put these ideas together by considering in detail two developmental achievements: in chapter 9, we consider the transition from nonreaching to reaching for an object in infancy. In chapter 10, we consider the development of the object concept and, in particular, the transition from the A-not-B error to successful search for a hidden object.

Chapter 9

Knowledge from Action: Exploration and Selection in Learning to Reach

In chapter 8, we illustrated the seamless dynamics of time in the development of novel locomotor skills, and the understanding of object properties and novel word meanings. We argued that each act—at whatever age or level of skill—had within it nested scales of activity: the actions in the here and now that are inextricably tied to the immediate dynamic context, the history of actions in the past that built the attractor landscape, and the molding of the future landscape in the repeated acts of the here and now. We showed that from the messy details of real time—from the variability and context sensitivity of each act—global order can emerge, order we characterized as ontogenetic process and progress. Knowledge, we concluded, is not a thing, but a continuous process; not a structure, but an action, embedded in, and derived from, a history of actions.

In this chapter, we continue these themes in discussing infants' learning to reach. Specifically, we show that infants' individual actions in context are the very stuff of development; that actions are selected as categories of knowledge from exploration of the inherent variability and noise of a biological system. What is remarkable about the reaching story is both the individuality of the immediate solutions *and* the global convergence of the solutions as learning proceeds. Because the ability to control the limbs for adaptive ends is knowledge—it requires an understanding of the body and its relation to the environment—this example paints an especially detailed picture of the process of acquiring knowledge. We emphasize throughout that while movement—and its associated variables—are more overt and continuously measurable than purely mental activities, thought and action arise in real and developmental time through the same dynamics. There is no logical distinction between the *process* of forming and adaptively matching a motor category and forming and adaptively matching a perceptual category.

Learning to Reach: The Nature of the Task

Learning to reach is fundamental for all subsequent perceptual-motor learning. It is the means by which infants learn about objects directly and through many modalities: sight, haptics, proprioception, sound, and taste. Infants are highly motivated to reach and grasp objects, at first to convey them to their mouths for oral exploration, and later for more complex exploration using their hands and eyes. As we detailed in chapter 7, reaching and grasping set in motion a perception-action cycle whereby new motor skills open new opportunities for perceptual-motor exploration, which in turn sets new tasks for the action system to solve, and so forth.

What is the origin of this important behavior? What are its precursor abilities and by what means do infants improve? These questions have engaged many theorists and researchers. Before pursuing our dynamic version, it is useful to review some of the conventional theoretical approaches. Here, as in other perceptual, motor, and cognitive domains, we find the traditional explanations lacking.

One group of explanations is essentially nativistic. Halverson (1931, 1933), working with Gesell, concluded that reaching improved primarily through the increasing "dominance of cortical control" (1933, p. 40). In the Gesellian tradition, cortical maturation is inherent with growth, and growth, in turn, is a product of the genes. Bower and Trevarthen are proponents of a more contemporary nativism, claiming reaching to be a form of innate knowledge, akin to the innate knowledge of object properties claimed by Spelke and her colleagues. The evidence in favor of this view is that newborn infants are reported to extend their arms toward visual targets or in the direction of their head and gaze (Bower, Broughton, and Moore, 1970; Hofsten, 1982; Trevarthen, 1974, 1984.) Reaching, therefore, is neither novel nor learned; it is an already prefigured representation uniting vision and prehension that only needs refinement and tuning. Bower (1989), for instance, endows newborns with understanding formal properties of stimulation, the "higher order, modality-free form" (p. 30).

The second group of theories can best be characterized as having a constructionist flavor, focusing primarily on the building of a map of vision and hand. The classic account of Piaget, from which we quoted in chapter 7, depicts reaching as constructed from the mutual mapping of the seen and felt hand and the seen toy. Piaget believed that, initially, hand and eye belonged to two separate schemata and only through mutual interaction and integration would infants come to know that they could grasp something that they also saw. Bruner and Koslowski (1972; Bruner, 1973) proposed another kind of constructionist view. They suggested that mature reaching was built from component parts, and that the developmental task was to correctly order and integrate the parts. Thus, the problem was not so much integrating the disparate streams of perception and action, but learning to program the awkward, undifferentiated, and poorly coordinated components.

The innatist solution suffers from the usual problem of logical infinite regress; if reaching is prefigured in the genes, and later in the brain, how did it get there? How does it get out? In addition, the empirical evidence is equivocal. Newborns may extend their arms in the presence of a visually interesting sight, but their movements are not visually guided to the object. Hofsten (1982) believed that the newborn synergy seemed to be more of an attentional response—infants may be aroused by interesting displays and extend their arms—than a movement signifying intention to grasp and manipulate. It is also important to note that the conditions under which newborns perform these "prereaching movements" are very constrained and specific—when maximally alert, upright, and posturally supported. The functional importance of these movements is unclear. In addition, there is no observable continuity between newborn arm extensions and later reaching. Indeed, the frequency and quality of arm movements change dramatically during the first 4 months, including a period where they are nearly impossible to elicit (Hofsten, 1984).

Constructionist positions also run afoul of data. While the central role of vision in accurate reaching and grasping cannot be disputed, we may question whether reaching really emerges from a cycle of look at object, look at hand, move hand, compare hand and object, compute difference, move hand again, look-move-compare. Indeed, it looks at though the very first attempts to reach, while usually elicited by a seen object, can also be elicited by a sounding object, and most important, do not require a seen hand or arm. The evidence for hand-object matching is a period of intense hand-regard or hand-object looking seen around the time of reaching onset. But Piaget saw mutual hand-object regard in his children only *after* they brought the hand in the vicinity of the target, that is, they had already somehow learned to get their hands close to the desired object. White, Castle, and Held (1964) reported a prolonged period of hand regard as evidence for a hand-object match. But note that they studied reaching development in a group of institutionalized infants, whose rearing conditions could be considered quite significantly impoverished, as they lay supine in their cribs for nearly all their waking hours. Given this relative visual and motor deprivation, their hands were perhaps the most interesting and attention-grabbing sights around.

The most compelling evidence for the minimal use of vision for guiding first reaches comes from a recent study by Clifton, Muir, Ashmead, and Clarkson (1993). These researchers followed a group of infants longitudinally, testing their reaching ability both in the light and in the dark to glowing or sounding objects. They found that at the time of their very first reaches, infants were equally proficient when reaching in the light or the dark, and in the dark, to either the glowing or sounding toy. This equivalence continued for many months. The dark condition, where the infants could not see their hands and localized the toy by sound alone, did not disrupt their performance. Only later in the first year, when grasping became more accurate and differentiated, did vision significantly aid reaching performance (Bushnell, 1985).

Learning to Reach: A Dynamic Approach

If reaching is neither prefigured nor constructed by the progressive mapping of the hand and the eye, where does the new behavior form come from? The study undertaken by Thelen and her colleagues (Thelen, Corbetta, Kamm, Spencer, Schneider, and Zernicke, 1993) was designed from a dynamic systems approach. Their focus was not to search for the essential, innate components, or for the single cause of visual-motor mapping. Instead, the focus was on reaching as an instance of an *emergent* perceptual-motor pattern. The assumption behind this work is that reaching is acquired through the soft assembly of mutually interacting, equivalent, multiple-component structures and processes within a context. All of these components are essential for the final skill to emerge, but one or more components may act as the control parameter or rate-limiting element.

This dynamic view generates a different set of assumptions to guide a study of reaching onset from a nativist or constructionist view. The study by Thelen et al. of reaching looks very different from the typical developmental study which tests hypotheses and looks for single causes. Thelen et al. measured behavior repeatedly in the same children at multiple levels, from success in contacting a toy to muscle patterns—and at multiple time scales, from the fractions of sections that make up a single reach to the multiples of minutes in which a reach to a toy is practiced in a single session, to the weeks and months over which qualitative shifts in reaching behavior emerge. The study of multiple levels and time scales— the sheer variety of kinds of measures and the magnitude of the empirical task Thelen et al. set before themselves—derives directly from the foundational assumption that reaching emerges in a complex *nonstationary* system. This study thus provides an example of *how* to begin a dynamic systems account of an emerging ability.

The comprehensive examination of multiple levels and time scales is pertinent to four specific empirical questions. First is the question of the infant's *intrinsic dynamics*. In the dynamic systems view, infants *discover* reaching from an ongoing background of other nonreaching postures and movements. In other words, *before* reaching begins, the system has a landscape with preferred attractor valleys that may be more or less deep, and that reflect both the infant's history and his or her potential for acquiring new forms. This landscape constitutes the infant's *intrinsic dynamics*. Describing the intrinsic dynamics at each point in developmental time requires studying the trajectories of behavior in real time and how they stay the same amd how they change.

Second is the integration of *time scales*. Understanding the transition from nonreaching to reaching requires the integration of real time and developmental time. It is real-time behavior that invites transitions in emergent action and that enables changes in landscape. *What* changes when infants convert their nondirected movements to the task of reaching for an object? Because of the assumption that reaching comes neither from a dedicated "reaching" device nor pops out de novo, but is discovered from other movements, the researchers did not measure reaches alone. Rather, they presented infants with attractive objects within a longer session where motor variables were recorded, so that the transition from nonreaching behavior to reaches could be captured. Thus, they recorded transitions on two time scales: one, the real time of the trial where the toy was presented and the infant had to recruit a pattern of action, and the second developmental time scale, where patterns of stability may evolve and dissolve.

Third is the discovery of the *control parameter*. In the initial study of the development of a complex system, the control parameters are unknown and the control parameter—the emergence of that final component that causes the transition from nonreaching to reaching—could be at any level in the system. When the control parameter is unknown, emergent patterns must be studied at multiple levels. In the present case, Thelen et al. studied not only the trajectories of hands moving in space and patterns of joint coordination but also the *forces* used to move the limb, and the muscle patterns underlying the generation of movement. They also added a "naturalistic" component which allowed for rich description of movements, postures, and activities that might contribute to the onset and improvement of reaching.

Fourth is the choice of an appropriate *collective variable*. Recall that a collective variable is a condensation of the degrees of freedom that expresses the cooperative system dynamics and their change over time. The collective variable is thus the dependent measure of developmental change in a system. The proper collective variable is not obvious a priori; it is not logically derived but empirically derived. In the present case, a simple performance measure—Did infants actually grasp the toy?—is an insufficient *dependent measure* of the development of the reaching system. Grasping a toy can be done in many ways, with an equivalent outcome, yet it can arise from very different processes. Much previous research has documented that after reach onset, infant reaches become progressively straighter and somewhat faster over the first year (Fetters and Todd, 1987; Halverson, 1931, 1933; Hofsten, 1991; Mathew and Cook, 1990). Should "directedness of reach" be the collective variable? Which collective variable from among all possible collective variables indexes change in the most sensitive manner?

In overview, putting these four considerations together, the study of Thelen et al. examined multiple levels of behavior at multiple time scales in children before their first reach and during the transition to reaching for objects. Since previous research had not provided answers to *why and how* infant reaches emerge and improve, the *control parameters* responsible for shifts in the system's behavior remained to be identified. Thus, the point of the study is to map the system's dynamics in order to discover points of change—*phase shifts*—so that the underlying control parameters can be identified and then, as spelled out in the case of walking in chapter 4, manipulated experimentally.

The study involved four infants, Nathan, Gabriel, Justin, and Hannah, whose reaching movements were observed weekly from 3 weeks until 30 weeks and every other week thereafter. The reach sessions consisted of a standard procedure: infants were supported in a nearly upright seat and presented with attractive toys at shoulder height. The manner of presentation varied with the age and interest of the child; most often the parent or the experimenter presented the toy, but when infants were distracted by the social interaction, an apparatus swung the toy in front of the infant. Three-dimensional position-time data were collected from the joints of both arms, along with electromyographic (EMG) recordings from one arm and the lower back. These data, along with detailed anthropometric measurements of the limbs, allowed for a large number of kinematic (time-space), kinetic (force), and muscle pattern data to be collected and calculated. Readers are referred to Thelen, Corbetta, Kamm, Spencer, Schneider, and Zernicke (1993) for details of data collection and analysis. In addition to this instrumented observation of reaching, in a second laboratory visit, infants played on the floor in a seminaturalistic session. Parents were told to play normally with their infants; experimenters began each 2-minute play session by placing infants in different postures—supine, seated, or prone—and in half the session infants were given an interesting overhead mobile. These play sessions were coded continuously for infants' posture and locomotion, head position, manual activity, and gaze. Analysis of this massive data set is still in progress. Nonetheless, we present results on the reaching transition, and on the full year of reaching for one infant, Nathan, which illustrate the dynamic assembly of action in context.

The Transition to Reaching

Where does reaching come from? What is the nature of the phase shift—from no reaching to be able to reach and grab objects? What are the control parameters that engender the emergence of this novel form? And once infants have discovered a solution, how do they subsequently use and modify the action? In dynamic terms, how does the pattern stabilize?

As we discussed in chapter 3, the critical dimension for identifying stable states and transitions is the time scale of the change in relation to the time scale of the observation. In order to study transitions as they happen, the time scale of observation must be smaller than the time scale of change. If, for example, reaching emerges gradually over months, observing the dynamics every 3 weeks would be sufficient to identify the transition and the scale of change. If, however, infants acquire and improve the skill very quickly, such an observation schedule would miss the dynamics of the phase shift. (In reality, of course, the ideal observation time scale must be tempered with what is feasible given volunteer subjects and the time-and-effort limits of the observers.)

With a weekly observation schedule, it was possible to identify with reasonable precision the onset of reaching, defined as the infants lifting and extending their arms to make repeated contacts with the presented toy while looking at it. The infants need not, and did not always grasp the toy at first contact; it was sufficient that they contacted it. To characterize the transition, Thelen et al. described both spontaneous movements and goal-directed reaching movements at the week of reach onset and at the 2 weeks preceding and following onset.

The four infants reached this motor milestone at very different ages. Moreover, the individual character of the transitions suggested that each infant acquired reaching by solving different problems. This makes complete sense from our dynamic theory. Novel forms arise from the self-organizing properties of complex systems through the loss of the stability of old patterns and the ability of the system to explore new forms of coordination. At any point in time, the current state of the system depends both on the environmental and task support of the moment, and on the history of the system, the embodiment of the arrow of time. Thus reaching will emerge specifically in regard to each infant's current movement status, which in turn is a product of his or her continuing developmental trajectory. In short, the task of reaching *was not the same* for the four infants, given their individual *intrinsic dynamics*, and it required individual, on-line solutions.

Let us explain. First, consider what is needed for an infant to be able to reach a desired object. What subsystems need already be in place before the action—even in primitive form—can emerge? First and foremost, infants must want to get the toy, presumably motivated by the desire to explore the object orally, since the mouth is the ultimate destination of objects in young infants. Both everyday and laboratory observations indicate that this motivation is high: (1) infants will orally explore objects placed in their hands long before they reach and grasp them alone; (2) infants can be seen to make mouth-opening movements in the presence of visually attractive sights at 1 month old and earlier (Jones, 1992); (3) infants evidence interest in attractive objects by visual fixation and tracking, also long before they can reach and grab. In addition, G. Smith (1992) has described rhythmic cycles of hand grasping and mouthing several weeks before reach onset. These movements look as though infants are treating the grasped hands as an object and regularly transporting them into the mouth. Second, in order to reach, infants must have a good, if not perfect, understanding of object location in three-dimensional space. By 3 months, infants have rather good convergence and acuity. As we discussed in chapter 7, by this age infants are also likely to be using multiple visual cues to provide depth information. At the time of first reaches, these depth cues may not be finely tuned, but are sufficient to allow infants to get their hands pretty close to the objects offered, which are usually large and colorful and have many edges and contours. Finally, in order to reach, infants should have a sufficiently stable head and trunk posture to provide a constant visual image and to allow the arm to be extended without disrupting the postural stability completely. This last skill may be critical, as we explain later.

What, then, is the developmental trajectory of learning to reach? What are the possible control parameters in the emergence of this novel form? The answers to these questions depend on the *intrinsic dynamics* of the system prior to transition; these dynamics differ in each infant. Here we contrast the two infants who represented the initially most-active baby, Gabriel, and the quietest baby, Hannah.

Adult Reaching
Before we proceed with the description of early reaches in Gabriel and Hannah, it is instructive to view the kinematic and kinetic profiles of skilled reaching in adults to compare the patterns seen in infancy. Reaching in adults has been extensively studied, and there are many models of how the brain may control the arm to produce the smooth, efficient, reproducible patterns characteristic of these highly practiced movements. When adults were given the same task as the infants in the longitudinal study, to reach and grasp a toy at midline, shoulder height, and an arm's length in front of them, they produced kinematic, kinetic, and muscle activation patterns that varied little within and between subjects. For instance, consider the movements produced by one female subject who was instructed to reach for the object starting with her hand either at her thigh or at her mouth and either fast or slowly. When viewed from above (figure 9.1), the trajectories of her hand traced a reproducible path each time, with the fast movements somewhat straighter than the slow ones; the curved paths are typical. The hand velocity profiles in figure 9.2 also had the characteristic smooth, single peak of acceleration and deceleration, with the same amplitude and characteristic frequency for each trial repetition. At the level of joint coordination (figure 9.3), a similar regularity was observed, with a smooth lifting of the shoulder and extension of the elbow and wrist. As has been noted frequently in studies of skilled reaching, the coordination of the three joints extended to the changes in velocity (figure 9.4), with shoulder, elbow, and wrist accelerating and decelerating in close synchrony. Next, we see a similar regularity at the level of the joint torques. The muscle torques at the shoulder (plotted in figure 9.5) show that the smooth kinematic changes reflected a high degree of control of the forces that produced them. Finally, the patterns of muscle activation recorded by EMG revealed characteristic triphasic, reciprocal activation patterns, well delineated and repeatable over several trials of reaching (figure 9.6). The patterns seen in this single subject were highly similar to those in the other adults studied. In sum, with this simple and constrained task, skilled reachers had discovered

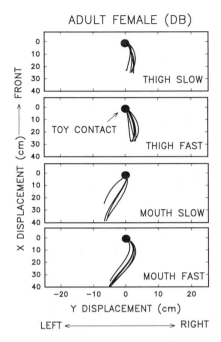

Figure 9.1
Hand trajectories of an adult reacher. Reaches from two starting positions (thigh and mouth) and two speeds (fast and slow), viewed in the *x, y* plane, as if the viewer were poised above the hand.

smooth, efficient solutions that were highly invariant over repetitions within and between individuals.

With these patterns in mind, we now ask how, at the first time they successfully reach out, infants accomplish the same task.

Gabriel: From Flapping to Reaching

Gabriel was a motorically very active infant, who reached for the toy first at 15 weeks. In the weeks before his actual arm extension to contact the toy, he engaged in fast, vigorous "flapping" movements both in social interactions and when looking at the toy. In figure 9.7, we show an example of Gabriel's spontaneous movements of both arms the week before reach onset. The plots at the top of the figure show the trajectory of his hands as projected on a plane in front of him and as a dynamic representation on a *phase plane.* The phase plane plots the displacement of his hand in the left-to-right direction vs. its velocity. Several features are worthy of note. First, the energetic, rapid, and regular cycling of both hands in equivalent spaces suggests that both hands were being driven simultaneously. Both the trajectory and phase-plane plots are time-independent. When these same data are plotted as a time series (velocity vs. time; figure 9.8), it can be clearly seen that both hands speed up and slow down in a coordinated fashion.

Second, Gabriel's spontaneous movements are far from random thrashings. The phase plane describes, as a collective variable, the mutual relation between the position of the hand and its energy dissipation. In this case, both hands had

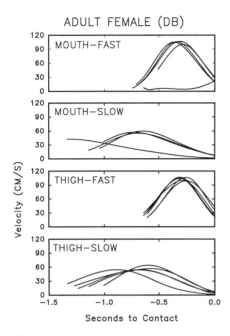

ADULT FEMALE (DB)

Velocity (CM/S)

MOUTH—FAST

MOUTH—SLOW

THIGH—FAST

THIGH—SLOW

Seconds to Contact

Figure 9.2
Velocities of the reaches depicted in figure 9.1. Reaches are plotted from time of contact (0.0).

higher velocity, as Gabriel moves toward the body (from right to left in the right hand and from left to right in the left hand). But in both hands the smooth ellipses suggest the behavior of a damped spring with a periodic forcing function (Abraham and Shaw, 1984). That is, as Gabriel exhibited these excited arm-flapping movements, the intrinsic dynamics of his arms produced timing and pattern that are topographically similar to that of a physical spring with particular stiffness, damping, and forcing characteristics. As we saw in chapter 4, infants' limbs, when under few or no task constraints, can exhibit remarkable self-organizing patterns that emerge from the physical characteristics of bones, joints, and muscles and the energetic and metabolic characteristics of an excited baby. The phase plane of Gabriel's arms describes a classic *cyclic attractor.*

When Gabriel's visual attention was captured by the toy, and his motivation caused him to become aroused by that sight, his arms behaved like springs! Clearly, these wildly flapping movements, while certainly not random, were also not adequate to perform what we infer to be Gabriel's intended goals—to get the toy and put it in his mouth. The task for Gabriel, then, was to somehow disrupt this attractor, to scale some control parameter to which the system is sensitive, and to shift the attractor to a *point attractor,* that is, a stable, single endpoint, hopefully in the vicinity of the toy. Imagine a damped pendulum or spring, which once set in motion does not receive any additional energy kicks. Eventually, it will come to rest at a single point, and on the phase plane this would result in decreasing spirals to a final point (see figure 3.7). If we are correct and reaches are discovered from the ongoing dynamics—the intrinsic dynamics of the arms—then reaches should be embedded in these ongoing movements, and

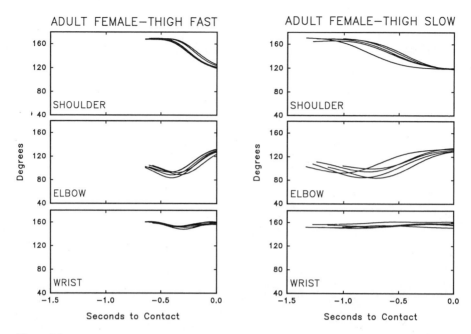

Figure 9.3
Coordination of the shoulder, elbow, and wrist joints for the reaches from the thigh starting position depicted in figure 9.1. Decreasing joint angles indicate flexion. By convention, flexion at the shoulder is lifting the arm. Reaches again are plotted from time of contact on the right.

indeed we should be able to detect the mechanisms by which Gabriel converts one attractor regime into the more adaptive task structure.

This conversion of a spontaneous flapping movement into a directed extension toward the toy is illustrated in figure 9.9. In the top panels of the figure are the two-dimensional projections of the path of Gabriel's hand during an 8-second segment from the week of first reaching, which included a seemingly undirected "flap" back and away from the toy which preceded and was continuous with a movement up and toward the toy. The speed of these movements was high and there were many changes of direction, indicated by peaks in the velocity profile shown below. Gabriel reduced the speed of his movement only within the last fraction of a second before contact. The next set of panels show the patterns of action of the shoulder, elbow, and wrist joints that underlie this movement segment. These kinematics reveal rapid flexions of the shoulder and a rather stiff elbow, characteristic of Gabriel's spontaneous flapping movements in the weeks before reaching onset. Although he flexed and extended his elbow and wrist before contact in this example, in many of his early reaches he kept his elbow stiff.

What kinds of forces lay beneath these movement patterns? In the bottom graph of figure 9.9 are the torques associated with the same segment. Recall from chapter 4 that torques are forces that rotate limbs around their joint centers. Through the techniques of inverse dynamics, which uses measured accelerations and limb masses to calculate forces, it is possible to partition the sources of the forces moving limbs into active and passive components (see Schneider, Zer-

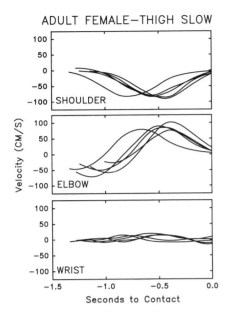
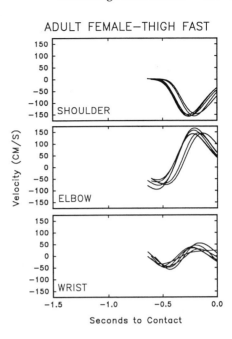

Figure 9.4
Velocities of the joint-angle rotations of the slow reaches starting from the thigh, as depicted in figure 9.1. Note close correspondence of velocity changes in all three joints.

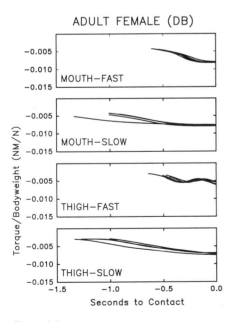

Figure 9.5
The total amount of force produced at the shoulder for the subset of reaches depicted in figure 9.1 for which data were available. The important point here is the stable pattern within reaches in each condition.

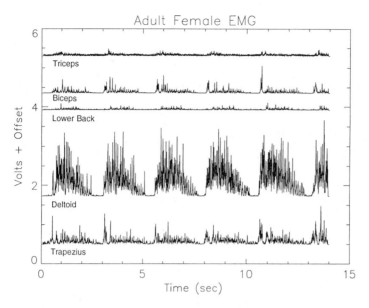

Figure 9.6
Patterns of muscle activation detected by surface EMG from an adult performing successive reaches.
Monitored muscles are the biceps, triceps, deltoid, trapezius, and the spinal extensor muscles. Note
the repeatable triphasic pattern.

nicke, Jensen, Ulrich, and Thelen, 1990). The passive components are the forces
moving limbs that arise from gravity (GRA) and from the movements of other
parts of the body that are mechanically transmitted to the limb segment, that is,
the forces on the elbow resulting from the movement of the shoulder (MDT, or
motion-dependent forces). The active forces are those produced by the contraction of the muscles and from other elastic properties of the tissues (MUS). Because
Gabriel was moving fast and forcibly, his flapping movements generated high
MDT at the shoulder, which were counterbalanced by high MUS forces. What is
most notable is that within the segment of movement directed toward the toy,
Gabriel successively modulated his high torques as he approached the toy.

The pattern of muscle contractions shown in the panel to the right and above
reveals how Gabriel converted his uncontrolled flapping movements into a directed action. Compare the pattern of muscle contractions that adult reachers
use when asked simply to move their hand from their laps to an object placed at
shoulder height and at arm's distance. In contrast to the well-delineated pattern
of reciprocal muscle activation of adult skilled reachers, Gabriel demonstrated
massive co-contraction of both shoulder and upper arm movements during the
reach toward the toy. Such co-contraction has the effect of stiffening the arm,
reducing its compliance, or "give," and thereby damping down the wild, high-
velocity flapping movements that Gabriel could not direct toward the toy and
that would cause him to swipe rather than have a controlled contact.

In the first week of reach onset, all of Gabriel's reaches came from his ongoing
flapping movements, which were characterized by movement primarily at the
shoulder, with high velocities, high motion-dependent torques, and using ex-

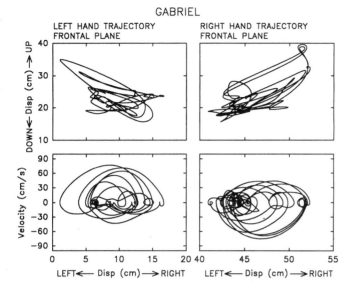

Figure 9.7
Hand trajectories and phase plane plots of 14 seconds of Gabriel's spontaneous movements at the week before reach onset. *Top panel,* The path of both hands in the frontal (*y,z*) plane. Imagine the infant facing the page, with his left and right hands tracing a path on screens in front of him. There was no toy contact. *Bottom pane,* The same movements plotted as phase planes with the hand displacement in the lateral plane vs. the velocity. The rounded trajectories indicate that the velocity varied smoothly with the displacement, a dynamic characteristic of springs and pendulums. The topological similarity of the trajectories suggests behavior of a *limit cycle attractor.* (From Thelen et al., 1993. Reprinted with permission.)

tensive co-contraction. Thus, Gabriel voluntarily adjusted his muscle patterns to "tame" and exploit his arm-spring system to convert a cycle attractor pattern into a point attractor, much as a naturally damped spring reaches a point equilibrium.

Hannah: Solving a Gravity Problem
It is instructive now to contrast Gabriel's initial solution to getting the toy to that adopted by the infant Hannah, whose intrinsic dynamics presented her with a much different problem. In contrast to Gabriel, Hannah was a quiet, contemplative infant who was also visually alert and socially responsive, but motorically less active. Before reaching onset at 22 weeks, she preferred sitting with her hands on her chest or in her mouth or engaging in small, slow movements. Several weeks before she extended her arm up and outward herself to get the toy, she grasped and manipulated it when her parent handed it to her.

Hannah's spontaneous movements before reach onset had much lower average hand speeds and muscle torques than the other infants (Thelen et al., 1993). Thus, reaching presented a different challenge. She did not need to tame unbridled forces and wildly swinging arms. Rather Hannah needed to generate sufficient force in her shoulder to lift her arm against gravity, and in her elbow to counteract the natural flexor position of her arms.

From this low-activity background, Hannah generated smooth and quite mature-looking first reaches. Note in figure 9.10 that the exemplar reach was initiated

GABRIEL

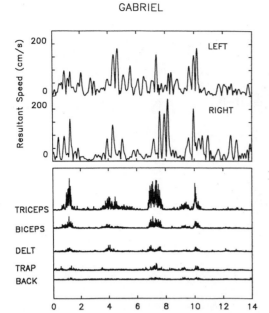

Figure 9.8
Resultant three-dimensional velocities for right and left hands and corresponding EMG of right arm muscles and lower back for Gabriel's spontaneous movements at the week preceding reach onset. (From Thelen et al., 1993. Reprinted with permission.)

from a quiet position with a small lateral and backward loop, followed by the hand moving directly to the toy, although she overshot it. The reach was relatively slow in duration and speed, with few changes of direction, and looked more like the adult pattern (see figure 9.1) than did Gabriel's first attempts. Whereas Gabriel mostly kept his elbow stiff, Hannah in this and other reaches showed more compliant joints (see Thelen et al., 1993), which sometimes moved in coordinated fashion, as in the exemplar (lower left panel, figure 9.10). Also, in dramatic contrast to Gabriel, Hannah's slow movements did not generate high MDTs and indeed, her muscle torques worked primarily against gravity (bottom panel). However, her muscle firing patterns were quite similar to Gabriel's in showing primarily coactivation. (Indeed, none of the infants had the precise muscle patterns of adult reachers.)

Hannah's problem was different from Gabriel's, but it was also the same. She, like Gabriel, had to adjust the energy or forces moving her arm—in her case to make her arm sufficiently stiff or forceful to lift it off her lap. What Gabriel and Hannah had in common, therefore, was *the ability to modulate the forces they delivered to the arms* to change their ongoing, but nonfunctional patterns to movements that brought their hands close enough to the toys for them to make contact. Their solutions were discovered in relation to their own situations, carved out of their individual landscapes, and not prefigured by a synergy known ahead by the brain or the genes.

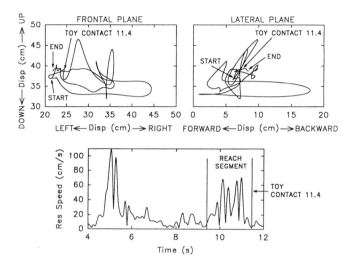

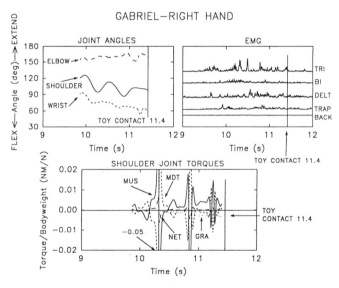

Figure 9.9

Exemplar trial at reach onset showing conversion of spontaneous flapping into reach for Gabriel's right hand. *Top panels, left,* 8-second hand path in the frontal plane; *right,* the same hand path in the sagittal plane (viewed from Gabriel's right side, as he faces the origin of the plot.) *Center panel,* resultant three-dimensional velocity for the same segment showing high-velocity flap at 4 to 6 seconds and flap into reach at 9.5 seconds. *Middle left panel,* rotations of the shoulder, elbow, and wrist joints for the flap into reach segment indicated in the *center panel.* Flexion, decreasing joint angles at elbow and wrist, and lifting the arm with shoulder flexion. *Middle right panel,* EMGs of five muscle groups for the entire 8-second segment. Note phasic co-contraction at the first flap and tonic co-contraction at the flap into reach. *Bottom panel,* Torques at the shoulder associated with the same segment. Negative torques work to flex the joints. *NET,* sum of all torques rotating the shoulder joint; *GRA,* torques due to the pull of gravity; note that gravity is extensor at the shoulder. *MDT,* torques rotating the shoulder that result from the movement of the other, mechanically linked segments of the arm; *MUS,* torques rotating the shoulder arising from muscle contraction and tissue deformation. (From Thelen et al., 1993. Reprinted with permission.)

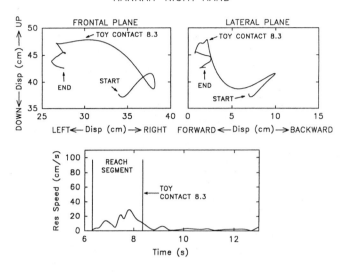

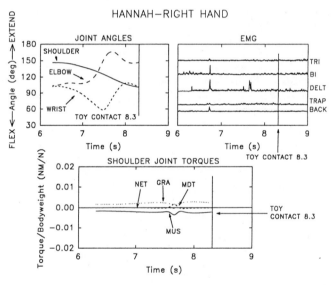

Figure 9.10
Exemplar trial for Hannah's right hand at reach onset showing smooth reach segment initiated from a quiet starting position. *Top panels*, 8-second hand path in the frontal plane and lateral planes. *Middle panel*, Resultant three-dimensional velocity for the same segment showing a slower reach with fewer reversals than for Gabriel. *Lower left panel*, Rotations of the shoulder, elbow, and wrist joints for the reach segment. Note slow flexion of the shoulder with adjustments confined to the elbow and wrist. *Lower right panel*, EMGs from the 8-second segment with the reach segment indicated by *vertical lines*. Note co-concentration of triceps, biceps, and deltoid with small activity in the lower back. *Bottom panel*, Torques at the shoulder associated with the same segment. Very low MUS counteracts gravity with small MDT. (For abbreviations, see legend to figure 9.9) (From Thelen et al., 1993. Reprinted with permission.)

Reaching Onset: The Discovery of a New Form

It is a primary tenet of a dynamic systems theory of development that behavior is not symbolically represented in the system or programmed in the absence of the here-and-now context in which it performed. This means that as infants encounter their environments in ever-changing ways, and as their environments, in turn, afford ever-new encounters, infants must *discover* novel patterns of action that allow a fit between their desires and their opportunities.

The contrast between how Gabriel and Hannah realized their common goal—getting the toy and stuffing it into their mouths—dramatically illustrates that behavior is *process* and *relations* and not instructions and performance. As they faced the problem of how to get the object dangling in front of them, these infants were neither tabulae rasae nor bundles of algorithms. Rather, they each had a unique set of *intrinsic dynamics*, a collective of temperament, attention span, abilities, muscle physiology, energy level, and so on, that determined the movement (or nonmovement) of their arms and their postural tone. This is what they had to work with, the space in which their systems lived, and from which they must *autonomously and individually* discover a solution. Indeed, at reach onset, what Gabriel and Hannah had in common was their desire to get the toy, and their eventual successful contact. What other common processes and relations did they also share that allowed them to find their individual solutions?

How the central nervous system (CNS) controls the arm and hand for reaching and grasping is a question of central importance in motor neuroscience and robotics. Gabriel and Hannah, and every reacher, must work to solve Bernstein's degrees-of-freedom problem, which we discussed in chapter 4. This means that each reacher must recruit a heterogeneous assembly of individual parts—neurons, muscle fibers, bones, joints, metabolic processes—with nearly unlimited possibilities of combinations into a single-purpose device, the hand and arm, which goes quickly and efficiently to the desired object. As Bernstein pointed out, there are no unique or deterministic solutions to this movement problem. Many combinations of joint angles can produce a hand trajectory, as can countless combinations of individual muscle patterns or sums of active and passive forces.

What, then, does the CNS actually control? Scientists observing and modeling human arm trajectory formation have proffered several alternative hypotheses to account for the smooth, fast, and efficient movements illustrated in figures 9.1 through 9.6. Note that in these typical profiles, the hand traversed nearly a straight path to the target, with a characteristic velocity profile, the joints flexed and extended almost simultaneously, and the hand opened and closed at precisely the right moment to anticipate the object's size and weight. Also, mature reachers used muscle forces efficiently and not excessively to initiate and brake movements and to stabilize the reach against unwanted interactive forces.

One group of models suggests that the brain directly controls the direction of the hand path through continual visual comparisons between the actual and intended trajectory (e.g., see Morasso, 1981). Another group of models also focuses on the trajectory—the kinematics—but suggests that the CNS plans reaches to be smooth and graceful by minimizing the irregularities in the path of the hand (Hogan, 1984). A third theory focuses on how the brain calculates the correct pattern of joint-angle changes in order to move the hand correctly in three-dimensional space (e.g., Soechting and Ross, 1984). Since muscle contraction must underlie movement control, yet another model focuses on that level, suggesting that it is the relative timing of the activation of the limb agonists and antagonists that determines the resulting kinematic regularities (Gottlieb, Corcos, and Agarwal, 1989). Each of these engineering solutions addresses some of the known qualities of human arm trajectory formation, but each also fails at the most critical juncture—to explain how actions remain flexible and skilled in the face of inevitable and often unpredictable perturbing forces arising internally from the movement of the limb or externally from the environment. Nor do any of the models provide an account of how any particular level of control *develops*. Since people are not born knowing instinctively how to reach, a performance model must also be developmentally realistic.

Indeed, these developmental data do not support models that consider trajectory, joint angles, or muscle patterns to be the controlled variable. At reach onset, Gabriel and Hannah appeared to plan their movements at none of these levels. Their reaches were visually triggered by the sight of the toy, but there was no obvious continual visual correction either in their head and gaze behavior or in the movement trajectory itself, which as often moved *away* from the target as toward it (Thelen, unpublished observations). Along with the compelling data from Clifton et al. (1993), which showed early reachers to be equally proficient in the dark as in the light, it seems unlikely that initial reaches represent on-line visual monitoring of the hand in relation to the object. Likewise, infants produced hand trajectories from a great variety of patterns of joint-angle coordination. This variation was apparent not only between the four infants studied but even within single infants, whose coordination varied from reach to reach. Finally, as in infant kicking, the muscle activation patterns showed considerable co-contraction, with nonspecific and variable synergies, suggesting that initially infants did not produce reaches from a preexisting stereotyped, or reflex-like response.

What these developmental data do support is a group of models that suggest the CNS is actually working on the dynamic and ensemble characteristics of the entire controlled limb rather than its movement pathway or the firing patterns of the muscles. More specifically, these models propose that limbs behave like springs with masses attached, where the nervous system changes the overall response dynamics by altering the limb's compliance (dynamic stiffness) (Berkenblit, Feldman, and Fukson, 1986; Feldman, 1966; Polit and Bizzi, 1978; Hogan, Bizzi, Mussa-Ivaldi, and Flash, 1987). In these views, there are no explicit a priori instructions or programs for either the trajectory of the hand, joint-angle coordination, or muscle-firing patterns. Instead, the CNS sets up initial stiffness conditions in the limb in relation to the current position of the arm, the target, and the intended movement goals so that when the movement is initiated, the spring-like qualities of the limb determine its final position, or final equilibrium point. Imagine adjusting the stiffness of a mass spring. When energy is imparted to the spring, it will oscillate with an amplitude and frequency and come to rest as determined by its inherent stiffness and damping characteristics. Likewise, the time and space details of the trajectory of the hand and the patterns of the joint rotations emerge as a consequence of these initial stiffness adjustments. The kinematic properties need not be explicitly represented anywhere because they arise secondary to the dynamics.

While there is little evidence that very young infants can plan and execute trajectories at the level of the kinematics of the hand or joints, there is considerable support for the possibility that the physiological mechanisms for detecting dynamic force fields and imposing compliance control of the limb are in place very early in life. These are likely to include lower-level stretch reflexes, probably mediated at the spinal level, which function to control the length of muscles in response to changes in load (Houk, 1979; Myklebust, Gottlieb, and Agarwal, 1986) and the use of agonist-antagonist coactivation, which stiffens the entire limb or limb segment (Feldman, 1980; Hogan et al., 1987). Coactivation, or the mutual contraction of agonist-antagonist pairs, is a primary mechanism for changing limb stiffness (Place your left hand around your upper arm and try to stiffen the whole limb.) Indeed, young infants show extensive co-contraction as a means of motor control, not only in the arms but in the legs, neck, and torso as well (Thelen and Fisher, 1983; Hadders-Algra, Van Eykern, Klip-Van den Nieuwendijk, and Prechtl, 1992).

Thus, the first reaches of Gabriel and Hannah, and of the other two infants observed (Thelen et al., 1993), are each individually discovered solutions to the problem of how to adapt their spontaneous movement dynamics to their intentional goals and the perceptual characteristics of the desired objects. More specifically, they initially accomplish this match through modulating and exploiting their intrinsic movement dynamics, using the resonant frequencies of their springlike arm, but also adjusting the tension on those springs. Their initial attempts produced rather crude and awkward reaches, with jerky and circuitous pathways to the toy. But the movements did get their hands close enough to the toy to start the process of more precise calibration. Once the novel form is discovered through these self-organizing processes, the system has something to work on. It is this continuing process of adaptive matching that we address in the next section.

Matching Intention and Intrinsic Dynamics

Even in the 2 weeks following their reach onset, Gabriel and Hannah (and the other two infants studied) began to adapt their crude initial reaches to the demands of the reaching task. There was little discernible change in their hand trajectories—they still performed jerky, irregular, and indirect movements toward the toy—and they showed variable and inconsistent patterns of joint coordination. Where improvement was evident was in the variables indexing levels of force control—in the velocity of the hand, the torques at the shoulder, and in an estimate of the stiffness of the system.

What is remarkable in the infants' patterns of adaptation is that they were *individually* appropriate. Consider figures 9.11 and 9.12, which show the changing velocities of Gabriel's and Hannah's hands as they approached the objects. In these figures, all analyzable reaches were normalized to the time of toy contact and the resultant speed of the hand plotted for the 3 seconds preceding contact. At the week of onset, these profiles demonstrate Gabriel's high-velocity flaps and Hannah's much slower movements. Over the next 2 weeks, Gabriel learned to slow down and damp his movements, noticeable especially in the last 0.5 second before contact. Hannah, in contrast, decided to speed up and indeed

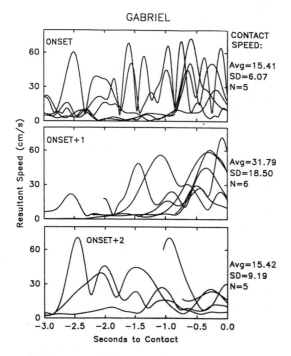

Figure 9.11
Resultant speed of the hand trajectories of all analyzable trials at the week of reach onset and the following 2 weeks, when Gabriel contacted the toy. Only the hand making first contact is plotted. Reaches are plotted from contact (0.0) and the preceding 3 seconds. (From Thelen et al., 1993. Reprinted with permission.)

produced very adult-looking velocity profiles with a somewhat bell-shaped speed curve, but also slowing down just before contact. Recall from the adult data that the most mature reach strategy was a rapid approach, but then decelerating to allow the hand to configure for grasping and to avoid swiping. Although their reaches were far from skilled, these infants appeared to be approaching a more efficient strategy.

The search for a good reach was also reflected in a force variable, the muscle torque generated at the shoulder. The muscle torque is the controlled torque, and may be generated both to rotate the joint and to counteract unwanted passive forces. At onset week, Gabriel generated very high torques, shown in figure 9.13, in dramatic contrast to Hannah's movements (figure 9.14). Gabriel learned rapidly that his wild movements were not doing the job and by 2 weeks after reach onset had modulated them consistently. Hannah was exploring faster, more forceful movements, reflected in larger and more varied torques in the weeks after onset.

Finally, we see compelling evidence of individual strategies in the plots of figures 9.15 and 9.16, estimates of the overall *stiffness* of the system. Although the stiffness (tension) cannot be measured directly, it can be estimated by considering the maximum velocity of a movement in relation to the distance the limb has moved. The underlying assumption is that there needs to be more

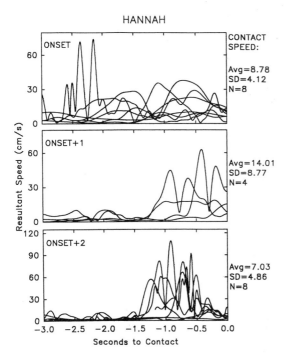

Figure 9.12
Resultant speed of the hand trajectories of all analyzable trials at the week of reach onset and the following 2 weeks when Hannah contacted the toy. Only the hand making first contact is plotted. Reaches are plotted from contact (0.0) and the preceding 3 seconds. (From Thelen et al., 1993. Reprinted with permission.)

tension to move a joint faster for a given distance (think of a tight vs. a loosely coiled spring). For this estimate, we identified each unit of acceleration and deceleration (Hofsten's *movement units*; Brooks, Cooke, and Thomas, 1973; Hofsten, 1982). Each unit has associated with it a hand path. Thus, each point represents the peak velocity displacement value for a movement unit, plotted by seconds prior to toy contact for all analyzable reaches. The regression of these two variables estimates the stiffness. Gabriel became less stiff both in the second before contact and in the weeks succeeding onset. This suggests that he modulated his flapping as he approached the toy, *and* that he became more compliant overall as the weeks progressed. Hannah, who reached with low stiffness in onset week, became much more stiff as her reaches became faster.

Action as an Emergent Category

These detailed pictures of two infants discovering how to reach and, even within 2 weeks, learning how to match their movements to a task, provide an entry into the dynamics of a developmental phase shift. At this transition, the control parameter appeared to be the regulation of arm stiffness, that is, gaining sufficient control of this system quality to get the hand in the vicinity of the toy at an appropriate speed. Although the transition from no reaching to reaching was

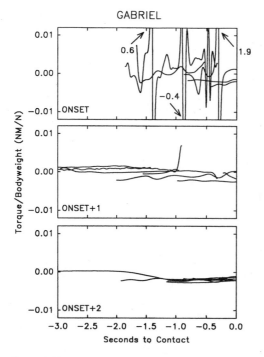

Figure 9.13
Shoulder MUS torques of the segments of the trajectories plotted in figure 9.11 (Gabriel) where dynamic data could be calculated. Negative MUS means that the muscles were contracting to flex the shoulder primarily to counteract gravity. High spikes of MUS are associated with rapid movements generating high MDT. (For abbreviations, see legend to figure 9.9.) (From Thelen et al., 1993. Reprinted with permission.)

discontinuous, the processes engendering this newly discovered control must be continuous in nature. Although Gabriel and Hannah were not performing arm-extended reaches, they were not inactive in the 3 to 4 months preceding this milestone. By the time they had produced their first reaches in the experimental context, they had months of perceptual-motor experience in a visually complex, gravitational environment, filled with reachable objects. They have acquired improved visual tracking, accuity, and binocular vision, along with more stable head control and control of their trunks. Moving and perceiving in this perceptually complex world provided them with the varied, reentrant, time-locked multimodal takes on how the world looks, feels, sounds, tastes, and smells. Most important, as they moved their heads and limbs when they were crying, excited, relaxed, or drowsy, they explored various energy levels and the consequences of various scales of activation in muscles, joints, skin, and vestibular receptors. At the same time they were feeling their body dynamics in terms of muscle stiffness and compliance, they were seeing and feeling the consequences of their movements in many situations and gravitational orientations.

Although goal-directed reaching is a wondrous and complex perceptual motor act, it unnecessary to presume that the system must come with this complexity. The system only needs the most simple motivational impulses—keep interesting

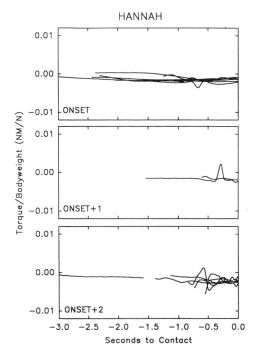

Figure 9.14
Shoulder MUS torques of the segments of trajectories plotted in figure 9.12 (Hannah) where dynamic data could be calculated for Hannah. Note increasing magnitude and variability of MUS at onset +1 and +2 seconds. (From Thelen et al., 1993. Reprinted with permission.)

things in sight, get them in your mouth—to set the self-organizing processes in motion. As we proposed in earlier chapters, the correlated input sets up neural groups that act like attractors that may be progressively strengthened or weakened, depending on the infants' own perceptual motor activities and the consequences of their actions. In the case of Gabriel and Hannah, and the other infants in the study, exploration of their intrinsic dynamics allowed them to discover individually appropriate solutions—speed up or damp down—in order to get their hands near their desired goals.

Over the next 2 weeks, the infants gained knowledge; they formed a category of appropriate stiffness controls—or equilibrium points—that could transport their hands to the toy from a variety of starting positions. Indeed, the hallmark of these self-assembled skills is, as Bernstein pointed out, their equifinality, the ability to execute the same task using different patterns of coordination. Each reach over those 2 weeks was an effort to match current abilities to the location of the toy. By the repeated matching effort over each day, the infants established a more general category of efficient and stable solutions. Would these solutions generalize to all reaching situations, for example, from different postures, to different locations in space, and so on? The naturalistic data suggest not immediately. When observed in the more varied and natural play situation, infants reached several weeks earlier when seated upright than when supine (Schoeny, 1992, and Thelen's unpublished observations). Reaching from supine is more

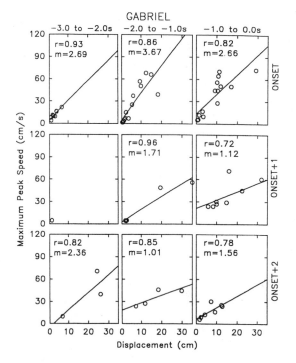

Figure 9.15

Arm stiffness estimation for Gabriel's reach segments at 3 to 2 seconds, 2 to 1 second, and 1 to 0 second prior to contact during the week of onset and the 2 following weeks. Each point of the scattergram represents the displacement as a function of the maximum peak speed for a single "movement unit." Regression lines give an estimation of arm stiffness. Steep slopes indicate high stiffness, slopes near 0 indicate a lack of stiffness. See discussion in Thelen et al., 1993, however, on the debate on the meaning of this estimate. (From Thelen et al., 1993. Reprinted with permission.)

difficult energetically (consider the effort needed to hold a book and read in bed) and presumably infants must learn a new set of stiffness ranges to accomplish that more-challenging task. But with increasing experience reaching in different postures and locations, infants acquire general category knowledge of how much muscle force is needed to lift their limbs and scale their energy appropriately for varied goals.

Again, these data illustrate the integration of time scales so central to our dynamic approach. Developmental change is engendered by the same process of exploration and discovery that led to the first reaches. Development is a continual process of learning by doing.

Although the infants in the study all learned within a few weeks of reach onset to appropriately modulate the forces moving their arms, they were anything but proficient reachers. Their movements were still jerky and indirect and they often batted at the toy or missed it completely. What their initial reaching attempts did was to get their hand "in the ballpark," close enough to provide information about what it feels like and looks like to grab the toy, or to just miss it. From this, and the evidence of Clifton et al. (1993), it seems likely that the first reaches involved the seen toy and the felt hand. The control parameter was initially the

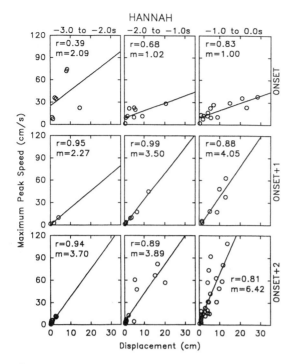

Figure 9.16
Arm stiffness estimation for Hannah's reach segments at 3 to 2 seconds, 2 to 1 second, and 1 to 0 seconds prior to contact during the week of onset and the 2 following weeks. Each point of the scattergram represents the displacement as a function of the maximum peak speed for a single "movement unit." Regression lines give an estimation of arm stiffness. Steep slopes indicate high stiffness, slopes near 0 indicate a lack of stiffness. (From Thelen et al., 1993. Reprinted with permission.)

appropriate scaling of muscle activation; once infants can produce these ballpark reaches, we suspect (although did not test) that visual monitoring of hand and target may become more important.

Nathan: Exploration and Selection over the First Year

It is well known that over the first year, reaches become straighter and smoother, and that infants anticipate the object to be grasped with anticipatory opening and closing of the fingers. According to a dynamic view, this process of gradual improvement in the skill should also be a product of exploration and selection. That is, infants would initially produce many hand path, joint coordination, force, or muscle patterns that could be used to reach from different starting conditions, but that they would eventually select only a small subset of smooth and efficient solutions.

The data for one infant, Nathan, for whom analysis is complete for the entire first year, clearly illustrate the dual processes of exploration and selection. Consider first the control of his hand speed. It is important to approach an object to be grasped with a movement that is not too fast. A swipe does not allow for proper hand and finger control for grasping and a movement that is too slow may miss a moving object and requires strong muscle contractions to keep the arm suspended. Hand speed is a reasonable collective variable indexing the control of forces in the spatial context of approaching the toy. In the top panel of figure 9.17 are plotted the average speeds of Nathan's hand for all analyzable reaches over the first year. The data are normalized to the toy contact and include 3 seconds before the contact to show the reach itself and the movements before the reach (Typically, a moderately paced mature reach takes less than 1 second.) The three-dimensional plot shows the seconds before contact and Nathan's age on the x and y axes and the average hand speed on the vertical or z axis. The bottom panel shows age-related changes in the average speed at the point of contact.

Note that in the weeks after he started to reach at 15 weeks, Nathan had a great range of velocities in the portion of the movement that approached the toy.

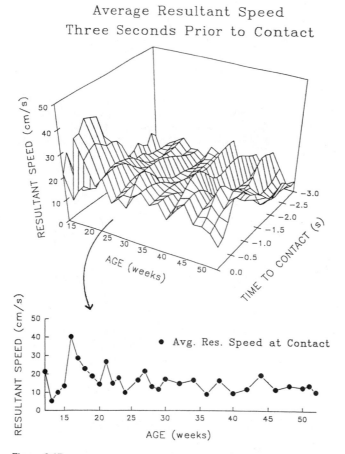

Figure 9.17
Developmental changes in the reach speed for one infant, Nathan, for the first year. *Top panel,* Continuous three-dimensional resultant hand speed 3 seconds prior to contact to toy contact; x axis is age, y axis is time to contact, and z axis is the speed. Note increasingly modulated speed prior to contact with age. *Bottom panel,* Average resultant speed at toy contact.

Even during the middle part of the first year, he used fast movements in some weeks and slow movements in other weeks. Indeed, not until the last months of the first year did Nathan scale his movements consistently, settling on the bell-shaped velocity curve in the last second before the reach and approaching the toy with a well-modulated speed.

A direct path to the object is also the signature of good reaches, and may also be considered a good collective variable. Figure 9.18 is also a three-dimensional landscape, but now plotting Nathan's average distances from the toy as he approached it. Again, note that most of the year was marked by great variability. In some weeks, Nathan approached the toy by advancing his hand in regularly decreasing distances; in other weeks his progress was erratic. Most noteworthy is the decreasing variability in the last few months of the year of the last 0.5 second prior to contact, again indicating that from the variability of the earlier period, Nathan had selected a more efficient strategy.

Overall, Nathan did not show linear improvement in these two collective variables. Rather, he showed a period after reach onset of great variability as he explored a wide range of forces and spaces. During the middle part of his first year, from about weeks 30 to 45, his reaching plateaued, but still varied from session to session. It was as though during this period reaching was "good enough," and there was little impetus for change. Finally, in the last month or so, he discovered more consistent spatial and force values. Because observations were terminated at 1 year, it is unknown whether additional gradual or dramatic changes ensued.

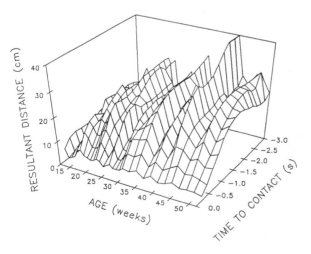

Average 3D Distance from Toy
Three Seconds Prior to Contact

Figure 9.18
Developmental changes in the hand trajectory (distance from the toy) for Nathan over the first year. Continuous distance from the toy 3 seconds prior to contact to toy contact; x axis is age, y axis is time to contact, and z axis is the resultant (three-dimensional) distance from the hand to the toy.

If we accept that control of hand speed and direction condense the degrees of freedom and index the levels of underlying control, then we can also ask about the dynamics of the contributing subsystems. Can we identify potential control parameters—subsystems whose changes engender systemwide reorganizations, that act as the agents of developmental change? Figure 9.19 is a summary of the changes in some component subsystems contributing to reaching dynamics over the first year. The central plot repeats the collective variable of the average speed of the hand at toy contact, showing the period of Nathan's active exploration until week 20, continued variability until week 32, a more stable plateau until week 46, and a final period of quite stable performance of controlled hand speed. Above and below the graph are qualitative descriptions of behavioral and kinetic variables and patterns of muscle activation associated with the kinematic changes.

First, let us look at the forces and the muscle patterns that produce control of hand speed. Not surprisingly, there is a correspondence between the shifts in

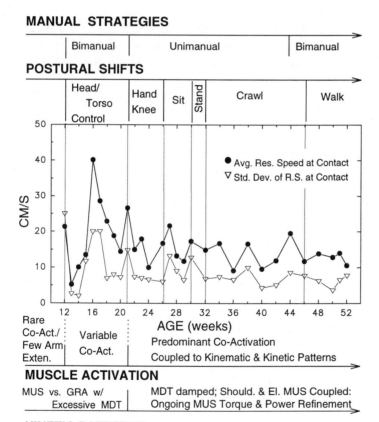

Figure 9.19

Changes in multiple subsystems underlying reaching improvement over the first year. *Center panel* is average hand speed at contact with the toy. Text above and below gives qualitative descriptions of related changes in muscle activation patterns, forces, interlimb coupling, and posture. (For abbreviations, see legend to figure 9.9.)

control at the behavioral level and in the mechanisms beneath that control. Note first that the period of initial high variability in hand contact control was mirrored in equally poor control of the forces that moved the arm segments (Zernicke and Schneider, 1992). Nathan often generated uncontrolled, high-velocity movements and used his muscle activation to counteract the high motion-dependent torques generated by his flapping actions. Or in quieter weeks, muscle power was used to counteract gravity. Several months after reach onset, Nathan became more adept at damping down his flapping movements, and he used his muscle activity more selectively and efficiently. Importantly, as the year progressed, Nathan was able to couple the control of forces at the shoulder and elbow, creating more coordinated control of the entire limb segment.

Exploration and selection were especially evident in the patterns of muscle activation associated with Nathan's reaches (Spencer, Kamm, and Thelen, 1992). At reaching onset, Nathan's muscle patterns, the timing of the onset of the arm and shoulder flexor and extensor muscles, was highly variable, and rarely showed any discernible patterns. (Recall that well-practiced adults reach with a stable pattern of reciprocal activity in biceps and triceps, for example.) During the period of variability in the hand contact velocity, Nathan also used variable muscle patterns, but within that variability some reaches showed clear coactivation patterns. Later in the first year, with the stabilization of the collective variable, he also settled in on a pattern of primarily coactivation. This is not an adult pattern, but it is a coordinated and not random pattern that effectively controls the limbs.

Through months of producing reaches, Nathan learned to control his muscles to produce more smoothly coordinated and appropriate reaching. What about other associated behavior? Although the collective variable, the hand speed, was measured only for the hand that first contacted the toy, reaching in Nathan (and the other infants) was often a two-handed activity (Corbetta and Thelen, 1993). Most notably, when Nathan began reaching, he primarily used both hands together, although both hands sometimes did not contact the toy simultaneously. He shifted dramatically to unimanual reaching at week 20, and continued to use one hand, primarily but not exclusively the right hand, until the last few months of the year when he just as dramatically shifted again to two-handed reaching (Corbetta and Thelen, 1993). Shifts in bimanual coordination have been frequently observed in infant hand use, but the transitions have remained unexplained (e.g., see Goldfield and Michel, 1986). Why, in the global progression to lateral hand dominance, do infants show these puzzling, and seemingly unsystematic shifts in coordination and preference?

A systems view of reaching provides some clues to the potential control parameters. The first phase shift—from Nathan's primarily bimanual hand use to unimanual preference—was associated with his first period of more stable hand speed control. The second shift to bimanual activity again coincided with the highly consistent velocity control of the last months. Indeed, in a detailed examination of the patterns of torque control, Corbetta and Thelen (1993) showed that Nathan was first able to use one hand alone only when he was able to control the forces of the reaching hand and effectively damp the "overflow" of energy across the two-handed synergy. This suggests that the initial period of bimanuality reflected poorly controlled energetic movements, and inability to differentiate control between the limbs.

In the period from 12 to 20 weeks, therefore, Nathan learned from his repeated practice of reaching not only to modulate the forces controlling one hand but also to surpress the associated movements of the other hand. Naturally, it is not efficient to whip both hands toward a small object when only one hand is needed to grasp it. Through repeated perception and action, a more stable and adaptive movement emerged.

What about the second shift to bimanual reaching toward the end of the year? We can only speculate here. However, it was at this time that Nathan began to use two hands cooperatively, for example, to use the left hand to hold a box while the right hand inserted a toy. This shift to bimanuality may reflect this change in intention and foreshadow improvements in bimanual skill.

To this point, we have been describing changes in multiple levels of the reaching system. Are there any systemwide parameters that might account for the several phases of increasing control? The longitudinal study included measures of ongoing behavior less directly related to reaching per se. Schoeny (1992) reported Nathan's postural preferences over the first year as the time spent in particular postural configurations. As would be expected, at certain ages, particular postures were especially "attractive"; Nathan was most stable in these postures, and preferred to assume them when he was perturbed. Figure 9.19 demonstrates that the system-wide postural dynamics were not unrelated to reaching, which is traditionally not conceived of as a postural task.

For example, in weeks 12 to 20, when Nathan was most variable in his hand speed control, he was also gaining control of his head and torso. His assumption of hands-and-knees posture, sitting, and standing, all requiring strength in the back and neck muscles and the ability to move the arms independently at the shoulder, were associated with his next level of arm speed control. Crawling again indexed another reaching plateau, and there was a strong association between Nathan's walking independently and the most stable control of his arm.

We must be appropriately cautious about these results. They reflect current work on only one infant, and they report only associations, which may identify, but do not confirm, potential control parameters. The direction of causality is not known. Do the processes leading to or resulting from learning to walk facilitate improvements in arm control, or vice versa? These questions can only be answered by experimental manipulation, as we suggested in chapter 4.

Even more important from a dynamic perspective is that the agents of change may themselves change. Because the system is dynamic and nonlinear, it is more sensitive to different control parameters at 12 weeks than at 52. For example, while destabilizing the trunk may disrupt reaching at 12 weeks, it is probably ineffective in moving the system at 1 year. By 1 year, the attractor is sufficiently deep—the motor category is sufficiently general—that infants can reach from many postures, in many situations, and toward objects near and far. At 1 year, improvements in reaching probably involve subtle changes in the efficiency of force control, or perhaps in the timing of bimanual coordination. Single-cause explanations are insufficient to capture this rich, multidimensional dynamic.

Knowledge from Action and Action from Knowledge

What is happening when infants convert their undirected movements into functional reaches and subsequently learn to become smooth and efficient? As we have argued previously, movement must be considered as a perceptual category—a time-locked association of neural activations which cohere because of their repeated, varied, and reentrant nature within a functional task context. Within this task context infants are acting and learning from acting what levels of arm stiffness, trunk stabilization, bilateral damping, and so on best meet the task demands of grabbing an item located in three-dimensional space in order to transport it to the mouth. They are learning to convert the natural springlike qualities of their arms—qualities which must be perceived through exploration—into efficient reaching devices.

This learning is knowledge, as is knowledge about the physical properties of objects in the world: the understanding of edges, contours, collisions, slopeness, and so on. The activation patterns created by reaching create expectancies, direct attention, marshall cognitive resources, and act dynamically, as do the patterns of activities traditionally considered more cognitive. Both are products of activities in the here and now, and owe their configurations to the demands of the here and now. And both have histories and futures.

To this point, we have told a number of developmental stories with common themes. We have shown how common processes described at the abstract level of dynamics, and at the more mechanistic level of neural activation patterns and forces, can account for some of the fundamental skills of infancy: locomotion, reaching, and the ability to categorize, learn, and remember. We have emphasized throughout that these domains are not separate, but form interwoven fabrics of causality. A new skill in one domain—a new motor milestone, or success at a Piagetian cognitive task—often appears as if the precursors to that skill should be privileged in that domain. But we have seen that the story is always more complex, and often surprising—fat changes motor skills, motor skills change cognitive abilities. In the next chapter, we analyze one of the most striking and engaging new skills in infancy—the ability to remember the location of a hidden object—to show the dynamic matrix of perception and action that supports this cognitive milestone.

Chapter 10

Real Time, Developmental Time, and Knowing: Explaining the A-Not-B Error

Chapter 9 provides a clear example of dynamic systems theory applied to development. In that chapter, we showed how the global structure of reaching emerges in and through the *details* of real-time processes. A reach is a dynamic ensemble that does not exist separately from the actions of muscles and joints, from limbs with biomechanical and kinematic properties, and from infants' motivation to reach and group objects. The global structure of a reach is *not reducible* to these components, but is only explained by understanding how these components interact in real time. Moreover, developmental change becomes transparent only by understanding how individual reaches in real time are modified by and, in turn, modify the components. Thus reaching is not preformed, nor is development pushed forward by magical maturational processes. Rather, the development of reaching is a result of changes in the heterochronic underpinnings of the behavior itself—changes that emerged from the activity of the organism.

That action and cognition are a dynamic ensemble is the core assumption of a new developmental theory and a new empirical approach to the study of change. In this chapter, we apply dynamic principles to infants' understanding of objects and in particular to one milestone in that understanding—the A-not-B error. In explaining the A-not-B error we again show how knowing is created in activity.

The A-Not-B Error

In his theory of how infants construct an understanding of the unitary, bounded, and persistent nature of objects in time and space, Piaget (1952) proposed six successive reorganizations of mental structure—the six stages of the sensorimotor period. Piaget derived this theory of successive qualitative shifts in mental structure from observations of dramatic changes in his own infants' behaviors toward objects. None of these shifts was as enigmatic as the one he used to define stage 4 of the development of the object concept.

The intriguing behavior, the A-not-B error, emerges in a hide-and-seek task with objects. In this task the experimenter hides a tantalizing object in location A, for example, under a bucket, while the infant watches. After some time, usually a few seconds, the infant is allowed to search for the object. The stage 4 infant does search and successfully finds the object. This A trial is repeated several times. On the critical trial, the experimenter hides the object in location B, for example, under a different bucket, while the infant watches. The surprising behavior of the stage 4 infant is this: when allowed to retrieve the object, the infant searches in location A—not the place where the infant saw the object disappear but the place where the infant last found the object. According to Piaget, the A-not-B error occurs because infants do not represent the object as continuing in space and time independently of their own perceptions or actions. Babies younger than 7 months do not make the A-not-B error because they do not search for hidden objects. Infants older than 12 months typically do not make the A-not-B error because they successfully search where they saw an object last disappear. Only for a brief period in development, then, does the qualitatively unique A-not-B error occur. Yet, during this time, the error is robust and would seem a signal event in the development of cognition.

Because the A-not-B error is so dramatic and so clearly demarcates a stage between less and more mature understandings of object permanence, it is not surprising that the phenomenon has been so highly studied. What is surprising is that a vast bank of empirical research has not led to a coherent theory (see Bremner, 1985; Harris, 1987; Wellman, Cross, and Bartsch, 1987). In our view, theoretical attempts at integration have been stymied by two factors: the search for single causes and the competence-performance distinction.

The empirical question driving experiments on the A-not-B error has been: Do stage 4 infants *really believe* that an object hidden in location B actually exists in location A? To answer this question researchers have designed two sorts of studies: (a) those seeking to demonstrate that infants possess the critical competence (Do infants *really* know where the object is?), and (b) those seeking to discover the performance variables such as memory, attention, or spatial knowledge that mask the supposed underlying competence (If they know it, how come they can't do it?). As an example of the first kind of study, Baillargeon and Graber (1988) developed a version of the A-not-B task that did not require infants to actually search and retrieve an object. Instead, Baillargeon and Graber used a habituation paradigm like those discussed in chapters 6 and 8 to show that infants "really knew" that objects are found where they are hidden. In their study, infants watched an object as it was hidden, watched a brief distractor event, and then watched as the object was retrieved. Infants in the possible condition saw the object retrieved from where it was hidden. Infants in the impossible condition saw the object retrieved from a different location. Infants looked at the retrieval event more in the impossible than possible condition. Baillargeon and Graber concluded that infants *really know* about the *permanence* of objects in space and time but that this competence is somehow masked by the task requirements of manually searching in the A-not-B task.

A line of research consistent with the second question—uncovering the performance variables that mask competence—is Diamond's (1990a,b) recent research on the development of the A-not-B error in relation to the maturation of the frontal lobe. Diamond explains the A-not-B error in terms of a failure of inhibitory control, and specifically an inability to inhibit prepotent response tendencies. Diamond, like Baillargeon and Graber, argues that infants "know where the reward is even when they reach back to where they last found it" (Diamond, 1990b, p. 662). The problem for the infant, in Diamond's view, is not in the knowing, but in the inhibiting of the reaching.

One difficulty with such a competence approach to the A-not-B error is that it leaves unexplained a large body of evidence which shows that this error depends systematically on a number of context-specific factors. In other words, the transition is not simply having the knowledge vs. not having the knowledge, or being able to inhibit a reach or not inhibit a reach. Rather, using our conventional dynamic depiction, the developmental trajectory looks like that illustrated in figure 10.1. Early in development, there is one deep attractor: infants do not reach for completely hidden objects and cannot be induced to do so. At the other end, there is another very deep attractor: infants always search at B—the location at which they saw the object disappear. In the developmental landscape, the A-not-B error belongs to the bumpy terrain between the two valleys. The point, put differently, is that the error—in that brief stage of development in which it occurs—is variable.

Herein lies the critical idea. If real-time behavior and developmental time are continuous, if the context-specific forces that assemble behavior in real-time search tasks are the same forces that cause developmental change, *then the variability of the A-not-B error*, the contexts in which it does and does not occur, are the key to understanding the transition from not searching for hidden objects to searching correctly for them.

The structure of this chapter is as follows. First, we review the evidence on task and context effects on the occurrence of the A-not-B error in infants from 8 to 10 months of age. That is, we look at real-time task effects in the transition period from not searching for hidden objects to searching correctly. Second, from the evidence on context effects, we propose what the system might be like— what the components are that give rise to these effects. Third, we consider developmental time—how changes in the system and its components may explain the developmental trend. That is, we use our dynamic systems account of real-time context effects to provide an account of the phase shifts into and out of the stage 4 error. Fourth, we ask the question of what drives development. We

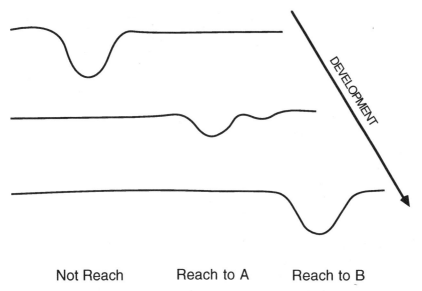

Not Reach   Reach to A   Reach to B

Figure 10.1
Changing attractors in the A-not-B task with development.

specifically consider and reject Diamond's proposal that developmental change in this task is driven by the maturation of frontal cortex. Finally, we ask what competence is: What do infants know and how is knowing related to search behavior?

Context Effects

There may well be more published studies on the A-not-B error than on any other phenomenon in developmental psychology. In tests of many of the specific hypotheses driven by different theoretical reasons, experimenters have manipulated all aspects of the task. These include the visual properties of the hiding locations, their transparency, the distance between them, the number of hiding places, the delay between hiding and search, search for people vs. objects, search at home vs. in the laboratory, and several other factors. What experimenters have found is that they nearly all matter in one way or another, and if not alone, then in combination.

Wellman et al. (1987) attempted to bring order to this literature through a meta-analysis of reported results. Meta-analysis is a statistical procedure that combines results from published studies to investigate the effects of independent variables on some dependent variable. In a meta-analysis, experimental conditions in published studies—not individual subjects—are the unit of analysis. Wellman et al. used the dependent measure of the proportion of infants who demonstrated the target behaviors on the critical trial when the object was hidden at location B: the error of searching at location A or the correct behavior of searching at location B. In their analysis, Wellman et al. found four variables to be critical in determining the number of infants who did and did not make the A-not-B error. These are: (a) the age of the infants; (b) the delay between the time the object is hidden and when the infants are allowed to search; (c) the number of hiding locations; and (d) the distinctiveness of the containers. These task effects consistently emerge as critical and they are left unexplained by current theory. In the rest of the chapter, we apply a dynamic systems account.

The Data to Be Explained
We briefly summarize here the major results of the meta-analysis by Wellman et al. We describe the task conditions and the *developmental functions* in those task conditions. Wellman et al. reported the results of their analyses in several ways. One presentation was in terms of whether more infants made the response than expected by chance, fewer made the response than expected by chance, or the number of infants making the response did not differ from that expected by chance. We used this information principally in constructing the generalized developmental functions we seek to explain. Thus, for example, the developmental function drawn at the top of figure 10.2 was derived from four points suggested by the meta-analysis of 8-month-olds in the standard condition: at 0-second delay and the 1-second delay, the number of infants searching at A and the number of infants searching at B are not greater than chance. At the 3-second and 5-second delay, the number of infants searching at B is greater than chance. Thus, we draw a generalized developmental function to capture the effects of delay at this age by drawing a smooth function that connects equal likelihood of

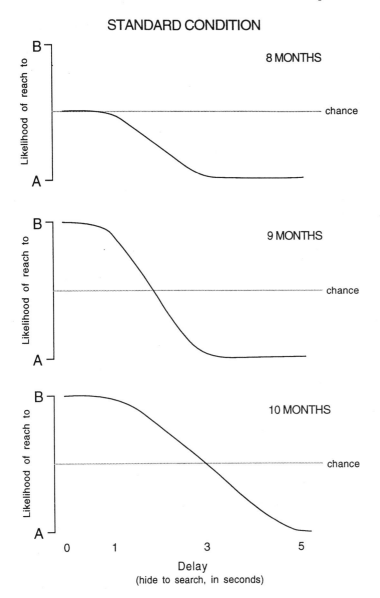

Figure 10.2
Likelihood that the subjects in an experiment will all reach to A, all reach to B, or as a group show change level performance with some subjects reaching to A and some reaching to B. (Derived from the results of the meta-analysis conducted by Wellman et al.)

searching at A and B at the two brief delays to the strong likelihood of searching at B at the long delays.

Delay in Standard Two-Location Tasks The standard two-location version of the A-not-B task follows closely Piaget's task. There is a single desired object, two horizontally displaced locations separated by a small distance and marked by two *identical* covers and backgrounds. The meta-analysis of published results in this task revealed two factors that determined whether infants searched correctly or not: the age of the infants and the delay between hiding and when the infant was allowed to search. Figure 10.2 shows the generalized developmental functions suggested by the analysis of Wellman et al. for 8-, 9-, and 10-month-olds when the delay between hiding and search was 0, 1, 3, or 5 seconds. The figure shows that 8-month-olds do not reliably make the error at 0- and 1-second delays but do systematically make the error at the longer delays of 3 and 5 seconds. Nine-month-olds, in contrast, search correctly at 0 seconds, and systematically make the error at 3- and 5-second delays. Ten-month-olds search correctly at 0- and 1-second delays and systematically make the error at 3- and 5-second delays. Thus, we see systematic change in the developmental functions that relate the likelihood of correct search to the length of delay between hiding and search.

Visually Distinctive Hiding Locations These functions, however, are not the same across all task contexts. One variation that matters is whether the containers are visually distinctive. In the standard task, when the containers are identical, infants make the error. When the containers are different colors or patterns, infants to not make the error. Figure 10.3 shows the suggested developmental functions in conditions in which the two hiding locations were distinguished by properties other than their location in space. Again, we see clear changes in the developmental functions that relate the likelihood of correct search to the length of delay between hiding and search. However, these functions are different from those in the standard nondistinctive cover version of the task. At no age level do children systematically make the A-not-B error. Instead, the proportion of children making the error either does not differ reliably from chance or children search correctly. Eight-month-olds do not systematically search in location B at any delay; 9-month-olds search correctly at 0- and 1-second delays; and 10-month-olds search correctly at 0-, 1-, and 3-second delays.

Multiple Locations The number of hiding locations also alters the likelihood of errors and the functions relating age and delay. Indeed, it is in this condition only that 8-month-olds search correctly. In the multiple-location tasks, infants are presented with as many as six locations, all with visually identical backgrounds and covers. In these multilocation studies, location A is usually at one extreme and location B is at the other extreme. The developmental functions suggested by the meta-analysis of results from experiments using multiple hiding locations are shown in figure 10.4. The developmental functions suggest that even 8-month-olds will correctly search at B on the critical trial given no delay and multiple locations, but will systematically make the error at long delays. Nine-month-olds systematically search correctly at 0- and 1-second delays, but make the error at 5-second delays. Ten-month-olds systematically search cor-

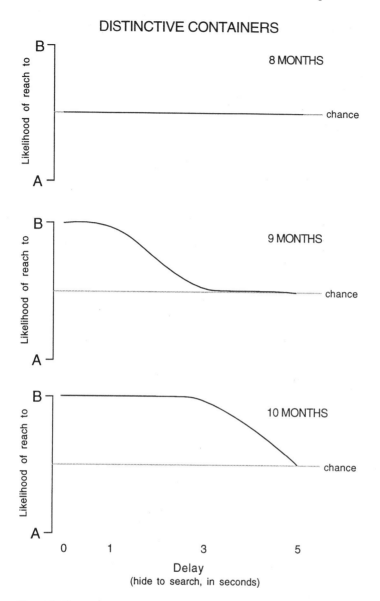

Figure 10.3
Likelihood that the subjects in an experiment will all reach to A, all reach to B, or as a group show chance level performance with some subjects reaching to A and some reaching to B. (Derived from the results of the meta-analysis conducted by Wellman et al.)

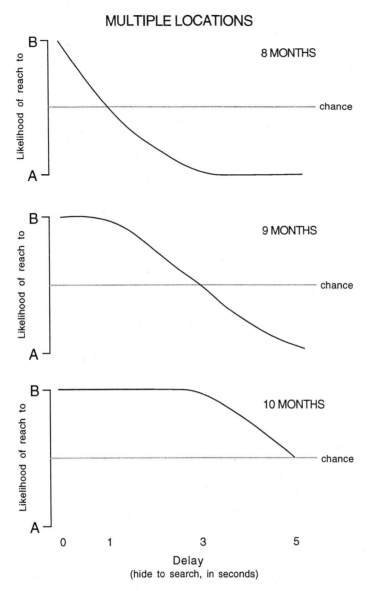

Figure 10.4
Likelihood that the subjects in an experiment will all reach to A, all reach to B, or as a group show chance level performance with some subjects reaching to A and some reaching to B. (Derived from the results of the meta-analysis conducted by Wellman et al.)

rectly at 0-, 1-, and 3-second delays. Overall, then, multiple locations increase the likelihood of correct search. Why should this be?

If we look across figures 10.2, 10.3, and 10.4, we see clear order in the data; development is showing clear directional growth to errorless search regardless of task context. Across all the contexts, there is small but progressive change: with age children can withstand longer and longer delays. But we can also see that in this brief developmental period of the A-not-B error, infants' performances depend on the task context. Thus, there are three aspects of the phenomenon to be explained: (a) the changing context effects of 8-, 9-, and 10-month-olds, (b) the ability of infants to withstand longer delays with increasing age, and (c) the error itself. We suggest all three are manifestations of a single developing system and that the context effects, the developmental changes, and the error itself all emerge in and *grow out of behavior,* that is, grow from the activity of the system itself.

A Systems Account

Our account builds on the ideas we offered in chapters 6 and 8 about emergent cognition in the time-locked interactions of what and where systems. In our account of the A-not-B error, we propose that development emerges in the interaction of three systems: a what system, and two where systems. At each point in time, we propose that from these three systems six simultaneous mappings are being made: each system maps the physical events in the world to its own activity and each system maps the activity of the other systems to its own activity. The three heterogeneous systems and their reentrant connections are illustrated in figure 10.5. They include the two where systems of looking and reaching, and the what system of perceiving the static visual properties of objects. We propose that task-specific behaviors of the A-not-B error and developmental

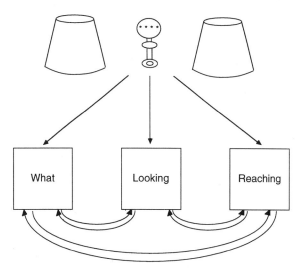

Figure 10.5
Couplings between looking and reaching systems.

changes in search behavior emerge in the interactions of these three systems with events in the world and with one another. We propose that task-specific behaviors and development happen because the reentrant mappings between the three systems create an internal landscape. Through this landscape, the history of experiences, the just-previous activity of the system, and the immediate input jointly cause behavior. The specific dynamic account of the A-not-B error that follows shares much with, and derives from, the work of Acredelo (1990) and Bertenthal, Campos, and Barrett (1984).

A preliminary caveat is in order. Our goal here is to show how dynamic systems can explain both real-time activity and the developmental trend and we attempt to do so in concrete and simple ways that illustrate how dynamic systems approaches may work as real testable theories in development. To do this, we make simplifying assumptions about the operations of the component systems and their interactions—simplifying assumptions that are surely wrong because each one of these systems is a complex system in and of itself and, as we discuss later, the very complexity and developmental course of the components may contribute substantially to the observed developmental trend. Nevertheless, we believe our account captures some fundamental truths about search behavior, task context, and development, and in so doing shows the promise of dynamic systems.

Recall that there are three *always relevant* determiners of the activity of a dynamic system: the intrinsic dynamics, the just-preceding events, and the immediate sensory input. The intrinsic dynamics reflect the long-term history of the system—in evolution and in development. The intrinsic dynamics depend on the specific characteristics of the component systems and the couplings between them. The immediately preceding events, the very recent history of the system, have their effects through representational momentum and transient changes in coupling strength, transient changes that are brought about by the *specific sequence of internal and external events* in real time. Finally, there is the sensory input at the moment.

We build our account of the A-not-B error by concentrating on the sensory input and how the sequence of internal and external events in the task itself determines the occurrence of the error. We do this by concentrating first on context effects at one age level—8 months. We then consider development and how the intrinsic dynamics, and thus the transient dynamics, might change to yield the developmental trend illustrated in figures 10.2, 10.3, and 10.4.

Explaining the Context Dependencies in Eight-month-old Performances
The time course of events in the standard two-location task runs approximately as follows (we notationally mark points in this continuous event to help in describing the activity of the component systems and the trajectories).

$t_{(1)}$	The infant sees and watches an interesting toy.
$t_{(2-4)}$	The infant watches as the experimenter moves the toy to location A.
$t_{(5)}$	The infant sees the toy disappear at location A.
$t_{(6)}$	The infant watches the experimenter's hand leave location A and return to center.

$t_{(7-n)}$ The infant is restrained some variable time period (n) and is released at t(n).

$t_{(n + 1-n + 2)}$ The infant manually reaches toward location A.

$t_{(n + 3)}$ The infant retrieves the interesting toy.

This event is then repeated some number of times (m = 2 in most studies) and then the critical test event—hiding at location B—occurs as follows:

$t_{m(1)}$ The infant watches the interesting toy.

$t_{m(2-4)}$ The infant watches as the experimenter moves the toy to location B.

$t_{m(5)}$ The infant sees the toy disappear at location B.

$t_{m(6)}$ The infant watches the experimenter's hand leave location B.

$t_{m(7-n)}$ The infant is restrained some variable time period and is released at time t_{mn}.

What we want to explain is the 8-month-old infant's behavior at this point in time—time $t_{m(n + 1)}$. Does the infant reach to location A or B? How does that behavior depend on the delay (n), the hiding location distinctiveness, and the number of locations?

We can understand the in-task events just prior to this critical point in time as a trajectory of internal mental activity—a trajectory that arises in context from perceiving objects, looking, and reaching. In the interest of clarity, we again make simplifying assumptions about how the level of activity in each of our component systems might be related to the input, just as we did in our account of infants' perception of possible and impossible events in chapter 8. Again, to aid in plotting our theoretical trajectories of mental activity, we denote states of activity by whole numbers such that the similarity of stimulus events and corresponding activity levels within a single component system are ordered by these numbers. Table 10.1 lists these activity levels at each point in time in the three component systems in the standard two-choice task with identical covers and *no delay* between hiding and search during the A phase of the task and the B phase of the task. This is a context in which 8-month-olds at the critical test moment do not systematically search at either location A or B: they neither consistently make the error nor search correctly. We describe what the numbers in table 10.1 represent—what the activity levels are over the course of events for each component below:

The What System—Perceiving the Static Properties of Objects
The principal objects that an infant may attend to in the A-not-B task are the interesting toy, the covers, and the experimenter's hand. We assume that the pattern of internal activity based on the static properties of these objects is highly dissimilar for the three key objects of toy, cover, and hand since they share few properties. The pattern of activity for the two hiding-place covers is, of course, the same (or nearly so) because the covers in the standard task are identical. For the purposes of explication and in order to plot the trajectories of internal activity, we will use the following values to represent the internal activity for each of the critical objects in our account: toy (in experimenter's hand)—8; experimenter's hand alone—4; cover at A—2; cover at B—2. We also assume that the what

Table 10.1
Hypothetical activity values of the what, where-looking and where-reaching systems used to construct representational trajectories for 8-month-olds in the standard condition with 0-second delay[a]

	Time	Steps	What	Look	Reach
Activity levels in the A phase	1	toy	8	4	4
	2	toy moved to A	8	3	4
	3	toy moved to A	8	2	4
	4	toy moved to A	8	1	4
	5	toy disappears at A	2	1	4
	6	hand at center	4	4	4
	7	0 delay look toward A	2	3	4
	8	0 delay look toward A	2	2	4
	9	0 delay look toward A	2	1	4
	10	reach and retrieve toy	8	1	1
Activity levels in the B phase	1	toy	8	4	4
	2	toy moved to B	8	5	4
	3	toy moved to B	8	6	4
	4	toy moved to B	8	7	4
	5	toy disappears at B	2	7	4
	6	hand at center	4	4	4

[a] Values plotted just until critical test event of noting where the infant reaches.

component operates on the objects that the infant is looking at and that looking behavior is highly influenced by movement in the stimulus field. Thus the numbers in the *what* column at the top of table 10.1 correspond to the infant watching the toy [$t_{(1)}$]; watching the toy transported to location A [$t_{(2-4)}$]; seeing the cover at A [$t_{(5)}$]; watching the experimenter's hand move away from A; looking at the cover as the infant reaches [$t_{(7,8)}$]; and looking at the toy [$t_{(9)}$]. An identical course of activity is shown in the what system of phase B—the critical test trial—up until $t_{(7)}$, the point in this event that we hope to predict.

The Looking System
We assume that the level of activity in this system depends on *where* the infant is looking. For the present purposes, we represent the activity level in this component in terms of the lateral position of direction of gaze relative to location A and location B. Looking at A is represented by the value of 1 and looking at B is represented by the value of 7. The sequence of looking behavior thus described in the Look column of table 10.1 in phase A is as follows: looking toward midline where the experimenter is holding the toy [$t_{(1)}$]; tracking the movement of the toy to A [$t_{(2-5)}$]; looking at A as the toy is hidden [$t_{(5)}$]; tracking the hand toward midline as the experimenter moves away from location A [$t_{(6)}$]; looking at location A as the infant reaches [$t_{(7,8)}$]; and looking at location A as the toy is found [$t_{(9)}$]. The bottom of table 10.1 describes the analogous pattern of looking *toward location B* up to $t_{(7)}$ the point at which one hopes to predict what the infant does.

The Reaching System

This system is like the looking system in that its activity level depends on *locations* in the world. The activity level in this hypothesized system is determined by the felt direction of a reach—with 1 representing reaches in the direction of A, 7 representing reaches in the direction of B, and the values 2 to 6 representing reaches in between these two extremes. Also, we use the value 4 as a default value to indicate no reach during the delay period in which the infant is restrained. The hypothesized activity levels in this system are given in table 10.1 in the third column. In the A phase of the experiment, the infant is restrained and is not reaching until the last step in our description of the events. Thus the activity level in the reaching system is at the default value of 4 until the last step in the A phase of the experiment, at which point it is at value 1 as the infant correctly reaches toward the A location.

Note that the pattern of activity we describe here is a description of the hypothetical internal events that arise from the felt movements of reaching. It does *not* explain why the infant reached to A in the first place in this phase of the experiment. We do, however, offer an explanation in the course of our following account. But first we concentrate on what happens in the critical B phase when the infant is released to reach.

Trajectories—Eight-month-olds, Standard Condition, No Delay

The values in table 10.1 may be used to plot trajectories of one force (the stimulus input) on the time-locked activity in the three systems. Because it is difficult to see the fine points of the trajectories in three-dimensional representations, we show, instead, in figure 10.6, three two-dimensional plots. These represent three planar views of the three-dimensional state space.

What by Look   The representation at left shows the activity level in the what system as a function of the activity level in the look system. The thicker trajectory portrays the joint activity in the two systems during the A phase. The thinner black line portrays the trajectory of activity in the two systems as the events unfold in the B phase. Following the same reasoning we used in chapters 6 and 8, we propose that the repeated experience of the A phase of the experiment sets up a transient attractor. That is, the thick trajectory may be thought of as the low point and center of a valley formed by the A phase of the experiment. Levels of activity that come close to that trajectory will tend to be captured by it.

In the *what-by-look* phase portrait, the A and B trajectories start at similar points in the state space but move in opposite directions. Critically, however, the end of the phase B trajectory, the point at which the infant is released to reach, and the point we want to predict, is close to the phase A trajectory that corresponds to a reach toward A. Should the mental activity levels *in the B phase of the experiment*, therefore, be pulled into this attractor? Perhaps.

What happens when the infant is released to reach in phase B will depend not just on its location in the state space and the sensory input at that moment but also on the representational momentum—the *reentered* activity in the three systems. At a 0-second delay—when the moment of release and reach immediately follow the return of the experimenter's hand from location B to the center—the representational momentum, the momentum in the internal activity itself, may

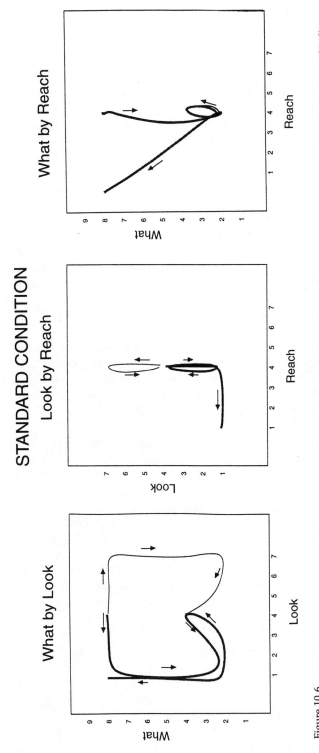

Figure 10.6
Three planar views of the trajectory of joint activity in the three-coupled system. *Thick line*, attracting trajectory formed during the A phase; *thin line*, trajectory in B phase up to the moment of reach.

be *away* from the phase A trajectory. Critically, however, the likelihood that there is sufficient momentum in the phase B trajectory to avoid it being captured by the phase A attractor will *decrease* with increasing delay.

Look by Reach   The middle state space shows the time-locked activity of the look and reach systems as the events unfold in phase A (thick trajectory) and in phase B (thin black trajectory). Again, the phase B trajectory ends close to the hypothesized attracting trajectory that has emerged from the prior experience of phase A. However, whether that attracting trajectory captures performance at the critical moment in phase B again depends on the representational momentum, that is, on the reentrant influences of the just preceding activity from each of the three systems on one another. And again, the force of any representational momentum away from the phase A attractor will decrease with increased delay between hiding and search.

What by Reach   The state space at right shows the time-locked activity of the what and reach systems. Again, the thick trajectory represents the attracting trajectory of activity from the experience of the A phase and the thin black trajectory represents the time-locked activity of the two systems in phase B. Here one can see that in this plane, the trajectory of phase B activity falls directly on the phase A trajectory. This is because the static visual properties and the physical restraint on reaching are identical in phase A and phase B up to the critical moment. Should the infant in phase B then reach toward A? If these two systems—what and reach—were all that were operative, the answer would clearly be yes. But they are not; the relevant pattern of activity is in the three-dimensional space defined by joint reaching, looking, and seeing. We next consider what the patterns of activity of the whole suggest for the behavior of 8-month-olds in the standard task.

Explanation of Eight-month-olds' Behavior in the Standard Task
By the meta-analysis of Wellman et al., 8-month-olds show chance level performances at 0- and 1-second delays—neither systematically searching at A or B, but systematically and incorrectly searching at A after 3- and 5-second delays. By our analysis, the chance level of performance with 0-second delay—the delay represented by the trajectories in figure 10.6—occurs because with 0-second delay the representational momentum of the phase B trajectory is sufficient, that although the pattern of activity may be distorted in the direction of A it is not invariably captured by the phase A trajectory. Put in other words, the single experience of watching the displaced hiding event sets up competing representational momentum sufficient to sometimes disrupt the previous pattern. There is, in this state of affairs, no strong pull in one direction or another and chance aspects of the events or internal activity may push individual infants one way (reach to A) or another (reach to B).

What happens as the infant is restrained longer and prevented from reaching? Activity in the three systems does not stop when there is a delay. The internal activity in each system at any given moment during the delay will be determined by the intrinsic dynamics, representational momentum, and unsystematic internal and external events during the delay. Over the time delay, these unsystematic influences, without the directional force of specific sensory input, will cause the pattern of activity to drift. And since the end of the B trajectory is relatively near the A trajectory and because the A trajectory may have more momentum because of its repeated activity, it becomes more likely with increasing delay that the system's activity will fall into a reach toward A.

We summarize the transient dynamics, the changing attractor strengths in the A vs. B direction that emerge in this task, in figure 10.7. This figure summarizes through its hills and valleys the *likelihood* that the system (indicated by the ball in the center of the terrain) will move in a particular direction: (a) At the beginning of the experiment, the landscape is relatively flat; there is no greater tendency to look in the A direction than in the B direction. (b) Given the reentrant mapping of the what, look, and where systems, however, an attractor on the A side will form as the infant watches the object hidden in A. Thus, when the infant is released, the infant reaches correctly to A. (c) The time-locked sensory events and their reentrant effects that constitute a reach and successful search at A will strengthen the A attractor. (d) Watching the object hidden at B causes—in the same way as watching an object hidden at A causes—a shallow attractor to form. At the critical point in the experiment, the infant sits between the two attractors and may reach either to A or to B. With increasing delays, it is increasingly likely that the infant's activity will be captured by the deeper attraction of a reach to A.

Eight-month-olds and Distinctive Containers
Given two distinctive hiding locations marked by different colors or patterns, 8-month-old infants show chance level performances *at all delays*. Our account

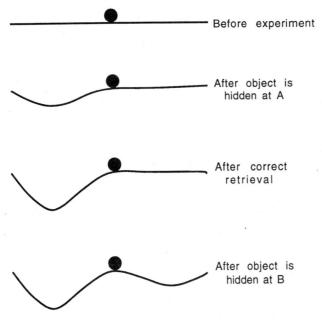

Figure 10.7
Changing attractors through the course of the standard task.

predicts such a context effect. Fewer errors are expected given distinctive locations at all delays because the phase A and phase B trajectories are not as near to each other as they are in the standard condition.

Table 10.2 gives the hypothetical activity levels in the distinctive container condition that we used to make our trajectories. The activity levels in phase A in the three component systems are identical to those of the standard task. Indeed, the only change in the hypothesized activity levels is in the what system at phase B step 6. Because the container at location B differs markedly in its static visual properties from the container at location A, the what system is hypothesized to have a markedly different pattern of activity when the infant looks at location B than when the infant looks at location A. Figure 10.8 shows the three planar views of the time-locked sensory input to the three systems. Note that in contrast to the trajectories of the standard condition, in no plane does the activity during phase B in the distinctive container condition fall on top of the attracting trajectory set up in phase A. In the three-dimensional state space of activity, the phase B trajectory is farther from the phase A trajectory.

What happens when the 8-month-old infant is released to reach in the distinctive container condition after 0 seconds of restraint? We illustrate the transient in-task dynamics in figure 10.9. Again, the hills and valleys summarize the *likelihood* at various points in the experimental task that the infant will reach to A or to B. The situation is like that illustrated for the standard task, except that at the critical point (step 4), the B attractor is relatively far from the deeper A attractor. When the infant is released to search, the potential for change is

Table 10.2
Hypothetical activity values of the what, where-looking and where-reaching systems used to construct representational trajectories for 8-month-olds in the distinctive container condition with 0-second delay

	Time	Steps	What	Look	Reach
Activity levels in the A phase	1	toy	8	4	4
	2	toy moved to A	8	3	4
	3	toy moved to A	8	2	4
	4	toy moved to A	8	1	4
	5	toy disappears at A	2	1	4
	6	hand at center	4	4	4
	7	0 delay look toward A	2	3	4
	8	0 delay look toward A	2	2	4
	9	0 delay look toward A	2	1	4
	10	reach and retrieve toy	8	1	1
Activity levels in the B phase	1	toy	8	4	4
	2	toy moved to B	8	5	4
	3	toy moved to B	8	6	4
	4	toy moved to B	8	7	4
	5	toy disappears at B	16	7	4
	6	hand at center	4	4	4

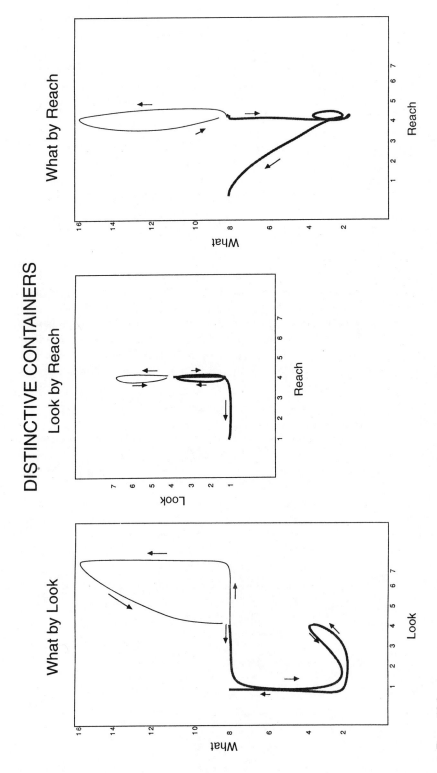

Figure 10.8
Three planar views of the trajectory of joint activity in the three-coupled system. *Thick line,* attracting trajectory formed during the A phase; *thin line,* trajectory in B phase up to the moment of reach.

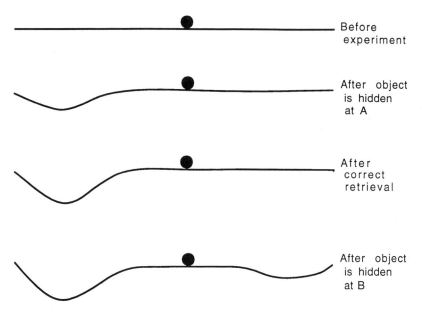

Before
experiment

After object
is hidden
at A

After
correct
retrieval

After object
is hidden
at B

Figure 10.9
Changing attractors through the course of the distinctive containers task.

comparable in both directions. Because the two attractors are far and the terrain between them flat, the likelihood of a search at A and B will not change over long delays. Unsystematic events during the delay are just as likely to drive the infant to A as to B.

What might these unsystematic events be that cause individual children to search at A or B on a given trial but that vary so across children and trials? One critical event suggested by Acredelo (1990; Acredelo, Adams, and Goodwyn, 1984) is spontaneous looking behavior. If the infant spontaneously (and perhaps randomly) looks to container A, the infant is likely to reach in that direction. If, however, the infant spontaneously looks to container B, the infant is likely to reach in that direction. In this example, a look one way or the other is a chance event that propels the system in a particular direction. However, given the coupling of the three systems, if we increase the likelihood of looking in the correct direction by context or by experience, we will increase the likelihood of a correct reach. We propose that this is what happens when there are multiple locations.

Eight-month-olds and Multiple Hiding Locations
In this task, the infant is presented with a line of five identical containers; the A container is at one end of the line and the B container is at the other. Given no delay in this task, 8-month-olds search correctly in phase B. At the 3- and 5-second delays, however, they systematically make the error, searching back at location A after watching the object disappear at location B. Why should 8-month-olds be correct at the 0-second delay in this condition but systematically search at the first hiding place with long delays? In dynamic terms, this effect of

number of hiding locations tells us that the experience of seeing an object transported past several containers and then hidden in the last container alters the
psychological task substantially. We propose that multiple locations significantly
alter the task space and thus changes the nearness of the mental trajectories of
phase A and phase B.

Table 10.3 summarizes the hypothesized activity levels in the three systems.
The two biggest changes are in the what and look systems that derive from the
experience of seeing the toy transported past the filler containers. When the
experimenter transports the toy from midline to its hiding location (A), the
experimenter will carry the toy past several filler containers. As the toy moves
past a container, there is some probability that the infant will momentarily look
away from the desired object and at the container. Thus the activity in the what
system will fluctuate during the transport of the toy—between toy and container
properties. The look system will also be perturbed—perhaps lingering longer or
looking back or forward to the containers that lie along the path the toy travels.
Two other changes in proposed internal activity as a function of sensory input
are proposed. The what activity for the two hiding locations A and B are slightly
different; although the two containers are ostensibly identical, their greater dis-

Table 10.3
Hypothetical activity values of the what, where-looking and where-reaching systems used to
construct representational trajectories for 8-month-olds in the multilocation container condition
with 0-second delay.

	Time	Steps	What	Look	Reach
Activity levels in the A phase	1	toy	8	7	7
	2	toy moved to A	8	5	7
	2a		2	4	7
	3	toy moved to A	8	3	7
	3a		2	2	2
	4	toy moved to A	8	1	7
	5	toy disappears at A	1	1	7
	6	hand at center	4	7	7
	7	0 delay look toward A	2	5	7
	7a		2	4	7
	8	0 delay look toward A	1	3	7
	9	0 delay look toward A	1	1	7
	10	reach and retrieve toy	1	1	1
Activity levels in the B phase	1	toy	8	7	7
	2	toy moved to B	8	9	7
	2a		2	10	7
	3	toy moved to B	8	11	7
	3a		2	12	7
	4	toy moved to B	8	13	7
	5	toy disappears at B	3	13	7
	6	hand at center	4	7	7

tance and neighbors make differences in shadows and other properties likely. Also, the psychological distance of locations A and B is presumed to be greater because of the greater actual distance and because the space between them is filled with objects.

Figure 10.10 shows the three planar views of the trajectories. In the what-look plane, the effect of filler containers is seen by the "wobbles" in the what-look trajectory in phase A as the desired toy is moved to hiding location A, and in the wobbles in the trajectory when the infant is allowed to search. The trajectory of activity in the what-look plane in phase B is also complex and contains wobbles. The trajectories in the look-reach plane are comparable to those in the standard and distinctive container conditions except the space has been expanded given the greater psychological distance of the two end containers. Finally, the A and B trajectories in the what-reach plane are also complex, showing an oscillating pattern that derives from alternating looks at the toy and the identical containers.

We suggest that the 8-month-old infant searches correctly initially because the momentum of the phase B trajectory with its added complexity pulls the infant to look back in the direction of B. This extra pull derives from the filler containers—from the wobbles in the trajectories. The filler containers help the infant by serving as reminders of the direction in which the toy is gone. Recall that specific contextual reminders increase the representational momentum of an event. The empty containers that marked the path when the experimenter hid the toy mark the path for the infant. The filler containers help pull looking along in the right direction because they remind the infant of what was seen when the object was hidden.

With sufficient delays, however, the A trajectory will become increasingly likely to capture the internal activity in the what, look, and reach systems because the A trajectory is strong and close to the B trajectory.

Evaluation of the Account of Eight-month-old Infants' Search Behavior
The above account of 8-month-old infants' search in three versions of the A-not-B task leaves much to be desired: the specific processes of the what, look, and where systems are far too simple. We have only tracked the possible time-locked interactions between the three systems as a function of the stimulus events. We have not taken into consideration the complex dependence of activity of each system on the activity of the others at each moment in time.

Nonetheless, the account serves as a model of how one might do developmental psychology under a dynamic systems framework. We have here an account of how context affects a behavior at a particular developmental time. In this account, we do not ask whether the behavior reveals some competence or not. We do not ask whether some conditions provide a better test of the infant's knowledge than others. Rather, we attempt an account that explains all the data—the global structure of search behavior and its variability in context. The account we offer, though simple and certainly not right in its entirety, is testable. And the kinds of tests it suggests are sure to reveal new and important facts about the complex system that generates the behavior of 8-month-olds in this task.

The best empirical tests of our account consist of perturbing the system—investigating context effects—and seeing how the system responds. For example, our account suggests that over the delay period, the internal activity of the what

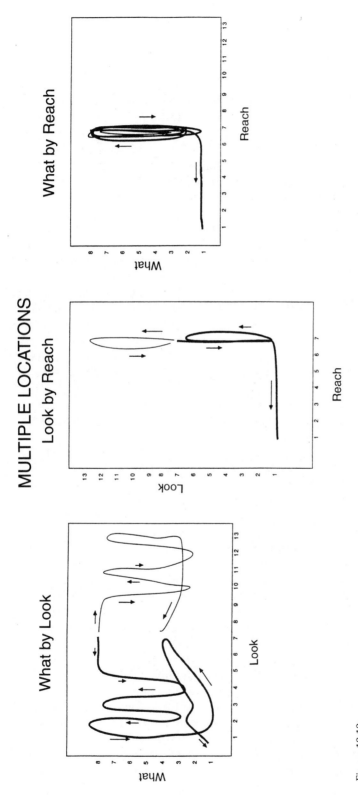

Figure 10.10
Three planar views of the trajectory of joint activity in the three-coupled system. *Thick line*, attracting trajectory formed during the A phase; *thin line*, trajectory in B phase up to the moment of reach.

and where systems is increasingly likely to drift into the A phase trajectory because there are not external forces on the systems (in the form of perceptual input) that keep the activity in the region corresponding to a search at B. If this is so, then external forces in the delay period that push the activity of component systems in the B direction should increase the likelihood of correct searches. We can test this as follows: after hiding the object at B, the hand, instead of returning to the center, could stay at B—moving to keep attention. If our account is correct, the infant should be more likely to search correctly.

We can also test the idea that multiple containers increased the likelihood of a correct search by adding distinguishing complexity to the internal activity that corresponds to looks to A and B locations. For example, we should be able to increase the likelihood of a correct search in phase B by any means that distinguishes the path to A from the path to B, say a red-striped road leading to A and a blue-dotted road leading to B, or if the object hopped to A but flew to B. We are beginning to test these ideas empirically and it seems likely that we will find support for our specific account. However, even if we do not, we will, by such studies of contextual influences, discover more about the components of the system and their interactions.

Our complex systems account of the contextual effects on 8-month-old behavior in the A-not B-task also provides a starting point for an explanation of developmental change. Why do the functions relating search success to context change as a function of age?

Development: Putting Real Time and Developmental Time Together

Nine- and 10-month-old infants perform differently than 8-month-olds in the same A-not-B task. This means that the intrinsic dynamics have changed. The landscape from which the here-and-now trajectory of mental activity emerges is different and thus the trajectory is different.

From the analysis of Wellman et al. of older infants' performances in the three task contexts, as summarized in figures 10.2, 10.3, and 10.4, we can infer something about the character of those changes. First, with development, the A and B trajectories must become farther apart in the state space. That is, there is a decreased probability that the A trajectory will capture the B trajectory. Second, the in-task experience of seeing an object hidden at B must create a trajectory with stronger representational momentum such that the mental activity created by the experience of the hiding at B continues during the period in which the infant is restrained from reaching. Greater representational momentum is needed to overcome drift toward the A attractor. These two changes—greater distance between the A and B trajectories and greater representational momentum—are easily explained by proposing that the what, look, and reach systems are *increasingly coupled* with development.

In our dynamic systems account, the mental activity in each system at any moment in time depends on its just-previous activity, and *two classes of inputs— those from the external world and those from the internal world*. The "internal world" inputs are the reentrant inputs from the activity of other components in the system. We can explain the developmental changes in the A-not-B task in terms of an increased dependence of the activity in each of the three systems on the activity in the others. This increased coupling will have the two effects of seg-regating the A and B trajectories in the state space and increasing the represen-tational momentum.

We can illustrate the effects of the first kind of change in table 10.4 and figure 10.11. The table and figure differ from table 10.1 and figure 10.2, the correspond-ing table and figure for 8-month-olds in the standard task, only by the activity of the reach system. In the present case, reach activity is made partially dependent on what is happening in the look system. The idea is that looking and reaching have become increasingly coupled so that the reach system—even when the infant is not actually reaching—reflects to some degree the activity of the look system. When we make the activity at each point in time in the reach system dependent in this way on the activity of the look system, the resulting A trajectory and B trajectory are farther apart in the state space: they are uniquely organized with differentiated patterns of activity. And thus, after watching an object being hidden at B, the infant should be less likely at all delays to be pulled toward a reach to A.

Increased coupling of the systems will not only make the events of the A and B phase of the experiment more distinct but such coupling will also create more powerful momentum. As the activity of each system depends more at each point in time on the just-previous activity in the other systems, then the internal activity will be less dependent on external, that is, immediate, sensory input. Stronger coupling means stronger *internal inputs* between components such that their activity can persist on their own in time. In other words, stronger coupling causes

Table 10.4
Hypothetical activity values of the what, where-looking and where-reaching systems used to construct representational trajectories for older infants in the standard condition with 0-second delay

	Time	Steps	What	Look	Reach
Activity levels in the A phase	1	toy	8	4	4
	2	toy moved to A	8	3	3.5
	3	toy moved to A	8	2	3
	4	toy moved to A	8	1	2.5
	5	toy disappears at A	2	1	2.5
	6	hand at center	4	4	4
	7	0 delay look toward A	2	3	3.5
	8	0 delay look toward A	2	2	3
	9	0 delay look toward A	2	1	2.5
	10	reach and retrieve toy	8	1	1
Activity levels in the B phase	1	toy	8	4	4
	2	toy moved to B	8	5	4.5
	3	toy moved to B	8	6	5
	4	toy moved to B	8	7	5.5
	5	toy disappears at B	2	7	5.5
	6	hand at center	4	4	4

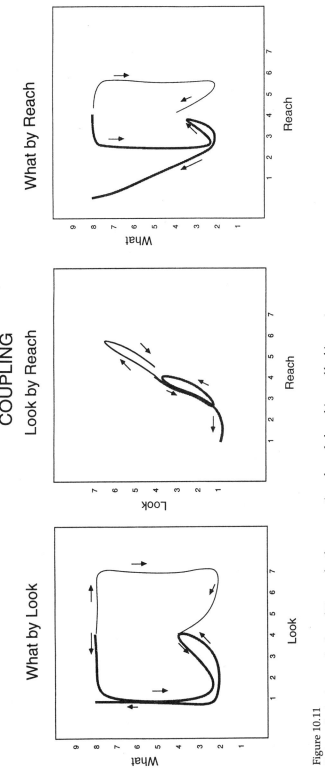

Figure 10.11
Trajectories in the standard condition under the assumption of coupled reaching and looking systems.

stronger representation momentum that lasts longer in time. Thus the idea of increased coupling of systems with development can explain why older infants search correctly over longer and longer delays than younger infants.

But why should coupling between systems increase between 8 and 10 months? In general, coupling will increase with the experience of time-locked activities. To the degree that two component systems have a history of complex time-locked activity, they will come to entrain each other and to mutually influence each other. Clearly, the coupling of what and where systems is promoted from the moment newborns open their eyes and look. But with each new motor skill and its associated attentional demands and opportunities, there is more opportunity for varied and reentrant activity. Thus, the coupling may become stronger and more refined when infants begin visually guided reaching. Coupling will undergo further developmental change as infants self-locomote and use looking and moving to navigate whole rooms. We propose that it is specifically this locomotor experience that promotes coupling of what and where in 8- to 12-month-old infants and thus is the critical event or control parameter for developmental changes in the A-not-B error.

There is considerable empirical evidence for this account. Infants who have had more experience self-locomoting are more successful on the A-not-B task (Bertenthal and Campos, 1990). Moreover, only self-locomotion that yields time-locked correspondences between where one looks, what one sees, and self-actions seems to benefit performance in the A-not-B task. As we noted in chapter 7, infants who belly-crawl and thus do not see where they are going do not show the advantage of self-locomotion in the A-not-B task (Kermoian and Campos, 1988). This fits perfectly with the account of development offered here. As infants move and explore, the time-locked activity of the component systems and their reentrant mapping produce connectivity and mutual influence among the components. The reentrant mappings in turn change the intrinsic dynamics, the landscape of the history of the system.

We have suggested that self-locomotion acts as a control parameter for the A-not-B task because infants' own activities produce an increased coupling of the look and reach systems, leading to a change in the intrinsic dynamics. Because infants with locomotor experience come into the A-not-B task with different intrinsic dynamics than nonlocomoting infants, the same real-time task elicits different mental trajectories. Indeed, there is solid empirical evidence specifically linking locomotor experience, visual tracking (the mechanism by which looking and reaching become coupled), and A-not-B performance. Infants who pay attention to the desired object, track it as it is moved to the B location, and watch the B location during the delay are more successful searchers at B (Acredelo, 1985; Horobin and Acredelo, 1986) Further, infants who have had more experience self-locomoting show greater visual attention to the desired object and the hiding locations in the A-not-B task (Acredelo et al., 1984).

This account unifies real time and developmental time in two ways. First, developmental time is continuous with and indeed fabricated from real-time experience. Second, we have provided a single account of context effects in both action and development. We explain the differences among 8-month-olds in different task contexts—in the standard task, with distinctive containers, in the multilocation task—with the same system that we use to explain developmental change. At 8 months, giving infants different hiding containers increases the distinctiveness of the mental activity associated with the phase A and phase B events. This distinctiveness is acquired developmentally through practice looking and moving. The fact that self-locomotion matters in the development of successful searches for hidden objects is precisely the kind of relation expected by the dynamic systems account of development. Development does not happen because internal maturational processes tell the system how to develop. Rather, development happens through and because of the activity of the system itself. Thus, the experiences engendered by self-produced mobility may be the control parameter for success in the A-not-B task.

We can test this account of development by exploring how the system responds "under perturbations," that is, in different contexts. For example, we may test our claim that a key component of developmental change is the increased coupling of the look and reach systems by manipulating contexts. If the increased coupling is what causes 10-month-olds to search more successfully than 8-month-olds, then we should be able to make 10-month-olds fail in their search by experimentally decoupling looking and reaching. Similarly, we should be able to increase 8-month-olds' correct searches by increasing or finding a substitute for the coupling.

Maturation or Development?

One of the assumptions of our account of the A-not-B error based on Edelman's theory of neuronal group selection (TNGS) is that the correlated activity of looking and reaching engenders real changes in brain circuits, strengthening the connectivity of groups receiving the multimodal, reentrant activity. We have not offered, however, any specifically anatomical account of where such circuits may be. An elegant alternative brain-based account of the A-not-B shift has been proposed by Adele Diamond. While we applaud Diamond's search for mechanism and her integrated evidence from human infants, infant and adult monkeys, and adult humans with brain lesions, we also believe her causal account is incomplete.

Diamond (1990a) proposed that the increased ability of infants aged between 8 and 12 months to search correctly over longer delays in the task is directly due to maturation of the dorsolateral prefrontal cortex. This area of the brain appears to be involved in responses that require both memory and the inhibition of a prepotent response. Prefrontal functioning is traditionally assessed by the delayed response test. And importantly, the delayed test is remarkably like the A-not-B task.

In both tasks, the subject watches as the experimenter holds up and then hides a toy in one of two identical hiding locations. The subject is then restrained for some variable amount of time and then allowed to search. In the version of the A-not-B task used by Diamond and in the delay task, the subject is prevented from looking at or straining toward the correct hiding location during the delay. The delay response differs from the A-not-B task in that the desired object is *not* hidden in A and then B with performance on B, the critical measure, but rather, the desired object is hidden in A and B in a randomly determined order with performance across trials the critical measure. Figure 10.12a shows the delays

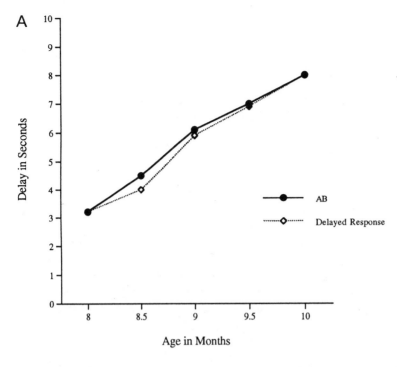

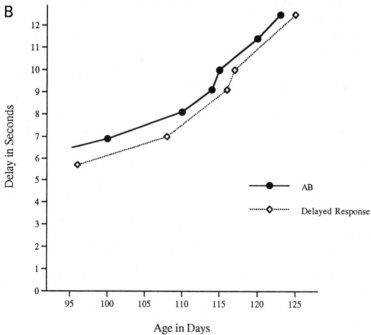

Figure 10.12
Developmental changes in infants (*a*) and in monkeys (*b*) in the delays at which successful searches can be achieved in the A-not-B and delayed response tasks.

(from test to search) at which infants first make the A-not-B error and at which performance falls below 88% in the delay task. Figure 10.12b shows the comparable results for infant rhesus monkeys. As is apparent, there is regular linear growth in both tasks for both species. Diamond (1990a) argues from this linear developmental progression that *maturation* of underlying neural structures is the likely cause of behavioral change.

The proposal that it is the maturation of the dorsolateral prefrontal cortex that controls performance in the delay response test is well supported by a variety of anatomical, physiological, pharmacological, and metabolic techniques (see Diamond, 1990a). Thus, for example, lesioning the prefrontal cortex in adult monkeys causes errors in the delayed response task and, in particular, an inability to withstand briefer delays. Diamond and her colleagues (Diamond and Goldman-Rakic, 1989; Diamond, Zola-Morgan, and Squire, 1989) have also shown that lesions in the dorsolateral prefrontal cortex in adult monkeys, but not lesions in the parietal cortex or the hippocampus, cause increased errors in the A-not-B task and specifically impair performance at longer delays. All in all, the evidence is quite compelling for the involvement of the dorsolateral prefrontal cortex in the A-not-B error.

Diamond argues that maturation of the prefrontal cortex enables the infant to inhibit prepotent, competing responses. By this argument, the type of errors infants make in the A-not-B and delayed response tasks should not be specific to those tasks or even to remembering the spatial location of hidden objects. In Diamond's view, infants who make the A-not-B mistake should have trouble in any task in which they must inhibit a dominant response. For example, infants' attempts to retrieve objects from transparent containers follow a similar course of development as the A-not-B task and delay response. In this object retrieval task, Diamond (1990b) presents infants with an attractive toy in plain view in a transparent box with one side open. The opening either faces the infant or is away from the infant. When the opening faces them, even 8-month-olds reach directly and retrieve the toy. However, they do not reach correctly when they must detour (reach to the side) to get the desired object. They can plainly see through the transparent container. Paradoxically, they can easily locate the side opening and make the detoured reach when the container is opaque. The better performance with opaque containers is predicted by Diamond's account because in that context there is no competing and dominant response to be inhibited during a sideways reach as there is in the case of the transparent container when a direct reach to the seen object (through the transparent walls) must be inhibited. Diamond argues from these results that infants can indeed remember where objects are and understand their permanence in space and time. Rather, the infants' central problem is seen as the inhibition of a prepotent response—the direct reach—due to the immaturity of the prefrontal cortex.

We find Diamond's behavioral evidence compelling; infants come to increasingly "inhibit" the "dominant" response, or in other terms, to adjust their responses to the fine details of the context. We also believe that the frontal lobe is involved in these tasks. But we question whether Diamond's argument constitutes an adequate explanation. How does the invocation of the "frontal lobe" *explain* development? How does the "immaturity" of the frontal lobe explain the specific behaviors that infants show in these tasks? What are the processes through which inhibition—in a particular task and at a particular time—is achieved? What makes a response "dominant?" And most important, what drives the development of the frontal lobe? What makes an immature frontal lobe mature? In our view, invoking the frontal lobe as the *cause* of behavior does not explain anything.

In contrast, our dynamic systems account answers the questions of process and cause. In our account "inhibition" is realized in specific tasks when two attractors are separated by sufficiently high ridges so that a trajectory in one task context is distinct from the trajectory in another task context. In our account, there is not some internal ability called "inhibition" that causes performance; rather inhibition *is the product* of a system in a particular context with particular dynamic properties.

What makes a response "dominant" in our account? In our view, "dominance" is determined by experience that creates a deep attractor *near* the region of the state space of internal activity that underlies the less-dominant response. The processes that make some behaviors more dominant than others and the processes of inhibition (which make "dominant" actions less dominant) are the very same and both are the products of a complex system in a specific task. For example, in everyday life, young immobile infants are given many opportunities to reach directly and very few where they must make detours. And, we suspect, successful detours (moving or reaching around something) dramatically increase with self-locomotion.

What makes an immature system mature? In our account, we specify the cause of developmental change: it is the activity of the complex system in real time. The same activities that make dominant actions dominant, the same real-time activities that cause the system to reorganize (through increased couplings) and thus create "inhibition," are the same activities that make the intrinsic dynamics of the system at 10 months different from what it was at 8 months.

Are we saying that the frontal lobe does not matter at all? No. None of our ideas are inconsistent with the involvement of the frontal lobe. We are suggesting, however, that Diamond may have cause and effect backward. For us, the causes of development are experiences that promote increased coupling of the what, look, and reach systems. This increased coupling may be instantiated by changes in the frontal lobe. The frontal lobe has projections from and to many other brain regions and thus may be involved in the integration and interaction of heterogeneous systems.

Diamond, in contrast, proposed that changes in the frontal lobe are the cause—the driver—of development. In reference to the results of Kermoian and Campos (1988) showing that belly crawlers did not show gains in the A-not-B task, Diamond specifically argued against self-locomotion as a causal force. She stated

> Maybe it is not the experience of crawling per se that is important here (or that the experience of belly crawlers is critically different from that of regular crawlers)—after all, why should crawling affect the ability to uncover a hidden object?. . . . maybe regular crawling is indicative of a maturational advance that is important both for crawling and other tasks as well. Regular crawling, but *not* belly crawling, usually requires a patterned movement of the limbs such that at any moment one is doing different things with the

arm and leg on one side of the body than with the contralateral arm and leg. [This] may require communication via the corpus callosum, between the SMA [an area in the frontal lobe] in each hemisphere so that one limb is inhibited from doing the same thing as the other limb. (1990c, p. 607)

There are both strong empirical and theoretical reasons to reject Diamond's defense of maturation. On empirical grounds, there is no evidence that the alternating limb action of crawling requires the frontal lobe. Well before they crawl, infants show well-organized patterns of alternating limb action in a variety of contexts, for example, when lying in the supine position and kicking or when vertically held above a moving treadmill (Thelen, 1986, Thelen and Ulrich, 1991). Limb alternation circuits are generally believed to be subcortical and likely even spinal (Grillner, 1981). Moreover, the evidence for self-locomotion as a critical experience for success in the A-not-B task is more than correlational: children who are experimentally given early self-locomotion experiences via walkers show more advanced levels of performance in search tasks (Bertenthal and Campos, 1990). Finally, developmental changes in frontal lobe electroencephalographic (EEG) patterns occur *after*, not before, self-locomotion (Bell and Fox, 1992).

There are also compelling theoretical reasons for not putting the cause of developmental change in the frontal lobe. If activity driven by internal and external events does not drive development, then what does? What is the developmental process that is "maturation?" Everything we know about biological development—from gene expression, to embryology, to neural and behavioral development—indicates that there is no such thing as a *nonexperiential component* to development (see Gottlieb, 1991a,b). Diamond asks "why should crawling affect the ability to uncover a hidden object?" The answer is that the relevant experiences for developmental process are not there by designed solution to some set of prescribed and preknown tasks. Rather, developmental process involves whole organisms as complex systems interacting with their environments.

What Is Knowing?

What does all this mean for Piaget's original conclusions from watching his own children search for objects in the "wrong" places? What do 8-, 9-, and 10-month-old children *know* about the permanence of objects? And what does the A-not-B error tell us about what they know?

The message from Baillargeon and Diamond is clear: infants "have" the object concept, but they just can't show it on the A-not-B task. Recall that in Baillargeon's many experiments, infants, after a familiarization, are surprised by events that are impossible because they violate the concrete permanence of objects. In Baillargeon and Graber's (1988) nonsearch version of the A-not-B task, infants were genuinely surprised when objects were retrieved from places different from where they were hidden. So if children "know" about objects when they just look, but are stupid about them when they look and reach, what do they really know? The question is much like the one raised about central pattern generators (CPGs) in chapter 1. If pattern never exists except within some context, what is the essence of pattern, or of knowing?

In our view, knowing is what infants do in both looking for and searching for hidden objects. Knowing is the process of dynamic assembly of the what system and the look system in relation to the task at hand within the intrinsic dynamics of the organism. We do not need to invoke represented constructs such as "object" or "extended in space and time." Logical structures for these constructs do not exist outside the task that invokes action.

Thus, knowing is a *product* of our dynamic system, not a causal prerequisite. Infants' looking and infants' reaching in the A-not-B task signifies knowing, actions that do not preexist their performance in real time. The intrinsic dynamics of a system may mean that particular patterns of knowing recur over and over in varieties of contexts and thus look as though they are directed by a single permanent structure, the CPG of knowing. Particular patterns of knowing may be highly stable through the activity of many coupled systems and thus *seem* unaffected by the details of the here and now, just as limb patterns can persist in the face of many perturbations. But just as the patterns of coordination emerge in dynamic interaction, so knowing cannot be crystallized and refined when its essence is flow.

In our final chapter we expand and evaluate this view of knowing and knowledge.

Chapter 11

Hard Problems: Toward a Dynamic Cognition

In this book, we have attempted an account of how knowing develops from doing. We began in chapters 1 and 2 by showing how current theoretical approaches left unexplained a central puzzle of human development: that within a species-typical global order of change the details were messy, fluid, idiosyncratic, and complex. We conclude by coming full circle: it is this very messiness and complexity that is the essence of development. What turning up the microscope reveals is that individual activity—real-time perceiving, moving, remembering—constitutes the driving force of change. When developmentalists present their subjects with a task to measure developmental status, they tap into not only the global order but also the child's real time attempts to do the task. True "competence" or "core knowledge" cannot be abstracted from the here-and-now dynamics of the task. The details are messy and fluid because problem solving is dynamic by its very nature. Solutions are always soft-assembled, and thus are both constrained by subjects' current intrinsic dynamics and potentially derailed or redirected by task conditions. It is precisely at this intersection of intrinsic dynamics and task where development moves forward because the fluid assembly allows for exploration and selection of more adapted solutions. The time scales are thus seamlessly interwoven; the components and their processes are of a piece.

On the way to our reconciliation of the global and local we offered very general principles of behavior in time, those of complex, nonlinear dynamic systems. Thus, in chapter 3, we showed how principles derived from physical systems could account for origins and change as one process. Using examples of infant leg coordination, in chapter 4 we applied these principles to real-time movements and their changes over developmental time. In particular, locomotor development was envisioned as a dynamic attractor landscape where movement configurations evolve and dissolve as new postures and tasks challenge the infant.

In our first chapters, we faulted current theory for ignoring biologically plausible mechanisms. Unlike information processing and other machine metaphors, a dynamic approach is compatible with developmental neurobiology and current theorizing in neuroscience. In chapter 5, we invoked Edelman's theory of neuronal group selection (TNGS) as the neural basis for a dynamic account. We reported how the basic processes of neuroembryology were themselves dynamic and contingent, and how these epigenetic processes built a brain wired to benefit from the time-locked properties of the input—the multimodal consequences of experience. The key process, as we argued in chapter 6, is the ability to form dynamic categories as the primitives of mental life right from the start. We showed how reentrant mapping and dynamic categories can explain—in terms of the here and now of neural activity—abilities in young infants assumed by some to be innate.

In chapter 7, then, we reviewed behavioral evidence that supported the TNGS. This included the primitive unity of the senses, the critical role of movement in forming early categories, and the context-tied nature of early remembering and forgetting. We tied these themes together in chapter 8 as we interpreted and reinterpreted several critical experimental phenomena in infants and children: locomotion over slopes, the detection of possible and impossible events, and the interpretation of novel words. In all three domains, our theme was, as before, the integration of real-time processes and developmental change. Chapter 9 contained a microanalysis of the real- to developmental-time shift in an investigation of learning to reach. We concluded that this novel form was neither preformed nor imposed, but individually discovered by infants as a match between their intrinsic dynamics and the constraints of the task at hand. Finally, in chapter 10, we integrated these themes to reinterpret one of the most extensively studied phenomena of infancy, Piaget's A-not-B error. We showed how a dynamic approach can unify seemingly disparate and even paradoxical findings. The key, we argued, was understanding the dynamics of the experimental situation and how babies' real-life activities changed the neural dynamics that supported their task performance. In particular, we pointed to self-produced locomotion as the process leading to changes in visual attention, which in turn facilitated correct search.

Now we turn to a number of issues raised by this account, but insufficiently addressed to this point. Although we have stressed the relations between the domains and levels, neural, perceptual-motor, and cognitive, that form the recurrent motifs of this book we have paid scant attention to other critical issues and implications. Thus, we want to clarify the status of several constructs that we introduced in the book but did not fully develop, and we want to extend the theory to levels we have not addressed. These include the questions of motivation and value, the role of the context, and especially social and cultural considerations in development, the relation of language and thought, and the issue of whether we are just promoting a newly costumed version of old associationism. The thrust of the chapter is to chip away at the toughest nut, the question of whether a dynamic approach can move away from sensorimotor and concrete operations into the domains of abstract reasoning and metacognition, thinking about thinking. We conclude that these higher-order processes are in principle no different from the less-abstract mental operations upon which they are ontogenetically based, and that, indeed, a common dynamic must unify all brain function as well as changes in brain and behavior.

Motivation: Where Does It All Come from?

We have tried hard to do away with the ghosts in the machine. We have argued, following Edelman, that the primitive state is a richly interconnected matrix that through mutual activation and entrainment constructs an ever more sharply defined functional reality. We saw how this process must include the correlated perception of events and perception of self-motion. But this process cannot take place without some *value* on behavior, without some activities being better than others. Edelman demonstrated the importance of value in his simulations of the TGNS in the Darwin automata. The process of change cannot begin in a value-neutral system. Something has to start the process in the first place. Something has to motivate infants to look, to reach, to mouth, to seek out information about their worlds. We have consistently emphasized the importance of exploration and selection, as the assembly of various cooperative interactions of the subsystems, and the retention of those synergisms that provide a functional match with the child's goals and capabilities within the environment. But what generates the engine for exploration? What passes judgment on what makes a functional match? Can these issues be addressed without reintroducing the homunculus?

Historically, the issues of motivation and its relation to behavioral change have been the province of learning theory, personality, attachment theory, and psychodynamics. There is little explicit incorporation of motivation in contemporary accounts of the development of perception, action, cognition, or language. The work of Kurt Lewin stands in the forefront as a motivational theory of development (Lewin, 1946.) Lewin, whose behavioral dynamics foreshadowed contemporary dynamic systems by over half a century, explicitly and elegantly assigns the engine for developmental change as changing fields of motivational forces. For Lewin, behavior begins with psychological *force*, a "tendency to act in a certain direction" (Lewin, 1946, p. 796). People develop within a life space, a psychological field of various activities that have different motivational valences or potencies. The valence determines whether and how strongly people move toward the activity. Cognitive change, according to Lewin, results when people learn new pathways to their goal activities. Development, then, is an elaboration and differentiation of the life space, from the simple force fields of infancy, to the highly complex goal space of the older child and adult. (We refer to Lewin's dynamics again in a later section.)

Motivational drive also played a predominant role in John Bowlby's (1969) classic work on attachment. Bowlby assigned the origins of attachment behavior to a "felt need for proximity" to a caregiver. According to Bowlby this motivation is instinctive. It is built in because staying close to a caregiver gives immature animals an enormous selective advantage; they survive longer to differentially reproduce. Given this initial motivational bias, infants recruit different kinds of actions toward this goal, actions that change as infants mature. When infants are immobile, crying effectively keeps mother close by. As infants develop mobility, they can follow their mothers by themselves. Facial expressions, vocal gestures, and later, language, are all subsumed under this broad motivational umbrella: keep Mom nearby for protection and comfort.

Since Lewin, cognitive theorists have been less direct in confronting motivational bias. Piaget believed that what impelled the organism forward was the need to adapt to the environment, to be in a state of equilibrium with it. This is a biological given. In a sense, then, one can consider Piaget's structural invariants of assimilation and accommodation, in the service of equilibration, as providing the continuing motor for change. Infants actively seek out aspects of the environment to feed into their existing mental structures, change their structures, and then seek out new aspects in the continuing dialectic. Indeed, Piaget used the metaphors of food seeking and consumption, as though the drive for mental equilibration is on a motivational par with the drive for nourishment. Why, Piaget asked, did 1-month-old Laurent persist in looking at his surroundings when he was seeing disjointed and incoherent images?

> What then is the motivating force of the child's behavior? There only re-mains the very need to look which can play this role. . . . In other words, if the child looks at moving objects it is simply because, at the beginning, they constitute an *aliment* [emphasis added] for the activity of the glance. Later when the various accommodations to distance, prominence, etc., enrich visual perception, the objects looked at serve as more differentiated *nourishment* for these multiple operations. (Piaget, 1952, p. 65)

Gibson (1988) also posited intrinsic motivational forces that impel infants to actively seek out "aliment" for the senses, to explore.

> A baby is provided by nature with some very helpful equipment to start its long course of learning about and interacting with the world. A baby is provided with an urge to use its perceptual systems to explore the world; and it is impelled to direct attention outward toward events, objects, and their properties, and the layout of the environment. (Gibson, 1988, p.7)

In the last several decades, the question of motivation per se has been over-shadowed by a concern over the relation between emotion and cognition (e.g., Izard, Kagan, and Zajonc, 1984; Lewis and Goldberg, 1969; McCall, 1972). Here the debate has centered on whether emotion is a consequence of cognition or whether it is a motive or drive producing action and thought. In the first case, cognitive processes result in emotional responses, for example, when mastery of a task produces enjoyment. Cognition, in this view, may also serve to interpret emotional responses, to label them, and to regulate their expression to socially acceptable situations. More directly relevant to the issue of motivation is the relation of emotion to learning. In several important papers, Watson (1966, 1972) reported that when infants learned to press a pillow or kick their legs to activate a mobile, they showed an increase of smiling and cooing in recognition of the contingency. As Lewis, Sullivan, and Michaelson (1984) point out, affect may serve both to energize performance—to direct infants' attention to the contin-gency and motivate their focus—and insure that they learn and remember the contingency through positive reinforcement. Indeed, these authors suggest, as have others, that the repeated positive experience of contingent stimulation results in a generalized expectation that individuals can act upon and manipulate the environment. This learned association, in turn, acts as a motivational force for further exploration, especially in novel situations.

With the exception of these emotion theorists, the bulk of contemporary cog-nitive developmental science has distanced itself from classic theories of learning and motivation. Lewin (or Freud) is not in the mainstream of developmental thinking, despite his immeasurable impact on personality theory and social science in general. Drive theorists such as Hull and Skinner are even less influ-ential, and their developmental progeny, social learning theory, has become less focused on motivation and more on social cognition, that is, the effects of cog-nitive development on social behavior (Bandura, 1986).

In the interests of a true systems approach, it is perhaps time to recognize and recover some of the shared territory. The construct of intrinsic urges and needs to seek out stimulation, novelty, mastery of the environment, or the like elevates the old concepts of drive from the purely physiological such as hunger or thirst to something that can be harnessed for higher cognition Logically, however, there is no difference between motivation to seek food and motivation to explore. When we get hungry, we poke in the refrigerator and cupboards until we find something to eat. Several hours later, we are hungry again. Likewise, an infant's attention is compelled toward an interesting toy and it just feels good to grab it and put it in the mouth. After a while, the baby is impelled to seek a new toy. In each the motivational construct introduces a bias into the system that says one activity is better than another given the current state of the organism and the stimuli in the environment. Learning does not happen without these biases. Although theorists have recognized the necessity for a motivational component, the nature of early motivation and its developmental changes have been poorly specified, especially in relation to perceiving, acting, and thinking. If a dynamic account is to be successful in spanning the time scales of action, learning, and development, we need to pay more attention to the questions of these needs and drives, the values of the system.

One issue that needs to be addressed in future work is just how specific or general the motivational component needs to be in order to set the system on the trajectory of learning from doing without installing knowledge devices. In Edelman's simulations, the values were simple: light is better than no light, contact is better than no contact. We think that a plausible developmental scenario can be written with equally simple biases in real human infants. Simple, relatively low-level valences—for edges, for movement, for light, for sounds in the range of human voices, for warmth, for touch—can initiate the developmental cascade. For example, Johnson and Morton (1991) argue that infants' strong attraction to faces begins with an initial orienting bias in newborns. This bias, the behavioral evidence suggests, favors the arrangement of several high-contrast "blobs" corresponding to the relative location of the eyes and mouth, likely mediated through subcortical pathways. Given that infants see such configurations in real faces close up during nursing, changing, and socializing, even a small initial valence toward that configuration would lead to rapidly strengthened neuronal groups in the presence of faces. As higher brain centers become more involved in the second and third months, the system will already be tuned toward facelike stimuli, insuring that infants will be positioned to acquire more information about faces. Indeed, preference for particular faces emerges by 4 months or so.

What is minimally needed to start such a process moving is a sensory system with some relatively unspecific tuned parameters and a value wash that keeps the organism preferring certain stimulus configurations over other values. Such values are not specific tutors. Having a bias in the system that says light is better than no light or human voices are better than auto horns does not endow the system with knowledge modules or conceptual primitives or the understanding of object properties. Rather, these are valences or tropisms similar to those exhibited by simple organisms and even by animals without nervous systems. That such valences might be contained within the architecture of the system does not put a ghost in the machine, or if it does, it is the ghost of life itself, for similar biases are exhibited even in single cells.

Infants come into the world with a rich set of adaptive biases, epigenetically acquired, but having strong selective value. These surely include the motivation to suck and seek nourishment, motivation for contact and warmth, preferences for certain moderate levels of sensory stimulation, and preferred dynamics (e.g., Turkewitz and Kenny, 1983). Taken together, these may well dispose the infant to pay particular attention to the sensory array emanating from other humans, the particular spatial and auditory frequencies of human faces and voices. The association of these constellations of attributes with other adaptive biases—food and warmth—builds quickly into the strong social relationships that become manifest in the first few months of life. That certain internal states and external stimuli are endowed with a particular hedonic tone—a scaled valence of pleasure or discomfort—constitutes the infant's value or motivational primitives. Edelman's automata suggest it is these biases that are essential and critical elements in the real-time processes of reentrant categorization, and thus at the core of the development of the mind (see also Cruz, 1992; Grossberg, Schmajak, and Levine, 1992, for accounts of motivation in learning simulations).

Rethinking Motivation

Here we begin to see a rapprochement between traditional learning theory, dynamics, the neural basis of learning ,and current concerns in cognitive development. Behavioral change in real time is predicated on the association of the animal's perception and action with some value state (reinforcement or punishment). Can we reconcile the value valence demanded by TNGS with a dynamic account of development, where behavior is epigenetic, emergent, and discovered?

Current neuroanatomical and neurophysiological evidence supports this integrated view. The basic wiring of the brain, Edelman's primary repertoire, strongly implicates a value component in all processes of learning and memory. That is, from the start, it appears that areas of the brain involved in emotion, arousal, and vigilance have access to, and are in turn accessed by, nearly all areas of higher brain function (the neocortex) and the structures involved in memory, learning, and action, as well as information about autonomic and endocrine functioning (Gray, 1991; Steinmetz, in press). This means that processes of neuronal group selection in basic perceptual categorization, memory, recall, and recategorization all take palce in this wash of affective valence. In particular, because of the dense and reentrant nature of the interconnected perception-action circuits and those responding to cues associated with reinforcement, neuronal groups may form that map the action with its emotional consequences.

Motivation and the Dynamic Landscape

Given that the neural anatomy and the physiology of reverberating circuits support the pervasive influence of motivational influences on learning and memory, we can now move up to a more macrolevel and depict the motivational component in terms of our metaphoric dynamic landscape introduced in chapter 4. In the last few years there have been several efforts to model drive states—motivational forces—as explicit dynamic systems (Killeen, 1989, 1991, 1992;

Townsend and Busemeyer, 1989). In these models, tendencies to do one activity over another can be conceptualized as forces driving behavior toward attractors, the strength of the attractor indicating the strength of the particular motivational valence associated with the stimulus or task space. Although these models are not developmental, they are nonetheless evocative.

This is whimsically illustrated by Killeen's (1991, p. 439) depiction of Buridan's ass (figure 11.1). Centuries ago the philosopher Buridan suggested that an ass placed equidistantly from two identical piles of hay would never be able to move. The ass, equally attracted to each pile, and presumably having to exert equal energy to get to either pile, could not generate the potential energy to leave his equilibrium position between the two piles. Killeen shows this in figure 11.1 as the now-familiar potential well. The ass needs an internal push or perturbation to start to move. If the forces act like the stretched springs, and the piles of hay are equally attractive, the ass will oscillate between them, being pulled back to pile B as it gets closer to pile A. Only if one pile is considerably more compelling will the animal generate enough motivational energy to climb the walls of the potential well. (If the piles of hay were replaced with two electric fences, the ass would be equally immobile, positioned between two repellors.)

Killeen's point is that the goal states act like behavioral attractors and the shapes of the potential wells indicate how readily and how swiftly the animal will move toward those attractors (or away from similarly configured repellors). Behavior itself creates a trajectory through a field of attractors and repellors. The

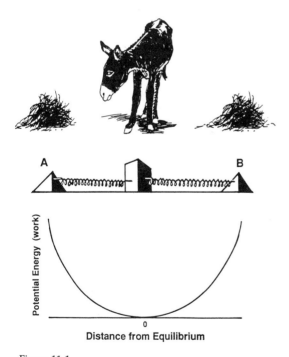

Figure 11.1
Top, Buridan's ass. *Middle*, Hypothetical forces acting on the ass. *Bottom*, The potential function. (From Killeen, 1991.)

trajectory can be direct and rapid toward a goal equilibrium state, or if the basins are shallow, the path can be meandering and slow, perhaps by chance captured by a nearby basin. Sometimes, like Buridan's ass, people are caught between two or more equally attractive or unpleasant goal states and vacillate in a state of indecision.

We can easily substitute a motivational landscape, therefore, for the locomotion landscape we introduced in chapter 4. Imagine, then, in figure 11.2, that the hills and valleys represent not particular leg configurations but the relative strength and stability of the forces impelling or repelling the infant toward various stimuli or tasks. Let us assume that at birth, certain simple stimuli have acquired, through natural selection, particular valence values. Thus the furrows might represent attractors for sucking when a nipple is in the mouth, or for warmth and physical contact, or for attending particular visual stimuli. Through learning in the manner we have described previously, not only may the behavior itself change but also the associations and strengths of the motivational drives propelling the performance of that behavior (Killeen, 1991). Additionally, the infant may learn to be a better perceiver of the stimuli that are associated with the motivational attractor.

That is, as infants move and perceive, as they explore the possibilities of the landscape, they meander among the various motivational basins depicted in figure 11.2. This exploration allows them to sample and be drawn into various attractors and match their actions with the affective consequences. Through the

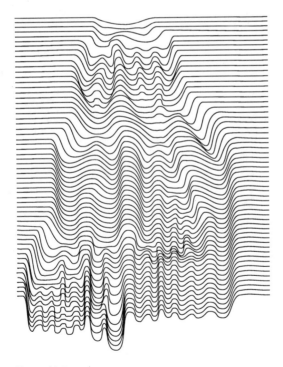

Figure 11.2
The locomotor landscape from chapter 4 as a generic landscape for the development of motivation or emotion.

processes of neuronal group selection, just as certain movements and perceptions form higher-order categories, these categories become associated with particular motivational attractors. Because of the emotional associations, they may subsequently attend to and remember the particulars of the perceptions and movements associated with that place on the landscape. When the emotional valence is not strong, any number of behavioral solutions may be good enough. Behavior can be flexible, somewhat determined by chance or whim, and diverse. When the emotional stakes are high, children will learn effective strategies quickly—they will be more focused, more quickly recruited, and less able to be distracted or perturbed by internal or external factors.

As an illustration, imagine that the furrows on the top third of figure 11.2 represent an infant's motivation to explore—to look, feel, and taste objects that can be reached and grasped. This is a compelling motivation, but of moderate strength, allowing infants to choose among several behavioral options, to move from one object to another, or to be distracted when a social opportunity intervenes or when they get hungry or sleepy. Within these moderate attractors, however, motivational strength will change. For instance, the motivation to put an object in the mouth for exploration decreases during the first year, as exploration with hands and eyes increases (Bushnell and Boudreau, 1993; Gibson, 1988). Later, the motivational attractor associated with the mouth becomes associated with edible items; infants have learned to recognize a different category of things to be put in the mouth and to redirect the strength and goals of the motivational component. These changes are depicted as the hillocks changing depth and spread. Likewise, although infants may initially be attracted to very simple visual stimulus attributes, as they explore and acquire more complex and general categories of objects, other stimulus attributes become more compelling through their learned associations.

In contrast, let us focus on the series of valleys to the right of the attractor landscape. Imagine these are the motivational strengths of Bowlby's need for caregiver proximity. Although the behaviors subserving this attractor will change, the motivational strength starts strong and remains strong throughout. When this system is activated by the felt loss of caregiving, responses are rapid, strong, and not easily diverted. Other motivational drives are suppressed—exploration ceases, feeding stops—as all behavioral trajectories are sucked into this attractor furrow.

Thus, just as the real-time processes of perceiving and acting segue smoothly into the stuff of developmental change, so this motivational landscape, given only minimal initial biases, itself differentiates into a rich set of dynamic possibilities. The motivational landscape—potentials for perceiving and acting—lives in the same space as the behavioral state spaces. It is part and parcel of the same dynamic, just as the brain systems providing the affective valence are richly and densely interconnected with those of perceiving, acting, and thinking.

Toward an Affective Cognition
Such a systems perspective provides a theoretical basis not only for reconciling motivation and cognition but also for considering the nature of developing emotion. What does our consideration of valence have to do with the felt experience of positive or negative affect—emotion—and its expression? Using a dy-

namic systems perspective, Fogel and his colleagues (Fogel and Thelen, 1987; Fogel, 1992; Fogel, Nwokah, Dedo, Messinger, Dickson, Matusov, and Holt, 1992) have suggested that just as cognition or developmental stages are not "things" in the brain, so emotions are also dynamically emergent. In a new theory of emotion, Fogel et al. propose that emotion is part of the same dynamic as other aspects of perception, action, cognition, and social behavior:

> We postulate that emotion is not felt experience alone, nor a pattern of neural firing, nor an action such as smiling. Emotion is the process that emerges from the dynamic interaction among these components as they occur in relation to changes in the social and physical context. . . . From a dynamic systems perspective, coherent emotions can be conceived of as relatively stable patterns that are continually constructed by a complex and dynamic process of interaction among the components. (Fogel et al., 1992, p. 129)

As emergent, self-organized processes, emotions like cognitions are fluid, context-sensitive, nonlinear, and contingent. As with other emergent categories, infants learn through everyday social activities to assign meaning—to form categories—from what is initially a more diffuse match between self and environment. As infants engage in social discourse, they produce actions, perceive their felt consequences, and view the reciprocal activities of the social partner, often in a game of mutual matching and turn-taking. Just as stable categories of world understanding emerge in the TNGS, so stable categories of affect become associated with certain perceptual-motor categories. (Meltzoff [1993] has also suggested that perceptual-motor mapping between infant and adult is the source of the understanding of emotional expression both in oneself and in others.)

Thus, the motivational landscape can just as easily be interpreted as one showing the differentiation of emotional experience and expression. From an initial bias, a diffuse attractor landscape with a few deep wells, infants, through their repeated experience producing and perceiving emotional states and their associated activities, come to acquire a more complex, differentiated set of stable basins of attraction. Along the way, some associations are lost, while others are diverted to new social situations. In this way, the social and cultural expectations become part and parcel of the felt emotions and of the activities that communicate those felt emotions to others. These activities, again, may be thought of as layered and completely intersecting with the landscapes of motivation and cognition.

Kurt Lewin Rediscovered

We conclude our consideration of motivation and a dynamic cognition with a tribute to Kurt Lewin, who drew dynamic motivational landscapes 50 years ago. Thus, our journey through contemporary dynamic systems and neuroscience in search of motivational primitives has led us full circle back to Lewin's remarkable vision. Although Lewin is all but forgotten as a developmental theorist (he is not mentioned in a recent textbook [Miller, 1989]), his account has a particularly contemporary relevance. Lewin was a true systems theorist. In order to understand behavior, Lewin claimed, "the person and his environment have to be considered as *one* constellation of interdependent factors" (1946, p. 793). A given physical setting has meaning only as a function of the state of the individual in that setting. Conversely, individual traits do not exist outside of the settings in which they are displayed. Thus, the goal in explaining behavior is to characterize this life space scientifically, and then to discover the function that links behavior to that life space.

As we mentioned previously, Lewin characterizes the life space as a field of forces—attractors and repellors in our dynamic translation—with varying strengths. People move dynamically through this force field depending on their location in the space, their needs, previous history, and so on. Forces—motivations—may compete, conflict, overlap, or sum depending on these dispositional characteristics within the specified environment. Learning involves finding a pathway, or adding structure, to an unspecified place in the life space. As children carve new pathways, new life spaces open up and in turn become differentiated, with new and more specific areas of attraction or repulsion.

Lewin's developmental dynamic is beautifully illustrated in figure 11.3. Life spaces are depicted as layered force fields, with certain attractor basins and varying zones corresponding to the potency of the forces. The parameters of the life space have several dimensions: size, degree of specifity, the separation between reality and "irreality," and the size and distance of the influence of psychological processes across time. The top panel (*a*) represents the life space of a younger child. It is smaller, less well differentiated, and there is little separation between reality and fantasy, either in the present or the immediate past or the future. In contrast, development (*b*, older child) results in more accessible and known areas of the space, a greater distance between reality and the spaces of wishes and fears, and both a longer psychological history and a more well-defined knowledge of what to expect in the future.

According to Lewin, cognition or the solutions to how to maneuver in these spaces comes from needs. "The cognitive structure of the life space is influenced by the state of the needs" (1946, p. 810). Meaning is imparted on perception only in relation to the intensity of the needs and what Lewin calls the "fluidity" of the related areas of the space. In our terms, we would think of this as the relative flexibility of the cooperative subsystems in allowing exploration and selection of alternative patterns. In short, Lewin sees cognition as soft-assembled, motivationally driven, task-flexible, individual, historical, and functional.

It is just these qualities of mental life, we argue in the next section, that allow so-called higher forms of cognition to dynamically emerge. Language, logic, consciousness, imagination, and symbolic reasoning are not "above" the processes of motivated perception, categorization, and action that we have been describing. Rather they are part and parcel of these processes, seamless in time and mechanism. Above all, we maintain, higher cognition is developmentally situated. It grows from and carries with it the history of its origins. In particular, cognition is *embodied* and *socially constructed*. How a dynamic theory supports an embodied and socially constructed cognition is the subject of the next sections.

The Origins of an Embodied Cognition

In chapter 2 we claimed that the study of cognitive development had reached a crisis. The crisis was the result of the confrontation between theories of the

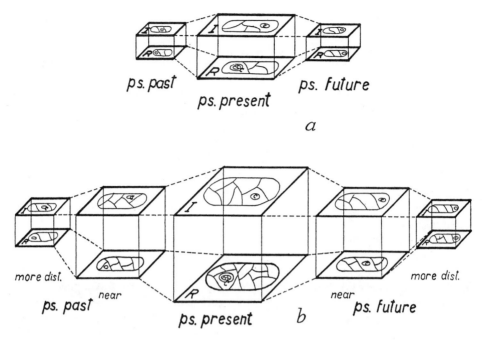

Figure 11.3
Lewin's psychological space (*ps.*) landscapes depicted as layered systems of force fields with R = reality and I = "irreality," showing the connection between the motivational forces in the past, present, and future. The *top panel* depicts the life space of a younger child; the *bottom*, that of an older child.

nature of mind and real data about real children. From a lofty view, human cognition has been characterized as symbolic, rational, encapsulated, structured, and algorithmic. But the data on how we develop mind does not fit these descriptions of the end-state. When we turned up the microscope on how real children did real tasks, we found that thinking looked messy, fluid, contextual, and often less than rational. We have argued in this book that what we know about the brain and what we know about development lead us to a completely different picture of the end-state.

Recently, several philosophers of mind have offered an alternative to the predominant characterizations of human cognition as reflecting an objectivist view of mind (Johnson, 1987; Lakoff, 1987a,b; Varela, Thompson, and Rosch, 1991). The term *objectivist* refers to the belief that there are objective truths in the world that people understand by mental constructions that symbolically represent these truths. Piaget epitomizes an objectivist view of mind. What Piaget saw as the endpoint of development was a mind designed to understand the world through relentless logic. What development leads to is a series of propositional structures that impart meaning to a logical world only understood through these symbolic constructions. Thus, in Piagetian theory, infants and children must shed their subjective, context-grounded, and illogical solutions for the ideal abstractions of formal logic. Piaget began his inquiry with the endpoint—a rational, Kantian knower endowed with abstract structures that evolved to fit the way the world worked. He built his developmental story backward, in a sense. From his understanding of the ideal adult knower, he then interpreted his developmental observations—which in themselves are without peer—to end up with a Swiss logician, a transcendent rationalist. When we shed these preconceptions of what the end-state should look like, we are free to interpret the developmental story—both Piaget's and our own data—in very different ways indeed.

The anti-objectivist philosophers argue that objectivist views of mind, by emphasizing mind's rational, mentalistic, abstract, conceptual, and a priori attributes, fall short of accounting for entire realms of human experience. These are the physical, emotional, perceptual, imaginative, a posteriori, and practical aspects of everyday existence. As we claimed in the first section of this chapter, it is these motivational currents, this contact with the real stuff of life, that energizes our activities and focuses and enlarges our thoughts. These thinkers reject the assumption, so common in contemporary cognitive science, that mind works like a digital computer. They suggest that knowing—categorizing the world, acting in it, giving the world meaning, and reflecting upon our acts—is at core nonpropositional, fluid, messy, imaginative, emergent, constructive, metaphorical, and above all dynamic. They consider knowledge as not above experience, but directly grounded in it. They see the very essence of meaning as part and parcel of our perceptions of the world and our very bodily activities in it. Meaning is constructed from the ways in which we see, and hear, and feel and act to solve problems within our cultures of home, work, and community.

Johnson and Lakoff applied the term *embodied* to capture the emergence of thinking from real experience. Varela, Thompson, and Rosch (1991) used the term *enactive cognition* to capture similar ideas. The notion of an embodied cognition is this: humans can and do use propositional logic to describe and think about their experiences. However, the stuff that our logic works on is nonpropositional and, indeed, is totally based on bodily experience. We deal with our perceptions and actions in terms of fluid, dynamic, contextual categories, patterns of organization, which form the very grist for our engagement of meaning. In an enactive cognition, meaning in the most abstract sense cannot be separated from actions. Meaning has its origins in actions and is made manifest—created—in real time and through activity.

One of the important sources of embodied meaning is our generalized experience of *physical containment*. As Johnson writes:

> Our encounter with containment and boundedness is one of the most pervasive features of our bodily experience. We are intimately aware of our bodies as three-dimensional containers into which we put certain things (food, water, air) and out of which other things emerge (food and water wastes, air, blood, etc.). From the beginning, we experience constant physical containment in our surroundings (those things that envelop us). We move in and out of rooms, clothes, vehicles, and numerous kinds of bounded spaces. We manipulate objects, placing them in containers (cups, boxes, cans, bags, etc.). In each of these cases there are repeatable spatial and temporal organizations. In other words, there are typical schemata for physical containment. (Johnson, 1987, p. 21)

Johnson goes on to show how these schemata pervade our thinking and language, how in the abstract metaphorical sense, we understand the world through the physical relations of containment. This is reflected in our understandings of prepositions such as *in, out, over,* and *near.* We understand these physical relations, according to Johnson, because we have acted them and felt them and seen them. But our bodily experiences are carried into even more abstract realms, those of metaphor and imagination. Consider, for example, our understanding of the prepositions *in* and *out* as part of our generalized categories of containment. Phrases such as *leave out, pick out,* or *take out* can have a purely physical meaning having to do with orientation. But look what happens to the meaning of *leave out* in the following two sentences:

(1) Leave out that big log when you stack the firewood.
(2) I don't want to leave any relevant data out of my argument. (From Johnson, 1987, p. 35)

In the first sentence, the phrase reflects simple physical relationships. But in the second, we make a metaphorical leap. There is no physical presence of *data* in an *argument.* We have construed an *argument* to be like a container, holding data that we can add or remove. Arguments are not logically equivalent to containers, but they are like them *if we can project containment* onto other venues of our experience. This requires a fluid, expressive, emergent use of the categories of *in* and *out.*

We believe that our dynamic systems account of cognition and action suggests a developmental mechanism by which these revealing extensions are acquired. In particular, we can speculate how some of the examples we have provided in this book can lead directly to a second of Johnson's pervasive image schemata, that of physical *force.*

We must control forces to move our bodies through space. Indeed all our causal relations with our environment require some sort of forceful interaction, as we act on objects or they act upon us. As Johnson says, "Since our experience is held together by forceful interactions, our web of meanings is connected by the structure of such activity" (p. 42). He then goes on to show how force gestalts pervade our language and meaning through force schemata: all our verbs expressing compulsion, blockage, counterforce, diversion, enablement, attraction, and so on are root metaphors derived and understood through our experience as force-producing and force-receiving beings. Even more remarkably, Johnson shows how the modal verbs such as *can, may, must, should, could, might*—verbs that have perfectly legitimate logical structure in the language and can be expressed as propositional structure—can also be understood in a more root, experiential sense. These verbs of possibility, necessity, and permission carry with them the meanings of overcoming barriers, impulsion, and other force-related acts on the environment. Johnson maintains these understandings are prelinguistic. The concept of *must* or *can* need not be learned from language, but from everyday acts of force, of moving limbs and body around barriers, of grabbing things within reach, of controlling forceful interactions between your bottom and the chair, and so on.

A Developmental Account of Force Embodiment

The construct of an embodied cognition gives new meaning to the activities of infants and young children learning to control their bodies. In chapters 4, 8, and 9, we have given accounts of infants acquiring simple motor skills: how to walk, to reach, to kick their legs to activate an overhead mobile, and to navigate down slopes. In each case, we claimed that the tasks were learned because infants have some motivation to reach a goal—get across the room, grab a toy, see an interesting event, or hug Mom—and have harnessed forceful interactions with their bodies in order to do so. Walking requires mastering dynamic balance, not allowing the forces of gravity to topple your pendulum, and creating the correct impact between foot and floor. To reach, infants need to deliver the appropriate amount of force to their arms to either lift them off their laps or control their enthusiastic flapping movements, and then to brake their reach to contact the toy. Activating the mobile is a matter of increasing the frequency and strength of muscle contractions to the legs. Successful traversal of the slope requires accurate assessment of slopeness and individual locomotor skill, and matching the type and scale of locomotor movements to the incline.

In each case, we suggested that infants come to acquire solutions through exploration: generating movements in various situations and feeling and seeing the consequences of those movements. When faced with a novel task—the overhead mobile or the slope—infants come into the situation with some understanding acquired through other movements generated either spontaneously or to accomplish goals. Although the task challenge is new, the process of moving and perceiving is continuous in time. Even the most common actions, the everyday poking, squishing, banging, bouncing, cruising, and babbling, give the child information about his or her movements in interaction with the world.

What we suggest here is that, through the processes of neuronal group selection, the reiterative, correlated reentry of movements and their perceptual consequences, infants come to acquire categories of knowledge. They individually learn how much force is appropriate to get their hands to the toys, as we saw with Gabriel and Hannah in chapter 9. But these infants are also learning about their legs, their heads, their postural stability, all of which involve some scaling of forces and result in forceful interactions with the environment. In particular, we suggest that through the experiences of learning to control forces in a wide variety of specific situations, a more general category of understanding emerges. From the experience of "force on slopes," "force with mobiles," "force reaching for toys," and so on, infants learn to remember and generalize the higher-order concept of "force in general." Recall in Rovee-Collier's experiment that it was experience with several, varied mobiles that allowed infants to remember appropriate kicking to mobiles in general and not just to the stimulus-bound situation of their training. In real life, of course, experience is highly varied as infants deal with many toys, different postures, surfaces, people, and so on. According to the TNGS, it is this continual forming and storing of varied categories that is the foundation for emergent higher-order abstractions.

The cycle of challenge, exploration, discovery, and new challenge within the motor skill domain occupies a large part of an infant's waking hours. Indeed, we speculate that the solutions to force interactions with the world are so pervasive and foundational in infancy and indeed throughout life, that they are carried along, so to speak, into the very fabric of all cognition. This process can be illustrated with a simple model. Imagine, as in figure 11.4, that in some abstract mental state space we represent solutions to the force problems we described as four clouds. We use clouds to indicate their dynamic, nonstructural, process-like character; in dynamic terms we can consider these as attractor basins. Initially, as the experiments with mobiles and slopes indicate, the solution spaces are small and constrained. Infants learn solutions specific to their postures, locations, or other particulars of the context. The clouds are separate; an action in a particular context is influenced by that context, and a limited, similar history, as indicated by figure 11.4,1. However, as infants gain a wide range of experience, these clouds enlarge, the solutions are generalized, an action in one context is influenced by a history of actions in a wider variety of contexts (figure 11.4,2). Eventually, the solution spaces intersect where the common aspects of each solution overlap (figure 11.4,3). In this case, it is as if there were a superordinate category of abstract force that had emerged from these specific experiences. This abstract knowledge of force is not a representation, however, disconnected from its specific instances. It is *in* the processes of interacting neuronal groups, processes that carry their history with them, processes identical to how infants learned "mobileness" or "slopeness" (see figure 11.4,3).

If, as we have suggested, a history of experience with bodily forces accompanies very many of our solutions in daily life, the abstraction cloud would become

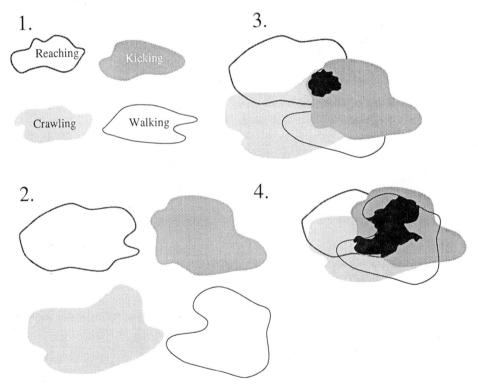

Figure 11.4
Model for the embodiment of the concept of *force*. See text.

very large indeed (figure 11.4,4). The force cloud would emerge not only by perceiving to act but also by thinking about acting, by planning to act, and by talking about acting. In dynamic terms, we could imagine that from these specific, real-time experiences a wide attractor basin would emerge, so that very many experiences in life would be captured by this basin. Meaning, a global similarity across diverse individual cognitive acts, a *seemingly* common core, a *seemingly* single abstract idea, literally grows from the commonalities of a multitude of everyday experiences. In this way, thought becomes developmentally constructed. The seamless web of time and process gives bodily foundations to emergent, higher-order abstractions. The root relationships are built early, before language, and these embodied relationships continue to exist after language, both independently of it and through it. The notion is that we have lived in these intersections so thoroughly, they are so embedded and embodied, that we can "leave out" data from an argument and understand the extensions from the literal meaning. Or we can realize that the word *must* (force) involves a forceful compulsion at its very root. In his deconstruction of other embodied image schemata—balance, pathways, links, attraction, matching, contact, object, mass-count, center-periphery, scale, superposition, and so on—Johnson concludes that they are *"pervasive, well-defined, and full of sufficient internal structure to constrain our understanding and reasoning* [Johnson's emphasis]" (Johnson, 1987, p. 126).

> By virtue of such superimpositions our world begins to take shape as a highly structured, value-laden, and personalized realm in which we feel the pull of our desires, pursue our ends, cope with our frustrations, and celebrate our joys. Much of the structure, value, and purposiveness we take for granted as built into our world consists chiefly of interwoven and superimposed schemata of the sort just described. (pp. 125–126)

The theme of this book has been to show that the "world begins to take shape" in infancy through the dynamic processes we have described. Because the thread of time is unbroken, and because bodily experience—perceiving and acting—form the primeval interactions with the world, cognition must be embodied. Because knowing is dynamic and not encapsulated, because it is trajectories and process rather than structure and computation, higher order understanding can self-organize from the real-time solutions of everyday life. There need not be a ghost in the machine, a knower in the head, or special devices.

Toward a Social Embodiment of Knowledge

In this book, we have focused on the individual perceiving, acting, and knowing. We characterized the individual as first and foremost a problem solver, generating and selecting adaptive matches to the challenges of the environment. Sometimes, as in the A-not-B error, individuals get caught in "local" solutions, captives, so to speak, of the peculiarities of their intrinsic dynamics and the current constraints of the task. At other times, they escape these local eddies and in dynamic phase shifts, discover new adaptive matches.

In the real world, of course, individuals never search and explore the solution spaces entirely on their own. From the moment of birth, learning and developing are social. Family and peers are as intimately a part of the world of infants and young children as are the objects and surfaces with which they live. And unlike their physical counterparts, humans create an intricate dynamic, with both partners mutually changing as their relationships proceed.

While we have not focused on the social aspects of early development, we believe the account we offer here is both consistent with theories of the social construction of knowledge and in fact offers a biologically plausible mechanism for such a process. Indeed, we agree with Fogel (1993) that meaning is imparted by relationships within the family, school, community, and culture in a way identical to how actions of the body become "embodied" in thought. Because social information and social problem-solving are so entirely pervasive in the here and now of everyday activities, commonalities of such encounters create a very large cloud, an enormous attractor basin that pervades every aspect of thought, imagination, and language. Commonalities arise, in turn, through the specifics of the culture; meaning cannot, therefore, be disentangled from the local activities that create it.

Theories of the social embeddedness of thought have roots in John Dewey (1916) and, more recently, in the renewed interest in the Russian psychologist L. S. Vygotsky (1978, 1986; see Luria, 1976; Rogoff, 1982; Wertsch, 1985; Cole 1985). The essence of Vygotsky's theory is that children's cognitive development progresses, and can only be understood, as a social activity. Family, peers, and teachers, and through them, the culture of the society as a whole, provide not only the content and structure of mind but the very nature of consciousness. Through social discourse and language, children participate in and absorb a sociohistorical context, which they subsequently incorporate into their thought and language. Vygotsky, like Dewey before him, believed it was the child's active participation in the culture, the sharing of mutual activities, often with a partner who knows more of the culture's values and tools, that is the engine of change. Thus, as in our dynamic account, new adaptations emerge from the seamless dynamic of time scales. What the child does in the here and now is both a product of activities in the past and the substrate for actions in the future.

In the Vygotsky tradition, Rogoff (in press) has characterized the dense, mutual interactions of children in social contexts as occurring on three different planes of focus. The metaphor of *apprenticeship* captures the process whereby children learn culturally organized activities through practice in contexts arranged by others to promote participation by the less experienced. Schools, organized clubs and activities, lessons, all provide children with culturally sanctioned tools and materials, values, and constraints. Rogoff labels as *guided participation* activities that take place on the interpersonal plane. This includes all the mutual actions of individuals and social partners in structured activities. One of the partners may guide the other in formal or informal ways or structure the environment to facilitate certain activities. All partners, though, are active participants, even when the participation in not symmetrical—one partner may be just watching. Important in Rogoff's construct is that what organizes guided participation is the mutual task and the seeking of mutual solutions. This may be very specific to getting a job done—solving a puzzle, reading a map—or simply spending enjoyable time together. Rogoff's third level of description is that of *participatory appropriation*. This is the process by which individuals change and thus "become prepared to engage in similar activities in a different manner" (p. 17). She contrasts her term with the notion of *internalization* as used by Vygotsky. Children just do not absorb information and incorporate it, a transformation from the external to the internal. Rather, she claims, "it is the children's active participation itself as being the process by which children gain facility in an activity."

> The dynamic approach of participatory appropriation does not define cognition as a collection of stored possessions (such as thoughts, representations, memories, plans) but rather treats thinking, re-presenting, remembering, and planning as active processes that cannot be reduced to the interaction of stored objects. . . . Instead of studying a person's possession or acquisition of a capacity or a bit of knowledge, the focus is on the active changes involved in an unfolding event or activity in which people participate. Events and activities are inherently dynamic. . . . Change and development . . . are assumed to be basic. (Rogoff, in press, pp. 17–19)

A dynamic systems approach to cognition and action provides a biological ground for cultural and contextual accounts of human cognition. Beginning with the simple assumptions that thought and action are soft-assembled, fluid, and task-driven, we built a case for mental life as emergent from the activities of everyday life. We argued in the previous section that meaning itself is action in the context of our history, our common experience. As the culture in all its manifestations infuses our everyday life, meaning is suffused with the shared aspects of that culture. Meaning is activity in context in a system with a dynamic history, and thus meaning comes with interpretive values, beliefs, and tendencies shared by the culture and the family within it. There are no logical structures abstracted from these meanings, as each cognitive act creates its own meaning.

Talking and Perceiving: An Interactive Cognition

One aspect of culture as pervasive as the forces harnessed to reach, hit, and kick is language. Children grow in a sea of words, words coupled with perceiving, acting, thinking, wanting. The heterogeneous, disjunctive, redundant, and coupled neuronal groups jointly involved in real-life language use will, through their reentrant influences, evolve deep and broad attractors. Thus, the shared history of language, like the shared history of bodily forces and culture, will shape individual real-time cognitive acts. All that we do—talking about acting, planning to act, thinking about acting, perceiving to act—will bring along this history of language experiences.

Our view of language's role in development thus places us close to the Whorfians. Although we accord language no *special* status, we propose, as did Whorf (1956), that language shapes thinking and perceiving. Historically, the idea that language could alter perception has been most controversial. If perception is universal and uninfluenced by language, then perception is a bedrock on which language can be built. If, in contrast, what is perceived and therefore what is knowable from one's own interactions with the world depends on language, then there is no single truth. What is knowable is relative. Many believe that the perception-language controversy has been resolved in favor of a constant and universal perceptual system (see Glucksberg, 1988). Recently, however, there have been increasing reports to the contrary (e.g., Choi and Bowerman, 1991;

Gentner and Rattermann, 1991; Lakoff, 1987b; Sera, Reittinger and Castillo, 1991; Smith, 1993; Smith and Sera, 1992). We shall briefly consider one result.

One way to study perception-language interactions is to study the end-states of perception in people who grew up speaking different languages. Another way is to examine developmental dependencies between changes in perception and language. Smith and Sera (1992; Smith, 1991) used the second approach and they reported dramatic changes in children's perception of dimensions as a function of children's knowledge of dimension words. Specifically, they found a marked increase between the ages of 2 and 3 years in children's matching of sizes to loudnesses. Two-year-olds did not match bigger objects to louder sounds but children 1 year older did so uniformly and unambiguously. Moreover, individual children's performances in the perceptual matching task were determined by whether they knew the words *big, little, loud,* and *quiet.* Children who knew the words made the cross-dimension matches.

Smith and Sera found a quite opposite developmental course in children's matching of sizes and shades of gray. Two-year-old children robustly and uniformly matched bigger objects to darker shades of gray, but older children did not. Instead they matched sizes and darknesses randomly. Moreover, it was the older children who knew the words *big, little, dark,* and *light* who did *not* match bigger sizes to darker grays. It was specifically the young children who *did not know* the words *dark* and *light* who matched bigger to darker.

Thus, Smith and Sera found one perceived correspondence that increased with language learning and one that decreased. They hypothesized that language learning, along with other forces, created the perceived correspondence between "quantitative" dimensions that we take for granted as adults. They speculated that English's special treatment of positive pole terms and use of the word *big* as a general scalar, as in "big noises," promoted the formation of an abstract idea of "moreness"—an abstract idea that we view as like the "cloud" attractors for the idea of force in figure 11.4. Smith and Sera further argued that the early perceived relation between bigger and darker was directly countered by language's reorganization of perceived magnitude and specifically by English's use of the words *dark* and *light* to refer to the color gray as well as the intensity of illumination. Moreover, they speculated that for individuals growing amid languages that do not conflate the words for colors and for lights, in languages like the West African Yoruba, big might be perceptually like dark gray throughout development.

Smith and Sera's results and their interpretation suggest that perception is no bedrock for language. Words are not pristinely mapped onto already formed perceptual categories without touching and changing those same categories. Rather, learning words, like learning to reach or crawl, changes the perceptual landscape. What we perceive depends on our history of experience and that history includes language. Language, like kicking, like moving into and out of containers, like turn-taking with a social partner, is one dynamic component in the complex history of interactions that create cognition.

This idea, that knowing a language alters perceiving, is one that directly counters the view of cognitive development as flowing in only one direction—from percepts to concepts to language, ever higher and ever more abstract. Our vision of cognition instead is of simultaneous and continuous interactions across and between levels in all directions—from perception to language and from language to perception. This idea of a developing cognitive system as the holistic result of *mutual* dependencies is illustrated by a metaphor offered by van Geert (1993). He likens development to the evolution and colonization of an island biotope. Perception and language can be thought of as two species in this biotope. The adaptation of each species depends on the other and on all other species on the island. No adaptations can be understood in isolation. Moreover, it makes no sense to ask, as in the traditional formulation of the Whorfian hypothesis, whether one species *determines* the other. The outcome of development, the structure of the island biotope as a whole and the adaptations of the individual species, is best understood as a dynamic system of continuous interaction and mutual influence.

Fodor (1983) rejected this idea of cognition as a high-dimensional system with many mutual dependencies and context sensitivities on the grounds that such a cognitive system would not be scientifically studiable. This book and its companion volume (Smith and Thelen, 1993) provide evidence to the contrary. To understand the developmental process through which multiple parts continuously and fluidly influence one another, we must study the dynamic organization of cognition as a complex system and empirically discover its points of stability, instability, organization, and reorganization.

Symbolic Thought in a Dynamic Cognition

We introduce another metaphor here—one that illustrates the radical difference between our conception of dynamic cognition and the more traditional computational view. This metaphor also sets the stage for our consideration of what some might claim to be the signal strength of computational theories and the fatal flaw of our dynamic theory. That watershed issue is symbolic thought.

The metaphor was offered by van Gelder (1992) and it derives from a 19th century engineering problem involving a steam engine that drives a flywheel connected to some machinery. The problem is that the speed of the flywheel must remain constant despite irregular and continuous fluctuations in the workload on the engine and the steam pressure. How could one design a device, called a governor, to maintain a constant flywheel speed? Van Gelder considers first a computational solution that contains the following: a tachometer for measuring the speed of the wheel, a device for calculating the throttle valve adjustment, a throttle valve adjustor, and an executive to handle the sequencing of operations. Note that within this device are representations (measures) of the steam pressure, the speed, and so forth. Indeed, this computational governor works—just like the traditional metaphor of cognition—by the manipulation and passing of representations from one component to the next.

A computational governor probably could be built that would work. But it is unlikely that it would work as well as or adapt as intelligently and fluidly to changes in workload and pressure as does the simple and elegant device invented by James Watt in the early 1800s. A version of Watt's device, the centrifugal governor, is illustrated in figure 11.5. The centrifugal governor consists of a vertical spindle geared into the main flywheel so that it rotates at a speed directly dependent upon that of the flywheel itself. As van Gelder writes:

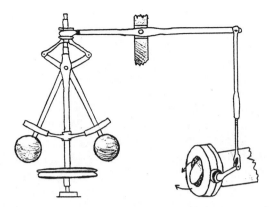

Figure 11.5
A version of Watt's centrifugal governor. See text.

Attached to the spindle by hinges were two arms, and on the end of each arm was a metal ball. As the spindle turned, centrifugal force drove the balls outwards and hence upwards. By clever arrangement, the arm motion was linked directly to the throttle valve. The result was that as the speed of the main wheel increased, the arms raised, closing the valve and restricting the flow of steam; as the speed decreased, the arms fell, opening the valve and allowing more steam to flow. The result was that the engine adopted a constant speed, maintained with extraordinary swiftness and smoothness in the presence of large fluctuations in pressure and load. (van Gelder, 1992, p. 3)

Watt's governor accomplishes its tasks in a radically different way than the computational device—in a way that allows for intelligent and continuous context sensitivity and a global order *without representations or computations*. Watt's governor does not represent anything; it just does the job. It does a near-perfect job because at every point in time, everything is dependent on everything else. The raising of the arms, the motion of the throttle valve, the speed of the flywheel are not connected in a linear progression. No behavior of the system is prior to or a progenitor of another; rather, all are simultaneously products and causes in a complex and self-modifying stream of activity in time. Note also that Watt's device is smart; it *embodies* (although it does not represent) as much knowledge as the computational governor. We propose that cognition is like the smartness of Watt's centrifugal governor—an activity emergent in the simultaneous and continuous interactions of a myriad of heterogeneous forces. Of course, the theory of cognition that we have laid out in this book is not like the centrifugal governor in one critical way: cognition develops. We must envision a centrifugal governor that through its own activity changes its very components and the manner of their interaction. We believe that this vision of the developing centrifugal governor offers a good metaphor for cognition—one that encapsulates the ideas we have presented in this book. It illustrates what we mean by an *enactive* system: cognition is the *activity* of a complex system; each moment in time is created through the dynamic interactions of many components and each moment creates the next.

There are some who might argue that van Gelder's metaphor is an apt one for our theory of cognition and one that reveals the fatal flaw. Their argument against our theory might go as follows: imagine some people whose lifework was to be a governor for a steam engine. If people devoted themselves to keeping the flywheel steady, they would not *just do the job*. They would think about it, they would talk about it, they would invent machines to do it for them, they would devise theories to explain it, they would write poetry to immortalize it. To borrow an example from Gleitman, Gleitman, and Shipley (1992), weaving people but not weaving spiders know what they know about weaving and often they know what they know in ways that enable them to bring this knowledge to bear in new contexts and to communicate this knowledge to others. Could the centrifugal governor ever know how it keeps the flywheel steady?

Without careful thought, it might seem that the computational model offers an easy solution to the deep problem of metacognition and symbolic thought. The computational governor, unlike the centrifugal one, consists of individuated structures that measure (represent) things. To explain how such a device might think about keeping the flywheel steady or invent a system of symbols to stand for the various steps in the procedure, we need only explain how the device looks down on its own cognitive processes and makes them accessible to consciousness. In this view, metacognition and explicitly symbolic thought are built out of the very same representations that do the job of more ordinary cognition.

This kind of explanation is pervasive throughout cognitive development. One example can be seen in discussions of phonemes. Phonemes are postulated (in many theories) to be the representational units of speech perception and speech production (see Harris and Coltheart, 1986). Phonemes are also (more or less) explicitly represented by the letters of the alphabet. Alphabets thus can be viewed as the external manifestation of internal symbols and their invention as evidence for phonemes' internal reality (Gleitman and Rozin, 1977). Other cognitive domains in which we explicitly manipulate phonemes, as in teaching reading, writing poetry, theorizing about phonology, and talking pig latin can also be viewed as using the very same representations that underlie the perception and production of speech. Thus all of cognition is one kind of thing: the explicit symbolic manipulations of doing logic, drawing maps, and counting are overt versions of what all cognitive process is. We illustrate these ideas in cartoon form in figure 11.6. Metacognition and explicitly symbolic thought consist of gaining access to the unconscious representations and making them conscious, transportable, and explicitly manipulable (Rozin, 1976). Note in this tradition, reflection and introspection are perfectly good routes to uncovering the structure of cognition.

The seductive ease in explaining symbolic thought in the computational account is illusory. Representational entities such as phonemes do not exist, even for the most ardent symbol theorist, in palpable form like adjustor valves, flywheels, or letters on a piece of paper. If we were to look into the brain, we would not see symbols. The symbolic level is not reducible to the physical level but is transcendent of physical form. Here lies the problem: if symbolic representations are transcendent of the physical stuff they are made of, then by what real-time

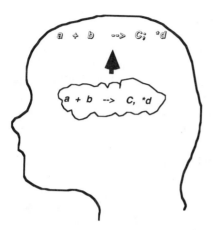

Figure 11.6
Cartoon of one possible relation between symbolic thought and ordinary cognition.

processes in real living people are they made consciously known? The ideas of symbols and access and consciousness will ultimately have to be grounded in real processes, real time, and real matter.

Connectionist models have been offered as an alternative to computational models and as a way of getting symbols out of real live matter. The basic idea is that when simple, unintelligent components, like neurons, are connected in the right way, they have interesting global properties and these global properties exhibit characteristics that are symbol-like and thus give rise to symbolic thought (Smolensky, 1988; Clark and Karmiloff-Smith, in press).

Varela, Thompson, and Rosch (1991) use the example of genes to illustrate the idea of *emergent* symbolic representations:

> For many years biologists considered protein sequences as being instructions coded in the DNA. It is clear, however, that DNA triplets are capable of predictably specifying an amino acid in protein if and only if they are embedded in the cell's metabolism, that is, in the thousands of enzymatic regulations in a complex chemical network. It is only because of the emergent regularities of such a network as a whole that we bracket out the metabolic background and thus treat triplets as codes for amino acids. (p. 101)

In other words, there is for DNA triplets (in context) a global order that is sufficiently regular that those DNA triplets can be treated as symbolic units, what we call "genes." Although genes are not independent of the substratum whence they emerge, they are a useful theoretical construct, a "shorthand" that can *stand for* the more complex and context-dependent processes of real DNA triplets.

Karmiloff-Smith (1992) has suggested that cognition is like "genes" and DNA triplets. She proposes that the causal stuff of cognition is realized in the distributed processes of highly connected components, but the global stabilities that emerge in these distributed and context-sensitive patterns may be redescribed in symbolic terms—as the biologist redescribes the activity of DNA triplets in their cellular context. Karmiloff-Smith calls this process representational redescription. She suggests that cognition is two kinds of things—distributed activity in a complex network of interactions *and* the redescription of that activity in terms of internally represented symbols. We illustrate Karmiloff-Smith's idea of emergent symbols in the cartoon of figure 11.7. This cartoon is like the one we used to depict the symbolic computational account, only here there are not precisely the same representational entities at lower and higher levels; rather, at the lower levels are messy interactive networks and at the higher levels are their symbolic redescriptions.

There are advantages to this explicitly hybrid account of cognition. Cognition is grounded in the body and in distributed patterns of brain activity. And there are symbols that are needed because people do think about and act on such externally realized symbols such as words, letters, and maps. Moreover, this account explicitly recognizes symbols as a shorthand, a convenience like "genes," that stand for more fluid and context-dependent processes.

Despite these advantages, the hybrid account retains key disadvantages—indeed, in our view, the fatal flaw of the computational account. The hybrid model still sees cognition as flowing in one direction, from lower, messier perception to higher, more-abstract thought. Symbolic thought is still a "raising up" and "redescription" of the more basic processes, a transcendent layer on top of real brain activity, rather than a product of the global activity itself. This is a highly problematic idea. If phonemes, for example, are "really" global patterns of activity across a complex network, what, then, looks down at that global pattern and redescribes it in explicitly symbolic terms? What, where, are these explicitly symbolic representations if *they* are not also distributed patterns of activity in time? Who does the redescribing? Is consciousness the ghost in the machine? If we are going to invoke ghosts, we might as well do it for the dynamic account as well as the computational one. There is no advantage for symbol

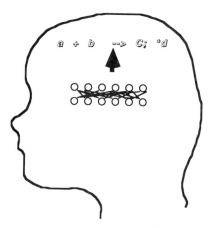

Figure 11.7
Another cartoon of one possible relation between symbolic thought and ordinary cognition.

theorists here. The ghost in the machine can just as well "look at" and "make conscious" the centrifugal governor as well as the computational one.

Our point is that we must ultimately explain consciousness and symbolic thought in real processes and in the activity of real living matter. When we do, the explanation will look like the centrifugal governor, like a complex dynamic system. Figure 11.8 illustrates our vision of symbolic thought. The figure shows complexly interacting neuronal groups of the kinds proposed by Edelman and used by us in chapters 6, 8, and 10 to explain developing cognition. Only here there are many heterogeneous systems (though far less than in the brain!). Each neuronal group has its own time-locked take on external *and* internal events. The pattern of activity in any one system will depend at each moment of time on its mapping to the external world, its just-previous state, and the reentrant mapping from a myriad of other neuronal groups. These patterns of neuronal group activity will recruit and be recruited by one another and will over time educate one another.

Where lies symbolic reasoning in this dynamic system? Throughout this book we have shown how "ordinary" cognition and behavior may be explained in the emergent patterns of activity of a complex system such as that illustrated in figure 11.8. Reconsider the example of weaving: weaving at a particular moment in time will consist of complex interactions across many neuronal groups. The activity in these groups will be timelocked to each other and to events in the world. *Thinking* about weaving also consists of interaction among neuronal

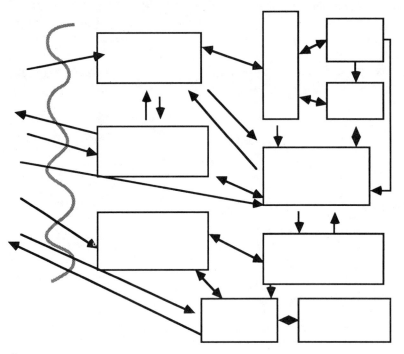

Figure 11.8
Our view of both symbolic thought and ordinary cognition.

groups in real time. Thinking, like weaving, is a *behavior,* a product of the entire system's activity. However, the patterns of activity that are weaving and the patterns of activity that are thinking about weaving are not the same nor is one in any way contained within the other or "raised up" to form the other. Weaving and thinking about weaving will not involve all the same components nor will they involve them in the same way. There will be overlapping components, overlapping histories, but the total ensembles will be different. Thinking about weaving cannot be taken apart to find out what really happens when we weave. Introspecting cannot give us information about cognition because introspecting is not a window onto mind but a behavior like any other behavior of this complex system. We, like the symbolic computational theorist, view cognition as all one kind; but in our view, it is all embodied, all distributed, all activity, all a complex event in time.

We believe that our theory of activity-driven, reentrant, high-dimensional cognition offers the best hope for understanding symbolic thought. We propose that symbolic thought, like walking up and down slopes, like the A-not-B error, like interpreting novel words, is emergent in activity and in the products of those activities in the physical world and on us. As we act and explore our world, our actions will produce concrete *physical* changes in that world that we may perceive. By perceiving the products of activity and the reentrant mapping of that perceiving onto the ongoing activity from which it emerged, we create *external* symbols and discover their value.

An example may be seen in the early emergence of spatial classification. People commonly display their knowledge of object categories by grouping objects in space, for example, by putting all the balls close together in one pile and all the boxes close together in another pile that is physically separated from the first. Thus, classifying uses space symbolically: nearness *stands for* similarity and farness *stands for* dissimilarity. The use of space to represent similarities was recognized by Inhelder and Piaget (1964) as an indicator of higher intellectual functioning and is widely used as a measure of intelligence in standardized tests. Children begin to spontaneously classify objects—to use space to indicate perceived similarities and differences—at around 18 months of age (e.g., Gopnik and Meltzoff, 1987; Sugarman, 1983).

Namy and Gershkoff-Stowe (1993) have suggested how children might discover the symbolic use of space in their spontaneous play with objects. They found that 18-month-old children who did not yet spontaneously classify objects on their own could be made to do so if they were given play experiences that promoted interaction with only one kind of object while rejecting the other. For example, in one experiment, children were given a transparent shape sorter into which only one kind of object fit. In this task, the children played with that one object and ignored all other kinds. This experience caused the children in a separate task to spatially classify—to make multiple spatial groups of like objects. Namy and Gershkoff-Stowe suggest that the original practical desire of playing with one kind of object led to like objects being gathered together in close proximity (on the table or in the bottom of the transparent shape sorter). They suggest further that *seeing* like objects gathered together gave children the very idea of using space to represent likeness and difference. In this way, the symbolic use of space may have emerged from the external *physical* products of behavior and the reentrant mapping of these perceived products onto internal activity. These results and Namy and Gershkoff-Stowe's interpretation offer an instantiation of what Karmiloff-Smith might mean by representational redescriptions. Note, however, that in this account, the only symbols are external: space on the table is a symbol for similarity. Perceiving, thinking, classifying, wanting, however, are not symbols; they are behaviors made manifest in the activity of a complex dynamic system.

These ideas of symbolic thought developing through the external manifestations of behaving are classic ones in developmental psychology (Luria, 1976; Vygotsky, 1962; see also Premack, 1976; Smith, 1993). These classic ideas fit well with our conception of a complex system that is continuously part of an ongoing world—both a product and a cause that makes changes in itself and in the world.

Paradigm Shifts

We close by asking where our account of cognition fits in the theoretical scheme of things. There are several issues that are commonly used to pigeonhole theories and put them in their supposed place. Does development proceed through innate plans or learning? Is there one general set of cognitive processes and learning procedures or are knowledge and process domain-specific and modular? Is learning simply associationist or is it constrained by evolutionary history?

We cannot answer these questions. We cannot say yes or no to innate or learned, domain-specific or domain-general, associationist or constrained. These are old questions, old controversies, which do not apply—are not even easily discussable—in our new view of cognition.

Activity in the world, real-time activity, makes development happen in our theory, but this is not learning in the usual sense and it is not a denial of evolutionary history. The heterogeneous processes of real brains, with their multiple convergent and divergent connections, are the intrinsic dynamics from which activity emerges. The nature of these heterogeneous components, their initial state and couplings, will determine the direction that development can take. But we are not nativists; development does not unfold according to some prespecified plan. There is no plan! We posit that development, change, is caused by the interacting influences of heterogeneous components, each with its own take on the world. These are not encapsulated modules; indeed, development happens, behavior is fluid and adaptively intelligent because everything affects everything else. Domain-specific versus domain-general is not a division that has meaning in this theory. We posit that development happens because of the time-locked patterns of activity across heterogeneous components, but this is not an associationist theory of mind. We are not building representations of the world by connecting temporally contingent ideas. We are not building representations at all! Mind is activity in time—the real time of real physical causes.

These old saws of metatheoretical discussions are no longer relevant because our dynamic systems theory constitutes a radical restructuring of how we conceptualize cognition and mind. Thomas Kuhn (1962), in his study of theory change in the history of science, suggested that paradigm shifts in science consist of three related changes: (a) the domain of phenomena accounted for, (b) the nature of the explanations that are acceptable, and (c) the very concepts and issues at the center of theory. It is difficult, perhaps impossible, to see clearly what one is doing when one is in the midst of doing it. Yet, it seems to us that psychology and cognitive science are in the midst of a paradigm shift. Our theory suggests a radical restructuring of the phenomena—a shift from competence and structures to variability, change, and process. Our theory suggests that explanations in terms of structures in the head—"beliefs," "rules," "concepts," and "schemata"—are not acceptable; acceptable explanations will ground behavior in real activity. Our theory has new concepts at the center—nonlinearity, reentrance, coupling, heterochronity, attractors, momentum, state spaces, intrinsic dynamics, forces. These concepts are not reducible to the old ones.

Mitchell Feigenbaum talked about the corresponding conceptual shift in understanding fluid dynamics:

> There's a fundamental presumption in physics that the way you understand the world is that you keep isolating its ingredients until you understand the stuff that you think is truly fundamental. Then you presume that the other things you don't understand are details. The assumption is that there are a small number of principles that you can discern by looking at things in their pure state—this is the true analytic notion—and then somehow you put these together in more complicated ways when you want to solve more dirty problems. If you *can*. In the end to understand you have to change gears. You have to reassemble how you conceive of the important things that are going on. . . . It requires a different way of thinking about the problem. (Feigenbaum, quoted in Gleick, 1987, p. 185)

Epilogue

What can a dynamic approach do? A dynamic approach can change the way you think about development and it can change the way you conduct research in development.

Once we began to view development from a dynamic and selectionist approach, we found the ideas so powerful that we could never go back to other ways of thinking. Every paper we read, every talk we heard, every new bit of data from our labs took on new meaning. We planned experiments differently and interpreted old experiments from a fresh perspective. Some questions motivating developmental research no longer seemed important; other, wholly new areas of inquiry begged for further work.

We see these changes as liberating. The overall result is a rejection of the dualism that pervades theory and research and the freedom to study development for what it is—process and change.

In this book, we have argued that progress in understanding is not well served by the old dualistic thinking: structure vs. function, nature vs. nurture, brain vs. behavior, perception vs. cognition, mind vs. body, competence vs. performance, learning vs. development. What we have substituted instead is an approach that considers dynamics at all levels, where continuity and change can be accommodated under a single theoretical umbrella and where the dualistic boundaries are erased.

This liberation from dualistic thinking about development has important implications for conceptualizing and conducting research. In these final few pages, we suggest three ways in which dynamic thinking can change empirical work.

1. A new meaning for time. A dynamic approach erases the distinctions between acting, learning, and developing and considers only change occurring at different scales of time. As a consequence, it demands that, when designing and interpreting studies, we understand what the child experiences *during the experiment*— and what the child does *in everyday life*—as affecting how the child behaves in the here and now of the test situation. What are the potential patterns of activity created by these experiences? What do they share in common with experimental test events? What is the nature of the input in everyday life, and the real-life multimodal correlations? How do these experiences become part of stable memories, that is, categories of experience that may then generalize to related situations? Thinking dynamically liberates us from encapsulating the test situation from the ongoing life of the child.

2. A new meaning for variability. A dynamic approach elevates variability, both within and between individuals, into an essential element in the developmental process. Variability is a metric of stability and a harbinger of change. Variability is also the essential ground for exploration and selection.

It is liberating to view old data and design new experiments in this light. When performance is variable, it may mean that we are tapping a system in transition and that there are multiple pathways or timetables for change. It may indicate the interaction between the individual's intrinsic dynamics—what they bring to the task as a result of organic and historical factors—and the task itself. These interactions are important and interesting, as they may reveal the opportunities and constraints of the process. The studies of shape bias in chapter 8 and of reaching in chapter 9 stand as examples of how variability can illuminate process.

We encourage our readers to reach into their file cabinets where they store the studies they did not publish because their ANOVAs did not detect significant effects. If errors of design or execution are not at fault, think dynamically and use the variability as data. Does the variability itself change over time? Are individual children variable between measures or are they pursuing consistent, but different pathways? Are there systematic patterns of exploration? Then, are there task manipulations that can shift these patterns?

3. A new respect for individuality. Finally, taken together, we believe a dynamic approach liberates developmental researchers from the tyranny of group-by-age comparisons and legitimizes alternative study designs. In particular, we encourage dense, multidimensional longitudinal studies using a few subjects where we can learn, not necessarily how *all* children effect some developmental transition, but in detail, how *a few* children do it. Such designs require extraordinary rigor, creativity, and dedication and would ideally be conducted by a multidisciplinary group in order to integrate dynamics at several levels of analysis. Such studies are an essential step in integrating dynamics over levels and time scales.

The final test of dynamics in development, of course, is in its usefulness to a wide range of scholars. We hope readers will accept the challenge of this new way of thinking and working and we look forward to the report card.

References

Abraham, R. H., and Shaw, C. D. (1984). In R. H. Abraham (Ed.), *Dynamics—The geometry of behavior* (Vols. 1–4). Santa Cruz, CA: Aerial Press.

Abraham, R. H. (1987). Dynamics and self-organization. In F. E. Yates (Ed.), *Self-organizing systems: The emergence of order* (pp. 599–613). New York: Plenum Press.

Acredelo, L. (1990). Behavioral approaches to spatial orientation in infancy. In A. Diamond (Ed.), *The development and neural bases of higher cognitive functions* (pp. 596–612). New York: National Academy of Sciences.

Acredelo, L. P. (1985). Coordinating perspectives on infant spatial orientation. In R. Cohen (Ed.), *The development of spatial cognition* (pp. 115–140). Hillsdale, NJ: Erlbaum.

Acredelo, L. P. (1988). Infant mobility and spatial development. In J. Stiles-Davis, M. Kritchevsky, and U. Bellugi (Eds.), *Spatial cognition: Brain bases and development* (pp. 156–166). Hillsdale, NJ: Erlbaum.

Acredelo, L. P., Adams, A., and Goodwyn, S. W. (1984). The role of self-produced movement and visual tracking in infant spatial orientation. *Journal of Experimental Child Psychology, 38,* 312–327.

Adolph, K. E. (1993). *Perceptual-motor development in infants' locomotion over slopes.* Unpublished doctoral dissertation, Emory University, Atlanta.

Adolph, K. E., Eppler, M. A., & Gibson, E. J. (1993a). Crawling versus walking. Infants' perception of affordances for locomotion on slopes. *Child Development. 64,* 1158–1174.

Adolph, K. E., Eppler, M. A., and Gibson, E. J. (1993b). Development of perception of affordances. In C. Rovee-Collier and L. P. Lipsitt (Eds.), *Advances in infancy research* (Vol. 8, pp. 51–98). Norwood, NJ: Ablex.

Alexander, R. M. (1984). Walking and running. *American Scientist, 72,* 348–354.

Anokhin, P. K. (1964). Systemogenesis as a general regulator of brain development. *Progress in Brain Research, 9,* 54–86.

Armstrong, S. L., Gleitman, L. R., and Gleitman, H. (1983). What some concepts might not be. *Cognition, 13,* 263–308.

Aslin, R. N., and Smith, L. B. (1988). Perceptual development. *Annual Review of Psychology, 39,* 435–474.

Ausabel, D. (1957). *Theory and problems of child development.* New York: Grune & Stratton.

Bahrick, L. E. (1983). Infants' perception of substance and temporal synchrony in multimodal events. *Infant Behavior and Development, 6,* 429–451.

Bahrick, L. E., and Watson, J. S. (1985). Detection of intermodal proprioceptive-visual contingency as a potential basis of self-perception in infancy. *Developmental Psychology, 21,* 963–973.

Baillargeon, R. (1986). Representing the existence and the location of hidden objects: Object permanence in 6- and 8-month-old infants. *Cognition, 23,* 21–41.

Baillargeon R. (1987a). Object permanence in 3.5- and 4.5-month-old infants. *Developmental Psychology, 23,* 655–664.

Baillargeon, R. (1987b). Young infants' reasoning about the physical and spatial properties of hidden objects. *Cognitive Development, 2,* 179–200.

Baillargeon, R. (1991). Reasoning about the height and location of a hidden object in 4.5- and 6.5-month-old infants. *Cognition, 33,* 13–42.

Baillargeon, R. (1992). The object concept revisited: New directions in the investigation of infants' physical knowledge. In C. E. Granrud (Ed.), *Visual perception and cognitions in infancy* (Vol. 23). Hillsdale, NJ: Erlbaum.

Baillargeon, R., and Graber, M. (1987). Where's the rabbit? 5.5 month infants, representation of the hidden object. *Cognitive Development, 2*, 375–392.

Baillargeon, R., and Graber, M. (1988). Evidence of location memory in 8-month-old infants in a nonsearch AB task. *Developmental Psychology, 24*, 502–511.

Baillargeon, R., Spelke, E. S., and Wasserman, S. (1985). Object permanence in five-month-old infants. *Cognition, 20*, 191–208.

Baltes, P. B. (1987). Theoretical propositions of life-span developmental psychology: On the dynamics between growth and decline. *Developmental Psychology, 23*, 611–626.

Bandura, A. (1986). *Social foundations of thought and action.* Englewood Cliffs, NJ: Prentice-Hall.

Barnsley, M. (1988). *Fractals everywhere.* New York: Academic Press.

Barsalou, L. W. (1987). The instability of graded structure: Implications for the nature of concepts. In U. Neisser (Ed.), *Concepts and conceptual development: Ecological and intellectual factors in categorization* (pp. 101–140). New York: Cambridge University Press.

Bates, E. (1979). *The emergence of symbols: Cognition and communication in infancy.* New York: Academic Press.

Bates, E., and Elman, J. (1993). Connectionism and the study of change. In M. H. Johnson (Ed.), *Brain development and cognition* (pp. 623–642). Cambridge, MA: Blackwell.

Bateson, P. P. G. (1987). Biological approaches to the study of behavioural development. *International Journal of Behavioral Development, 1987, 10*, 1–22.

Beek, P. J. (1989). *Juggling dynamics.* Amsterdam: Free University Press.

Bekoff, A. (1985). Development of locomotion in vertebrates: A comparative perspective. In E. S. Gollin (Ed.), *Comparative development of adaptive skills: Evolutionary implications* (pp. 57–94). Hillsdale, NJ: Erlbaum.

Bekoff, A., and Kauer, J. A. (1982). Neural control of hatching: Role of neck position in turning on hatching movements in post-hatching chicks. *Journal of Comparative Physiology, A, 145*, 497–504.

Bekoff, A., and Kauer, J. A. (1984). Neural control of hatching: Fate of the pattern generator for the leg movements of hatching in post-hatching chicks. *Journal of Neuroscience, 4*, 2659–2666.

Bell, M., and Fox, N. A. (1992). The relations between frontal brain electrical activity and cognitive development during infancy. *Child Development, 66*, 1142–1164.

Bernstein, N. (1967). *Coordination and regulation of movements.* New York: Pergamon Press.

Berkinblit, M. B., Feldman, A. G., and Fukson, O. I. (1986). Adaptability of innate motor patterns and motor control mechanisms. *The Behavioral and Brain Sciences, 9*, 585–638.

Bertalanffy, L. von. (1968). *General system theory.* New York: George Braziller.

Bertenthal, B. I. (1990). Application of biomechanical principles to the study of perception and action. H. Block and B. I. Bertenthal (Eds.), *Sensory-motor organizations and development in infancy and early childhood*, pp. 243–260. The Netherlands: Kluwer Academic Publishers.

Bertenthal, B. I., and Campos, J. J. (1990). A systems approach to the organizing effects of self-produced locomotion during infancy. In C. Rovee-Collier and L. P. Lipsitt (Eds.), *Advances in infancy research, Vol 6* (pp. 1–60). Norwood, NJ: Ablex.

Bertenthal, B., Campos, J., and Barrett, K. (1984). Self-produced locomotion: An organizer of emotional cognitive, and social development in infancy. In R. Emde and R. Harmon (Eds.), *Continuities and Discontinuities* (pp. 175–210). New York: Plenum Press.

Bigelow, A. E. (1992). Locomotion and search behavior in blind infants. *Infant Behavior and Development, 15*, 179–189.

Bloom, L. (1973). *One word at a time.* The Haque: Mouton.

Boller, K., Rovee-Collier, C., Borovsky, D., O'Connor, J. and Shyi, G. (1990). Developmental changes in the time-dependent nature of memory retrieval. *Developmental Psychology, 26*, 770–780.

Borovsky, D., and Rovee-Collier, C. (1990). Contextual constraints on memory retrieval at 6 months. *Child Development, 61*, 1569–1583.

Bower, T. G. R. (1986). Repetitive processes in child development. *235*, 38–47.

Bower, T. G. R. (1989). *The rational infant: Learning in infancy.* New York: Freeman.

Bower, T. G. R., Broughton, J. M., and Moore, M. K. (1970). Demonstration of intention in the reaching behaviour of neonate humans. *Nature, 228*, 679–681.

Bowlby, J. (1969). *Attachment and loss. Volume 1: Attachment.* New York: Basic Books.

Bradley, N. S., and Smith, J. L. (1988a). Neuromuscular patterns of stereotypic hindlimb behaviors in the first two postnatal months. I. Steppping in normal kittens. *Developmental Brain Research, 38*, 37–52.

Bradley, N. S., and Smith, J. L. (1988b). Neuromuscular patterns of stereotypic hindlimb behaviors in the first two postnatal months. III. Scratching and the paw-shake response in kittens. *Developmental Brain Research, 38,* 69–82.

Brainerd, C. J. (1978). The stage question in cognitive-developmental theory. *The Behavioral and Brain Sciences, 1,* 173–182.

Bremner, J. G. (1985). Object tracking and search in infancy: A review of data and a theoretical evaluation. *Developmental Review, 5,* 371–396.

Brent, S. B. (1978). Prigogine's model for self-organization in nonequilibrium systems: Its relevance for developmental psychology. *Human Development, 21,* 374–387.

Brent, S. B. (1984). *Psychological and social structures.* Hillsdale, NJ: Erlbaum.

Bril, B., and Breniere, Y. (1992). Postural requirements and progression velocity in young walkers. *Journal of Motor Behavior, 24,* 105–116.

Bronfenbrenner, V. (1979). *The ecology of human development.* Cambridge, MA: Harvard University Press.

Brooks, V. B., Cooke, J. J., and Thomas, J. S. (1973). The continuity of movements. In R. B. Stein, K. G. Pearson, R. S. Smith, J. B. Redford (Eds.). *Control of posture and locomotion* (pp. 257–272). New York: Plenum.

Bruner, J. S., and Koslowski, B. (1972). Visually preadapted constituents of manipulatory actions. *Perception, 1,* 3–14.

Bruner, J. S., and Olver, R. R. (1963). Development of equivalence transformations in children. *Monographs of the Society for Research in Child Development,* No. 28.

Bryant, P. E., and Trabasso, T. R. (1971). Transitive inferences and memory in young children. *Nature, 232,* 456–458.

Bullock, M., Gelman, R., and Baillargeon, R. (1982). The development of causal reasoning. In W. J. Friedman (Ed.), *The developmental psychology of time.* New York: Academic Press.

Bushnell, E. M. (1985). The decline of visually guided reaching during infancy. *Infant Behavior and Development, 8,* 139–155.

Bushnell, E. M., and Boudreau, J. P. (1993). Motor development in the mind: The potential role of motor abilities as a determinant of aspects of perceptual development. *Child Development, 64,* 1005–1021.

Butler, J., and Rovee-Collier, C. (1989). Contextual gating of memory retrieval. *Developmental Psychobiology, 22,* 533–552.

Cairns, R. (1988). Spoken comments at the centennial celebration of the Department of Psychology, Indiana University, Bloomington.

Carey, S. (1985). *Conceptual change in childhood,* Cambridge, MA: MIT Press.

Chapman, M. (1988). *Constructive evolution. Origins and development of Piaget's thought.* Cambridge: Cambridge University Press.

Chi, M. T. H. (1978). Knowledge structures and memory development. In R. S. Siegler (Ed.), *Children's thinking: What develops?* (pp. 73–95). Hillsdale, NJ: Erlbaum.

Chi, M. T. H., and Koeske, R. D. (1983). Network representations of knowledge base: Exploring a child's knowledge and memory performance of dinosaurs. *Developmental Psychology, 19,* 29–39.

Choi, S., and Bowerman, M. (1991). Learning to express motion events in English and Korean: The influence of language-specific lexicalization patterns. *Cognition, 41,* 83–121.

Chomsky, N. (1965). *Aspects of the theory of syntax.* Cambridge, MA: MIT Press.

Chomsky, N. (1986). *Knowledge of language: Its nature, origin, and use.* New York: Praeger.

Clark, A., and Karmiloff-Smith, A. (in press). The cognizer's innards: A psychological and philosophical perspective on the development of thought. *Mind and Language.*

Clark, E. V. (1972). How children describe time and order. In C. A. Ferguson and D. I. Slobin (Eds.), *Studies of child language development* (pp. 585–606). New York: Holt, Rinehart, & Winston.

Clifton, R. K., Muir, D. W., Ashmead, D. H., and Clarkson, M. G. (1993). Is visually guided reaching in infancy a myth? *Child Development, 64,* 1099–1110.

Cohen, A. H. (1992). The role of heterarchical control in the evolution of central pattern generators. *Brain, Behavior, and Evolution, 40,* 112–124.

Cohen, A. H., Holmes, P. J., and Rand, R. H. (1982). The nature of coupling between segmental oscillators of the lamprey spinal generator for locomotion: A mathematical model. *Journal of Mathematical Biology, 13,* 345–369.

Cohen, L. B., and Salapatek, P. (1975). *Infant perception: From sensation to cognition.* New York: Academic Press.

Cole, M. (1985). The zone of proximal development: Where culture and cognition create each other. In J. V. Wertsch (Ed.), *Culture, communication, and cognition: Vygotskian perspectives* (pp. 146–161). Cambridge: Cambridge University Press.

Corbetta, D., and Thelen, E. (1993). Shifting patterns of interlimb coordination in infants' reaching: A case study. In S. P. Swinnern, H. Heuer, J. Massion, and P. Casaer (Eds.), *Interlimb coordination: Neural, dynamical and cognitive constraints* (pp. 413–438). New York: Academic Press.

Cowan, W. M. (1978). Aspects of neural development. *International Review of Physiology, 17,* 150–191.

Cruz, C. A. (1992). Knowledge-representation networks: Goal direction in intelligent neural systems. In D. S. Levine and S. J. Leven (Eds.), *Motivation, emotion, and goal direction in neural networks* (pp. 369–410). Hillsdale, NJ: Erlbaum.

Damasio, A. R. (1989). Time-locked multiregional retroactivation: A systems-level proposal for the neural substrates of recall and recognition. *Cognition, 33,* 25–62.

Davis, D. W. (1991). *Treadmill-elicited stepping in low birthweight infants born prematurely.* Unpublished doctoral dissertation, Indiana University.

DeCasper, A. J., and Fifer, W. P. (1980). Of human bonding: Newborns prefer their mothers' voices. *Science, 208,* 1174–1176.

Delcomyn, F. (1980). Neural basis of rhythmic behavior in animals. *Science, 210,* 492–498.

DeLoache, J. S. (1987). Rapid change in the symbolic functioning of young children. *Science, 238,* 1556–1557.

Devaney, R. (1986). *An introduction to chaotic dynamical systems.* New York: Addison-Wesley.

Dewey, J. (1916). *Democracy and education: An introduction to the philosophy of education.* New York: Macmillan.

Diamond, A. (1988). Differences between adult and infant cognition: Is the crucial variable presence or absence of language? In L. Weiskrantz (Ed.), *Thought without language* (pp. 337–370). Oxford: Clarendon Press.

Diamond, A. (1990a). Development and neural bases of AB and DR. In A. Diamond (Ed.), *The development and neural bases of higher cognitive functions* (pp. 267–317). New York: National Academy of Sciences.

Diamond, A. (1990b). Developmental time course in human infants and infant monkeys, and the neural bases of inhibitory control in reaching. In A. Diamond (Ed.), *The development and neural bases of higher cognitive functions* (pp. 637–676). New York: National Academy of Sciences.

Diamond, A. (1990c). Discussion. In A. Diamond (Ed.), *The development and neural bases of higher cognitive functions* (pp. 1–25). New York: National Academy of Sciences.

Diamond, A., and Goldman-Rakic, P. S. (1989). Comparison of human infants and rhesus monkeys on Piaget's AB task. Evidence for dependence on dorsolateral prefrontal cortex. *Experimental Brain Research, 74,* 24–40.

Diamond, A. S., Zola-Morgan, S., and Squire, L. (1989). Successful performance by monkeys with lesions of the hippocampal formation on AB and object retrieval, two tasks that mark developmental changes in human infants. *Behavioral Neuroscience, 103,* 526–537.

Donaldson, M. (1978). *Children's minds.* New York: W. W. Norton.

Edelman, G. M. (1987). *Neural Darwinism.* New York: Basic Books.

Edelman, G. M. (1988). *Topobiology: An introduction to molecular embryology.* New York: Basic Books.

Edelman, G. M. (1989). *The remembered present: A biological theory of consciousness.* New York: Basic Books.

Edelman, G. M. (1992). *Bright air, brilliant fire. On the matter of mind.* New York: Basic Books.

Edelman, G., and Gall, W. (1979). The antibody problem. *Annual Review of Biochemistry, 38,* 699–766.

Ehri, L. (1976). Comprehension and production of adjectives and seriation. *Journal of Child Language, 3,* 369–384.

Engel, A. K., König, P., Kreiter, A. K., Schillen, T. B., and Singer, W. (1992). Temporal coding in the visual cortex: New vistas on integration in the nervous system. *Trends in Neurosciences, 15,* 218–227.

Ettlinger, G., and Wilson, W. A. (1990). Cross-modal performance: Behavioral processes, phylogenetic considerations and neural mechanisms. *Behavioural Brain Research, 40,* 169–192.

Fagen, J. W., Morrongiello, B. A., Rovee-Collier, C., and Gekoski, M. J. (1984). Expectancies and memory retrieval in three-month-old infants. *Child Development, 56,* 936–943.

Fagen, J. W., and Rovee-Collier, C. (1983). Memory retrieval: A time-locked process in infancy. *Science, 222,* 1349–1351.

Feldman, A. G. (1966). Functional tuning of the nervous system with control of movement or maintenance of a steady posture. III. Mechanographic analysis of execution by man of the simplest motor tasks. *Biophysics, 11,* 766–775.

Feldman, A. G. (1980). Superposition of motor programs—I. Rhythmic forearm movements in man. *Journal of Neuroscience, 5,* 81–90.

Felleman, D. J., and Van Essen, D. C. (1991). Distributed hierarchical processing in the primate cerebral cortex. *Cerebral Cortex, 1,* 1–47.

Fetters, L., and Todd, J. (1987). Quantitative assessment of infant reaching movements. *Journal of Motor Behavior, 19,* 147–166.

Fischer, K. W., and Bidell, T. R. (1991). Constraining nativist inferences about cognitive capacities. In S. Carey and R. Gelman (Eds.), *Constraints on knowledge in cognitive development* (pp. 199–236). Hillsdale, NJ: Erlbaum.

Flavell, J. H. (1970). Concept development. In P. H. Mussen (Ed.), *Carmichael's manual of child psychology* (Vol. 1). New York: Wiley.

Fodor, J. A. (1972). Some reflections on L. S. Vygotsky's "thought and language." *Cognition, 1,* 83–95.

Fodor, J. A. (1976). *The language of thought.* New York: Crowell.

Fodor, J. A. (1983). *The modularity of mind.* Cambridge, MA: MIT Press.

Fodor, J. A. (1987). Modules, frames, fridgeons, sleeping dogs, and the music of the spheres. In J. G. Garfield (Ed.), *Modularity in knowledge representation and natural language understanding* (pp. 25–36). Cambridge, MA: MIT Press.

Fogel, A. (1992). Movemment and communication in human infancy: The social dynamics of development. *Human Movement Science, 11,* 387–423.

Fogel, A. (1993). *Developing through relationships: Origins of communication, self, and culture.* New York: Harvester Wheatsheaf.

Fogel, A. (1993). *Developing through relationships: Communication, self, and culture in early infancy.* Cambridge: Harvester Press.

Fogel, A., Nwokah, E., Dedo, J. U., Messinger, D., Dickson, K. L. Matusov, E., and Holt, S. A. (1992). Social process theory of emotion: A dynamic systems approach. *Social Development, 1,* 122–142.

Fogel, A., and Thelen, E. (1987). The development of expressive and communicative action in the first year: Reinterpreting the evidence from a dynamic systems perspective. *Developmental Psychology, 23,* 747–761.

Forssberg, H. (1985). Ontogeny of human locomotor control. I. Infant stepping, supported locomotion, and transition to independent locomotion. *Experimental Brain Research, 57,* 480–493.

Fraiberg, S. (1977). *Insights from the blind.* New York: Basic Books.

Freeman, W. J. (1981). A physiological hypothesis of perception. *Perspectives in Biology and Medicine, 24,* 561–592.

Freeman, W. J. (1987). Simulation of chaotic EEG patterns with a dynamic model of the olfactory system. *Biological Cybernetics, 56,* 139–150.

Freeman, W. J. (1991). The physiology of perception. *Scientific American, 264,* 78–85.

Freeman, W. J., and Skarda, C. A. (1985). Spatial EEG patterns, nonlinear dynamics and perception: The neo-Sherringtonian view. *Brain Research Reviews, 10,* 147–175.

Frégnac, Y., and Imbert, M. (1984). Development of neuronal selectivity in primary visual cortex of cat. *Physiological Review, 64,* 325–434.

Freyd, J. (1983). The mental representation of movement when static stimuli are viewed. *Perception and Psychophysics, 33,* 575–581.

Freyd, J. J. (1992). Five hunches about perceptual processes and dynamic representations. In D. Meyer and S. Komblum (Eds.), *Attention and performance XIV: A silver jubilee,* Hillsdale, NJ: Erlbaum.

Freyd, J. J., and Finke, R. A. (1984). Representational momentum. *Journal of Experimental Psychology: Learning, Memory, & Cognition, 10,* 126–132.

Gallistel, C. R. (1980). *The organization of action: A new synthesis.* Hillsdale, NJ: Erlbaum.

Garfield, J. (1987). *Modularity in knowledge representation and natural language understanding.* Cambridge, MA: MIT Press.

Gasser, M., and Smith, L. B. (1991). The development of the notion of sameness: A connectionist model. *Proceedings of the Thirteenth Annual Conference of the Cognitive Science Society, 719–723*.

Gelman, R. (1969). Conservation acquisition: A problem of learning to attend to relevant attributes. *Journal of Experimental Child Psychology, 7*, 167–187.

Gelman, R. (1972). The nature and development of early number concepts. In H. W. Reese and L. P. Lipsitt (Eds.), *Advances in child development and behavior*. New York: Academic Press.

Gelman, R., and Gallistel, C. R. (1978). *The child's understanding of number*. Cambridge, MA: Harvard University Press.

Gelman, S. A., and Coley, J. D. (1991). Language and categorization: The acquisition of natural kind terms. In S. A. Gelman and J. P. Byrnes (Eds.), *Perspectives on thought and language: Interrelations in development* (pp. 146–196). Cambridge: Cambridge University Press.

Gelman, S. A., and Markman, E. M. (1987). Young children's inductions from natural kinds: The role of categories and appearances. *Child Development, 58*, 1532–1541.

Gelman, S. A., and Medin, D. L. (1993). What's so essential about essentialism? A different perspective on the interaction of perception, language, and concrete knowledge. *Cognitive Development, 5*, 157–168.

Gentner, D. (1989). The mechanisms of analogical learning. In S. Vosniadou and A. Ortony (Eds.), *Similarity and analogical reasoning* (pp. 199–241). Cambridge: Cambridge University Press.

Gentner, D., and Rattermann, M. J. (1991). Language and the career of similarity. In S. A. Gelman and J. P. Byrnes (Eds.), *Perspectives on thought and language: Interrelations in development*. Cambridge: Cambridge University Press.

Georgopoulos, A. P. (1986). On reaching. *Annual Review of Neurosciences, 9*, 147–170.

Georgopoulos, A. P. (1988). Neural integration of movement: Role of motor cortex in reaching. *The FASEB Journal, 2*, 2849–2857.

Georgopoulos, A. P. (1990). Neurophysiology of reaching. In M. Jeannerod (Ed.), *Attention and performance XIII* (pp. 227–263). Hillsdale, NJ: Erlbaum.

Georgopoulos, A. P. (1991). Higher order motor control. *Annual Review of Neurosciences, 14*, 361–377.

Georgopoulos, A. P., Kettner, R. E., and Schwartz, A. B. (1988). Primate motor cortex and free arm movements to visual targets in three-dimensional space. II. Coding of the direction of movement by a neuronal population. *The Journal of Neuroscience, 8*, 2928–2937.

Gesell, A. (1939). Reciprocal interweaving in neuromotor development. *Journal of Comparative Neurology, 70*, 161–180.

Gesell, A. (1945). *The embryology of behavior*. New York: Harper.

Gesell, A. (1946). The ontogenesis of infant behavior. In L. Carmichael (Ed.), *Manual of child psychology* (pp. 295–331). New York: Wiley.

Gesell, A., and Ames, L. B. (1940). The ontogenetic organization of prone behavior in human infancy. *The Journal of Genetic Psychology, 56*, 247–263.

Ghiselin, M. T. (1969). *The triumph of the Darwinian method*. Chicago: University of Chicago Press.

Gibson, E. J. (1969). *Principles of perceptual learning and development*. Englewood Cliffs, NJ: Prentice-Hall.

Gibson, E. J. (1988). Exploratory behavior in the development of perceiving, acting, and the acquiring of knowledge. *Annual Review of Psychology, 39*, 1–41.

Gibson, E. J., and Walk, R. D. (1960). The "visual cliff." *Scientific American, 202*, 64–71.

Gibson, E. J., and Walker, A. (1984). Development of knowledge of visual and tactual affordances of substance. *Child Development, 55*, 453–460.

Gibson, J. J. (1979). *The ecological approach to visual perception*. Boston: Houghton-Mifflin.

Glass, L., and Mackey, M. C. (1988). *From clocks to chaos. The rhythms of life*. Princeton, NJ: Princeton University Press.

Gleick, J. (1987). *Chaos: Making a new science*. New York: Viking.

Gleitman, L. R., Gleitman, H., and Shipley, E. (1972). The emergence of the child as grammarian. *Cognition, 1*, 137–164.

Gleitman, L. R., and Rozin, P. (1977). The structure and acquisition of reading I: Relation between orthographics and the structure of language. In A. S. Reber and J. Scarborough (Eds.), *Toward a psychology of reading*. Hillsdale, NJ: Erlbaum.

Gleitman, L. R., and Wanner, E. (1982). Language acquistion: The state of the state of the art. In E. Wanner and L. R. Gleitman (Eds.), *Language acquisition: The state of the art* (pp. 3–51). Cambridge: Cambridge University Press.

Glucksberg, S. (1988). Language and thought. In R. J. Sternberg and E. E. Smith (Eds.), *The psychology of human thought* (pp. 214–241). Cambridge: Cambridge Univerity Press.

Goldberger, A. L., and Rigney, D. R. (1988). Sudden death is not chaos. In J. A. S. Kelso, A. J. Mandell, and M. F. Shlesigner (Eds.), *Dynamic patterns in complex systems* (pp. 248–264). Singapore: World Scientific.

Goldfield, E. G., and Michel, G. F. (1986). The ontogeny of infant bimanual reaching during the first year. *Infant Behavior and Development, 9,* 81–89.

Goldman-Rakic, P. S. (1987). Development of control circuitry and cognitive function. *Child Development, 58,* 601–622.

Goodman, N. (1955). *Fact, fiction and forecast.* Indianapolis: Bobbs-Merrill.

Gopnik, A., and Meltzoff, A. N. (1987). The development of categorization in the second year and its relation to other cognitive and linguistic developments. *Child Development, 58,* 1523–1531.

Gottlieb, G. (1961). Developmental age as a baseline for determination of the critical period in imprinting. *Journal of Comparative and Physiological Psychology, 54,* 422–427.

Gottlieb, G. (1991a). Epigenetic systems view of human development. *Developmental Psychology, 27,* 33–34.

Gottlieb, G. (1991b). Experiential canalization of behavioral development: Results. *Developmental Psychology, 27,* 35–39.

Gottlieb, G. (1991c). Social induction of malleability in ducklings. *Animal Behavior, 41,* 953–963.

Gottlieb, G. L., Corcos, D. M., and Agarwal, G. C. (1989). Strategies for the control of voluntary movements with one mechanical degree of freedom. *Behavioral and Brain Sciences, 12,* 189–250.

Gould, S. J., and Lewontin, R. C. (1979). The spandrels of San Marco and the Panglossian paradigm: A critique of the adaptationist programme. *Proceedings of the Royal Society of London (B), 205,* 581–598.

Gray, J. A. (1991). The neuropsychology of temperament. In J. Strelau and A. Angleitner (Eds.), *Explorations in temperament; International perspectives on theory and measurement* (pp. 105–128). New York: Plenum.

Grebogi, C., Ott, E., and Yorke, J. A. (1987). Chaos, strange attractors, and fractal basin boundaries in nonlinear dynamics. *Science, 238,* 632–638.

Greco, C., Hayne, H., and Rovee-Collier, C. (1990). Roles of function, reminding, and variability in categorization by 3-month infants. *Journal of Experimental Psychology: Learning, Memory & Cognition, 16,* 617–633.

Greene, P. H. (1982). Why is it easy to control your arms? *Journal of Motor Behavior, 14,* 260–286.

Greenfield, P. M. (1991). Language, tools and brain: The ontogeny and phylogeneny of hierarchically organized sequential behavior. *Brain and Behavioral Sciences, 14,* 707–784.

Greenough, W. T. (1991). Experience as a component of normal development: Evolutionary considerations. *Developmental Psychology, 27,* 14–17.

Greenough, W. T., Black, J. E., and Wallace, C. S. (1987). Experience and brain development. *Child Development, 58,* 539–559.

Grillner, S. (1975). Locomotion in vertebrates: Central mechanisms and reflex interaction. *Physiological Reviews, 55,* 247–304.

Grillner, S. (1981). Control of locomotion in bipeds, tetrapods, and fish. In V. B. Brooks (Ed.), *Handbook of physiology,* Vol. 3: *Motor control* (pp. 1179–1236). Bethesda, MD: American Physiological Society.

Grillner, S. (1985). Neurobiological bases of rhythmic motor acts in vertebrates. *Science, 228,* 143–149.

Grossberg, S., Schmajuk, N., and Levine, D. S. (1992). Associative learning and selective forgetting in a neural network regulated by reinforcement and attentive feedback. In D. S. Levine and S. J. Leven (Eds.), *Motivation, emotion, and goal direction in neural networks* (pp. 37–62). Hillsdale, NJ: Erlbaum.

Gustafson, G. E. (1984). Effects of the ability to locomote on infants' social and exploratory behaviors: An experimental study. *Developmental Psychology, 20,* 397–405.

Hadders-Algra, M., Van Eykern, L. Al., Klip-Van den Nieuwendijk, A. W. J., and Prechtl, H. F. R. (1992). Developmental course of general movements in early infancy. II. EMG correlates. *Early Human Development, 28,* 231–251.

Haken, H. (1977). *Synergetics: An introduction.* Heidelberg: Springer-Verlag.

Haken, H. (Ed.). (1985). *Complex systems: Operational approaches in neurobiology, physics, and computers.* Heidelberg: Springer-Verlag.

Haken, H. (1987). Synergistics: An approach to self-organization. In F. E. Yates (Ed.), *Self-organizing systems: The emergence of order* (pp. 417–434). New York: Plenum Press.

Hall, W. G., and Bryan, T. E. (1980). The ontogeny of feeding in rats. II. Independent ingestive behavior. *Journal of Comparative and Physiological Psychology, 93,* 746–756.

Halverson, H. M. (1931). Study of prehension in infants. *Genetic Psychological Monographs, 10,* 107–285.

Halverson, H. M. (1933). The acquisition of skill in infancy. *Journal of Genetic Psychology, 43,* 3–48.

Hanson, S. J. (1990). Meiosis networks. In D. S. Touretsky (Ed.), *Advances in neural information processing systems II.* (pp. 533–541). San Mateo, CA: Morgan Kaufman.

Haroutunian, S. (1983). *Equilibrium in the balance: A study of psychological explanation.* New York: Springer-Verlag.

Harris, P. L. (1987). The development of search. In P. Salapatek and L. B. Cohen (Eds.), *Handbook of infant perception* (Vol. 2). New York: Academic Press.

Harris, M., and Coltheart, M. (1986). *Language processing in children and adults.* London: Routledge & Kegan Paul.

Hasan, Z., and Stuart, D. G. (1988). Animal solutions to problems of movement control: The role of proprioceptors. *Annual Review of Neurosciences, 11,* 199–223.

Held, R. (1985). Binocular vision—Behavioral and neural development. In V. Mehler and R. Fox (Eds.), *Neonate cognition: Beyond the blooming buzzing confusion* (pp. 37–44). Hillsdale, NJ: Erlbaum.

Held, R., and Hein, A. (1963). Movement produced stimulation in the development of visually guided behavior. *Journal of Comparative and Physiological Psychology, 56,* 872–876.

Heriza, C. B. (1988). Organization of spontaneous leg movements in preterm infants. *Physical Therapy, 68,* 1340–1346.

Hildebrand, M. (1989). Vertebrate locomotion: An introduction. How does an animals' body move itself along? *BioScience, 39,* 764–765.

Hinde, R. A. (1961). The establishment of the parent-offspring relation in birds with some mammalian analogies. In W. H. Thorpe and O. L. Zangwill (Eds.), *Current problems in animal behaviour* (pp. 175–193). Cambridge: Cambridge University Press.

Hofsten, C. von. (19823). Eye-hand coordination in the newborn. *Developmental Psychology, 18,* 450–461.

Hofsten, C. von (1984). Developmental changes in the organization of prereaching movements. *Developmental Psychology, 20,* 378–388.

Hofsten, C. von (1989). Motor development as the development of systems: Comments on the special section. *Developmental Psychology, 25,* 950–953.

Hofsten, C. von (1991). Structuring of early reaching movements: A longitudinal study. *Journal of Motor Behavior, 23,* 280–292.

Hogan, N. (1984). An organizing principle for a class of voluntary movements. *Journal of Neuroscience, 4,* 2745–2754.

Hogan, N., Bizzi, E., Mussa-Ivaldi, F. A., and Flash, T. (1987). Controlling multijoint motor behavior. In K. B. Pandolf (Ed.), *Exercise and sport science reviews* (Vol. 15, pp. 153–190). New York: Macmillan.

Hood, L., and Bloom, L. (1979). What, when, and how about why: A longitudinal study of early expressions of causality. *Monographs of the Society for Research in Child Development,* Serial No. 181.

Horobin, K., and Acredolo, L. P. (1986). The role of attentiveness, mobility history, and separation of hiding sites on stage IV search behavior. *Journal of Experimental Child Psychology, 41,* 114–127.

Horowitz, F. D. (1987). *Exploring developmental theories: Toward a structural/behavioral model of development.* Hillsdale, NJ: Erlbaum.

Houk, J. C. (1979). Regulation of stiffness by skeletomotor reflexes. *Annual Review of Physiology, 41,* 99–114.

Huttenlocher, P. R. (1990). Morphometric study of human cerebral cortex development. *Neuropsychologia, 28,* 517–527.

Inhelder, B., and Piaget, J. (1964). *The early growth of logic in the child.* London: Routledge & Kegal Paul.

Izard, C. E., Kagan, J., and Zajonc, R. B. (Eds.) (1984). *Emotion, cognition, and behavior.* Cambridge: Cambridge University Press.

Jackson, E. A. (1989). *Perspectives of nonlinear dynamics.* Cambridge: Cambridge University Press.

Jeannerod, M. (1985). *The brain machine. The development of neurophysiological thought* (English translation by David Urion). Cambridge, MA: Harvard University Press.

Jenkins, W. M., Merzenich, M. M., and Recanzone, G. (1990). Neocortical representation dynamics in adult primates: Implications for neuropsychology. *Neuropsychologia, 28,* 573–584.

Jensen, J. L., Thelen, E., and Ulrich, B. D. (1989). Constraints on multi-joint movements: From the spontaneity of infancy to the skill of adults. *Human Movement Science, 8,* 393–402.

Johnson, J., and Newport, E. (1989). Critical period effects in second language learning: The influence of maturational state on the acquisition of English as a second language. *Cognitive Psychology, 21,* 60–99.

Johnson, K. E. (1992). *The effect of expertise on hierarchical systems of categorization.* Unpublished doctoral dissertation, Emory University. Atlanta, GA.

Johnson, M. (1987). *The body in the mind: The bodily basis of meaning, imagination, and reason.* Chicago: University of Chicago Press.

Johnson, M. H. (1990). Cortical maturation and the development of visual attention in early infancy. *Journal of Cognitive Neuroscience, 2,* 81–95.

Johnson, M. H., and Morton, J. (1991). *Biology and cognitive development: The case of face recognition.* Oxford: Blackwell.

Jones, S. S. (1992). The importance of mechanism for interpreting neonatal matching of adult behaviors. Presented at the International Conference on Infant Studies, Miami, May 1992.

Jones, S. S., and Smith, L. B. (1993). The place of perception in children's concepts. *Cognitive Development, 8,* 113–140.

Jones, S., Smith, L., and Landau, B. (1991). Object properties and knowledge in early lexical learning. *Child Development, 62,* 449–516.

Jones, S., Smith, L., Landau, B., and Gershkoff-Stowe, L. (1992). The developmental origins of the shape bias. Presented at the Boston Child Language Conference, October 1992.

Jordan, M. I. (1990). Motor learning and the degrees of freedom problem. In M. Jeannerod (Ed.), *Attention and performance XIII* (pp. 796–836). Hillsdale, NJ: Erlbaum.

Juszyk, P. W. (1989). Perception of cues to clausal units in mative and non-native languages. Presented at the Biennial Meeting of the Society of Research in Child Development, Kansas City, March 1989.

Kaas, J. H. (1991). Plasticity of sensory and motor maps in adult mammals. *Annual Review of Neurosciences, 14,* 137–167.

Karmiloff-Smith, A. (1992). *Beyond modularity.* Cambridge, MA: MIT Press.

Karmiloff-Smith, A. (1992). Nature, nurture and PDP: Preposterous, developmental postulates? *Connection Science, 4,* 253–269.

Keil, F. C. (1981). Constraints on knowledge and cognitive development. *Psychological Review, 88,* 197–227.

Keil, F. C. (1989). *Concepts, kinds, and cognitive development.* Cambridge: Cambridge University Press.

Kellman, P. J., and Spelke, E. S. (1983). Perception of partly occluded objects in infancy. *Cognitive Psychology, 15,* 483–524.

Kellman, P. J., Spelke, E. S., and Short, K. (1986). Infant perception of object unity from translatory motion in depth and vertical translation. *Child Development, 57,* 72–86.

Kelly, M. (1992). Using sound to solve syntactic problems. *Psychological Review, 99,* 349–364.

Kelso, J. A. S., and DeGuzman, G. C., (1991). An intermittency mechanism for coherent and flexible brain and behavioral function. In J. Requin and G. E. Stelmach (Eds.), *Tutorials in motor neuroscience* (pp. 305–310). Amsterdam: Kluwer.

Kelso, J. A. S., Holt, K. G., Kugler, P. N., and Turvey, M. T. (1980). On the concept of coordinative structures as dissipative structures: II. Empirical lines of convergence. In G. E. Stelmach and J. Requin (Eds.), *Tutorials in motor behavior* (pp. 49–70). New York: North-Holland.

Kelso, J. A. S., Holt, K. G., Rubin, P., and Kugler, P. N. (1981). Patterns of human interlimb coordination emerge from the properties of non-linear limit cycle oscillatory processes: Theory and data. *Journal of Motor Behavior, 13,* 226–261.

Kelso, J. A. S., Mandell, A. J., and Shlesinger, M. F. (Eds.). (1988). *Dynamic patterns in complex systems.* Singapore: World Scientific.

Kelso, J. A. S., and Scholz, J. P. (1985). Cooperative phenomena in biological motion. In H. Haken (Ed.), *Complex systems: Operational approaches in neurobiology, physics, and computers* (pp. 124–149). Heidelberg: Springer-Verlag.

Kelso, J. A. S., Scholz, J. P., and Schöner, G. (1986). Non-equilibrium phase transitions in coordinated biological motion: Critical fluctuations. *Physics Letters A, 118,* 279–284.

Kermoian, R., and Campos, J. J. (1988). Locomotor experience: A facilitator of spatial cognitive development. *Child Development, 59,* 908–917.

Killeen, P. R. (1989). Behavior as a trajectory through a field of attractors. In J. R. Brink and R. Haden (Eds.), *The computer and the brain: Perspectives on human and artificial intelligence* (pp. 53–82). Amsterdam: Elsevier.

Killeen, P. R. (1991). Behavioral geodesics. In D. S. Levine and S. J. Leven (Eds.), *Motivation, emotion, and goal direction in neural networks* (pp. 91–114). Hillsdale, NJ: Erlbaum.

Killeen, P. R. (1992). Mechanics of the animate. *Journal of the Experimental Analysis of Behavior, 57,* 429–463.

Kitchener, R. F. (1982). Holism and the organismic model in developmental psychology. *Human Development, 25,* 233–249.

Konner, M. (1991). Universals of behavioral development in relation to brain myelination. In K. R. Gibson and A. C. Petersen (Eds.), *Brain maturation and cognitive development: Comparative and cross-cultural perspectives* (pp. 181–223). New York: Aldine de Gruyter.

Kugler, P. N., Kelso, J. A. S., and Turvey, M. T. (1980). On the concept of coordinative structures as dissipative structures. I. Theoretical lines of convergence. In G. E. Stelmach and J. Requin (Eds.), *Tutorials in motor behavior* (pp. 3–47). New York: North-Holland.

Kugler, P., Kelso, J. A. S., and Turvey, M. T. (1982). On the control and coordination of naturally developing systems. In J. A. S. Kelso and J. E. Clark (Eds.), *The development of movement control and coordination* (pp. 5–78). New York: Wiley.

Kuhl, P. K., and Meltzoff, A. N. (1982). The bimodal perception of speech in infancy. *Science, 218,* 1138–1141.

Kuhn, D., and Phelps, E. (1982). The development of problem-solving strategies. In H. Reese and L. Lipsitt (Eds.), *Advances in child development and behavior* (Vol. 17, pp. 2–44). New York: Academic Press.

Kuhn, T. S. (1962). *The structure of scientific revolutions.* Chicago: University of Chicago Press.

Kuo, Z. (1967). *The dynamics of behavior development: An epigenetic view.* New York: Random House.

Lakoff, G. (1987a). *Women, fire, and dangerous things: What categories reveal about the mind.* Chicago: University of Chicago Press.

Lakoff, G. (1987b). Cognitive models and prototype theory. In U. Neisser (Ed.), *Concepts and conceptual development: Ecological and intellectual factors in categorization* (pp. 63–100). Cambridge: Cambridge University Press.

Landau, B., Smith, L., and Jones, S. (1988). The importance of shape in early lexical learning. *Cognitive Development, 3,* 299–321.

Laszlo, E. (1972). *Introduction to systems philosophy.* New York: Harper & Row.

Lee, D. N., and Aronson, E. (1974). Visual proprioceptive control of standing in human infants. *Perception and Psychophysics, 15,* 529–532.

Lehrman, D. S. (1970). Semantic and conceptual issues in the nature-nurture problem. In L. B. Aronson, E. Tobach, D. S. Lehrman, and J. S. Rosenblatt (Eds.), *Development and the evolution of behavior* (pp. 17–52). San Francisco: Freeman.

Lerner, R. M. (1978). Nature, nurture, and dynamic interaction. *Human Development, 21,* 1–20.

Lewin, K. (1946). Behavior and development as a function of the total situation. In L. Carmichael (Ed.), *Manual of child psychology* (pp. 791–844). New York: Wiley.

Lewis, M., and Goldberg, S. (1969). Perceptual-cognitive development in infancy: A generalized expectancy model as a function of mother-infant education. *Merrill-Palmer Quarterly, 15,* 81–100.

Lewis, M., Sullivan, M. W., and Michaelson, L. (1984). The cognitive-emotional fugue. In C. E. Izard, J. Kagan, and R. B. Zajonc (Eds.), *Emotion, cognition, and behavior* (pp. 264–288). Cambridge: Cambridge University Press.

Lewkowicz, D. J., and Turkewitz, G. (1980). Cross-modal equivalence in early infancy: Auditory-visual intensity matching. *Developmental Psychology, 16,* 597–607.

Lockman, J. J. (1990). Perceptuomotor coordination in infancy. In C-A, Hauert (Ed.), *Developmental psychology: Cognitive, perceptuo-motor, and neuropsychological perspectives* (pp. 85–111). Amsterdam: North-Holland.

Lorenz, K. (1937). The companion in the bird's world. *Auk, 54,* 245–273.

Luria, A. R. (1976). *Cognitive development: Its cultural and social foundations.* Cambridge, MA: Harvard University Press.

Madore, B. F., and Freedman, W. L. (1987). Self-organizing structures. *American Scientist, 75,* 252–259.

Mandler, J. M., Bauer, P. J., and McDonough, L. (1991). Separating the sheep from the goats: Differentiating global categories. *Cognitive Psychology, 23,* 263–299.

Markman, E. M. (1989). *Categorization and naming in children: Problems of induction.* Cambridge, MA: MIT Press.

Marler, S. (1991). The instinct to learn. In S. Carey and R. Gelman (Eds.), *The epigenesis of mind: Essays on biology and cognition* (pp. 37–66). Cambridge, MA: MIT Press.

Marr, D. (1982). *Vision.* San Francisco: Freeman.

Mathew, A., and Cook, M. (1990). The control of reaching movements by young infants. *Child Development, 61,* 1238–1258.

McCall, R. B. (1972). Smiling and vocalization in infants as indices of perceptual-cognitive processes. *Merrill-Palmer Quarterly, 18,* 341–347.

McGraw, M. B. (1932). From reflex to muscular control in the assumption of an erect posture and ambulation in the human infant. *Child Development, 3,* 291–297.

McGraw, M. B. (1940). Neuromuscular development of the human infant as exemplified in the achievement of erect locomotion. *Journal of Pediatrics, 17,* 747–771.

McGraw, M. B. (1945). *The neuromuscular maturation of the human infant.* New York: Columbia University Press.

McGraw, M. B. (1946). Maturation of behavior. In L. Carmichael (Ed.), *Manual of child psychology* (pp. 332–369). New York: Wiley.

McMahon, T. A. (1984). *Muscles, reflexes, and locomotion.* Princeton, NJ: Princeton University Press.

Medin, D., and Ortony, A. (1989). Psychological essentialism. In S. Vosniadou and A. Ortony (Eds.), *Similarity and analogical reasoning* (pp. 179–195). New York: Cambridge University Press.

Meltzoff, A. N. (1990). Towards a developmental cognitive science: The implications of cross-modal matching and imitation for the development of representation and memory in infancy. In A. Diamond (Ed.), *The development and neural bases of higher cognitive functions* (pp. 1–25). New York: New York Academy of Sciences.

Meltzoff, A. N. (1993). The centrality of motor coordination and proprioception in social and cognitive development: From shared actions to shared minds. In G. J. P. Salvelsbergh (Ed.), *The development of coordination in infancy* (pp. 463–496). Amsterdam: North-Holland.

Meltzoff, A. N., and Borton, R. W. (1979). Intermodal matching by human neonates. *Nature, 282,* 403–404.

Mendelson, M. J., and Haith, M. M. (1976). The relation between audition and vision in the human newborn. *Monographs of Society for Research in Child Development, 41,* Serial No. 167.

Merzenich, M. M., Allard, T. T., and Jenkins, W. M. (1990). Neural ontogeny of higher brain function: Implications of some recent neurophysiological findings. In O. Franzn and P. Westman (Eds.), *Information processing in the somatosensory system* (pp. 293–311). London: Macmillan.

Merzenich, M, M., and Kaas, J. H. (1980). Principles of organization of sensory-perceptual systems in mammals. *Progress in Psychobiology and Physiological Psychology, 9,* 2–42.

Miller, P. H. (1989). *Theories of developmental psychology* (2nd ed.). New York: Freeman.

Mjolsness, E., Sharp, D. H., and Reinitz, J. (1990). A connectionist model of development. (Report YALEU/DCS/RR-796) Department of Computer Science, Yale University, New Haven, CT.

Morasso, P. (1981). Spatial control of arm movements. *Experimental Brain Research, 42,* 223–227.

Morton, J., and Johnson, M. H. (1991). Conspec and Conlern: A two-process theory of infant face recognition. *Psychological Review, 98,* 164–181.

Mountcastle, V. B. (1980). *Medical physiology* (14th ed.). St. Louis: C. V. Mosby.

Movshon, J. A., and Van Sluyters, R. C. (1981). Visual neural development. *Annual Review of Psychology, 32,* 477–522.

Mpitsos, G. J., Creech, H. C., Cohan, C. S., and Mendelson, M. (1988). Variability and chaos: Neurointegrative principles in self-organization of motor patterns. In J. A. S. Kelso, A. J.

Mandell, and M. F. Shlesigner (Eds.), *Dynamic patterns in complex systems* (pp. 162–190). Singapore: World Scientific.

Muchisky, M., Gershkoff-Stowe, L., Cole, E., and Thelen, E. (1993). The epigenetic landscape revisited: A dynamic interpretation. Manuscript submitted for publication.

Murthy, V. D., and Fetz, E. E. (1991). Synchronized 25–35 Hz oscillations in sensorimotor cortex of awake monkeys. Abstracts of Society of Neuroscience 21st Annual Meeting, New Orleans, November 1991.

Myklebust, B. M., Gottlieb, G. L., and Agarwal, G. C. (1986). Stretch flexes of the normal infant. *Developmental Medicine and Child Neurology, 28,* 440–449.

Namy, L., and Gershkoff-Stowe, L. (1993). A microgenetic analysis of the origins of classification. Presented at the meeting of the Society for Research in Child Development, New Orleans, March 1993.

Newport, E. L. (1990). Maturational constraints on language learning. *Cognitive Science, 14,* 11–28.

Nosofsky, R. M. (1986). Attention, similarity, and the identification-categorization relationship. *Journal of Experimental Psychology: General, 115,* 39–57.

Oppenheim, R. W. (1981). Ontogenetic adaptations and retrogressive processes in the development of the nervous system and behaviour: A neuroembryological perspective. In K. J. Connolly and H. F. R. Prechtl (Eds.), *Maturation and development: Biological and psychological perspectives* (pp. 73–109). London: Spastics International and William Heinemann.

Osherson, D., Stob, M., and Weinstein, S. (1986). *Systems that learn.* Cambridge, MA: MIT Press.

Overton, W. F. (1975). General systems, structure, and development. In K. F. Riegel and G. C. Rosenwald (Eds.), *Structure and transformation: Developmental and historical aspects* (pp. 61–81). New York: Wiley.

Oyama, S. (1985). *The ontogeny of information: Developmental systems and evolution.* Cambridge: Cambridge University Press.

Patla, A. E. (Ed.). (1991). *Adaptability of human gait. Implications for the Control of Locomotion.* Amsterdam: North-Holland.

Pearson, K. (1987). Central pattern generation: A concept under scrutiny. In H. McLennen (Ed.), *Advances in physiological research* (pp. 167–185). New York: Plenum.

Pearson, K. G., and Duysens, J. (1976). Function of segmental reflexes in the control of stepping in cockroaches and cats. In R. M. Herman, S. Grillner, P. S. G. Stein, and D. G. Stuart (Eds.), *Neural control of locomotion* (pp. 519–537). New York: Plenum.

Pearson, K. G., Ramirez, J. M., and Jiang, W. (1992). Entrainment of the locomotor rhythm by group Ib afferents from ankle extensor muscles in spinal cats. *Experimental Brain Research, 90,* 557–566.

Piaget, J. (1951). *Play, dreams, and imitation in childhood.* New York: Norton.

Piaget, J. (1952). *The origins of intelligence in children.* New York: International Universities Press.

Piaget, J. (1952). *The origins of intelligence.* New York: Norton.

Piaget, J. (1954). *The constructin of reality in the child.* New York: Basic Books.

Piaget, J. (1955). *The construction of reality in the child.* London: Routledge and Kegan Paul (Original French edition 1937).

Piaget, J. (1970). *Psychology and epistemology.* New York: Norton.

Piaget, J. (1971). *Biology and knowledge.* Chicago: University of Chicago Press.

Piaget, J. (1976). *The grasp of consciousness: Action and concept in the young child.* Cambridge, MA: Harvard University Press.

Piaget, J. (1985). *The equilibration of cognitive structures: The central problem of intellectual development.* Chicago: University of Chicago Press. Originally published in 1975.

Piaget, J. (1987). *Possibility and necessity.* Minneapolis: University of Minnesota Press.

Pick, H. L., and Pick, A. D. (1970). Sensory and perceptual development. In P. Musson (Ed.), *Carmichael's manual of child psychology* (Vol. 1, pp. 773–847). New York: Wiley.

Pinker, S. (1987). The bootstrapping problem in language acquisition. In W. Demopoulas and A. Marras, (Eds.), *Language learning and concept acquisition.* Norwood, NJ: Ablex.

Pinker, S. (1989). *Learnability and cognition: The acquisition of argument structure.* Cambridge, MA: MIT Press.

Plunkett, K., and Marchman, V. (1989). Pattern association in a back propagation network: Implication for language acquisition. Center for Research in Language, University of California Technical Report No. 8902, San Diego, CA.

Polit, A., and Bizzi, E. (1978). Processes controlling arm movements in monkeys. *Science, 201,* 1235–1237.

Posner, M. I. (1980). Mental chronometry and the problem of consciousness. In P. W. Jusczyk and R. M. Klein (Eds.), *The Nature of thought: Essays in honor of D. O. Hebb* (pp. 95–114). Hillsdale, NJ: Erlbaum.

Prechtl, H. F. R. (1986). Prenatal motor development. In M. G. Wade and H. T. A. Whiting (Eds.), *Motor development in children: Aspects of coordination and control* (pp. 53–64). Dordecht, Netherlands: Martinus Nijhoff.

Premack D. (1976). *Intelligence in ape and man.* Hillsdale, NJ: Erlbaum.

Prigogine, I., and Stengers, I. (1984). *Order out of chaos: Man's new dialogue with nature.* New York: Bantam.

Pylyshyn, Z. W. (1978). When is attribution of beliefs justified? *Behavioral and Brain Sciences, 1,* 592–593.

Quine, W. V. O. (1960). *Word and object.* Cambridge, MA: MIT Press.

Rapp, P. E., Albano, A. M., and Mees, A. I. (1988). Calculation of correlation dimensions from experimental data: Progress and problems. In J. A. S. Kelso, A. J. Mandell, and M. F. Shlesinger (Eds.), *Dynamic patterns in complex systems* (pp. 191–205). Singapore: World Scientific.

Reed, E. S. (1982). An outline of a theory of action systems. *Journal of Motor Behavior, 14,* 98–134.

Reeke, G. N., Jr., and Edelman, G. M. (1984). Selective networks and recognition automata. *Annals of the New York Academy of Science, 426,* 181–201.

Reese, H. W., and Overton, W. F. (1970). Models of development and theories of development. In L. R. Goulet and P. B. Baltes (Eds.), *Life-span development psychology: Research and theory* (pp. 115–145). New York: Academic Press.

Robertson, S. S., Cohen, A. H., and Mayer-Kress, G. (1993). Behavioral chaos: Beyond the metaphor. In L. Smith and E. Thelen (Eds.), *A dynamic systems approach to development,* Cambridge, MA: MIT Press.

Rock, T. (1973). *Orientation and form.* New York: Academic Press.

Rogoff, B. (1982). Integrating context and cognitive development. In M. E. Lamb and A. L. Brown (Eds.), *Advances in developmental psychology* (Vol. 2, pp. 125–170). Hillsdale, NJ: Erlbaum.

Rogoff, B. (in press). Observing sociocultural activity on three planes: Participatory appropriation, guided participation, apprenticeship. In A. Alvarez, P. del Rio, and J. V. Wertsch (Eds.), *Perspectives on sociocultural research,* Cambridge: Cambridge University Press.

Rolls, E. T., and Williams, G. V. (1987). Sensory and movement-related activity in different regions of the primate striatum. In J. S. Schneider and T. I. Kidsky (Eds.), *Basal ganglia and behavior: Sensory aspects and motor functioning* (pp. 37–59). Bern: Hans Huber.

Rosch, E. H. (1973). Natural categories. *Cognitive Psychology, 4,* 328–350.

Rose, S. A., and Ruff, H. A. (1987). Cross-modal abilities in human infants. In J. D. Osofsky (Ed.), *Handbook of infant development* (pp. 318–362). New York: Wiley.

Rosenbaum, D. A., and Saltzman, E. (1984). A motor-program editor. In W. Prinz and A. F. Sanders (Eds.), *Cognition and motor processes* (pp. 51–61). Heidelberg: Springer.

Rovee, C. K., and Rovee, D. T. (1969). Conjugate reinforcement of infant exploratory behavior. *Journal of Experimental Child Psychology, 8,* 33–39.

Rovee-Collier, C. (1990). The "memory system" of prelinguistic infants. In A. Diamond (Ed.), *The development and neural bases of higher cognitive functions* (pp. 517–542). New York: New York Academy of Sciences.

Rovee-Collier, C. K., and Gekoski, M. J. (1979). The economics of infancy: A review of conjugate reinforcement. In H. W. Reese and L. P. Lipsitt (Eds.), *Advances in child development and research* (Vol. 13, pp. 195–255). New York: Academic Press.

Rovee-Collier, C. K., Griesler, P. C., and Early, L. A. (1985). Contextual determinants of retrieval in three-month-old infants. *Learning and Motivation, 16,* 139–157.

Rovee-Collier, C., and Hayne, H. (1987). Reactivation of infant memory: Implications for cognitive development. In H. W. Reese (Ed.), *Advances in child development and behavior* (Vol. 20, pp. 185–238). New York: Academic Press.

Rozin, P. (1976). The evolution of intelligence and access to the cognitive unconscious. In J. M. Sprague and A. A. Epstein (Eds.), *Progress in psychobiology and physiological psychology* (Vol. 6). New York: Academic Press.

Rumelhart, D. E. (1989). The architecture of mind: A connectionist approach. In M. I. Posner (Ed.), *Foundations of cognitive science* (pp. 133–160). Cambridge, MA: MIT Press.

Rumelhart, D. E., and McClelland, J. L. (Eds.). (1986). *Parallel distributed processing: Explorations in the microstructure of cognition. Vol. I: Foundations.* Cambridge, MA: Bradford Books/MIT Press.

Sameroff, A. J. (1983). Developmental systems: Contexts and evolution. In P. H. Mussen (Ed.), *Handbook of child psychology* (4th ed.). *Vol. I: History, theory, and methods* (pp. 237–294). New York: Wiley.

Schieber, M. H., and Hibbard, L. S. (1993). How somatotopic is the motor cortex hand area? *Science, 261,* 489–492.

Schiller, P. H. (1986). The central visual system. *Vision Research, 26,* 1351–1386.

Schiller, P. H. (1993). The effects of V4 and middle temporal (MT) area lesions on visual performance in the rhesus monkey. *Visual Neuroscience, 10,* 716–746.

Schmidt, H., Spelke, E. S., and LaMorte (1986). The development of Gestalt perceptions in infancy. Presented at the International Conference on Infant Studies, Los Angeles, April 1986.

Schmidt, R. A. (1975). A schema theory of discrete motor skill learning. *Psychological Review, 82,* 225–260.

Schneider, K., Zernicke, R. F., Ulrich, B. D., Jensen, J. L., and Thelen, E. (1990). Understanding movement control in infants through the analysis of limb intersegmental dynamics. *Journal of Motor Behavior, 22,* 493–520.

Schoeny, M. (1992). Relations between laboratory measures of reaching and behavior in a natural setting. Presented at the International conference on Infant Studies, Miami, May 1992.

Scholtz, J. P., Kelso, J. A. S., and Schöner, G. (1987). Nonequilibrium phase transitions in coordinated biological motion: Critical slowing down, and switching time. *Physics Letters, A, 123,* 390–394.

Schöner, G., and Kelso, J. A. S. (1988). Dynamic pattern generation in behavioral and neural systems. *Science, 239,* 1513–1520.

Sera, M., Reittinger, E., and del Castillo Pintado (1991). Developing definitions of objects and events in English and Spanish speakers. *Cognitive Development, 6,* 119–142.

Sera, M., and Smith, L. B. (1987). Big and little: Nominal and relative uses. *Cognitive Development, 2,* 89–112.

Shaw, R. (1984). *The dripping faucet as a model chaotic system.* Santa Cruz, CA: Aerial.

Sherrington, C. S. (1906). *The integrative action of the nervous system.* New Haven: Yale University Press (2nd ed. 1947).

Shields, P. J., and Rovee-Collier, C. (1992). Long-term memory for context-specific category information at six months. *Child Development, 63,* 245–259.

Shiffrin, R. M., and Schneider, W. (1977). Controlled and automatic human information processing: Perceptual learning, automatic attending, and a general theory. *Psychological Review, 84,* 127–190.

Shirley, M. M. (1931). *The first two years: A study of twenty-five babies. Vol. 1. Postural and locomotor development.* Minneapolis: University of Minnesota Press.

Siegler, R. S. (1978). The origins of scientific reasoning. In R. S. Siegler (Ed.), *Children's thinking: What develops?* (pp. 109–147). Hillsdale, NJ: Erlbaum.

Siegler, R. S. (1989). Mechanisms of cognitive development. *Annual Review of Psychology, 40,* 353–380.

Siegler, R. S., and Crowley, K. (1991). The microgenetic method. *American Psychologist, 46,* 606–620.

Siegler, R. S., and Jenkins, E. A. (1989). *How children discover new strategies.* Hillsdale, NJ: Erlbaum.

Sinclair de Zwart, H. (1969). Development psycholinguistics. In D. Elkind and J. H. Flavell (Eds.), *Studies in cognitive development* (pp. 315–366). New York: Oxford University Press.

Singer, W. (1986). The brain as a self-organizing system. *European Archives of Psychiatry and Neurological Sciences, 236,* 4–9.

Singer, W. (1990). The formation of cooperative cell assemblies in the visual cortex. *Journal of Experimental Biology, 153,* 177–197.

Singer, W., Artola, A., Engel, A. K., König, P., Kreiter, A. K., Löwel, S., and Schillen, T. B. (1993). Neuronal representations and temporal codes. In T. A. Poggio and D. A. Glaser (Eds.), *Exploring brain functions: Models in neuroscience* (pp. 179–194). New York: Wiley.

Singer, W., Gray, C., Engel, A., König, P., Artola, A., and Bröcher, S. (1990). Formation of cortical cell assemblies. In Cold Spring Harbor Symposium, *Quantitative Biology* (Vol. IV, pp. 939–952), Cold Spring Harbor Press.

Skarda, C. A., and Freeman, W. J. (1987a). Simulation of chaotic EEG patterns with a dynamic model of the olfactory system. *Biological Cybernetics, 56,* 139–150.

Skarda, C. A., and Freeman, W. J. (1987b). How brains make chaos in order to make sense of the world. *Behavioral and brain sciences* (Vol. 10, pp. 161–195). New York: Cambridge University Press.

Skarda, C. A., and Freeman, W. J. (1981). A physiological hypothesis of perception. *Perspectives in Biology and Medicine, 24,* 561–592.

Smith, G. (1992). Spatial and temporal characteristics of hand-to-mouth movements in the first year. Presented at the International Conference on Infant Studies, Miami, May 1992.

Smith, J. L. (1986). Hindlimb locomotion of the spinal cat: Synergistic patterns, limb dynamics, and novel blends. In S. Grillner, P. S. G. Stein, D. G. Stuart, H. Forssberg, R. M. Herman, and P. Wallen (Eds.), *Neurobiology of vertebrate locomotion* (pp. 185–208). Hampshire, England: Macmillan.

Smith, J. L., and Zernicke, R. F. (1987). Predictions for neural control based on limb dynamics. *Trends in Neuroscience, 10,* 123–128.

Smith, L. B. (1989). A model of perceptual classification in children and adults. *Psychological Review, 96,* 125–144.

Smith, L. B. (1991). Perceptual structure and developmental process. In G. R. Lockhead and J. R. Pomerantz (Eds.), *The perception of structure* (pp. 297–316). Washington, DC: American Psychological Association.

Smith, L. B. (1992). Real time and developmental time: Insights from novel word interpretation. Presented at the Symposium on Dynamic Systems in Psychology, American Psychological Association, August 1992, Washington, DC.

Smith, L. B. (1993). The concept of same. *Advances in Child Development and Behavior, 24,* 215–252.

Smith, L. B. (in press). Stability and variability: The geometry of children's novel word interpretations. In F. Gilgen and F. Abraham (Eds.), *Chaos theory in psychology.* Westport, CT: Greenwood Press.

Smith, L. B., and Heise, D. (1992). Perceptual similarity and conceptual structure. In B. Burns (Ed.), *Percepts, concepts, and categories* (pp. 234–272). New York: Elsevier.

Smith, L. B., Jones, S. S., and Landau, B. (1992). Count nouns, adjectives, and perceptual properties in children's novel word interpretations. *Developmental Psychology, 28,* 273–289.

Smith, L. B., Rattermann, M. J., and Sera, M. (1988). ''Higher'' and ''lower'': Comparative and categorical interpretations. *Cognitive Development, 3,* 265–284.

Smith, L., and Sera, M. (1992). A developmental analysis of the polar structure of dimensions. *Cognitive Psychology, 24,* 99–142.

Smith, L. B., Sera, M., and Gattuso, B. (1988). The development of thinking. In R. J. Sternberg and E. E. Smith (Eds.), *The psychology of human thought* (pp. 366–391). Cambridge: Cambridge University Press.

Smith, L. B., and Thelen, E. (Eds.). (1993). *A dynamic systems approach to development: Applications.* Cambridge, MA: MIT Press.

Smolensky, P. (1986). Information processing in dynamical systems: Foundations of harmony theory. In D. E. Rumelhart and J. D. McClelland (Eds.), *Parallel distributed processing* (Vol. 1, pp. 194–281). Cambridge, MA: MIT Press.

Smolensky, P. (1988). On the proper treatment of connectionism. *Behavioral and Brain Sciences, 11,* 1–74.

Soechting, J. F., and Ross, B. (1984). Psychophysical determination of coordinate representation of human arm orientation. *Neuroscience, 13,* 595–604.

Soja, N., Carey, S., and Spelke, E. (1991). Ontological categories guide young children's induction of word meanings: Object terms and substance terms. *Cognition, 38,* 179–211.

Spelke, E. S. (1976). Infants' intermodal perception of events. *Cognitive Psychology, 8,* 533–560.

Spelke, E. S. (1979). Perceiving bimodally specified events in infancy. *Developmental Psychology, 15,* 626–636.

Spelke, E. S. (1984). The development of intermodal perception. In L. B. Cohen and P. Salapatek (Eds.), *Handbook of infant perception.* New York: Academic Press.

Spelke, E. S. (1985). Preferential looking methods as tools for the study of cognition in infancy. In G. Gottlieb and N. Krasnegor, (Eds.), *Measurements of audition and vision in the first year of postnatal life* (pp. 323–364). Norwood, NJ: Erlbaum.

Spelke, E. S. (1988). Where perceiving ends and thinking begins: The apprehension of objects in infancy. In A. Yonas (Ed.), *Perceptual development in infancy: The Minnesota Symposia in Child Psychology* (Vol. 20, pp. 197–234). Hillsdale, NJ: Erlbaum.

Spelke, E. S. (1990). Origins of visual knowledge. In D. N. Osherson, S. M. Kosslyn, and J. M. Hollerbach (Eds.), *An invitation to cognitive science: Visual cognition and action* (pp. 99–128). Cambridge, MA: MIT Press.

Spelke, E. S. (1990). Principles of object perception. *Cognitive Science, 14,* 29–56.

Spelke, E. S., Breinlinger, K., Macomber, J., and Jacobson, K. (1992). Origins of knowledge. *Psychological Review, 99,* 605–632.

Spelke, E. S., Hofsten, C. V., and Kestenbaum, R. (1989). Object perception in infancy: Interaction of spatial and kinetic information for object boundaries. *Developmental Psychology, 25,* 185–196.

Spencer, J., Kamm, K., and Thelen, E. (1992). Longitudinal study of EMG activation relative to reaching kinematics kinematics and kinetics in the first year. Presented at the Annual Meeting, Society for Neuroscience, Anaheim, CA, October 1992.

Stehouwer, D. J. (1988). Metamorphosis of behavior in the bullfrog (*Rana catesbeiana*). *Developmental Psychobiology, 21,* 383–395.

Stehouwer, D. J., and Farel, P. B. (1983). Development of hindlimb locomotor activity in the bullfrog. (*Rana catesbeiana*) studied in vitro. *Science, 219,* 516–518.

Stehouwer, D. J., and Farel, P. B. (1984). Development of hindlimb locomotor behavior in the frog. *Developmental Psychobiology, 17,* 217–232.

Stein, B. E., and Meredith, M. A. (1993). *The merging of the senses.* Cambridge, MA: MIT Press.

Steinmetz. J. E. (in press). Brain substrates of emotion and temperament. In J. E. Bates and T. D. Wachs (Eds.), *Temperament: Individual differences at the interface of biology and behavior.* Washington, DC: American Psychological Association.

Stent, G. S. (1984). Semantics and neural development. In S. C. Sharma (Ed.), *Organizing principles of neural development* (p. 156). New York: Plenum.

Stillings, N. (1987). Modularity and naturalism in theories of vision. In J. L. Garfield (Ed.), *Modularity in knowledge representation and natural language understanding* (pp. 383–402). Cambridge, MA: MIT Press.

Strauss, S. (1982). Ancestral and descendant behaviors: The case of U-shaped behavioral growth. In T. G. Bever (Ed.), *Regressions in mental development: Basic phenomena and theories* (pp. 191–220). Hillsdale, NJ: Erlbaum.

Streri, A., and Pecheux, M. G. (1986). Tactual habituation and discrimination of form in infancy. A comparison with vision. *Child Development, 57,* 100–104.

Sugarman, S. (1983). *Children's early thought: Developments in classification.* Cambridge, MA: Cambridge University Press.

Sutherland, D. H., Olshen, R., Cooper, L., and Woo, S. L. Y. (1980). The development of mature gait. *Journal of Bone and Joint Surgery, 62,* 336–353.

Swinney, H. L., Horsthemke, W., McCormick, W. D., Noszitczins, Z., and Tam, W. Y. (1988). Temporal and spatial patterns in chemical systems. In J. A. S. Kelso, A. J. Mandell, and M. F. Shlesinger, (Eds.), *Dynamic patterns in complex systems* (pp. 112–120). Singapore: World Scientific.

Taylor, C. R. (1978). Why change gaits? Recruitment of muscles and muscle fibers as a function of speed and gait. *American Zoologist, 18,* 153–161.

Telzrow, R. W., Campos, J. J., Kermoian, R., and Bertenthal, B. I. (1992). Evidence for effects of motoric development on psychological processes: Studies of infants with myelodysplasia. Unpublished manuscript.

Templin, M. C. (1957). *Certain language skills in children.* Minneapolis: University of Minnesota Press.

Thelen, E. (1979). Rhythmical stereotypies in normal human infants. *Animal Behaviour, 27,* 699–715.

Thelen, E. (1981). Kicking rocking, and waving: Contextual analysis of rhythmical stereotypies in normal human infants. *Animal Behaviour, 29,* 3–11.

Thelen, E. (1984). Learning to walk: Ecological demands and phylogenetic constraints. In L. P. Lipsitt (Ed.), *Advances in infancy research* (Vol. 3, pp. 213–150). Norwood, NJ: Ablex.

Thelen, E. (1985). Development origins of motor coordination: Leg movements in human infants. *Developmental Psychobiology, 18,* 1–22.

Thelen, E. (1986). Treadmill-elicited stepping in seven-month-old infants. *Child Development, 57,* 1498–1506.

Thelen, E. (1988). Dynamical approaches to the development of behavior. In J. A. S. Kelso, A. J. Mandell, and M. F. Schlesinger (Eds.), *Dynamic patterns in complex systems* (pp. 348–369). Singapore: World Scientific.

Thelen, E. (1989). Self-organization in developmental processes: Can systems approaches work? In M. Gunnar and E. Thelen (Eds.), *Systems in development: The Minnesota Symposia in Child Psychology* (Vol. 22, pp. 77–117). Hillsdale, NJ: Erlbaum.

Thelen, E. (1991). Timing in motor development as emergent process and product. In J. Fagard and P. H. Wolff (Eds.), *The development of timing control and temporal organization in coordinated action* (pp. 201–211). Amsterdam: Elsevier.

Thelen, E. (1993). Timing and developmental dynamics in the acquisition of early motor skills. In G. Turkewitz and D. Devenny (Eds.), *Timing as an initial condition of development* (pp. 85–104). Hillsdale, NJ: Erlbaum.

Thelen, E., Bradshaw, G., and Ward, J. A. (1981). Spontaneous kicking in month-old infants: Manifestations of a human central locomotor program. *Behavioral and Neural Biology, 32,* 45–53.

Thelen, E., Bril, G., and Breniere, Y. (1992). The emergence of heel strike in newly walking infants: A dynamic interpretation. In M. Woollacott and F. Horak (Eds.), *Posture and gait control mechanisms* (pp. 334–337). Eugene, OR: University of Oregon Books.

Thelen, E., and Cooke, D. W. (1987). The relationship between newborn stepping and later locomotion: A new interpretation. *Developmental Medicine and Child Neurology, 29,* 380–393.

Thelen, E., Corbetta, D., Kamm, K., Spencer, J., Schneider, K., and Zernicke, R. F. (1993). The transition to reaching: Mapping intention and intrinsic dynamics. *Child Development, 64,* 1058–1098.

Thelen, E., and Fisher, D. M. (1982). Newborn stepping: An explanation for a "disappearing reflex." *Developmental Psychology, 18,* 760–775.

Thelen, E., and Fisher, D. M. (1983). The organization of spontaneous leg movements in newborn infants. *Journal of Motor Behavior, 15,* 353–377.

Thelen, E., Fisher, D. M., and Ridley-Johnson, R. (1984). The relationship between physical growth and a newborn reflex. *Infant Behavior and Development, 7,* 479–493.

Thelen, E., Fisher, D. M., Ridley-Johnson, R., and Griffin, N. (1982). The effects of body build and arousal on newborn infant stepping. *Developmental Psychobiology, 15,* 447–453.

Thelen, E., Kelso, J. A. S., and Fogel, A. (1987). Self-organizing systems and infant motor development. *Developmental Review, 7,* 39–65.

Thelen, E., Ridley-Johnson, R., and Fisher, D. M. (1983). Shifting patterns of bilateral coordination and lateral dominance in the leg movements of young infants. *Developmental Psychobiology, 16,* 29–46.

Thelen, E., and Ulrich, B. D. (1991). Hidden skills: A dynamic systems analysis of treadmill stepping during the first year. *Monographs of the Society for Research in Child Development,* Serial No. 223, 56 (1).

Thelen, E., Ulrich, B., and Niles, D. (1987). Bilateral coordination in human infants: Stepping on a split-belt treadmill. *Journal of Experimental Psychology: Human Perception and Performance, 13,* 405–410.

Townsend, J. T. (1992). Chaos theory: A brief tutorial and discussion. In A. F. Healy, S. M. Kosslyn, and R. M. Schiffrin (Eds.), *From learning theory to connectionist theory: Essays in honor of William K. Estes* (Vol. 1). Hillsdale, NJ: Erlbaum.

Townsend, J. T., and Busemeyer, J. R. (1989). Approach-avoidance: Return to dynamic decision behavior. In C. Izawa (Ed.), *Current issues in cognitive processes* (pp. 107–133). Hillsdale, NJ: Erlbaum.

Trabasso, T. (1977). The role of memory as a system of making transitive inferences. In R. V. Kail and J. W. Hagen (Eds.), *Perspectives on the development of memory and cognition* (pp. 333–365). Hillsdale, NJ: Erlbaum.

Trabasso, T., and Riley, C. A. (1975). The construction and use of representations involving linear order. In R. L. Solso (Ed.), *Information processing and cognition: The Loyola Symposium* (pp. 381–409). Hillsdale, NJ: Erlbaum.

Trevarthen, C. (1974). The psychobiology of speech development. In E. H. Lenneberg (Ed.), *Language and brain: Developmental aspects. Neurosciences Research Program Bulletin* (Vol. 12, pp. 570–585). Boston: Neurosciences Research Program.

Trevarthen, C. (1984). How control of movement develops. In H. T. A. Whiting (Ed.), *Human motor actions: Bernstein reassessed* (pp. 223–261). Amsterdam: North-Holland.

Tucker, M., and Hirsh-Pasek, K. (1993). Systems and language: Implications for acquisition. In L. B. Smith and E. Thelen (Eds.), *A dynamic systems approach to development: Applications* (pp. 359–384). Cambridge, MA: MIT Press.

Turkewitz, G., Birch, H. G., Moreau, T. Levy, L., and Cornwell, A. C. (1966). Effects of intensity of auditory stimulation on directional eye movements in the human neonate. *Animal Behaviour, 14,* 93–101.

Turkewitz, G., Gardner, J. M., and Lewkowicz, D. L. (1984). Sensory/perceptual functioning during early infancy: Implications of a quantitative basis of responding. In G. Greenberg and E. Tobach (Eds.), *Conference on levels of integration and evolution of behavior* (pp. 167–195). Hillsdale, NJ: Erlbaum.

Turkewitz, G., and Kenny, P. A. (1982). Limitations on input as a basis for neural organization and perceptual development: A preliminary theoretical statement. *Developmental Psychobiology, 15,* 357–368.

Ulrich, B. D., Ulrich, D. A., and Collier, D. (1992). Alternating stepping patterns: Hidden abilities in 11-month-old infants with Down Syndrome. *Developmental Medicine in Child Neurology, 34,* 233–239.

van Geert, P. (1993). A dynamic systems model of cognitive growth. Competition and support under limited resource conditions. In L. Smith and E. Thelen (Eds.), *A dynamic systems approach to development: Applications* (pp. 265–332). Cambridge, MA: MIT Press.

van Gelder, T. (1992). What might cognition be if not computation? Indiana University Cognitive Science Research Report 75.

Varela, F., Thompson, E., and Rosch, E. (1991). *The embodied mind.* Cambridge, MA: MIT Press.

Vereijken, B. (1993). Infant treadmill stepping: Effects of training. Presented at the Biennial Meeting, Society for Research in Child Development, New Orleans.

Vereijken, B., and Thelen, E. (1993). Effects of training on infant treadmill stepping. Manuscript submitted for publication.

Vygotsky, L. S. (1978). *Mind in society: The development of higher psychological processes.* Cambridge, MA: Harvard.

Vygotsky, L. S. (1986). *Thought and language.* Cambridge, MA: MIT Press.

Waddington, C. H. (1966). *Principles of development and differentiation.* New York: Macmillan.

Waddington, C. H. (1977). *Tools for thought: How to understand and apply the latest scientific techniques of problem solving.* New York: Basic Books.

Walley, A. (1993). The development of spoken word recognition. *Development Review* (in press).

Wallman, J. (1979). A minimal visual restriction experiment: Preventing chicks from seeing their feet affects later responses to mealworms. *Developmental Psychology, 12,* 391–397.

Watson, J. S. (1966). The development of and generalization of contingency awareness in early infancy. *Merrill-Palmer Quarterly, 10,* 223–228.

Watson, J. S. (1972). Smiling, cooing and "the game." *Merrill-Palmer Quarterly, 18,* 323–339.

Watson, S. J., and Bekoff, A. (1990). A kinematic analysis of hindlimb mobility in 9- and 10-day old chick embryos. *Journal of Neurobiology, 21,* 651–660.

Weisel, T. N., and Hubel, D. H. (1965). Comparison of the effects of unilateral and bilateral eye closure on cortical unit responses in kittens. *Journal of Neurophysiology, 28,* 1029–1040.

Weiss, P. A. (1969). The living system: Determinism stratified. In A. Koestler and J. R. Smithies (Eds.), *Beyond reductionism: New perspectives in the life sciences* (pp. 3–55). Boston: Beacon Press.

Wellman, H. M., Cross, D., and Bartsch, K. (1986). Infant search and object permanence: A meta-analysis of the A-not-B error. *Monographs of the Society for Research in Child Development, 54,* No. 214.

Wellman, H. M., Cross, D., and Bartsch, K. (1987). A meta-analysis of research on stage 4 object permanence: The A-not-B error. *Monographs of the Society for Research in Child Development, 5*(3).

Werner, H. (1957). The concept of development from a comparative and organismic point of view. In D. B. Harris (Ed.), *The concept of development* (pp. 125–148). Minneapolis: University of Minnesota Press.

Wertsch, J. V. (1985). *Vygotsky and the social formation of mind.* Cambridge, MA: Harvard University Press.

West, B. J., and Goldberger, A. L. (1987). Physiology in fractal dimensions. *American Scientist, 75,* 354–365.

West, M. J., and King, A. P. (1987). Settling nature and nurture into an ontogenetic niche. *Developmental Psychobiology, 20,* 549–562.

White, B. L., Castle, P., and Held, R. (1964). Observations on the development of visually directed reaching. *Child Development, 35,* 349–364.

Whiting, H. T. A., (Ed.). (1984). *Human motor actions: Bernstein reassessed.* Amsterdam: North-Holland.

Whorf, B. L. (1956). Languages and logic. In J. B. Carroll (Ed.), *Language, thought and reality: Selected writings of Benjamin Lee Whorf* (pp. 233–245). Cambridge, MA: MIT Press. (Originally published in 1940).

Wohlwill, J. F. (1962). Form perception to inference: A dimension of cognitive development. *Monographs of the Society for Research in Child Development, 27,* 87–112.

Wolff, P. H. (1987). *The development of behavioral states and the expression of emotions in early infancy. New proposals for investigation.* Chicago: University of Chicago Press.

Woollacott, M. (1990). Changes in posture and voluntary control in the elderly: Research findings and rehabilitation. *Topics in Geriatric Rehabilitation, 5,* 1–11.

Wynn, K. (1992). Addition and subtraction by human infants. *Nature, 358,* 749–750.

Yates, F. E. (1987). *Self-organizing systems: The emergence of order.* New York: Plenum.

Yonas, A., and Granrud, C. E. (1985). The development of sensitivity to kinetic, binocular, and pictorial depth information in human infants. In D. Ingle, M. Jeannerod, and D. Lee (Eds.), *Brain mechanisms and spatial vision* (pp. 113–145). Dordrecht, Netherlands: Nijhoff.

Zanone, P. G., and Kelso, J. A. S. (1991). Experimental studies of behavioral attractors and their evolution with learning. In J. Requin and G. E. Stelmach (Eds.), *Tutorials in motor neuroscience* (pp. 121–133). Dordrecht, Netherlands: Kluwer.

Zelazo, P. R. (1984). The development of walking: New findings and old assumptions. *Journal of Motor Behavior, 15,* 99–137.

Zelazo, P. R., Zelazo, N. A., and Kolb, S. (1972). "Walking" in the newborn. *Science, 177,* 1058–1059.

Zernicke, R., and Schneider, K. (1992). Changes in dynamics of reaching during the first year. Presented at the International Conference on Infant Studies, Miami, May 1992.

Author Index

Subject Index